SOUTHERN
BY THE
GRACE OF GOD

"The people of the Confederate States have made themselves famous. If the renown of brilliant courage, stern devotion to a cause, and military achievements almost without a parallel, can compensate men for the toil and privations of the hour, then the countrymen of Lee and Jackson may be consoled amid their sufferings. From all parts of Europe, from their enemies as well as their friends, from those who condemn their acts as well as those who sympathize with them, comes the tribute of admiration. When the history of this war is written, the admiration will doubtless become deeper and stronger, for the veil which has covered the South will be drawn away and disclose a picture of patriotism, of unanimous self-sacrifice, of wise and firm administration, which we can now only see indistinctly. The details of extraordinary national effort which has led to the repulse and almost to the destruction of an invading force of more than half a million men, will then become known to the world, and whatever may be the fate of the new nationality, or its subsequent claims to the respect of mankind, it will assuredly begin its career with a reputation for genius and valor which the most famous nations may envy."

The London Times, 1862

SOUTHERN
BY THE
GRACE OF GOD

Michael Andrew Grissom

Library of Congress Cataloging-in-Publication Data

Grissom, Michael Andrew
    Southern By the Grace of God / Michael Andrew Grissom
        p. cm.
    Includes bibliographical references.
    ISBN-13: 978-0-9628099-8-9
    1. Southern States—Civilization. 1. Title
F209.G75 1990
975—de20   89-25568
                                            CIP

First printing, August 1988
Second printing, November 1988
Third printing, November 1989
Fourth printing, September 1990
Fifth printing, March 1992
Sixth printing, February 1994
Seventh printing, May 1995
Eighth printing, May 1997
Ninth printing, March 1999
Tenth printing, December 2001
Eleventh printing, February, 2007
Twelfth printing, July 2018
Thirteenth printing, November 2020

LITTLE DIXIE PUBLISHING COMPANY
LittleDixiePublishing@gmail.com

TABLE OF CONTENTS

Introduction

Thirty-three years ago, I sat down, took pen in hand, and attempted a defense against those individuals and organizations who were seeking to destroy every feature of our distinctive Southern culture. The year was 1987, and for almost twenty years demoniac forces had made alarming inroads. Confederate flags were being hauled down; streets, roads, schools, buildings, and memorial highways were being stripped of their names; even our holidays, such as the hallowed Confederate Memorial Day, were being removed from the calendar. And yet, amidst all the turmoil there was evident a slight flicker of pride yet unextinguished; consequently, it seemed prudent to emphasize the positive sentiment that remained. By 1988, I had finished writing *Southern By the Grace of God* with the aim of re-acquainting the older Southerner with his remarkable heritage and at the same time introducing the younger folks to it – Heaven knows, they're not getting it in school – in hopes that it might spur Southerners to take a stand against what was and is clearly a shameful case of ethnic cleansing and cultural genocide. The original preface, which follows these introductory remarks, gives evidence of the need for such a book as this.

But in spite of my optimistic approach, things got worse. Our pride had been severely wounded, and our enemies were growing stronger. In 1991, I noted the downward trend in *The Last Rebel Yell.*

"In addition to battling the press, Hollywood, and Yankees who can't forget we lost the War, we now have to fight the largest organized hate group in the United States – the NAACP. The leaders of that ignominious organization are desperately trying to revive the smoldering fires of contempt that served them well during the 1960s and '70s. Realizing that the so-called civil rights movement had pretty well run its course, this bunch laid out plans to revive it by driving a permanent wedge between blacks and whites in the South, hoping to fill up the coffers of the organization, which in turn, would insure the lucrative positions of its leaders. Cloaked in the diabolical disguise of "newly-detected racism," the plot called for a systematic dismantling of all icons and symbols of the Southern heritage. That meant Confederate flags, monuments, statues, commemorative plaques, state flags, holidays, festivals, ceremonies, and names of streets, dormitories, buildings, parks, rivers, and roads. In short, anything held sacred by Southern whites was to be challenged and swept away by any means, whether legal, legitimate, oppressive, or clandestine."

As *Southern By the Grace of God* began circulating and people became more acutely aware of what was being stolen from them, there arose a measure of pushback against the onslaught. In some cases, the Sons of Confederate Veterans and the United Daughters of the Confederacy led the fight; in other situations small groups of unorganized people showed up to oppose removing names, flags, and plaques. Even though some significant battles were lost, people consoled themselves with the belief that our most permanent treasures would be safe. How many times I heard comments that ran something like this: "At least, we still have our monuments. They can't take those down."

SOUTHERN BY THE GRACE OF GOD

We underestimated the enemy. They have succeeded in removing from public display virtually all Confederate flags. Hardly a school bearing the name of a Confederate hero remains in the South. School mascots have shed the once ubiquitous name of Rebels in favor of bears, lions, wolves, and wildcats. Virtually all public celebration of Confederate heritage has ceased, and formerly-observed state holidays have been relegated to simple "days of remembrance." Robert E. Lee's birthday, once the most widely observed Confederate holiday in the South, has been buried by Martin Luther King Day.

Under the withering assault of the NAACP, with the additional forces of Black Lives Matter and Antifa, a group of anarchists formerly known as Anti-Racist Action, *Dixie*, a simple song, yet sacred to the people of the South ever since it gave us hope during the dark years of the war, is now universally banned from public hearing. Where once we used to instinctively jump to our feet at the first sound of those stirring strains, it is doubtful that anyone under the age of 40 has ever even heard the song. Bands used to play it; radio stations signed off with it; school children sang it. But now it is, to borrow those famous words of Margaret Mitchell, "gone with the wind."

And for the past four years we have been horror-stricken witness to the unthinkable. Our enemies have, indeed, attacked our monuments. Elaborate works of art, rivaling the exquisite statues of Europe – most of them over one hundred years old, some carved from Italian marble by the most famous sculptors of the day, others cast in bronze in France – have been defaced, demolished, or dismantled and removed to undisclosed locations or, in the case of New Orleans, deposited in the city dump.

But how have these mental troglodytes managed to commit such crimes with absolute impunity? The simple answer: *race*. In fact, it is race that propels all of the modern anti-South hatred, and it is race that has always been the underlying argument used so effectively in removing the icons and celebration of our Southern heritage. Unfortunately, it is that little four-letter word that hamstrings the Southerner, rendering him fundamentally powerless in disputing demands for destruction of the things he holds dear. Southerners have been beaten into submission when it comes to race. They will avoid discussing race at all costs, preferring, rather, to talk about the moon. I give but one example of the white man's perplexing reluctance to respond to any proposal antithetical to his interests if it entails a discussion of race.

In 1974, I joined the 95th Division of the United States Army Reserves as a chaplain's assistant. It was the middle of May, and my unit left for summer camp at Fort Polk, Louisiana, two weeks later. Unlike most new reservists, I had not yet been to active duty and was as green as a gourd when it came to army life. In l974, the army was made up almost entirely of white men. We had one black man, Matthew O. Hooks, in our unit. Hooks, as we called him – everyone goes by last names in the army – was a bit older than most of us new recruits. He was an easy-going, pleasant man with a big smile, and everyone liked him.

At Fort Polk, the entire 95th Division, made up of units in Arkansas, Oklahoma, and Louisiana, was present for two weeks training. As a chaplain's assistant, my training was done along-side the chaplains and other chaplain's assistants from the three states. Some of our time was spent in class. The idea of "diversity training" was a new concept in 1974, so one day we all assembled in a large classroom to hear a presentation on racial insensitivity. The instructor, a career sergeant, was the second black man I ever saw in the 95th Division. As we sat, he gave us the most preju-dicial lecture I guess anyone could give. It was a film presen-tation of white people repeating those little rhymes that we had heard from our infancy, such as:

Eeeny, meeny, miney, moe;
Catch a nigger by the toe;
If he hollers, make him pay
Fifty dollars every day.

iv

Now, I didn't have a problem with the instructor's use of the little nursery rhyme, nor did I have a problem with other examples he used. My problem was that the intent of the whole presentation was to put a guilt trip on his white audience. No examples of black rhymes or use of words like "cracker" or "honky" or any of various pejorative terms used by blacks. None at all. The whole operation degenerated into an obvious attempt to portray blacks as eternally oppressed by evil white men – compliments of the U.S. Army. It was insulting in the extreme, and as I squirmed, waiting for one of the chaplains to confront this smirking black sergeant, I looked around, surveying the assemblage of captains, lieutenant colonels, and full-bird colonels in the room, and saw nothing but expressionless faces. It was as quiet as a funeral parlor. A room full of officers and yet not one of them made a peep. So, I, a raw recruit who hadn't even been to basic training and had just barely learned how to salute, raised my hand and was recognized by the black instructor; whereupon, I took him to task for his one-sided, insulting presentation. To my surprise, he acknowledged that it had been one-sided and said, whether he meant it or not, that he appreciated my contribution to his class.

But what of the other white men in the room? We took a short break outside, where I was immediately surrounded by several frightened chaplain's assistants who exclaimed in great alarm, "What are you trying to do? Start a race war!"

And so it was, and so it is. Paralyzed by that little four-letter word. And yet, that's the battering ram with which the nihilists break down the doors. They know that politicians and office holders from City Hall to the State House fear being called racist more than they fear a stroll through a Memphis neighborhood after dark; consequently, our enemies frame every argument for removing the elements of our cultural identity in terms of race. That is precisely why Southern office holders accede in almost every instance to the demands of the NAACP, Antifa, Black Lives Matter, and their young white lackeys who are always hanging around, spewing their scripted racial invective.

Nevertheless, let us briefly take our own look at some of the racial arrows in their quiver.

SLAVERY

Now, the desired reaction to the mere word itself is revulsion, repugnance, and antipathy, because that's the way we have been trained by Hollywood, the press, the schools, and, sadly, most of the mainline churches, to react. It has become our common collective reflex. Due to the fictional portrayal of antebellum slavery that has become our regular diet, we are made to believe that plantations existed for the sole purpose of beating and killing black men, raping black women, torturing both by all sorts of sordid measures, and generally enjoying the depravity. If you don't react with the proper amount of moral outrage, then they will brand you as a Nazi, a white supremacist, or a bigot.

But it hasn't always been that way. In the days of my youth, during which time the War for Southern Independence was less than 90 years in the past, still living were Confederate soldiers, former slaves, and even a few Union soldiers. In fact, Walter Williams, recognized as the last surviving Confederate soldier, passed away in 1959 at the age of 117. Had the lurid tales of Hollywood been circulating at the time, there were authentic voices who could have corroborated those enormities. After all, there were plenty of opportunities to do so given the constant media attention they were receiving as the last survivors of the antebellum South; yet, no such confirmation was forthcoming. We simply understood slavery to be an outdated institution, no longer needed or desired in the 20th century. Slavery had been a legal American system whereby owners of large tracts of land could purchase workers for the fields and hold them in bondage. Contrary to the titillating tales of Hollywood, slavery had not died of moral outrage but as an adjunct of the War of the 1860s.

SOUTHERN BY THE GRACE OF GOD

In the South of the mid-20th century, most people went to church. We knew from our study of the Bible that God had instituted slavery among the Jews and that Jesus had urged slaves to "be obedient to your masters," with a corresponding directive to masters to "give unto your servants that which is just and equal; knowing that ye also have a Master in heaven." Who among us would have dared criticize God or take Jesus to task for not condemning slavery in the New Testament?

Writing many years after the War Between The States, Victoria Clayton of Barbour County, Alabama, whose family had owned a plantation, described the prevailing Southern attitude towards antebellum slavery.

> We never raised the question for one moment as to whether slavery was right. We had inherited the institution from devout Christian parents. Slaves were held by pious relatives and friends and clergymen to whom we were accustomed to look up. The system of slave-holding was incorporated into our laws, and was regulated and protected by them. We read our Bible and accepted its teachings as the true guide in faith and morals. We understood literally our Lord's instruction to His chosen people, and applied them to our circumstances and surroundings:

>> Both thy bondmen and thy bondmaids, which thou shalt have, shall be of the heathen that are round about you; of them shall ye buy bondmen and bondmaids. Moreover of the children of the strangers that do sojourn among you, of them shall ye buy, and of their families that are with you, which they begat in your land: and they shall be your possession. And ye shall take them as an inheritance for your children

after you, to inherit them for a possession;
they shall be your bondmen for ever. . . .
(Leviticus XXV: 44-46)

We simply and naturally understood that our
slaves must be treated kindly and cared for spiri-
tually, and so they were. We felt that we were responsible to God for our entire household. [1]

To be sure, slavery can, indeed, be a reprehensible opera-
tion if practiced as in Africa, for instance, by Kamurasi, king of
Inyoro, Mutesa, king of Buganda, or Shaka, the notorious Zulu
potentate whom PBS incredulously tried to portray as a brilliant
African leader. Stanley Burnham of the Foundation for Human
Understanding reports that the Shaka of PBS and the Shaka of
history are not one and the same. Citing English trader Henry
Francis Fynn's visit to the Zulu kingdom, he notes some of
Shaka's routine activities.

On the first day of Fynn's arrival at court, ten men
were carried off to death, and he soon learnt that
executions occurred daily. On one occasion Fynn
witnessed the dispatch of sixty boys under the age of
twelve years before Shaka had breakfasted. . . . On
one occasion between four and five hundred women
were massacred because they were believed to have
knowledge of witchcraft. . . . One of Shaka's concubines was executed for taking a pinch of snuff from
his snuff-box. . . . It was the rule in Zululand that no
one might eat from any crop until the king had
partaken of the first-fruits of the year at a special
ceremony. . . . At the ceremony, the king was accustomed to have many people executed for no other
reason than to show his power and cause him to be
feared. . . . During a period of one year after Nandi's

[his mother] death, all women found to be pregnant were executed with their husbands. [2]

Peter Brimelow writes that Shaka, "founder of the Zulu Empire," killed "all his concubines' children, sometimes with his own hands, massacred some seven thousand of his own subjects to mark his mother's death, sliced open a hundred pregnant women to satisfy a fleeting interest in embryology, and ordered executions at whim daily until his assassination in 1828." [3]

Africans obtained their slaves by raiding neighboring tribes. In 1890, *The Century Magazine* featured an eyewitness account of slavery as practiced by Africans in the interior of the continent. Written by E.J. Glave, who accompanied famous explorer Henry M. Stanley – discoverer of the long-hidden sources of the Nile and Congo Rivers and intrepid rescuer of Dr. Livingstone, who had been lost in the African jungles for six years – the narrative is briefly excerpted here to give the reader an idea of how Southerners could honestly look upon their own "peculiar institution" as somewhat benign.

Here at Lukolela, for instance, I had hardly settled down in my encampment when I was introduced to one of those horrible scenes of bloodshed which take place frequently in all the villages along the Congo, and which will be enacted so long as the life of a slave is counted as naught, and the spilling of his blood of as little account as that of a goat or a fowl.

In this particular instance the mother of a chief having died, it was decided, as usual, to celebrate the event with an execution. At the earliest streak of dawn the slow, measured beat of a big drum announces to all what is to take place, and warns the poor slave who is to be the victim that his end is night. It is very evident that something unusual is about to happen, and that the day is to be given up to some ceremony. The natives gather in groups and begin studiously to arrange their toilets, don their gayest loin-cloths, and ornament their legs and arms with bright metal bangles, all the time indulging in wild gesticulations and savage laughter as they discuss the coming event. Having taken a hasty meal, they produce from their houses all available musical instruments. The drums are wildly beaten as groups of men, women, and children form themselves in circles and excitedly perform dances, consisting of violent contortions of the limbs, accompanied by savage singing and repeated blasts of the war horns, each dancer trying to outdo his fellow in violence of movement and strength of lung.

About noon, from sheer exhaustion, combined with the heat of the sun, they are compelled to cease; when large jars of palm wine are produced, and a general bout of intoxication begins, increasing their excitement and showing up their savage nature in striking colors. The poor slave, who all this time has been lying in the corner of some hut, shackled hand and foot and closely watched, suffering the agony and suspense which this wild tumult suggests to him, is now carried to some prominent part of the village, there to be surrounded and to receive the jeers and scoffs of the drunken mob of savages. The executioner's assistants, having selected a suitable place for the ceremony, procure a block of wood about a foot square. The slave is then placed on this, in a sitting posture; his legs are stretched out straight in front of him; the body is strapped to a stake reaching up the back to the shoulders. On each side stakes are placed under the armpits as props, to which the arms are firmly bound. Other lashings are made to posts driven into the ground near the ankles and knees.

SOUTHERN BY THE GRACE OF GOD

A pole is now planted about ten feet in front of the victim, from the top of which is suspended, by a number of strings, a bamboo ring. The pole is bent over like a fishing rod, and the ring fastened round the slave's neck, which is kept rigid and stiff by the tension. During this preparation the dances are resumed, now rendered savage and brutal in the extreme by the drunken condition of the people. One group of dancers surround the victim and indulge in drunken mimicry of the contortions of the face which the pain caused by this cruel torture forces him to show. But he has no sympathy from this merciless horde.

Presently in the distance approaches a company of two lines of young people, each holding a stem of the palm tree, so that an arch is formed between them, under which the executioner is escorted. The whole procession moves with a slow but dancing gait. Upon arriving near the doomed slave all dancing, singing, and drumming cease, and the drunken mob take their places to witness the last act of the drama.

An unearthly silence succeeds. The executioner wears a cap composed of black cock's feathers; his face and neck are blackened with charcoal, except the eyes, the lids of which are painted with white chalk. The hands and arms to the elbows, and feet and legs to the knee, are also blackened. His legs are adorned profusely with broad metal anklets, and around his waist are strung wildcat skins. As he performs a wild dance around his victim, a murmur of admiration arises from the assembled crowd. He then approaches and makes a thin chalk mark on the neck of the fated man. After two or three passes of his knife, to get the right swing, he delivers the fatal blow, and with one stroke of his keen-edged weapon severs the head from the body.

The sight of blood brings to a climax the frenzy of the natives; some of them savagely puncture the quivering trunk with their spears, others hack at it with their knives, while the remainder engage in a ghastly struggle for possession of the head, which has been jerked into the air by the released tension of the sapling. As each man obtains the trophy, and is pursued by the drunken rabble, the hideous tumult becomes deafening; they smear one another's faces with blood, and fights always spring up as a result, when knives and spears are freely used. The reason for their anxiety to possess the head is this: the man who can retain that head against all comers until sundown will receive a present for his bravery from the head man of the village. It is by such means that they test the brave of the village, and they will say with admiration, speaking of a local hero, "He is a brave man; he has retained two heads until sundown."

When the taste for blood has been to a certain extent satisfied, they again resume their singing and dancing while another victim is prepared, when the same ghastly exhibition is repeated. Sometimes as many as twenty slaves will be slaughtered in one day. The dancing and general drunken uproar is continued until midnight, when once more absolute silence ensues, in utter contrast to the hideous tumult of the day. [4]

Having arrived in the Congo in 1883, Glave, under the authority of Stanley, had made an 800-mile expedition up the Congo River where he established an outpost at Lukolela. From there, Glave penetrated even deeper the African interior, and it was from those sojourns that he detailed his "experiences bearing upon the subject of slavery among the natives themselves." He reported that all of the large villages around Lake Mantumba and the Ubangi River (Bolobo, Chumbiri, Lukolela, Butunu, Ngombe, Busindi, Irebu) rely principally upon the Balolo tribes for their slaves. A comparatively peaceful tribe, the Balolo were numerous and plentiful. "The wretched state of these Balolo has always saddened me, as intellectually they are a grade higher than the tribes surrounding them," wrote Glave. [5]

> Their small, unprotected villages are constantly attacked by the powerful roving tribes of the Lutumbe and Ngombe. These two tribes are voracious cannibals. They surround the Lolo villages at night, and at the first signs of dawn pounce down upon the unsuspecting Balolo, killing all the men who resist and catching all the rest. They then select the stronger portion of their captives and shackle them hand and foot to prevent their escape. The remainder they kill, distributing the flesh among themselves. As a rule, after such a raid they form a small encampment; they light their fires, seize all the bananas in the village, and gorge upon the human flesh. They then march over to one of the numerous slave markets on the river, where they exchange the captives with slave traders of the Lulungu River for beads, cloth, brass wire, and other trinkets. . . .
>
> A large trade is carried on between the mouth of the Ubangi and Lulungu rivers. The people inhabiting the mouth of the Ubangi buy the Balolo slaves at Masankusu and the other markets. They then take them up the Ubangi River and exchange them with the natives there for ivory. These natives buy their slaves solely for food. Having purchased slaves, they feed them on ripe bananas, fish, and oil, and when they get them into good condition they kill

them. . . . A great many other slaves are sold to the large villages on the Congo to supply victims for the execution ceremonies. . . .

Cannibalism exists among all the people on the Upper Congo east of 16° E. longitude, and is preva-alent to an even greater extent among the people inhabiting the banks of the numerous affluents. . . . I found trading somewhat difficult on this river, as the standard of value on the Ubangi was human life – human flesh. . . . During my first visit to the up-per waters of the Malinga River, cannibalism was brought to my notice in a ghastly manner. One night, I heard a woman's piercing shriek, followed by a stifled, gurgling moan; then boisterous laughter, when all again became silent. In the morning I was horrified to see a native offering for sale to my men a piece of human flesh, the skin of which bore the tribal tattoo mark of the Balolo. I afterwards learned that the cry we had heard at night was from a female slave whose throat had been cut. I was absent from this village of Malinga for ten days. On my return I inquired if any further bloodshed had taken place and was informed that five other women had been killed.

While in the Ruki River at the beginning of this year, I was furnished with another proof of the horrible fate of the slaves. At Esenge, a village near which I stopped to cut wood for my steamer, I heard ominous beating of drums and outbreaks of excited mirth. I was informed by one of the natives from the village that an execution was taking place. To my inquiry whether they were in the habit of eating human flesh, he replied, "We eat the body entirely." I further asked what they did with the head. "Eat it," he replied, "but first we put it in the fire to singe the hair off." [6]

The lucky ones were the African slaves who were fortunate enough to avoid the executions; but these poor souls were forced down the rivers to the coast, where they were sold to slave traders who loaded them onto ships crossing the Atlantic. Slaves were, by far, the most valuable cargo a ship could carry. Ships from Spain, Britain, Portugal, France, Denmark, Holland, and New England competed for this lucrative business.

There is hardly a word to adequately describe the misery of these Atlantic crossings. Depending upon the size of the ship, from 250-600 slaves might be crowded on board. Having been captured in the interior of the continent, the slaves had never seen an ocean, and yet water was to be their only view for the two-to-three month voyage as they lay chained to each other below deck just above the cargo holds. In some ships, they were laid below deck like spoons with almost no room to turn. In others, each man might lie in a space about four feet in width with a space above his head of 3-5 feet, hardly enough room to sit up, much less stand.

The sanitary conditions were horrible. In some cases, there were holes just above the bilges for defecating and urinating over the edge of the ship, but in some ships there were only slop jars, brimming with putrid waste. When manacled to another slave, it was difficult to get to a slop jar in time, especially if the poor creature had diarrhea – which was often the case. In a few days, the ship would reek with the smell of urine, feces, and vomit.

In rough seas, the portholes had to be closed, leaving the desperate creatures gasping for breath among the stench of human waste. Food was plentiful, owing to the desire of the captains not to lose a man and thereby lose a good deal of money, but food was served in a bucket, ten men to one bucket, leading to quarrels and infection. Even though they might be brought up on deck twice a week for fresh air, it wasn't enough to maintain health, and between 10% and 20% of them might be lost in transit. At times, the rate was even higher. The main causes of death were smallpox and dysentery, the latter caused by unsanitary conditions that left the men with diarrhea that became mucous and hemorrhagic. There are reports that some simply threw themselves overboard to escape their misery.

The men and women were separated as soon as the ship sailed. Women were usually not bound because they were not perceived as a threat; sometimes they were taken above deck to help in cooking, so their mortality rate was not as high.

Throughout the 350 years of the Atlantic slave trade, nearly 12 million African slaves made the trip, 42% of them going to the Caribbean and 38% to Brazil. Only 5% were brought to North America. The first slaver sailed from Boston in 1644, carrying slaves between Africa and the Caribbean. By 1700, Rhode Island had entered the slave trade, and for the next century 60% of the ships carrying slaves would be based in that tiny little state. Many of the powerful families in New England made their fortunes in the slave trade. An example is Elihu Yale, for whom Yale University is named. Yale was a notorious slave trader who orchestrated the slave trade in the Indian Ocean from Madagascar to Sumatra and grew rich from its spoils. While in India representing the East India Company, he instituted a rule requiring ten slaves to be on every ship sailing for Europe. Yet, today's social justice warriors have excused Yale and the slave merchants of New England while condemning the entire South for what was arguably the mildest form of involuntary servitude in the hemisphere. In short, they indict the entire plantation system in the Old South, laboring to connect the miserable slave trade, where there is no connection, with all the icons of our splendid heritage, demanding we reject everything identifiably Southern.

Let it be said that the contemptible slave trade was not the business of the South. It wasn't Southerners who crowded human beings into the stinking cargo holds of ships. It was the South, the Old South, the plantation South, that gave the poor wretches a home. In fact, the Confederate constitution of 1861 forbade the importation of slaves.

"Oh," but cries the naysayer, "I've seen movies, and I've read novels – why, I saw *Roots* on television!"

Often, we are treated to rare photos of horribly scarred blacks and told that it was the stripes of the lash of the overseer that put those marks on the backs of the subjects in the photos. Rarely, if ever, is a name provided – either of the slave or the owner – and rarely is there any documentation to prove that the scars are not the result of knife-fights and beatings between slaves themselves or of any number of bacterial infections that scarred the slave with horrible skin lesions. Nor do these 160-year-old photos carry documentation to show that they are of Southern blacks, Northern blacks, African blacks, or any number of black-skinned people scattered about the globe at the time. Their primary purpose is to inculcate in the American mind a hatred of the plantation South, thereby intimidating Southerners into silence.

Southern planters had perfected the process of successfully cultivating immense tracts of land, an endeavor which required large numbers of workers. Although the land mass of the South equaled or surpassed that of the North, by 1860 there were slightly less than 6 million white people in the South as opposed to 22 million in the Northern states. Owing to the scarcity of white workers, the plantations turned to slave labor. Some plantations consisted of as few as 10 slaves while larger plantations might consist of a thousand negroes cultivating several thousand acres. Many plantations were larger than the neighboring villages, and it is there, on those large plantations that South-haters like to imagine the substance of lurid novels and sensational movies.

Contrary to the wild imaginations and incendiary rhetoric of the propagandists, plantations were not scenes of mayhem and murder. They were self-contained communities no worse or better than the next village down the road. Isolated as they were in the rural South, large plantations were empowered by the state to adjudicate ordinary crimes and administer appropriate remedies. On some plantations, the owners set up juries of the slaves themselves to try fractious offenders and set their punishment; at times, however, the owner had to intervene and set aside the penalty decided upon by the slaves because it was often too severe. If a slave was killed or maimed, the crime would fall under the jurisdiction of the state, and the perpetrator, whether white or black, would have to stand trial in regular court.

Savage though they might have been when plucked from the jungle, these slaves were, after all, human beings and deserved to be treated as such. The master did not own the soul of the slave and had no right to brutalize him. Slaveholders, most of whom were Christian men, having bought the slave, owned the right to his labor. He was not a free agent; he worked for his owner. In return, the master clothed him, fed him, provided him a place to sleep, and gave him medical attention. When work was slow, the slave could hire out to a person in town, but the contract was between the employer and the owner, not the slave, so the wages were paid to the owner who in turn paid the slave his worth. An often overlooked benefit to the slave was his introduction to Christianity. Many a slave went on to become a preacher of the gospel.

But rather than waste breath trying to educate the self-righteous warriors of social justice, none of whom seem the least bit interested in being educated, let us take leave of their high-flown bombast and turn to the slave narratives of 1937, where former slaves describe plantation life in their own words.

During the Depression, the WPA paid unemployed workers to interview slaves in all of the Southern and border states. Most of these authentic interviews are first person accounts, recorded in the dialect of the former slave, while others were transcribed into regular English usage as third-person accounts. White people referred to their slaves as negroes, while slaves often referred to themselves as niggers, but interviewers were instructed to record the interviews in their entirety without any editing. Some are brief, and others are lengthy. Due to limited space, I have chosen some of the shorter ones. The following excerpts constitute only a handful of the WPA's 2300 interviews.

Charles Crowley, age unknown, Petersburg Virginia

My Marster and Mistess was good to me as well as all us slaves. Dey owned 'bout fifty head of Colored People. All de work I did wuz to play an' drive cows, being only a boy worked around as chillun, doin' dis an' dat, little things de white folks would call me to do.

Pete Arthur, Union, South Carolina

I was 'bout nine year ole when de big war broke loose. My pa and ma 'longed to de Scotts what libbed in Jonesville Township. When I got big 'nough to work, I was gib to de youngest Scott boy. Soon after dis, Sherman come through Union County. No, m'am, I nebber seed Sherman, but I seed some of his soldiers. Dat's de time I run off in de wood and not narry a soul knowed whar I was till de dus' had done settled in de big road.

Every Sunday, Marse Scott sent us to church in one of his waggins. White folks rid to church in de buggy and Marse went on de big saddle hoss.

John Cameron, age 95, Jackson, Mississippi

My old Marster was de bes' man in de worl'. I jes' wish I could tell, an' make it plain, jus' how good him an' old Mistus was. Marster was a rich man. He owned 'bout a thousand an' five hund'ed acres o' lan' an' 'round a hund'ed slaves. Marster's big two-story white house wid lightnin' rods standin' all 'bout on de roof set on top of a hill.

De slave cabins, 'cross a valley from de Big House, was built in rows. Us was 'lowed to sing, play de fiddles, an' have a good time. De cabins was kep' in good shape. Us ain never mine workin' for old Marster, 'cause us got good returns. Dat meant good livin' an' bein' took care of right. Marster always fed his slaves in de Big House.

De slaves would go early to de fiel's an' work in de cotton an' corn. Dey had different jobs.

De overseers was made to un'derstan' to be 'siderate of us. Work went on all de week lak dat. Dey got off from de fiel's early on Satu'd'y evenin's, washed up and done what dey wanted to. Some went huntin' or fishin', some fiddled an' danced an' sung, while de others just 'lazed 'round de cabins. Marse had two of de slaves jus' to be fiddlers. Dey played for us and kep' things perked up. How us could swing an' step 'bout by dat old fiddle music always a-goin' on! Den old Marster come 'roun' wid his kine'ly smile an' jov'al spir'ts. When things went wrong he always knowed a way. He knowed how to comfort you in trouble.

Now, I was a gardner or yard boy. Dat was my part as a slave. I he'ped keep de yard pretty an' clean, de grass cut, an' de flowers 'tended to an' cut. I taken dat work 'cause I laks pretty flowers. I laks to build frames for 'em to run on an' to train 'em to wine 'roun'. I could monkey wid 'em all de time.

When folks started a-comin' through talkin' 'bout a-freein' us an' a-givin' us lan' an' stuff, it didn' take wid Marster's slaves. Us didn' want nothin' to come 'long to take us away from him. Dem a–tellin' de niggers dey'd git lan' an' cattle an' de lak o' dat was all foolis'ness nohow. Us was a-livin' in plenty an' peace.

De war broke out spite 'o how Marster's niggers felt. When I seen my white folks leave for war I cried myself sick, an' all de res' did, too. Den de Yankees come through a-takin' de country. Old Marster refugeed us to Virginny. I can't say if de lan' was his'n, but he had a place for us to stay at. I know us raised 'enough food for all de slaves. Marster took care o' us dere 'til de war ended.

Den he come to camp late one evenin' and' tell us dat us was free as he was; dat us could stay in Virginny an' work or come to Mississippi wid him. Might nigh de whole passel bun'led up an' come back, an' glad to do it, too. Dar us all stayed til' de family all died. De las' one died a few years ago an' lef' us few old darkies to grieve over 'em. . . .

I's a Christian an' loves de Lawd. I expecks to go to Him 'fore long. Den I know I'se gwine see my old Marster an' Mistis a'gin.

Ezra Adams, 83, Swansea, South Carolina

De slaves on our plantation didn't stop workin' for old Marster even when dey was told dat dey was free. Us didn't want no more freedom dan us was gittin' on our plantation already. Us knowed too well dat us was well took care of, wid a plenty of vittles to eat and tight log and board house to live in. De slaves where I lived knowed after de war dat dey had abundance of dat somethin' called freedom, what they could not eat, wear, and sleep in. Yes, sir, dey soon found out dat freedom ain't nothin' 'less you is got somethin' to live on and a place to call home.

Isaac Adams, age 87, Tulsa, Oklahoma

My mammy belonged to Mr. Sack P. Gee. I don't know what his real name was, but maybe it was Saxon. Anyways, we called him Master Sack.

Old Mistress died when I was a baby so I don't remember anything about her, but Young Mistress was a winder! She would ride horseback nearly all the time, and I had to go with her when I got big enough. She never did go around the quarters so I don't know nothing much about the negroes Mr. Sack had for the fields. They all looked pretty clean and healthy, though, when they would come up to the Big House. He fed them all good, and they all liked him. . . .

I don't think my pappy was born in Louisiana. Alabama, maybe. I think his parents come off the boat because he was very black – even blacker than I am.

I seen the old Sack P. Gee place about twenty years ago, and it was all cut up in little pieces and all run down. Never would have known it was one time a big plantation ten miles long.

I seen places going to rack and ruin all around – all the places I lived at in Louisiana – but I'm glad I wasn't there to see Master Sack's place go down. He was a good man and done right by all his negroes.

Cornelia Winfield, age 82, Augusta, Georgia

My father and mother wuz house servants. My marster served my father's plate from his own table and sent it to him, every meal. He had charge of the workshop, and when marster was away he always stayed at the Big House to take care of my Missus and the children.

My mother was a seamstress and had three younger seamsters under her that she taught to sew. We made the clothes for all the house servants an' fiel' hans. My mother made some of the clothes for my marster and missus. My mother was a midwife, too, and useter go to all the birthings on our place. She had a bag she always carried, and when she went to other plantations she had a horse and buggy to go in.

All the slaves on our place wuz treated well. I never heard of any of 'em bein' whipped. I wuz ten years old when freedom come, and I always knowed I wuz to belong to one of marster's daughters. After freedom, my father and mother worked on just the same for marster. When my father died, marster's fam'ly wanted him buried in the fam'ly lot, but I wanted him to lie by my mother. All the planks any of our fam'ly was laid out on, my father kep'. When he came to Augusta, he brought all these planks and made this here wardrobe.

Willis Dukes, Madison, Florida
As reported by Pearl Randolph

Prayer meetings were very frequent during the days of the War, and very often the slaves were called in from the fields and excused from their labors so they could hold their prayer meetings, always praying God for the safe return of their master.

The master did not return after the War, and when the soldiers in blue came through that section the frightened women were greatly dependent upon their slaves for protection and livelihood. Many of these black men chose loyalty to their dead masters to freedom and shouldered the burden of the support of their former mistresses cheerfully.

Frank Adamson, 82, Winnsboro, South Carolina

I b'longs to de Peays. De father of dem all was Kershaw Peays. My marster was his son, Nicholas; he was a find man just to look at. My mistress was always tellin' him 'bout how fine an' handsome-like he was. He must of got used to it, however; marster grin ever time she talk like dat.

My pappy was bought from de Adamson peoples; they say they got him off de ship from Africa. He sho' was a man; he run all de other niggers away from my mammy an' took up wid her widout askin' de marster. Her name was Lavinia. When us got free, he 'sisted dat Adamson was de name us would go by. . . .

"Deed, I did work befo' freedom. What I do? Hoed cotton, pick cotton, 'tend to de calves and slop de pigs. . .

Us live in quarters. Our beds was nailed to de sides ob de house. Most of de chillun slept on pallets on de floor. Got water from a big spring. De white folks tend to you all right. Us had two doctors, Doctor Carlisle and Doctor James.

I see some money, but never own any then. Had plenty to eat: meat, bread, milk, lye hominy, horse apples, turnips, collards, pumpkins, and dat kind of truck.

Was marster rich? . . . He brag his land was ten miles square and he had a thousand slaves. . . . See them big rock columns down dare now? Dats all dats left of his grandness and greatness. Dey done move de whippin' post dat was in de backyard. Yes, suh, it was a 'cessity wid dem niggers. . . . I ain't complainin'. He was a good master, bestest in de lan', but he just have to have a whippin' post 'cause you'll find a whole passle of bad niggers when you gits a thousand of 'em in one flock. . . .

My young marsters was: Austin, Tom, and Nicholas. They was all right, 'cept dey tease you too hard maybe some time, and want to mix in wid de 'fairs of slaves 'musements.

LYNCHING

Almost as useful to the tear-'em-down crowd is the subject of lynching. Adding it to their arsenal, they employ it against the South as if they own it outright. The NAACP and all its satellite groups continually harangue the weary public with claims that lynching (1) happened only in the South, (2) happened only to blacks, and (3) it was only because of the race of those who were lynched that it even happened at all. Of course, disproving all of their platitudinous palavering is a mere matter of historical review.

Lynching, the punishment of a crime by a group of people, as opposed to retribution by a single person, has been a familiar feature of the American frontier as it pushed beyond civilization faster than trial courts could catch up with it. Punishment took many forms. It might involve riding a transgressor out of town on a rail, tarring and feathering, public flogging, or execution by hanging, burning, or shooting; however, it has recently become more narrowly associated in the public mind with hanging.

Its name can be traced back to a Col. Charles Lynch, who lived in Bedford County, Virginia during the Revolutionary War. Thieves had been stealing horses and selling them to the British army, but the only court for trying felonies was 200 miles away at Williamsburg, so by local consensus Col. Lynch's home was declared a courthouse. The colonel was the presiding judge and three of his neighbors acted as jurors. The court meted out punishment in various ways. Sometimes the accused was sentenced to a public whipping and at other times to being strung up by his thumbs until his behavior improved. After the war, Virginia's legislature allowed the judgments to stand, and the process became know as Lynch's Law.

Now, let us consider the first claim of the black activists, who want us to believe that lynching happened only in the South.

Of course, that proposition is demonstrably false. Lynching has taken place in every corner of the world at one time or the other. One need but go back to the seventh chapter of Acts and read about the stoning of Stephen by an angry mob who falsely accused him of blasphemy against Moses and God.

Closer to home, however, are the most notorious lynchings

that occurred in the American West, where the untamed frontier, so slow to be settled, lasted longer than at any other place in the country. Horse thieves were held in utter contempt out West, and "string him up" were the last words many a horse thief heard.

Most of the lynchings in the West were carried out for the crimes of theft and murder. On February 22, 1884, a mob, estimated from between 50 and 150 men took John Heath out of the Cochise County courthouse at Tombstone and hanged him from a telephone pole for his part in the widely reported Bisbee Massacre, where five outlaws robbed a general store in Bisbee and killed four people, including a peace officer and a woman who was expecting a baby. The five killers were tried, convicted, and sentenced to hang. John Heath was convicted as an accomplice but given life in prison. The mob was not satisfied, entered the jail, and lynched Heath.

Between 1850 and 1910, there were 87 lynchings in New Mexico and 48 in Arizona. During the same period, there were at least 143 lynchings in California, including two in San Francisco in 1851 and four more in 1856, all six hanged by the Committee of Vigilance. On May 12, 1892, John and Charles Ruggles robbed a stagecoach between Weaverville and Redding in northern California and killed the stage guard. The brothers were arrested and a trial was scheduled for July 24, but on July 28 masked men entered the jail, took the prisoners out, and hanged them in Redding. At least 163 Mexicans were hanged in California between 1848 and 1860.

During the Johnson County War in Wyoming, a range war between large landowners and new settlers coming into the region, there were several lynchings, one of which was carried out by several cattlemen who hanged Jim Averell and his wife, Ella Watson, better known as Cattle Kate. The double lynching of the Averells was followed by the lynching of Tom Waggoner, a horse trader from Newcastle, in June 1891.

That same year, in Rawlins, Wyoming, one of the town's prominent citizens, Dr. John E. Osborne, who later became governor of the state, participated in the vigilante hanging of a bandit by the name of George Parrott.

On January 8, 1882, James Sullivan, William Howard, and Benjamin Payne, were lynched by a mob in Seattle, Washington. On December 4, 1888, George Witherell was hanged from a telephone pole in Canon City, Colorado.

So, no, contrary to the purposes for which the enemy uses it, lynching was not endemic to the South.

But let us turn to their next hypothesis, wherein they claim that the only people ever lynched were blacks. This is absurd. If it were true, then none of the hangings just noted would ever have occurred. In those hangings, which sometimes involved Mexicans and Chinese, the preponderance of evidence shows that whites were the main target of lynching. Even in the South, statistics show that there were 567 white people lynched between 1882 and 1903. Nationwide, during the same period, there were 1,169 white people put to death by lynch mobs. It is nonsense to believe that blacks were the only people who were lynched.

All one has to do is remember the hanging in Marietta, Georgia, of Leo Frank, superintendent of the National Pencil Company. In 1913, Frank was charged with killing Mary Phagan, a child laborer at the pencil factory. Frank, a white man, was convicted and sentenced to death upon the testimony of the janitor, a black man. In June, the governor commuted Frank's sentence. On August 17, 1915, a group of men abducted Leo Frank from the Georgia prison farm at Milledgeville, drove him to Marietta, little Mary's hometown, and lynched him.

In Kentucky, the Simmons Gang had operated for years in the counties of Owen and Henry and were widely suspected of committing several robberies, thefts of cattle and horses, and cold-blooded murders. In September of 1877, Jim Simmons and four members of his gang were arrested. Several nights later, a mob took them from the Henry County jail and hanged them. All five of the Simmons Gang were white.

Not only were blacks not the only people lynched in the

South, blacks did some of the lynchings themselves. E. Merton Coulter, writing in *The South During Reconstruction,* tells of a lynching in Chicot County, Arkansas, where, in 1872, "armed negroes took three white men from jail, riddled them with bullets, and went about burning and pillaging."[7] Frank Shay, in *Judge Lynch: His First Hundred Years,* notes that blacks not only lynched whites but other blacks, as well. In 1908, for instance, in a recorded incident at Pine Level, North Carolina "an unnamed negro entertainer as lynched by negroes for putting on a poor show." In 1934, a thirty-year-old Negro was beaten to death in Caddo Parish "by members of his own race because of an alleged insult offered . . . to a colored girl." [8]

But now let us consider their preposterous claim that the only reason Southern blacks were lynched was that they were black. To believe that, one would have to discount the historical record of lynching in the West, where most of the hangings were of Caucasians. Additionally, it would be necessary to believe that no crimes had been committed by those who swung from the gallows. Recently, lynching enthusiasts have created a national lynching museum, purportedly designed "to acknowledge past racial terrorism." Nothing said about crimes committed by those who were lynched or the victims of such crimes. In fact, if you follow the propaganda you will come away with the notion that white people simply went out for a good time and hung a few negroes. Lynchings were not incidental to a picnic. But that is exactly what they would have us believe.

Lynchings, which naturally go against our collective sense of propriety and moral decency, resulted when community values were violated in the extreme, especially when it was feared that justice might not be served in the courts.

Southern lynchings were most numerous between the 1880s and the early 1920s, but by the mid-1930s, lynching had virtually disappeared. It is true that more blacks than whites were subjects of vigilante hangings during that period, but to say that this was the result of racial terrorism is to ignore the predicament in which the South found itself in the post-war years. Dwight D. Murphey, retired professor of business law at Wichita State University wrote,

> Most conspicuously, civilization itself, with all that it entails for everyone involved, white and black together, could not be restored and maintained if the white society were swamped by that of millions of people who had just emerged from slavery, with all that that entailed. . . One cannot overlook the fact that the defeated South contained the millions of newly-freed blacks, who at first maintained the habits of discipline that had been inculcated into them during slavery, but who, as time went on and a new generation emerged, began to lose those habits. [9]

In the American West, lynchings were the result primarily of murder and theft. In the South, most of them were the result of murder and rape. In 1893, a judge in Georgia, upon sentencing a young black man to death for the crime of rape, turned to the defendant and told him that his race "has many noble men and women who are exemplars in living upright, honest lives" but "I regret to notice that members of your race commit so many atrocious crimes, particularly among the younger class, some of which seem to be extremely vicious and hard-hearted." [10]

E. Merton Coulter writes that "slavery left the Negro illiterate and untrained for the responsibilities of freedom, with such weaknesses as lying and thieving exaggerated. He loved idleness, he had no keen conception of right and wrong, and he was improvident to the last degree of childishness." [11]

James Elbert Cutler, writing in *Lynch-Law: An Investigation into the History of Lynching in the United States*, said that "the worst instincts of the negro came to the front; the percentage of criminals among negroes increased to an alarming extent; many were guilty of crimes of violence of the most heinous and repulsive kind."[12] Even the famous black leader, WE.B. Dubois, spoke of "a class of black criminals, loafers, and ne'er-do-wells who are a menace to their fellows, both black and white."[13]

On August 21, 1901, newspapers in Texas and the Indian Territory carried stories about the burning on the previous day of a black man at the hands of a mob in Dexter, Texas, a small town just south of the Red River in north Texas.

About a week earlier, he had sneaked across a field toward a woman's house; but, upon seeing him, the lady put down all the windows and locked the doors. Going on to the next house, he found a Mrs. Caldwell at home, committed the outrage all women fear, then cut off the lady's head and dragged her body down into the storm cellar. When Mr. Caldwell came home, he followed a gruesome trail of blood down into the cellar where the poor man found his wife's decapitated body. The lady at the first house identified the black man, and the search was on. The killer had a club foot, so he was easy to follow by the tracks his deformed foot made in the dirt and sand. After eight days of searching, the murderer was found cowering in a field. According to newspaper reports, he had fled north across the Red River into Indian Territory, where he was captured by three men near Thackerville. As the group and their prisoner crossed back into Texas, heading south towards Whitesboro, rumors had it that a contingent of law officers were riding north in the direction of the slayer and his captors. It was then decided that he should be promptly lynched at Dexter, about twelve miles northwest of Whitesboro. Before long, a crowd of several hundred gathered in Dexter, watching as the criminal was lashed with chains and barbed wire to a large tree in front of the small town's two-story frame hotel, where corn stalks and husks were piled high around him. Newspapers state that upon the murderer's confession to the crime, Mrs. Caldwell's husband applied the match.

However grisly the scene, it must be noted that the villain was not lynched because he was black; he was killed because he had murdered Mrs. Caldwell.

SOUTHERN BY THE GRACE OF GOD

Ray Stannard Baker, historian, journalist, biographer, and recipient of the Pulitzer Prize, was the first prominent journalist to examine America's racial divide in his highly successful book, *Following the Color Line: An Account of Negro Citizenship in American Democracy.* Although his study inspired optimism among moderates and liberals, Baker, himself a political progressive, nevertheless clearly blamed blacks for the many lynchings to which whites resorted, both North and South, saying, "I found that this floating, worthless negro caused most of the trouble," adding that their crimes were marked by an almost "animal-like ferocity."[14]

Without a doubt, statistics show that more blacks were lynched in the South than were whites, but at the same time, statistics show that blacks committed disproportionately more murder, rape, and other serious crime than whites. In New Orleans, for instance, homicide rates between 1921 and 1922 among blacks were 46.7 per population of 100,000, while homicide rates among whites were only 8.4 per population of 100,000. Homicide rates in Memphis were 116.9 among blacks as opposed to 29.6 among whites. Atlanta showed a rate of 103.2 per 100,000 among blacks as opposed to only 15 per 100,000 among whites.

Now, it cannot be overstated that lynching is a revolting practice, and we can all be thankful that it is no longer a fixture in our American culture; but to claim that blacks were lynched merely because of the color of their skin is as absurd as to say that whites were lynched because of the color of their skin. It is even more insidious to demand that the magnificent monuments honoring our Confederate soldiers be demolished because of lynching, yet those who hate the South labor to make that connection in the public mind and especially in the minds of city councilmen, state legislators, mayors, and governors who hold the power to destroy the tangible evidences of our heritage.

It is most unfortunate that we, in our feeble efforts to save what remains of our splendid legacy, have to stoop to the level of debating our enemies over lynching and slavery, but the issue of race, as noted earlier in my introduction, is the battering ram with which they successfully, in fact gleefully, break down our resistance and pry from us a heritage that was once the envy of the civilized world. Ours was a band of cavaliers in a land, blessed of God with temperate climate and beauty unrivaled, desperately striving against all odds to repeat what their grandfathers had accomplished in 1781 when Cornwallis surrendered at Yorktown. Even though failing in our quest for independence, we strove mightily, played the game fairly, and arose from the ashes in the confidence of knowing that we were in the right.

The English, watching from afar, were much in sympathy with the Confederacy as it struggled in its infancy to win its independence. It was fervently hoped and widely believed that England would come to the aid of the South, but Prime Minister Palmerston dithered until it was too late. Shortly after the surrender at Appomattox, P.S. Worsely, an English scholar who in 1861 had translated Homer's *Iliad* from the original Greek, sent a complimentary copy to General Lee. On the flyleaf, he inscribed a poem of admiration to the great general.

To GENERAL R.E. LEE, the most stainless of living commanders, and, except in fortune, the greatest, this volume is presented with the writer's earnest sympathy and respectful admiration.

> The grand old bard that never dies,
> Receive him in our English tongue!
> I send thee, but with weeping eyes,
> The story that he sung.

SOUTHERN BY THE GRACE OF GOD

Thy Troy is fallen, thy dear land
    Is marred beneath the spoiler's heel.
I cannot trust my trembling hand
    To write the things I feel.

Ah, realm of tombs! But let her bear
    This blazon to the last of times:—
No nation rose so white and fair,
    Or fell so pure of crimes.

The widows' moan, the orphan's wail,
    Come round thee; yet in truth be strong!
Eternal right, though all else fail,
    Can never be made wrong.

An angel's heart, an angel's mouth,
    Not Homer's, could alone for me
Hymn well the great Confederate South,
    Virginia first, and LEE.

                          — P.S.W.

But with the end of the war came the beginning of eternal persecution. There is no end to it. For twelve years we were ransacked by carpetbaggers. Our state governments were plunged into debts that plagued us far into the 20th century. Taxes were wrung from us and paid out to Union veterans while our poor Confederate soldiers were unilaterally denied pensions. Bankrupted by Northern vultures, we were laughed at in our poverty, ridiculed in our desperation, and mocked in our humble existence. In the thirties, when we tried to escape the grinding poverty of the dust bowl, we were called Okies and became the pariahs of the West Coast. In the sixties, our magnificent institutions of learning were disrupted, our peaceful society destroyed, and our blacks and whites pitted against each other in the guise of civil rights. For the past fifty years our customs, speech, and religion have been mercilessly attacked. The self-righteous, all-powerful media rakes the muck and sets the pace in dismantling our very heritage. There is not a good white man nor a bad black to be found in the South. Our law enforcement officials are pot-bellied and corrupt. White men are lazy, full of hate, and always hanging around honky-tonks. Black men are brain surgeons and as pure as the driven snow, father of two and pillar of the community. White churches are full of hypocrites. Black churches are full of saints. The tell-tale mark of a bigoted community is the presence of a Confederate monument, and the poor old Confederate flag is to blame for every evil named among men.

I know of no other group of people, ethnic or otherwise, who are made to bear public censure day after day, year after year, for quietly memorializing their cultural heritage. Do we tell the Jew to forget the abominations of the Holocaust? No, we sit in sackcloth and ashes and console him in his grief. Is the Cherokee put on a guilt trip for moving his slaves down the Trail of Tears? No, we forget about the slaves and weep with the Indian, marking his miserable route with bronze tablets. Do we tell the black man to forget slavery? Heavens, no! We make it into something it wasn't and use every means at our disposal to inflame his passions against the Southern white. Do we tell the aging veteran to forget World War II and quit fighting his war? No, we meticulously manicure cemeteries in Europe where his fallen comrades sleep.

Surprisingly, however, throughout the interminable years of condemnation, there were a few welcome breaks worthy of mention. The first came shortly after the Spanish-American War in 1898, when Southern boys were seen for the first time in the service of the United States military. In fact, Confederate General Joe Wheeler served during the Spanish-American War as a major general in command of the cavalry, which included

Teddy Roosevelt's Rough Riders.

Following the Spanish-American War, in a spirit of reconciliation, President McKinley proposed that the federal government should begin caring for the graves of Confederate soldiers;
consequently, a Confederate section was created at Arlington
National Cemetery in 1900. In 1906, Congress provided for supplying headstones for Confederate soldiers who died in Northern
prisons and hospitals, and in 1929 the law was expanded to
include headstones for all Confederate soldiers wherever they
were buried.

In 1905, President Roosevelt returned hundreds of captured Confederate flags to the Southern states. The flags had been
lying in the basement of the War Department since the end of
the war and would have been returned in 1887 by President
Cleveland, the first Democrat to be elected after the war, but for
a bitter outcry from Republicans who were still bitter towards the
South. Angry invective hurled at both Cleveland and Southerners
in general, did not abate until they had defeated Cleveland in
the next election. It would be almost two more decades before
feelings subsided enough to allow Roosevelt, a Republican himself, to return the flags.

Additionally, the turn of the century seemed to herald a
new fascination with Dixie as trains began hauling thousands of
vacationing northerners down South By the 1920s Southern roads
had progressed to the extent that Northern tourists began
making their annual treks to Florida by automobile. Composers,
including the inimitable Irving Berlin, wrote and published
hundreds of songs about the "dreamy South." Al Jolson, called
"the world's greatest entertainer," recorded song after song of
Southern tunes like *Mammy, Swanee, and Rock-a-Bye Your Baby
With a Dixie Melody*. It was a surprising yet welcome era of good
feeling towards the South.

It was during this time that most of the monuments to
Confederate soldiers were erected. Some monuments had been
constructed during the 1880s and 1890s, but by the turn-of-the-

century the soldiers were growing old, giving impetus to a renewed drive for memorializing their bravery and sacrifice. In 1894, the wives, widows, daughters, nieces, and granddaughters of the aging soldiers met in Nashville and chartered the United Daughters of the Confederacy, an organization that would become known as "the monument builders." The war had reduced the South from its lofty position as the wealthiest part of the country to the poorest, and, bankrupt as it had become from the years of Reconstruction, funds for building monuments simply weren't there. The ladies of the UDC and the children of the South stepped up to the task, raising money pennies and nickels at a time, and paid for the construction of thousands of magnificent monuments across the South.

To a certain extent, the feeling of reconciliation can be said to have held through the centennial of the War Between the States. A few years prior to 1961, Congress established a Civil War Centennial Commission for the purpose of commemorating the four-year event and urged every state to establish its own Centennial Commission. From 1961 through the early part of 1965, thousands of events were held throughout the South in recognition of the bravery, sacrifice, and dedication to a cause that characterized Southerners of a century earlier. It was a time to unfurl the Confederate flag and carry it in parades, wave it from cars, and hoist it above courthouses. Alabama enthroned it above the state capitol; South Carolina did likewise; Oklahoma flew it in front of the state capitol in Oklahoma City. In anticipation of the centennial, Georgia placed the Confederate emblem so judiciously on their state flag that vexillologists hailed it as one of the most perfectly designed banners in the world. A resurgence of Southern pride spread across Dixie, and people were set to enjoy, even in defeat, their enviable legacy.

Enter the spoiler. The NAACP was not going to let this pass. Plans were laid to throw the entire operation into turmoil. No sooner had the Civil War Centennial Commission scheduled its first commemorative event, the reenactment of the bombardment of Ft. Sumter, than the New Jersey commission's delegation protested the celebration. Knowing full well that hotels in Charleston were segregated, the New Jersey commission appointed a member of the NAACP to its roster, then issued demands that their black member be accommodated in the same hotel as other members of the various state commissions. Delegations from New York, California, and Illinois joined the protest, resulting in the removal of the entire Centennial conference to the Charleston Navy Yard.

Thus began the unending demands of the civil rights activists, all timed to spoil the Centennial. The four-year commemoration became tinged with racial strife. America's historical observances and reenactments were interspersed with civil rights marches, sit-ins, protests, demonstrations and riots, and the blameless Confederate flag was skillfully linked with opposition to black demands. Busloads of Northern blacks, adroitly labeled "freedom riders," were sent into the Deep South to violate the South's separate waiting rooms, lunch counters, and restrooms. Confrontations with state and local police were instigated in many Southern cities. The Kennedy administration sued school boards all over the South, forcing white families to send their children to black schools. The federal government initiated a riot at Ole Miss when it sent truckloads of combat troops rolling onto the campus. It was all playing out according to plan. The Centennial had been coopted by the black power brokers and their collaborators. Yes, people sang *Dixie*, waved their flags, and gayly shouted, "Save your Confederate money, boys – the South shall rise again!" But their merriment was tempered by the ever-present cloud of racial unrest.

The four years of the Civil War Centennial had been a tremendous success – for the NAACP. They had managed to create a visceral connection between racial issues and the Confederacy, and from that false premise they launched a perpetual campaign to prevent the white South from deriving any pleasure in celebrating its own history.

It was the last time Southerners could count on unqualified public ceremony; henceforth, to hold an event connected with Confederate history was to invite protests, lawsuits, threats of violence, and condemnation by the media. Eventually, schools and mainline churches joined the increasingly strident voices that denounced Confederate history, calling it "un-American."

As the years passed, more and more radical thought took root. Extremists demanded the removal of anything and everything having the slightest connection with the Old South. Names of streets, roads, highways, schools, hospitals, mascots all had to go – and they did. But never satisfied, the social justice warriors have now turned their wrath upon even the hallowed graves of long-departed Confederate soldiers. Vandalism of tombstones and cemetery monuments by Black Lives Matter and other terrorist groups have become almost commonplace across the South.

During the Obama administration, the Department of Veterans Affairs received orders to stop providing headstones for Confederate soldiers. Cleverly hatched, the directive did not rescind the 1929 act of Congress but achieved the same goal by adding a stipulation that an application for a Confederate headstone could only be made by the next of kin. More than 150 years after the war, it is virtually impossible to find a next-of-kin for most Confederate soldiers. As a result, many Confederate soldiers will forever lie in unmarked graves.

Our magnificent monuments, nearly all of which are dedicated to the memory of the Confederate soldier, are being dismantled because, in the words of the radical social justice crowd, they "represent slavery and lynching" and "were raised for the purpose of intimidating blacks." Pure nonsense. That is insulting, indeed, to the memory of the ladies of the South who, in nearly every instance, raised the money to build these military memorials. Our statues of Jackson, Lee, and Forrest were erected for the same reason statues of Sherman, Sheridan, and Grant, were erected in the North. They were our heroes.

If our Confederate monuments were, as our detractors charge, erected to memorialize lynching and slavery rather than the battlefield bravery of our military forces, then how do they explain the Confederate monuments that line Confederate Avenue in Vicksburg National Military Park? Or, perhaps those monuments are next on their demolition list.

Besides, as pointed out by Professor Murphey, who is not a Southerner, the South's determination to survive was a natural human response to the twin disasters of War and Reconstruction.

> The white population, despite its defeat, possessed a fierce spirit made up of several reinforcing elements: of localism, of community, of defiance of and later freedom from external authority, of a tradition of independence and self-sufficiency, of "honor" as a cultural system . . . of quiet despair over defeat, and of determination about the imperative to establish as quickly and as securely as possible the foundations of civilized order.
>
> As to the latter of these points, many twentieth-century writers, speaking in a "politically correct" tone . . . deride white Southerners as having wanted to "keep blacks in their place" and to "maintain white supremacy." Here, their ideology blinds them. . . .
>
> The white South had not lost its will to exist. Because mainstream Americans in the late twentieth century largely have lost a will to maintain a nation based largely on their own identity, this is something our contemporaries are unwilling to understand. To declare the white South's will to exist "racist" is simply to declare hostility towards a given people and culture. [15]

Not only do we have to suffer the physical destruction of the evidences of our civilization, our political strength was reduced with the overthrow of the Democrat party in the South, another casualty of the 1960s. Until 1964, the "solid South," as it was called, could be counted on to send conservative, traditional, authentic Southern Democrats to Washington. But during our preoccupation with the Civil War Centennial, young Northern hippies, drunk on the idea of social justice, fanned out across Dixie during their summer recess from college, registering thousands of blacks with the goal of taking over the Democrat party in the South. In 1964, at their national convention in Los Angeles, the credentials committee of the Democrat party refused to seat the legitimate Mississippi delegation, recognizing instead a rival delegation consisting mostly of newly registered blacks. Six weeks earlier, Congress had passed the controversial civil rights act, a broad, sweeping directive that forced the South to comply with complete integration in virtually all aspects of Southern life.

Not surprisingly, the solid South began to crumble. In the presidential election of 1964, five of the Deep South states voted Republican for the first time since Reconstruction. Realizing the opportunity, northern Republicans set their sights on the South, and in no time Southerners began flocking to a political party that had once been anathema to them. With arms outstretched and promises aplenty, Republicans eventually scooped up most of the white voters in the South. As it turned out, however, Republicans, even though representing much of the conservative thought attractive to a Southerner, were not the least bit interested in the endangered culture of the South.

Too late we learned that a Southern politician had to check his "Southern" at the door – and he did just that, accepting the Yankee adulation of Abraham Lincoln, the man most responsible for destroying the South, and happily spreading the party's annual Lincoln Day Dinners across the South. Indeed, we found that not only do Republican politicians fail to speak against the cultural cleansing of the South, they are eager to promote it. In 1987, Henry Bellmon, Oklahoma's first Republican governor,

xl

removed the Confederate flag in front of the state capitol in Oklahoma City. Several years later, another Republican governor, Frank Keating, removed the Choctaw flag from the state capitol when he learned that it had been carried by Choctaws during the war. In Texas, it was George W. Bush who removed two plaques from the Texas Supreme Court building, which was constructed with funds that had been set aside for Confederate widows. The plaques had been there since the building was constructed in 1955, one bearing an inscription to the memory of Confederate soldiers from Texas. The other plaque featured a quote from Robert E. Lee, expressing his appreciation of the Texas troops. Both gone, thanks to a Republican governor.

A few years ago, Greg Abbott, another Republican governor, so adamantly opposed allowing the Sons of Confederate Veterans in Texas a specialty license plate, spent taxpayer money taking the issue all the way to the Supreme Court, who agreed with Abbott, thus denying them the license plate with their logo.

In Georgia, it was a Republican governor who, refusing to allow the people to vote on keeping the state flag with its Confederate emblem, offered up two or three choices, none of which were the flag that Georgians had loved since 1956, and thus rigged an election to change the flag to a design no one wanted.

Asa Hutchinson, a Republican who gained notoriety from his role in the impeachment of President Clinton, was eventually elected governor of Arkansas; whereupon, he began pushing for a change in the official description of the Arkansas state flag that would deny the fact that one of the three stars in the center of the flag stands for Arkansas's allegiance to the Confederacy.

In South Carolina, Republican Governor David Beasley began a push to have the Confederate flag removed from atop the statehouse. He had campaigned on a promise not the remove the flag, but of course, like many Republicans who after getting our votes turn around and bite us, he pressured the legislature to remove the flag. For his treachery, he received the John F.

Kennedy Profile in Courage Award, presented by none other than the U.S. Senator from Massachusetts, Ted Kennedy. His betrayal, however, Caused Beasley to be defeated for re-election by a Democrat, and the flag was safe again – but only for a while.

A Republican legislature, in some sort of coercive compromise, eventually removed the flag from the capitol dome, placing it on a pole behind a Confederate statue in front of the capitol. But it would take a Republican woman of Sikh Indian parentage, having no background in American culture, to banish it forever. Nimrata Randhawa, who ran for governor under the name of Nikki, pulled the same Republican trick, telling voters she was for keeping the flag flying, but after being elected she changed her mind and asked the Republican legislature to remove it, which they promptly did.

Republicans keep ripping us, and we keep voting for them. So what is the alternative? There is no alternative. The state apparatus, except in Virginia, is controlled by Republicans, while black Democrats control the cities, such as New Orleans, Dallas, and Memphis, all of which have destroyed their Confederate monuments. We have no port in the storm.

Regrettably, our people are partly to blame. We are distracted in the extreme. Not only are Southerners hopelessly addicted to their latest technological toys, completely disinterested in much of anything they can't find, play, or hear on their smartphones, they live and breathe sports. A ballgame can be found somewhere twenty-four hours a day. If it's not football, it's basketball. If it's not college sports, it's professional sports. No time for reading, learning, or understanding their own culture. No appreciation of the past. Just give them a sofa, a can of beer, and the remote control – so they can find the next ballgame.

In between ballgames, they turn to the radio talk shows to get their political views. Thousands – no, millions – of our folks hang onto every word that proceeds out of the mouth of Rush Limbaugh. A former radio sports announcer, Limbaugh has been clever enough to do something the rest of us have not been able to do: carve out a platform for spreading his political views – and make millions doing it. Rush Limbaugh's narrow life views can be summed up in one simple phrase: *Republicans good, Democrats bad*. Every idea has to be squeezed into that tiny box. Obviously no intellectual, he simply makes comments on the news of the day, lacing his tirades with smutty remarks and suggestive banter. But it is his hostility to the Confederacy, secession, and the principle of independence for which our ancestors fought and died that pose the danger. Too many of our people believe what they hear from Rush Limbaugh, Sean Hannity, Mark Levin, Glenn Beck, and other potentates of talk radio, none of whom are Southern. Hannity is from New York; Levin is from Pennsylvania; Beck is from Washington. Rush Limbaugh, who hails from the southeastern corner of Missouri, could qualify as Southern, but he doesn't seem to want that connection.

All of them rail against the Confederacy, hurling invective against the heroic leaders of our struggle for independence, reminding gullible listeners that it was – here we go again – Democrats who instigated what they snidely call "the rebellion." *Republicans good, Democrats bad.* Glenn Beck singles out Nathan Bedford Forrest for special denunciation, while Sean Hannity assails Confederate flag supporters and Mark Levin sneers at secession. When the attacks upon our statues, monuments, and tombstones began, the most any of them would do was make timid statements of dismay that "monuments were erected by people of another time who shouldn't be held to the same standards of today"– and then they moved on. No real interest in actually coming to our defense *because they are not Southern*.

Several of the talk show gurus brought on an odd Indian troublemaker from Bombay named Dinesh D'Souza, often de-scribed as a conspiracy theorist and political provocateur. D'Souza is a convicted felon with a checkered past which in-cludes outing gays when he wrote for the student newspaper at Dartmouth. So, why you might ask, is he the darling of the neo-conservative talking heads? Answer: He makes documentaries and movies about the Democrats of the Old South – you know, the ones who loved the Confederacy, the flag, and our legacy of Southern independent thought. Disparaging our ancestors, this foreigner's assessment of the Southern experience fits their simplistic patter perfectly: *Republicans good, Democrats bad.*

And this is where we are today. Our culture and its sacred icons are rapidly vanishing, and there has been virtually no response adequate to saving them. There are three primary reasons we fiddle while Rome burns.

(1) We are distracted by sports and endless entertainment.

(2) We exchange our birthright for political intrigue, and sit at the feet of those who hate us.

(3) The enemy has adroitly chosen a battlefield upon which we do not wish to fight.

I cannot reverse the downward trajectory. I can only present historical fact within theses pages with a fervent hope that it takes root among those who read it. But cold hard facts can accomplish only so much. After all, the generations younger than mine have never thrilled to the sounds of a band playing *Dixie*. They've never even heard a band play *Dixie*. They have never seen Confederate flags waving atop courthouses and state capitols. They have never sat in a movie theater watching *Gone With the Wind*, crying with Mammy and cheering when Scarlett shoots that Yankee bummer right between the eyes. They've never leaped out of bed on Saturday mornings to watch Nick Adams in *The Rebel* or anxiously anticipated seeing Tod Andrews on Thursday evenings as he portrayed Col. John S. Mosby in *The Gray Ghost*. Those experiences come around only once in a lifetime. All I can do is try to evoke as much mental imagery of that golden era as is humanly possible within the limitations of the printed page.

And now, Dear Reader, I invite you to turn the page and read the original preface to *Southern by the Grace of God*.

November 1, 2020   *Michael Andrew Grissom*

Three Oaks

Courtesy of *White Pillars*, by J. Frazer Smith, © 1941

D'Evereux

Courtesy of *White Pillars*, by J. Frazer Smith, © 1941

Preface

There is a popular slogan in the South today: AMERICAN BY BIRTH, SOUTHERN BY THE GRACE OF GOD. You'll see it on bumper stickers, car tags, T-shirts, baseball caps, and just about anything that lends itself to printing. It tells something about us – how we feel, how we think, how we perceive ourselves. Southerners, who enjoy a reputation for being among the most patriotic people in America, consider their Southern status as something special, something above and beyond the good fortune of being American. It's the icing on the cake.

Yes, there *is* something about the South. Oh, yes, just say it: *The South*. The words hang heavy with dewdrops, honeysuckle, and magnolia blossoms. Steamboat 'round the bend. Fields of snowy white cotton. Southern belles. Smiling faces. Laughter on the levee. It's a storied land of romance and chivalry, fabled in legend and song and unlike anything known upon this continent. When you speak of the north, the east, or the west, you are speaking of a direction; but when you speak of the South, you are speaking of a country, a time, a place. The Old South. Margaret Mitchell told us it was "gone with the wind" and to look for it only in books, for it is no more than a dream remembered."[1] But we refused to let go of it, and today it lives not only in books, but in our souls as well.

Yet, at the same time, the Margaret Mitchell of 1936 may well prove to have been somewhat of a prophetess after all. I don't know whether our past glory lives on in fewer of us or if it lives less well in all of us. One thing is for sure – we are edging ever more closely to the point of losing our Southern heritage. If we become even the slightest bit more detached than we already are and fail to pass it on to our young, it truly will be found only in books. It can be lost in only one neglected generation. If we fail to perpetuate so glorious a legacy, then it truly may be spoken of us what Tacitus wrote of those who frivolously existed under the Roman Empire: "We cannot be said to have lived, but rather to have crawled in silence, the young towards the decrepitude of age and the old to dishonourable graves." [2]

North and South have never been alike and never will be as long as we remain free men and women. From earliest colonial days, the states north of Virginia followed divergent paths from those to the south. Two cultures developed in opposite directions. About the only thing they shared in common was the same language, and even that they spoke with different dialects. Southerners developed a philosophy of complete independence and individual freedom and were relatively free from governmental restraint. It was a system which worked well in the thinly populated, though geographically large, South. It was basically a policy of non-interference; consequently, Southerners cared little how northerners, or anyone else, carried on their day-to-day affairs. On the other hand, the populous North embraced the notion of a strong central government in which its citizens necessarily gave up a bigger measure of individuality. This ideology of universal governmental management produced, by its very nature, a policy of interference, whereby northerners operated upon the theory that if it was good for the North then it ought to be good for the South. The arrogance that attaches to such a narrow view would lead directly to a disastrous war in 1861.

Considering the large expanse of land covered by the new United States and the early polarization of North and South, it is a marvel that we long existed as one country. A more logical course might have been peaceful coexistence as two strong allies, both of European descent, similar to the relationship between the United States and Canada. As noted in the paragraph above, our strained attempts at holding together two cultures so diametrically opposed resulted in a regrettable war which proved only that a form of government which relies upon strong centralization can force us to cohabitate.

Conquered militarily, the South was expected to capitulate in spirit as well, but to a shocked world, we laid down our arms and picked up our pens. Unconquered in will, even after the oppression of Reconstruction, we exchanged our battle of bullets for a battle of the minds. Our love for independence and freedom from governmental supervision of our lives lived on, even under a system that has become increasingly contrary to individual liberty. Today, the South is the conservative balance against that same old liberalism against which we defended and lost, and our dilemma is the struggle between our American patriotism and an American that moves further every year into the abyss of centralized rule.

Since Appomattox, or we might more precisely say, since Reconstruction ended in the 1870s, the battle to harness the stubborn Southerner has moved from the bloody fields of Virginia to the halls of Congress across the Potomac. Between that political body and the Supreme Court, our traditions, laws, customs, and very mannerisms have been the objects of contention; nevertheless, we have had the fortitude to withstand each onslaught, perpetuating our heritage and handing it down from generation to generation. Indeed, we seemed to have won something of a reprieve in the early part of this century. We stood side by side with our Northern counterparts in a World

War, and as a result those people seemed, suddenly, to have rediscovered the South, this time in a more favorable light. The war years and the 1920s were full of fascination with this land below the Mason-Dixon line. It seemed that nearly every other song was about Dixie, Swanee, or Mammy. *The Jazz Singer* ushered in an era of good feeling on the silver screen that reached its artistic apex in 1939 in *Gone With the Wind*. Right on into the '50s, moviegoers could pretty well count on a Southern gentleman and his belle cast as the suffering hero and heroine, while Yankees represented the eternal invading villains of the halcyon land of cotton. At least the movies had it right, and Southerners basked in the sunshine of cinematic vindication.

In writing a book, one has to answer as to why he undertook the project. He first has to answer to himself; then, he must justify his subject to his readers. There were various reasons leading to this particular endeavor, but I think he single most important motive was that it has become alarmingly apparent that the South's conception of itself has made a precipitous decline from the description in the preceding paragraph. Even though we do have this intuitive sense that we are *Southern by the Grace of God*, we are less and less sure as to the reason, especially now that our old foes have entered among the flock and have made some converts among us who rise up and flail us as readily, or more so, than those from without. It is tragic enough to succumb to an outside attack, but it is a pity, indeed, to watch our heritage being dismantled year after year at the very hands of *Southerners* themselves. It wasn't latter-day Yankees who banned the playing of *Dixie* at ballgames; it was spineless *Southern* school boards and squeamish administrators. It wasn't Washington officials who retired our proud Confederate flags from our courthouses and city halls; it was timid, waffling *local* officials.

Southerners have become confused in recent years by the abundance of negative literature about the South. Literature, like clothing, is of a faddish nature, and it's unfortunate that poor, tasteless, pessimistic writing has been the fashion for some time

now. Good material is relegated to the back shelf while the sensational commands the attention of the world, resulting in a vacuum where truth and pride of belonging wither.

It occurred to me that Southerners, no matter how stalwart or steeped in their heritage, could not withstand such a bombardment of demeaning criticism indefinitely. Then I remembered a Scripture from my youth. In the book of *Hosea*, God says, "My people are destroyed for lack of knowledge." It is an eternal principle, and I saw at once the answer to the current situation: Knowledge.

But where would one find that knowledge? Certainly not in the textbooks of our schools. It has been a continuing source of disappointment to see traditional heroes, values, and examples of valor culled every year from Southern history texts. Today, virtually every school system in the South is equipped with American history books produced in the north by northern authors. Is there not a scholar in the South who can author an American history text designed to instill pride in Southern youth? Maybe the question should be: Is there a state textbook committee or superintendent in the South who would adopt such a book if written? We definitely have a problem when children in the South are raised on the fables of *Honest Abe* while they're taught that their own forebears were the villains of our country's history.

Today, I think it would be difficult to find a student of high school age who could name two Confederate generals or one important battle of that unfortunate war which, for all its misery, welded the Southern states into a solid community of people who share a common heritage unmatched among civilizations of the world. What student can recount one single story of courage and heroism, even though our quest for independence is replete with extraordinary examples of valor?

It's been said that an author writes the book he can't find on the library shelf. As I pondered the deteriorating situation, it was becoming clear to me that Southerners – especially the deprived youth of today – desperately need a short course in their own heritage, and it was apparent was that there was no such book addressing that problem. There are books that deal with specific aspects of our heritage, but nothing that consolidates the aspects of our heritage into a concise reference for Southerners who need a general knowledge of their heritage without having to spend the rest of their lives sifting through library acquisitions in search of it.

Convinced of the need for such a book, I set out to compile a volume which would do four important things: (1) provide the Southerner with a general overview of his heritage, (2) instill in him a greater pride in being Southern, (3) point him in the direction for further pursuit of the separate elements of his heritage, and (4) alert him to the fact that the distinguishing marks of his culture are fading away in the hope that a conscious effort will be made to maintain his heritage for posterity.

Designed to be something of a handbook for Southerners, this work attempts to familiarize the Southerner with those elements of his heritage that are obvious as well as those which are so much an unconscious part of us that they go unnoticed and taken for granted. For instance, one chapter is devoted to a discussion of our delightful Southern accent, which for all its pleasing delivery, is becoming a thing of the past as we sit zombie-like in front of our TV sets, day in and day out, subconsciously mimicking its bland, robotic speech. Another chapter discusses the great tangible symbols of the South, such as our Confederate flag, our holidays, and *Dixie*, while one part of the book is devoted to a wide range of subjects, such as our religion, our music, and our food.

Much of the narrative is in the first person. I relied upon stories and illustrations from my own past that will, no doubt be reflective of similar situations in the Southern backgrounds of each reader. One chapter is full of tales told by Southerners, who are, of course, the master storytellers. Most of the stories are previously unpublished but have stood the test of time, surviving in the vernacular, giving us an insight into the events which captured the imagination of the average man, as opposed to the professional writer of history. The famous *Bell Witch* of Tennessee claims her place in this section, which also includes a tale of dead reckoning in *The Hangin' at Ada*.

Genealogy is more important than ever nowadays, and in that respect I believe our heritage is relatively healthy. One chapter was planned with the beginning genealogist in mind, giving him or her a brief boost in getting started on that mos fascinating of journeys into the past. For the reader interested in finding a Confederate ancestor in the family tree, I have included a comprehensive list of the major agencies across the South who hold Confederate records, along with mailing addresses and contact information for those repositories.

Near the center of the book are pages of old photographs, depicting family life, style of dress, modes of transportation, and architecture of yesteryear. Not only are the photographic plates entertaining, they are germane to the text – even more, they are essential to it. They present a picture of Southern life from shortly before the War Between the States through the first World War. Except for photographs of well-known Confederate heroes, most of the pictures are previously unpublished images of the average Southern citizen who, along with his neighbors, pulled himself up by his own bootstraps after the War and, by the proverbial sweat of his brow, raised the South back to prosperity. Collected from across the South over a period of years, the pictures come primarily from my own collection, with others borrowed from kind friends and several state archives. The photographic section is designed to give us a look at real people who are typical ancestors of Southerners like you and me. The photos give us a visual concept and help us put faces on the characters in the stories, underscoring the underlying theme of the whole book – pride in *our* Southern heritage.

Of course, no book about the South would be complete without a look at the disastrous war, that paradoxical event which brought so much suffering yet called Southern manhood to its finest hour. One chapter outlines that episode of Southern history with an honest approach toward laying the blame for that bloody conflict squarely where it belongs. A section about Southern heroes contains brief sketches of the lives of seven giants of the Confederacy, men who once graced the pages of our Southern history books and inspired the youth of the South to emulate their deeds. Then, we take a hard look at the era of Reconstruction, a period of time that is not as clear to modern Southerners as it should be, owing primarily to the efforts now underway to rewrite that nightmare into a nice little novel about social progress.

As I travel across the South, I come in contact with hundreds of people who are weary of malcontents and politicians who feed off negative causes and continuously haul Southerners before the court of public opinion hoping for a guilty verdict. Southerners have been worn down to the bone with the anti-South psychosis that has afflicted our critics for so many years. Even though some of our own were caught up in the slanderous lies and accusations of the radicals and have turned to self-destructive caviling, I believe there has been a recent turnaround. More and more Southern citizens are willing to uncloset themselves and stand against the tide, and it's even beginning to be somewhat fashionable to be Southern once again. There are a lot of Southerners who believe that the Confederate flag should still be flown, *proudly*; that the Southern accent should still be spoken, *proudly*; that *Dixie* should still be played, *proudly*; and that we should take great pride in knowing who we are – we of a splendid heritage. To those people this book is dedicated. Stand up and cheer!

Michael Andrew Grissom

Wynnewood, Oklahoma
January 1, 1988

Auburn

Courtesy of *White Pillars*, by J. Frazer Smith, © 1941

I

Southern

Let me state my case and state it certain: I love the South. No qualms, No apologies. No qualifiers. I love the South!

If you're looking for one of those trendy books in which the South is socially and politically dissected for the base purpose of defaming our fair region, you'd best pass this one up. This book reflects a genuine appreciation for the enchanted land of Dixie and the blessing we Southerners have of calling it home.

There's a curious phenomenon in the South today. It used to be that Yankees criticized everything we did, and we, with one indignant voice, rose up in our own defense; but, a while back they slipped up on some of our slower folks and taught them to criticize themselves. Now the Yankees lie back and watch this new breed of misguided Southerners do their braying for them. This new bunch has decided to call itself *The New South*. They like that. It helps them feel that they have risen above the rest of us and that their superior intellect has permitted them to shake off the vestiges of the Old South of their ancestors, which, of course, the Yankees have told us all along was bad, bad, bad.

In their litany of disavowals, there is nothing good south

of the Mason-Dixon Line. There is no joy to be had in being Southern, and they pine for the day when *South* will be spelled with a little *s*. They also like to be called *revisionists*. That sounds real good. Makes them feel superior even when someone calls them aside and suggests that they are actually whipping themselves. Undaunted, they point with great pride to the exploits of Lincoln and Webster while holding their New South noses over the graves of Calhoun and Lee. How odd! Do northerners waste one moment berating themselves? Do westerners curse the memory of Wyatt Earp and relentlessly search for something sinister in the westward movement?

But then, we've had to deal with other pests before, like boll weevils, fire ants, and mosquitoes, so we can probably ride out the storm until they catch up with the 1980s and realize that being Southern is fashionable now. And even though our home-grown critics command the major attention of the pejorative press, I truly believe that they are in the loud minority. Most of us, and I might even add, most Americans in general, would have to admit that 'way down deep inside, where we do our secret thinking, we like having a place called Dixie. It's a place of the heart; it's a place of romance, legend, and song; it's a place called home.

Yet, there are those outside the South, who after having read so much of that predictable garbage over the past twenty-five years, are afraid that they just can't bring themselves to love the South altogether. Their apprehension, fueled by the New South columnists who find financial success in vitriol, is all too common and somewhat expected by long-suffering Southerners. A simple remedy for their skepticism, however, is to be found in the form of a mere visit by these non-Southern folks to the embracing environs of the South. As they feel the warmth of the soothing southern breeze and come in contact with the friendly, accommodating natives, it pleases but doesn't surprise us to hear that familiar answer to our hospitable question, "How y'all like it down here?" With a smile that might be found on the face of an

2

Irish Sweepstakes winner, aforesaid visitors show evidence of being cured on the spot. "We love it!" And this usually in a *need-you-ask?* tone of voice.

Although some of our friends outside the South have been programmed to hold misgivings about Dixie, we Southerners know better, don't we? This is the land of our fathers, the land of our birth, and the land that we love. The special way we feel about our Southland has seldom been said so eloquently as by Edward Ward Carmack, former Congressman from Tennessee. Known as *Carmack's Pledge to the South*, these words, cast in bronze on the base of his statue in Nashville, were excerpted from a speech he delivered in the U.S. House of Representatives on April 22, 1898.

> The South is a land that has known sorrows; it is a land that has broken the ashen crust and moistened it with tears; a land scarred and riven by the plowshare of war and billowed with the graves of her dead; but a land of legend, a land of song, a land of hallowed and heroic memories.
>
> To that land every drop of my blood, every fiber of my being, every pulsation of my heart, is consecrated forever. I was born of her womb; I was nurtured at her breast; and when my last hour shall come, I pray God that I may be pillowed upon her bosom and rocked to sleep within her tender and encircling arms.

Quite an apt description of our attachment to this country called The South. We're not always conscious of our deep devotion to it, but let some quarrelsome stranger undertake to criticize the South, and we reflexively rush to its defense. Without hesitation, we take up for our country as decidedly as we would defend our own family, and it is then that the full realization of our devotion strikes us. It's there all right, completely intact. And it's a good, confident feeling to be attached to something which we can so highly regard.

There's a sense of belonging here in the South. a sense of permanence. We belong to something lasting. A school-teaching acquaintance of mine once told me how much she envied the fact that I was able to teach my history classes from a partisan viewpoint. Having grown up in the bland, generic, one-world age of education, she was deprived of that sense of personal involvement in her Southern heritage. She was teaching a course in Oklahoma history, frustrated by her inability to experience that great feeling of state pride and patriotic fervor for the South that she needed in order to transform historical facts into *heritage* for her deserving students. She knew something was missing. It was the *feeling*.

Those of us who have the feeling know that it's there. The question is: *Why* is it there? Why do we take such great pride in calling ourselves Southern? Why for instance, do people in Texas feel a kinship to people in Virginia, though separated by a distance of 1500 miles? And what is this bond that holds the separate Southern states together in a confederation of mutual affection? It doesn't seem to exist among other states – north, east, or west. Why do the governors of Southern states who attend the National Governors' Conference each year, hold their own supplemental gathering called the Southern Governors' Conference? Why this concept of *country within a country*, a concept inherent in Southerners yet foreign to other Americans?

The most obvious and general answer is that the Southern states share a common heritage. That is not to say that Southern states do not have anything in common with other states of the Union. Naturally, under our compact called the United States of America, all states hold several things in common, including our national day of independence, our English language, our republican form of government, our unity in two world wars, our mutual defense, and our national holidays, to mention but a few; however, despite these mutual aspects, there were, as early

4

as colonial days, events, customs, and circumstances which led to fundamental differences between North and South. These factors, some discernible, some entirely intangible, continued to produce a people below the Mason-Dixon Line who were similar to each other while polarizing them from those increasingly peculiar people north of it.

Most historians and philosophers agree that climate has a large impact upon the development of societies. Perhaps this factor alone became the foundation upon which our common heritage evolved. Though there is a wide variance in temperature from the hills of Tennessee to the coasts of Florida, especially in the wintertime, the entire South lies in a temperate zone. The southern summer is hot everywhere – and humid. The middle and upper South will see an occasional winter snow, but it is rare to have more than a flurry before mid-December, and nowhere in the South does snow stay on the ground for any appreciable length of time. Generally speaking, the South is warm, and when it does turn frigid for more than a short period of time, people seem to think that something has gone wrong.

To a large extent, climate dictates the occupations of a country's inhabitants. It definitely affects an agrarian society, determining altogether the type of cash crop that planters may grow, if it allows the growing of a profitable crop at all. The immigrant who settled from Virginia southward found that he could grow rice, tobacco, indigo, sugar cane, and eventually cotton, the crop that was destined to attain absolute supremacy in the South.

Cotton has to have a long growing season, its harvest being accomplished any time from September through January. In the old days of picking by hand a planter could get two or three pickings beginning in September. Rural schools stayed in session through July and August, turning out in September and October for the picking. Nowadays, mechanical pickers make one pass over the field rather late in the year, and it is not unusual to see fields of snowy white cotton after Christmas. Not acclimated to

5

the North, "King Cotton" dictated a life-style much different from that of the small farmer and the factory worker in the North. Growing cotton on a large scale required the planter to acquire huge parcels of land, thus his home had to be in a rural setting close to his fields even though it worked to isolate him and his family from the niceties of city life. As a result, self-sustaining plantations developed.

An agricultural society was developing in the South, with most of its citizens residing in the country. Southern towns were small. Even cities considered to be large were nowhere near the size of the populous northern cities. New Orleans was, by far, the largest city in the South in 1860, although it could boast of only 168,675 people. The next largest city was Charleston, South Carolina, with a mere 40,578. This rural society, based largely upon a cotton economy, was insuring a common bond among the Southern people. Across the South, farmers grew the cotton, and city dwellers, in one way or another, were connected with the operation, whether in marketing the planter's product or supplying his plantation needs. This is not to say that small independent farmers were to be found only in the North. The South abounded in small farms, some of which raised no cotton at all, especially in the hill country; but the farmer, like the city dweller, was inextricably linked to a cotton economy.

Those who make a study of the effects of climate upon people tend to attribute many ordinary customs of a particular society to the climatic conditions of the area. Such elemental considerations as food, speech, dress, personality traits, and social customs are to some degree mandated by the weather, they believe. For whatever reason, the South did give birth to many pleasing customs in this warm clime, many of which, thank goodness, we still enjoy today.

As the Southern states developed westward to the Republic of Texas and the Indian Territory, traditions and peculiarities from the southeast were spread into this new southwest territory, further solidifying our common heritage. One of the most noticeable similarities among Southerners, then and now, is the southern accent. Though there are regional differences, easily discernible among native Southerners, all variations of the dialect are similar enough in comparison to the accent of other regions that all of these variations are usually addressed as one brogue. One can hear this soft, nearly musical speech of rather slow delivery spoken from Oklahoma to Florida. It falls easy on the ear, is highly-inflected, and is one of those easily recognizable dialects often imitated in the theater. Though it has been an unfortunate practice among schools of journalism and speech to try to eradicate this southern dialect, most people thoroughly enjoy an opportunity to hear Southerners talk, and we should be thankful that it is one of those blessings that comes with the territory. It's just another one of those privileges of being Southern.

It's amusing to hear others try to duplicate our accent. I enjoy hearing northerners trying to use our infinitely useful little word *you'all*. More than once I've heard those smugly officious New York newscasters on their celebrated "evening news" trying to slip it in here and there amongst their carefully purified tones.

It seems quite funny to hear *y'all* without a Southern drawl preceding it or following closely behind, but then I guess we should give them plaudits for a least trying to improve their limited vocabulary, if not their Yankee dialect. I've always wondered how northerners, when speaking to more than one person at a time, manage to speak directly to each other without using the word *y'all*. In the South, we would never be able to ask a group of people if they were ready to go somewhere, or tell our relatives to come back and see us if it weren't for that handy l'il ole Southern pronoun.

One Southern lady, keenly aware and justly proud of her Southerness, was sure that her Bible hero, the Apostle Paul, was not only the greatest of the Apostles, but was also a Southerner. And she could prove it, she said, as she turned in her Bible to Ephesians 4:6, where she read Paul's words: "One God and Father of all, who is above all, and through all, and in *you all*." And it did absolutely no good to point out the fact that Paul could not have been Southern at all because he was a citizen of Rome, "Why that proves it," she said without batting an eye. "Rome is only fifty-two miles northwest of Atlanta!"

By 1860, Southerners had endured, persevered, and survived. Eleven states, Indian Territory, and large portions of three other states, Kentucky, Missouri, and Maryland, were decidedly Southern. Their culture was one, and it extended across a remarkably vast region, sometimes finding itself temporarily exported into areas as far north as southern Kansas Territory, a place which would, however, eventually prove to be unfertile ground for Southern culture. This common bond was already firmly established when, looming on the dark horizon, was a cataclysm which would once and forever seal those bonds of Southern identity. A savage war was about to burst upon these people in a fury that knew no bounds. The trials, tribulations, and unspeakable horrors of that epoch would, nevertheless, serve to weld them into a solid and singular entity sometimes referred to as the *Southern race*.

SOUTHERN BY THE GRACE OF GOD

The war itself was perceived in the South as an attack upon the family, an assault upon the South's family honor. And literally speaking, it was. Although it is difficult in our bloated population today for even Southerners to comprehend the literal intertwining of families in the Confederate South, we find that there was an actual blood kinship among the people of the Southern states that bound them together as tightly as did pride of section. It would be an amazing study with surprising results that one could make of the familial relationships of the antebellum South. The passing references to kinship among Confederate generals alone in the Southern biographies lead us to a sharper realization of the smallness and resulting closeness of the Southern population.

If we of the now heavily populated sunbelt could grasp the old cotton belt idea of population, we might more fully appreciate the vast amount of territory which was populated and so admirably administered by a comparatively small number of people laboring under the handicap of an oppressive war. With our gleaming Southern metropolises of one and two million inhabitants each, it is hard, indeed, to imagine the sparsity of the Confederate population. In 1860, there were only approximately five and a half million white people in the eleven states which comprised the Confederacy. That number is equivalent to the present population of the state of Georgia.

When we further consider the fact that families were large in those days, the perception of the brotherhood of the South comes even better into focus. Small populations and large families don't leave much room for anyone but kinfolks! Not to be overlooked is the predominance of the Scotch-Irish and their centuries-old custom of living their life's existence within the realm of their own clan, which naturally necessitated intermarriage between cousins of varying degrees. In *Gone With the Wind*, Scarlett O'Hara couldn't understand why Ashley Wilkes married Miss Melanie Hamilton instead of her. It was there, in the opening scenes of that classic, that Scarlett learned from her father about the importance of the clan. Mr. O'Hara gently explained that the Wilkes always married cousins.

This interrelated populace probably gave rise to the unique southern peculiarity of calling people *Aunt, Uncle, Cousin, Granny,* etc., who are actually not related at all. In most southern communities there are those who are known as Granny or Aunt somebody. Robert E. Lee was affectionately called *Marse Robert* (from the slave pronunciation of "master") and *Uncle Robert* by his men.

With an understanding of the clan South, which Andrew Lytle has called a *republic of families,* one can see that when the blow of war fell upon the South, it fell upon a family. A common enemy was at the door, and Southerners clung together in a desperate family struggle for survival.

The calamity of that long war did more than any one thing to create a veritable nation out of several Southern states, giving us a legacy of valor unsurpassed in the annals of history and a roll call of heroes whose bravery is yet unequalled and whose numbers are yet untold. Also born of that tragedy are the symbols of our Southern nationality: our proud Confederate flag, and *Dixie,* our Southern "national anthem." It is interesting to note that no other section of the United States can lay claim to its own special flag or song, and that no other group of states ever existed together as a separate nation in the manner of the southern states during the four years that they were known as the Confederate States of America. Small wonder, then, that Southerners possess this special bond that transcends state boundaries and gives full meaning to the term *sister states.*

When I was in high school and college, we laughed at a Southern comedian called Brother Dave Gardner. In 1963, he played to a sold-out audience at the Municipal Auditorium in Oklahoma City, and I was there, along with a college buddy of mine. Brother Dave, who hailed from Tennessee, was a strictly Southern comedian; he told jokes about the South that only Southerners could fully appreciate and understand. He could imitate our Southern drawl with hilarious perfection, and he made us laugh at ourselves with his witty satire and blatant comedy. He loved the South, and it was evident with every word he spoke and every joke he told.

On the night I attended, he took his text on the north, telling us that he didn't even believe in the north – that it was only a figment of our imagination. He said that he had never heard of anyone going north for a vacation. "Have you ever heard of anyone retiring to the north?" he yelled to uproarious laughter. "I think the only reason anyone lives up there is 'cause they got jobs there."

While the north was obviously getting the raw end of that deal, Brother Dave was making us proud that we lived in the South, even a South that was still feeling the negative economic impact of the twin disasters of War and Reconstruction nearly a century afterwards. Although poverty and lack of financial opportunity – our inheritance from the carpetbaggers – caused many of our bright young men and women to seek employment outside the South, we still possessed something that appealed to others, and Brother Dave was reminding us of it. People did take vacations in the beautiful South. People did retire to the warm regions of Dixie. Obviously, they were finding something attractive here, and Brother Dave was riding it high.

The South's strength lies in its people. It always has. Gerald O'Hara told Scarlett that land was all that mattered, that it's the only thing that lasts. He told her that she would always return to the land – to *Tara*. And she did. But the reason she returned and fought the elements and the carpetbaggers for her beloved land is that she had the tenacity and inward resolve to persevere. We Southerners, of all people, are possessed of the land, our "native soil" as we like to call it; but the strength of the Southern character is what sustains us through perilous times, of which the South has seen more than its share. A Texas minister recently admonished his congregation, saying "Tough times don't last; tough people do."

11

Tradition. Anathema to the throw-away culture of the jet age bunch. But Southerners aren't afraid of tradition. In fact, we are quite fond of it. We're not afraid of doing things the same way over and over. To the contrary, we enjoy saying, "This is the 40th Annual All-Night Singing at Overbrook." Never mind that it dwindled to nearly nothing in the 1970s, and only a handful of people showed up each year just to meet the annual requirements. At least it was held – to satisfy tradition. What we remember are the first fifteen years or so when thousands of people drove out to this Indian campground, centered around the old McAlester Baptist Church, to hear the biggest names in gospel music: The Happy Goodmans, The Dixie Echoes, The Blackwood Brothers. It took acres and acres of dusty pasture just to park the cars. The big old diesel buses were parked just behind the little open-air stage so that the gospel singers could step out of those traveling hotels dressed in the finest business suits and tuxedos that you ever saw. The lady singers wore exquisite floor-length gowns that dazzled the eye as much as the music thrilled the ear.

All this on a hot, humid Saturday night south of Ardmore, Oklahoma, in a clearing surrounded by gnarled old oak trees and a roughly circular arrangement of wooden buildings used by the Chickasaw Indians for church, camp meetings, and, upon this occasion, concessions, which included Indian pashofa along with hot dogs and cokes. You brought your lawn chairs or sat on the homemade wooden benches provided by the Indian church, and you dressed in sharp contrast to the famous singers, the summer night dictating the light, cool clothing you needed in order to survive the heat. The music was turned up as loud as it would go so that it could be heard all over the campground and above the sound of the rhythmic hand clapping of adoring fans.

That's what we remember -- the fun of it all. But what matters is that the announcer can welcome us to the 40th *annual* all-night singing. We have kept the tradition. And why do we leave the air-conditioned comfort of our modern homes to sit in the heat and dust of an August night at an old-fashioned Indian assembly ground which hasn't changed in forty years? That includes two outhouses which are difficult to visit after nine o'clock because electricity has never been run out to them. Why don't they just break down next year and hold this whole thing uptown inside a big air-conditioned church, complete with a modern his and hers? Well, because it's always been done this way. It's traditional. Besides, I believe Southerners have a practical perspective when it comes to modern conveniences. We enjoy the results of modern technology as much as anyone, but we aren't enslaved to its products. Allen Tate once said that he much preferred an indoor commode to an outhouse if he didn't have to kneel down and worship the thing before he used it.

Southerners have such an affinity for tradition that we seem to get as much kick out of starting traditions as we do in keeping them. It's sometimes amusing to hear a community announce its first annual rodeo. How do they know it will be an annual event until next year, or the next? Well, never mind. It's going to be a tradition.

I suppose the most enjoyable tradition among Southerners is the tradition of Southern cooking. Until a person has sat down to a country dinner of fried potatoes, fried okra, cornbread, tomatoes, blackeyed peas, and iced tea, he can't say he has fully sampled the culinary delights of the South. Yes, I know that people in the north call our blackeyed peas cowpeas, and I've heard that they actually feed them to the cows, but that's not the first mistake Yankees have made. Their first one was in landing at Plymouth Rock – by mistake. They were headed for the established colony of Virginia and got lost. At any rate, we eat our blackeyed peas, and somewhere along the line a tradition was born out of that lowly pea. If there is a Southern home in the land that doesn't serve blackeyed peas on New Year's Day, we need to find it and make a tourist attraction out of it – you know, a one-of-a-kind sort of place. Just when and how the tradition found its way into our heritage is not known to me, but it is the custom to eat blackeyed peas on New Year's Day if you want to have good luck in the coming year. Some people (my mother, for one) consider blackeyed peas only half of the tradition, claiming you must also have pork, be it bacon, ham, or, as my mother served, hog jowl. And we have never, never, never missed our blackeyed peas and hog jowl on New Year's Day. You think we want bad luck?

That l'il old pea gained its place in history, too. In 1863, the citizens of Vicksburg, plus 29,000 Confederate soldiers, were surrounded and besieged by Yankee armies under the command of two of the world's meanest Yankee generals, whose names I can't bring myself to mention whilst speaking of something as pleasant as the blackeyed pea. Let's just say that one of them was just plain lucky to have gotten his picture on a $50 bill, and the other one has a skunk named after him at Stone Mountain, Georgia. Those two Yankees actually thought that their combined force of nearly 70,000 could whip General Pemberton's 29,000 men who were surrounded by water and Yankee gun boats on one side and that huge bunch of Yankee foot soldiers on the other. When it became obvious that they were no match for us, the Yankees decided to wait until the troops and the people of Vicksburg starved to death. After a while, the food did run out; even the army mules were reportedly being eaten. Still, the citizens of Vicksburg, living in newly dug caves, continued to survive, along with their gallant army. The Yankees didn't know about that little blackeyed pea, and that's what the people were eating. Even the bread had run out, so Vicksburg was making a sort of bread out of their peas. It was a sticky, gooey mess, and it wouldn't keep in the humidity of a Mississippi summer, but it did its part in keeping a huge Yankee army busy for forty-nine days so that General Forrest could spend more time making hash out of the other Yankees wandering around in the middle South. No wonder we honor that humble little pea on the first day of the year! Even Robert E. Lee once said that the only unfailing friend the Confederacy ever had was the cornfield pea.

I think certain foods have become trademarks of the South,

and, again, it illustrates the cohesiveness of the region to find many of those foods popular all across the South, a geographical area covering half the length and half the width of the entire country. We're not talking about the fast-food items like pizza and battered fish, which have proliferated in chain stores across the South – and the rest of the nation – within the past twenty years. We're speaking of truly Southern dishes which were developed in Southern kitchens years ago before any food was fast.

Without a doubt the absolute number one all-time Southern favorite has got to be fried chicken. How could you have a church social or a picnic in the park without fried chicken? It's so intrinsically Southern that other parts of the country have now added it to their menus as a specialty item, calling it *Southern-fried chicken*. I was in college before I had ever heard that term. We simply called it fried chicken, and I didn't know there was any other way to fry that animal. There must be, though. Celia Mae Bryant, my former piano instructor at the University of Oklahoma, was prominent in national music circles; consequently, this gracious and charming lady kept a busy schedule which sometimes took her to New York and other foreign countries. Once, in a fine New York restaurant, she ordered fried chicken. When it arrived, obviously cooked without having been near the flour bin, and extremely hard to identify, a discussion ensued which eventually brought out the master chef. Mrs. Bryant, always finding humor in every situation, offered to go into the kitchen and show the cook how to fry chicken; whereupon, to her surprise, he readily accepted. She excused herself from her distinguished hosts, followed him into the kitchen, rolled up her sleeves, and taught the master chef how to properly flour chicken and fry it to a golden brown. It was such a hit that the management promised that Southern-fried chicken would henceforth be served as a regular menu item at that establishment.

Old-timers will tell you that nothing tastes as good as

food cooked in a cast iron skillet on a wood stove. Well, modern Southern cooks are glad to be free from the wood burning cook stove, but they hung on to those iron skillets. One lady in Ada, Oklahoma, said that she had used the same cast iron skillet for thirty-five years. She had raised all of her children and some of her grandchildren out of that skillet, and when it broke, an era was gone. She bought another one, but of course it didn't seem quite the same.

The skillet is an integral part of Southern cooking, for it seems that most of the best-loved Southern foods are those that are fried. Fried potatoes are a must on the Southern table, especially if you want to please the kids. Coming in at second place, and sometimes first, with just about everybody, is fried okra. Not that battered, frozen, deep-fried type of nugget you get in cafeteria lines or fast food restaurants. No, the real okra is coated in a mixture of flour and meal then fried in a little bit of grease over a medium-hot fire. About the only places you can find it done up right anymore is at home and in small town cafes. Okra can be boiled – and I like it that way – but I've never seen a kid yet that would eat it.

Southerners fry squash also. Cut into thin slices, floured, and fried until somewhat crispy, it tastes similar to fried green tomatoes, which are prepared in the same way. And in Tennessee they have to have their fried apples. Every meal in every restaurant is advertised with a helping of fried apples. Of course, the best known fish entrée in the South is catfish. That, too, is fried. Most of the many catfish restaurants in the South generally serve side dishes of brown beans, fried potatoes, and hush puppies; but the most enjoyable way to eat catfish is at an old-fashioned outdoor catfish fry, held in the park, or more often, out in the country at some neighbor's house.

Almost as popular as fried chicken is that universal favorite, barbecue. Wherever one goes, he isn't far from the smell of some restaurant or backyard grill slowly cooking pork, beef, or chicken in a highly seasoned barbecue sauce. Many restaurants specialize in nothing but barbecue, evidence of the popularity of barbecued meat. There are so many commercial barbecue sauces for the home cook that no one sauce has claimed the number one spot among loyal enthusiasts. The only requirement is that the bottle's label show that the barbecue sauce, like hot sauce, is manufactured somewhere in the South; otherwise, true barbecue connoisseurs won't trust it.

The list of scrumptious Southern foods is endless, and it is interesting to note how many different items are so indicative of the South. Just mention mashed potatoes, white gravy, corn-bread, or poke salad, and someone thinks of Dixie. Even local areas within the South have come to be known by their food. Gumbo reminds us of Louisiana, and chili of Texas. If there were no other reason to live in the South, Southern cookin' would be enough.

But there are other reasons, not the least of which is our fundamental belief in the goodness of religion. We're not afraid of religion here in the South. Separation of church and state is important to us – after all, we wrote the Constitution – but we've always relied heavily upon our common sense down here in Dixie, and it doesn't violate our collective conscience at all to have prayers in school or anywhere else we choose. I never atten-ded a high school or college football game where a public prayer wasn't offered for the safety of the participants and the attitude of the spectators. Sad to say, that custom has been replaced with " a moment of silence" at best, and nothing at all most of the time.

People in the South like to go to church. It may be the men who are in charge of the services, but I believe that the women are the real backbone of the church. Southern women are the ones who want their children raised and married in the church, and if they're not teaching a Sunday School class they're busy making cool-aid and cookies for Vacation Bible School or making things to sell at the annual church bazaar. They're involved, all of their adult lives, in an endless string of revivals, Bible studies, church suppers, youth activities, and visits to the old folks' home. And if someone in the hospital gets real bad off, they take turns sitting up with the sick person around the clock, relieving weary relatives to go home and get some sleep.

For, you see, religion in the South is that down home, get involved, deep down kind of religion that sort of takes quiet precedence over the other activities of life. It's basic. This is the Bible Belt. We don't spend much time debating each other over the Holy Trinity, the Virgin Birth, and Divine Inspiration of the Scriptures. Those truths were accepted long ago and are quite taken for granted in our religion. Nor would we be involved in the question of "to pray or not to pray" in our public schools if the Supreme Court could find something else to do for a while. The South, generally speaking, doesn't question its religion; instead, it tends to seek practical ways of employing its fundamental belief in religion. Granted, you will find different levels of commitment. Some rarely ever attend a worship service; still, they believe. Others are the regular, three-times-a-week faithfuls who, without fanfare, march steadily along in their pathways of duty. Then there are the truly colorful soldiers of the Faith, the evangelicals – those Christians who are very visible in the pursuance of their beliefs. With a zeal for spreading the Gospel and converting lost souls, they're the ones called dedicated by their admirers and fanatic by the doubters. They're the ones Hollywood loves to ridicule. They're also the ones with the biggest churches.

A lot of the old ways have vanished. Before we had refrigerated air, church buildings were designed with real windows which actually opened. That wasn't too long ago. I can remember those hot summer revivals when the wind was still and you were glad for any puff of air which might make its way through the open windows. The front door, usually a set of double doors, was always flung wide open to encourage some circulation. We lived in a small town and only a half block from the church house, so we always walked to church, followed all too often by two or three of our cats which we tried to scare into going back home. My mother would cringe when one of those cats would find its way in and start looking for one of us, especially when it would star that "meow" business. After a couple of episodes like that, she gave us strict orders to lock the cats in the garage before we left for church. Well, it was hard to find all of those cats at one time, and by the time we found most of them the ones we had locked up first were smarter than the others and would jump out every time we opened the door to put another one in. The worst night I can remember was the time our old mama cat walked down the aisle, wandered up on the stage, and rubbed back and forth around the preacher's legs until it grew tired of that. Then it jumped up into the big pulpit chair just to his left, where it spent the rest of the sermon giving itself one of those cat baths. My mother tried to act like it wasn't ours, but everyone knew.

Cats weren't the only thing that came in. Bugs were attracted to the lights. We had all kinds of bugs. Big bugs, little bugs, green bugs, brown bugs – and they all flew. On Sunday mornings there were the wasps, but at night it was mostly millers and June bugs. Big old scary June bugs. The girls sat there in holy terror while the boys snickered and hoped one would land on them. One night, as I sat in a pew on the back row, a June bug made an unexpected dive at me. Without thinking, I instantly raised my songbook which I just happened to be holding onto with both hands, and in one reflexive swat batted the thing several rows back up towards the front. Unfortunately, like a bullet it went down the back of a lady's dress. She kept the back two rows of us kids entertained for a good portion of the sermon by her desperate attempts to extract the beast without screaming or passing out from fright.

When it was hot, you could fan with one of those church fans. They were made of stiff cardboard, sometimes on a stick like the doctor uses when he wants you to say "Ah." Some were square and some were fan-shaped, and if they weren't on a stick they had a hole at the bottom for your thumb to go through for a good grip. There was usually a picture of Jesus walking on the water on one side and an ad for a funeral parlor on the other side. The picture was nice, but I didn't much like the thought of dying and being buried by Spiller Funeral Home.

Funerals were another activity which involved the good people of the church. Years ago, when a person died he was laid out at home after being embalmed. The family would sit up with the body until the day of the funeral, which was held at the home or the church. Nowadays, the body rests at the funeral parlor for the wake, and most funerals are still held at the church where the deceased worshipped. If churches did nothing more than what they do upon the death of someone in the community, they would be worth their keep. No matter how backslidden a person might be, when death comes the family looks to the church for aid. The family needs comfort; they need a preacher; they need a funeral service; they need food for the relatives coming in from everywhere. The church provides all of these services and sends flowers. If the person isn't very well-known and it looks like the crowd might be thin, church members will attend the service to save the family the embarrassment of a small turnout. In rural communities, where churches are small, many times all of the churches will pitch in to help feed the incoming family members, which sometimes can number a hundred or more. As Phil Harris once said, "That's what I like about the South."

Cooperation between denominations of sometimes very different persuasions is a highly prized virtue among Southern people. Shall we call it religious tolerance? Or is it merely a practical application of the theory of Southern hospitality? True enough, each church is jealous of its own religious turf and constantly vying for new converts in the community even under an occasionally awkward situation of contending for the same person. But regardless of the belief in each denomination that its own particular program and tenets of faith is superior to the church down the road, religious rivalry takes a back seat to genuinely friendly relations among the churches of the typical Southern community. When the Methodists throw their annual bazaar to raise money for redecorating the church parlor, everybody attends and makes a purchase, regardless of church affiliation. When the Baptists decide its time to knock doors and conduct a religious survey of the community, the Presbyterians and Pentecostals, along with other denominations, pitch in and the survey is accomplished in record time.

Two of my favorite examples of interfaith relations in the South concern the Church of Christ, of which faith I have been a lifelong member. In the small Oklahoma town of Wynnewood, a small band of us desired to establish a new congregation but could find no suitable building for holding our meetings. The Presbyterians, who owned the oldest church building in town, had dwindled to only a few members and had been forced to abandon regular worship. When approached with a request to rent their building until we could find a permanent place, their remaining elders decided to loan us the building rent-free. Their kindness went even further. They continued to pay the insurance, while one couple sent regular contributions to our new congregation. That arrangement lasted for nearly five years, at which point our little church was able to buy the building from the Presbyterians for a nominal sum. In a joint communion service, the Presbyterian Church was officially dissolved and the Church of Christ became new owners of the quaint old church house.

The second instance of another denomination coming to the rescue of the Church of Christ occurred in the pretty little town of DeRidder, Louisiana. Not too many years ago, while doing one of my regular summer camps in the army reserves at Fort Polk, I drove with my cousin into DeRidder, the county seat of Beauregard Parish. It was Wednesday night, and we were headed for Bible study, or as some call it, prayer meetin'. To our shock, all that greeted us were the charred remains of the former building. Neighbors informed us that the church house had

21

burned in the midst of a recent revival, and they gave us directions to a building where the church was meeting temporarily. As it turned out, we found the congregation holding their Bible study downtown in the Knights of Columbus Hall. It seems that the Catholic Church had salvaged the rest of the revival by immediately offering the Hall to the Church of Christ, with the additional understanding that it was at their disposal for as long as the church needed it.

And then there's the town so small that the only Jewish lady sends her children to Vacation Bible School at the Methodist Church.

Society in the rural South is more informal than it is in the city, and church is no exception. About two years ago, on a warm Sunday evening, a wasp found its way into our little, old-fashioned church building through the open doors in the foyer. It would circle for a while, bumping the lights every so often, and then suddenly burst into a kamikaze dive at some uneasy soul who was trying desperately to sit in the pew looking cool, calm, and collected, but who also knew that if the thing got on him he would have to come up fighting like the devil to keep from being stung. Tension mounted as the sermon wore on, every eye in the house on that wasp. The preacher had a habit of delivering his sermons from a position just in front of the mourner's bench (the first row). Behind him was the communion table which held the sacraments as well as the collection plates. Unbeknownst to the preacher, the wasp lit on the communion table directly behind him. As he continued to hold forth in proclaiming the Word, a very lively lady, well into her seventies, stood up and dashed down the aisle with her songbook in her hand. Thinking she must be leaving early, as she always went out the side door to the left, the young minister continued preaching. All of a sudden the lady, whose name was Delphia, made a sharp turn toward the preacher, raised her songbook over her head, and came crashing down on the resting wasp, the edge of her hymnal catching the rim of the collection plate on the downswing, flipping it into the air. The preacher ducked, and coins from the airborne collection plate sailed through the air. As the congregation was reeling from the spectacle and beginning to break into laughter, Delphia calmly replaced the collection plate and walked back to her seat. As things finally began to settle down, she offered her simple explanation. "Well, I didn't come to church to watch a wasp fly around; I came to hear a sermon."

Rural electrification of the South, as well as indoor plumbing and other modern conveniences, which didn't arrive in much of the rural South until the late 1940s and early 1950s, spelled the end of an old custom – the outdoor baptizin.' Indoor baptistries came to city churches much earlier than they did in the country, but at one time virtually all baptisms were held in a creek, river, or farm pond. Some churches would wait until there were several souls desiring immersion before scheduling a baptism. Summertime, for obvious reasons, was the most desirable season. The entire congregation would assemble on the banks of the creek and watch as the preacher waded out to a spot where he could stand a little over waist deep, followed by a line of people waiting to be baptized one at a time, each person wading a little closer to the preacher as his time approached. If you happened to be of the persuasion that baptism was an immediate and integral part of your profession of faith, your baptizin' might have to be accomplished in cold water. An old lady in the Church of Christ told me that she will never forget the day she was baptized because it was in November during a freak cold spell, and ice had to be chopped off the river so she could get into the water.

Church functions, even in small farm communities, were well-attended in the old days. Churches and schools were institutions about which the center of social life revolved. Not only were most people more visibly religious than they are today, the events provided even the less faithful with some place to go. It was a refreshing break from the lonely farm chores and isolation of the rural environment. And, of course, you went. No matter the occasion, you went. Everybody went.

Some of the most popular religious activities centered around music and were held in both schools and churches. Who hasn't heard of an *All Day Singin' and Dinner on the Ground*? Though still found today, especially among rural churches, but usually only on church anniversaries or homecomings, this old Southern tradition was enjoyed often in the not-so-long-ago. People arriving for the Sunday morning preaching were prepared to stay until the last rays of the sun beckoned them home. The morning church service, which might feature a few numbers by some of the special singers as a preview of what was to come, would end about noon, and the ladies would begin setting out the food which had been brought by most of those attending the event. As anyone who has ever been to one of those feeds can bear witness, the "vittles," which always featured an endless supply of fried chicken, were without equal anywhere this side of Heaven. After dinner (on the ground, of course, where blankets were spread) the singing would crank up back inside around the piano. All afternoon it would go on, congregational as well as specials. There were good song leaders there, and anyone who had a favorite song could get it led. The favorite songs were those that took up two pages in the songbook and had lots of "repeats." The louder you could sing, the better. Finally, when everyone was about sung out, people would reluctantly begin leaving, already looking forward to the next one.

During the 1920s and 1930s the *singing convention* was at its peak. Each community would get up a chorus of singers who would meet at the schoolhouse and practice for the monthly convention. They would pick the showiest and most difficult gospel song they thought they were capable of presenting and try to work it up to perfection, hoping to win the banner. My grandmother's group, representing the Pleasant Ridge community, had a blind piano player who was one of the best in the country. Dick Peevey was his name. He could play anything they could sing. Each month, the singing convention would be held in a different schoolhouse around the area, and the crowds would be tremendous. Southerners loved gospel music, and this was a chance to hear the very best of each community – all under one roof.

The very music they were singing was a tradition in itself, for gospel music, now known as *Southern Gospel*, is an original form of American music. Developed in the South, Southern gospel probably had its beginnings in antebellum days, but the dark days of Reconstruction witnessed a sharp increase in the popularity of this genre. With the advent of radio in the 1920s, Southern gospel became a fully developed and recognized form of American music, and it was the singing conventions that perpetuated it.

A company in Dallas, Texas, known as the Stamps-Baxter Music Company, became famous for its songbooks and singing schools. Each year, Stamps-Baxter would put out two brand new convention songbooks containing the latest gospel songs as well as the most popular old tunes. In later years, the music company reduced its output to only one per year, but that one might contain slightly more songs than the previous twice-a-year books. The songbook was printed in what were called shape-notes, a system of notation whereby each note of the scale was assigned a particular shape (square, diamond, triangle, etc.). *Do* was always a triangle, *mi* was always a diamond, and *sol* was round. All seven of the syllables had a shape, and singing was taught that way in what were known as singing schools, held at the local schoolhouse by a man who traveled around the South for that purpose. The community would get up enough money to hire a music teacher for about a week, and he would hold a singing school – another event widely attended in the rural South. And if you happened to be especially gifted and could somehow find the money, you could attend the Stamps-Baxter Singing School in Dallas.

Though the singing schools and singing conventions have all but disappeared, Southern gospel music itself endures at all-night singings, in concert halls, on radio and television, and on recordings. Even the curious shape-note songbooks continue to be used by some present-day religious organizations, mainly independent Baptists, Pentecostals, Mennonites, and the Church of Christ.

Probably one of the most popular events connected with the Southern church was the old brush arbor meeting, found generally throughout the rural South. As a practical thing it is gone now, although it is revived occasionally by a church looking for a change of pace from the normal springtime revival. Before air-conditioning changed the way we live, a church would often resort to going outside for a summer revival. For this occasion the men would build a brush arbor in the church yard. They cut small trees into poles eight or nine feet long and set them upright in the ground. Next, a framework of limbs or boards was nailed across the top of the poles to hold the brush, or small limbs, that were piled on top of the framework to make a roof.

Everyone went to the brush arbor meetin.' It didn't matter your denomination, you went to all of them. It was some place to go. You sat under the arbor on the old homemade benches and laid the babies down at your feet on little pallets of quilts. If there wasn't enough room, you made a pallet on the ground just outside the arbor, or, in the old days, took the sleeping children to the wagon. Every so often, so I've heard people laugh and say, someone got home with the wrong children. Well, it was dark out there where the wagons were parked, and all wagons looked pretty much the same in the dark. Electric lights finally replaced lanterns before brush arbors were entirely a thing of the past. The only one I can remember was strung with those yellow lights that we called bug lights because they were supposed to keep the bugs away. Whether that worked or not I can't remember.

Traveling evangelists of every denomination would come through the country holding revivals, either under a tent, under a brush arbor, or in the schoolhouse. Pentecostal revivals were the most interesting due to the demonstrable nature of that religion. One particular revival that my mother and dad remembered drew record crowds, mainly, it seems, because of the preachers – two young women who were quite attractive. Their names were Goldie and Vashti. One had black hair; the other was blond. Men who had never set foot in church were conspicuously more interested in religion during that revival. Some were even known to testify at that meeting who had never testified before nor have since.

The same war that divided the country north and south divided most of the religions as well. The southern wing of the large Baptist denomination became known as the Southern Baptist Convention, and, developing along more conservative lines than the northern Baptists, it grew into what is today the nation's largest protestant denomination. The Methodists, who were the largest group in the South at the time of the war, remained separated from their northern wing until recent years and were known after the war as the Methodist Episcopal Church South. A friend of mine tells about her mother, a Methodist who was born in Mississippi and raised on tales of hearing the big guns while the Confederates were trying to keep the Yankees out of Corinth. Solidly Southern, this elderly lady, when asked in later years to what denomination she belonged, straightened proudly and answered in a clear, unmistakable voice, "ME. Church, SOUTH," with emphasis on *South*!

They say that Southerners are also characterized by a special affinity for home. No matter how far a Southerner roams, his thoughts are always on home, and he longs to return there, even if he knows he probably never will. The old saying, "Home, Sweet, Home," often done in cross-stitch and framed to hang on the wall in the Southern home, is more than a saying down South. Somehow, they tell us, we seem to be more sensitive upon that point than perhaps others are. I guess we're just too close to it for objective analysis, but the observation does seem to have some merit. Those who deal in such things accuse us from our own work. Our literature, from Faulkner to folklore, is replete with reflections upon home, revealing the significance which

27

Southerners attach to the family circle. Even the land itself – the old home place – is sacred to our memory, and our music often speaks of home. Remembering the old plantatnion days, Al Jolson captured a uniquely Southern idea of home in his de-lightful *Mammy*.

> Mammy, Mammy —
> The sun shines east; the sun shines west.
> But I know where the sun shines best.
> Mammy, Mammy —
> My heart strings are tangled around Alabamy.
> I'm comin' — Sorry that I made you wait.
> I'm comin' — Hope that I'm not too late.
> Mammy, Mammy —
> I'd walk a million miles
> For one of your smiles,
> My mammy. [1]

Country music, being Southern in origin, is a natural ve-hicle for expressing the Southerner's strong attachment to home. Working in this idiom, Southern songwriters, often drawing upon personal recollections and emotions, consistently write about the Southerner's eternal longing for home. In 1963, country singer Bobby Bare had a giant hit with a song simply titled *I Wanna Go Home*.

> Last night I went to sleep in Detroit city.
> I dreamed about those cotton fields back home.
> I dreamed about my mother,
> Dear old Papa, sister, and brother;
> I dreamed about that girl
> Who's been waiting for so long.
>
> I wanna go home — I wanna go home.
> Lord, how I wanna go home.

STANDARD EDITION
MY MAMMY
THE SUN SHINES EAST — THE SUN SHINES WEST
As Sung By
AL JOLSON
In Sinbad
Words by
JOE YOUNG
and
SAM LEWIS
Music by
WALTER DONALDSON
Irving Berlin Inc.
MUSIC PUBLISHERS
1587 Broadway N.Y.

In 1969, famous Georgia songwriter Joe South tugged on our heartstrings with a song called *Don't It Make You Want to Go Home*. As he repeats the words of the chorus over and over at the end, it's hard to keep a dry eye.

> Don't it make you wanna go home, now —
> Don't it make you wanna go home;
> All God's children get weary when they roam,
> Don't it make you wanna go home —
> Tell me, don't it make you wanna go home. [3]

Then there's the old song we sing at church, J.B.F. Wright's *Precious Memories*. Here's the second verse.

> Precious father, loving mother,
> Fly across the lonely years.
> And old home scenes of my childhood
> In fond memory appears. [4]

Truly, *home* is the word that strikes the responsive chord with Southerners. Tennessee invited us to *Homecoming'86*, and Mississippi beckoned us to visit there because *It's Like Coming Home*. Perhaps one of the reasons we revere home so much is the fact that we Southerners have had to make our stand in the literal doorways of our homes. We've had our homes violated, and we've watched as family heirlooms went up in the smoke of an invader's fire, and I think it makes a difference. A man fights a desperate battle when he stands upon his own ground. When the guns blazed in the frenzied struggle at Shiloh, General Pat Cleburne, from neighboring Arkansas, remarked "The Tennesseans had more to fight for; the fight was for their homes and firesides." [5]

Southerners have a similar attachment to their native states for much the same reason. I used to enjoy watching the Southern states cast their votes at the national political conventions of the

Democrat party. "The *great* and *sovereign* state of Alabama, *heart of Dixie*, is *proud* to cast its twenty-six votes for . . ." None of that simple stuff," Connecticut votes for . . ." No, Sir! There's state pride down here in Dixie. Anyone who doubts that has never been here during football season. When Texas and Oklahoma do battle each year in the Cotton Bowl stadium at Dallas, it becomes more than a ball game. Like many classic rivalries across the South, state honor is at stake!

I had a professor at the University of Oklahoma who had moved down from New York. He was constantly frustrated by this idea of state loyalty. He couldn't comprehend our extreme pride in being an Okie, or a Texan, or a Floridian. Didn't we take more pride in being Italian, or Irish, or German? Goodness, at that tender age, we didn't know that we were three-quarter Scotch-Irish and one-quarter English – we would learn that later. All we knew was that OU had better beat TU or we'd never be able to show our faces in Dallas again!

Another professor, this one from California, was also having difficulty with our notion of state pride. He took it as an affront to his dignity as an educator that he was having to take a basic course in Oklahoma history as a requirement for retaining his professorship. It was essentially the same course all of us had taken in high school, but he was personally insulted and angry about the situation, and we students heard about it more than once. California had no such law – we heard that more than once, too – and ours was archaic and absurd! Of course, it did no good to tell him that most, if not all, Southern states consider it important that you know something about the state in which you are instructing its students. What it finally boils down to is that old matter of state pride, and it's hard to explain that to someone who comes from a state where there is no state pride. There again, it's another one of those Southern values we get from home. We're raised on it.

State consciousness isn't new to the South. Phoebe Yates Pember alludes to it in her reminiscences of the Confederate military hospital in Richmond. She succeeded in obtaining permission to segregate Confederate Marylanders from Virginians, and it was found that a general division of rooms by state served to keep down friction among the patients. Even Mary Boykin Chesnut, whose keen insight during the war makes her diary the most widely read journal to come out of the conflict, thought that little of consequence happened outside the scope of the eastern theater of the war – her immediate world.

That idea is still around. We grow up with the charmingly provincial notion that our particular state, somehow or another, played the key role in the defense of the Confederacy, and had it not been for such-and-such the victory might have been won. A natural but sometimes amusing outgrowth of that local pride is the feeling that "my state is the real South." When I began writing this book, I was living in Oklahoma. Upon moving to Nashville, I met a lady who, upon discovering that I was writing a book about the South, looked at me in astonishment and asked, "Well, do you think you can do that with the proper perspective – I mean, how can you write a book about the South if you've never lived here?" Only a few weeks later, I was visiting with another Nashville woman who had recently traveled to Charleston, South Carolina, where she toured several of those wonderful antebellum homes. At one house the hostess asked where she was from. When this Tennessean proudly replied that she was from Nashville, the hostess asked, "Do y'all consider yourselves Southern up there?" Then there's an Oklahoma friend of mine who had grown up in Louisiana. She explained to me one day that Arkansas, Tennessee, North Carolina, and "those states up there" are not really Southern, flatly stating, "Louisiana is the real South." And on it goes. . . .

One thing is certain. We're all claiming our Southern heritage, and we won't be talked out of it. It's a heritage unlike any other – a legacy of faith, honor, and home – and it's only natural that we cling to it like we do. Call it provincial. Call it sentimental. But it's the way we are, and I'm glad that's the way we are.

SOUTHERN BY THE GRACE OF GOD

Florida's Bellamy Brothers stated it perfectly in their hit song of 1979, *You Ain't Just Whistlin' Dixie.*

> You ain't just whistlin' Dixie —
> You ain't just slappin' your knee.
> I'm a grandson of the Southland, Boys —
> An heir to the Confederacy.
> You ain't just whistlin' Dixie,
> Cause the cattle-call's callin' me home.
> So put me down there where I wanna be;
> Plant my feet with Robert E. Lee;
> Bury my bones under a cypress tree;
> And never let me roam. [6]

Chivalry drew its last breath in the Old South. Descendants of gallant knights and ladies fair, Southerners became the last bastion of the old European traditions of the Middle Ages, where a man's word was his sacred honor and the sanctity of womanhood was defended with near religious fervor. Its fate was sealed by the troglodyte invaders from Washington who conquered us and instituted a new order, consigning the days of fair damsels and chivalrous knights to the pages of our memory.

Even so, the basic way we behave towards each other obviously has its roots in that old idealism. Our common courtesy grew from those foundations, and traces of that chivalrous legacy are still to be found in simple examples of refinement, such as the gentleman who habitually opens the door for a lady, or the child who has been trained to say "yes, ma'am" and "no, sir." One of the most respectful customs among us, one that must have sprung from our legacy of gallantry and courtliness, is the respect we show for the dead. When that dreary funeral procession winds its weary way toward the final resting place, I've seen bystanders cease their work and stand with heads uncovered in respect. In most Southern states it is customary to pull over to the side of the road and bring your vehicle to a halt until the procession has passed. I've seen traffic stop on busy interstate highways, an indication that Southerners haven't lost their perspective even in this fast paced world. In fact, that practice is now law in some states, but the reassuring part is in knowing that the custom gave birth to the law.

Southerners are true romantics in the classic style, with a passion for living and a zest for adventure; but that high-strung, emotional side of our nature is prudently balanced by the restraint which comes from a code of conduct befitting a lady or a gentleman, even if it had to be reinforced with a switch from time to time. Our parents still believed in part of that old idea of chivalry, and thank goodness they instilled it into us. As we grow older, our adherence to a system of manners and decorous behavior becomes a point of pride with us. That pride, not arrogant or boastful, comes from a gratitude for our past, a knowledge of who we are, and a confidence in knowing that we truly are *Southern by the Grace of God*.

As Carmack so aptly said, the South is a "land of legend and a land of song." Those among us who have come to a full realization of our rich heritage live with a deep satisfaction of being Southern. And there are those friends of the South who, though not blessed by so rich an inheritance as ours, are, nevertheless, attracted to it. Noted historian, Burke Davis, alludes to these admirers who hold a kind of mystical longing to be able to claim a part of the legacy we so often take for granted. Noting a surprising amount of pro-southern correspondence from the North and Midwest, Davis cited a letter from a sixteen-year-old boy in Pennsylvania: "Though I am a native of Gettysburg, I am a Johnny Reb in word, thought, and deed." And a young man from Warren, Ohio, wrote, "My only regret is that I was not born a Southerner." [7]

Abram Joseph Ryan was a Catholic priest from Virginia who, as a young man in his twenties, witnessed the destruction of his beloved South. He viewed with a heavy heart the ruins of a once-great civilization. But, as the famous "poet-priest of the

Confederacy," as he was later to become known, pondered the effects of the catastrophe, he was struck by the stamina, strength, and solidarity of the people who had suffered together and survived, living among the ruins. Life became a struggle against nature itself, but out of the wreckage of the war-torn South came the inspiration for one of his famous poems.

A LAND WITHOUT RUINS

Yes, give me the land
    Where the ruins are spread,
And the living tread light
    On the heart of the dead;
Yes, give me the land
    That is blest by the dust,
And bright with the deeds,
    Of the down-trodden just.

Yes, give me the land
    Where the battle's red blast
Has flashed on the future
    The form of the past;
Yes, give me the land
    That hath legend and lays
That tell of the memories
    Of long-vanished days.

Yes, give me the land
    That hath story and song
To tell of the strife
    Of the right with the wrong;
Yes, give me the land
    With a grave in each spot
And names in the graves
    That shall not be forgot.

Yes, give me the land
    Of the wreck and the tomb;
There's grandeur in graves —
    There's glory in gloom.
For out of the gloom
    Future brightness is born;
As after the night
    Looms the sunrise of morn.

And the graves of the dead
    With the grass overgrown,
May yet form the footstool
    Of Liberty's throne;
And each simple wreck
    In the way-path of might
Shall yet be a rock
    In the temple of Right. [8]

II

The Southern Accent

One of the defining characteristics of any culture is its language. From the unique words and phrases of the region to the inflection with which they are employed, a society is somewhat reflected in the speech of its people. Those who study linguistics have among them scholars who believe that the hot southern climate has had a languid effect upon the South's inhabitants, slowing down not only their actions but their speech as well; thus, we hear a more slowly delivered conversation, indicative of a slower life style. Others say that the weather has nothing to do with it, that it is a blend of several brogues from The British Isles. Whatever the case, it is – or was until TV-speak had its evil way with the younger generations – a delightful marker of our southern character.

If you've ever lived outside the South or had to be away long enough to begin noticing that something was missing, do you remember how nice it was to hear that first hint of a southern accent as you crossed back into Dixie? It's kind of pleasant and reassuring just to hear the waitress say, "How y'all doin' today? I'll never forget the first southern accent we heard coming home from a trip out west. We'd been to California for about two weeks and had begun to grow accustomed to the plain sound of the natives while they, in turn, had almost quit asking us to amuse them with our dialect. All across Arizona and New Mexico we heard not a syllable that sounded familiar, but as soon as we crossed the Texas state line we heard it. At a little cafe in the Texas panhandle, our waitress smiled and said, "Darlin', I'll be right with y'all in just a minute." As she sailed over to take an order at another table, my friend smiled, leaned over towards me, and whispered, "Southern." We had hundreds of miles to go, but we felt like we were almost home.

The South has been uniquely blessed with one of the most recognizable and agreeable dialects of the English language. There is no mistaking a southern accent. It matters not which local variation of the brogue is being spoken, any non-Southerner can readily identify the speech as *southern*. And there are, most assuredly, variations within the South. Take the east coast, for instance. There, the word "about" comes out sounding like "aboot," especially in tidewater Virginia and North Carolina, probably due to the old English influence. In Texas, the long "i" is about as flat and straight as a human can pronounce it, while people of the interior South, especially Georgians, would make a Yankee think they were testing his hearing by their frequent, repetitious use of "ya hear?" after every sentence. Of course, that is spoken like this: "ya heah?" or sometimes just "hyeah?"

Most of the characteristics of the dialect are, however, common to the whole region of the South, making it easy to identify. Most Southerners speak rather softly and in a rhythm that is smooth, at times even musical. It falls easy on the ears and is a highly inflected dialect, reflecting the expressive nature of Southerners. The language is one of constant diphthongs. A simple one-syllable word such as "there" comes out in a diphthongal "they-uh" sound. And that famous "r" consonant is never heavy, frequently sounding like no more than "ah," All in all, the southern accent is one of those rare gems that make life on this planet a little more interesting.

SOUTHERN BY THE GRACE OF GOD

Now, granted, most Southerners are not aware of the intricacies of their brogue. They grow up with it. It's second nature to them, just like walking. Of course, we certainly wouldn't expect a modern teenager to bother with a topic of such seemingly trivial proportions, would we? Well, not until his girlfriend, whom he cherishes more than anything else, turns up minus her Southern-belle accent! Just a few months ago, a sixteen-year-old boy from Hermitage, Tennessee, was recounting for me how that his girl friend had moved up north for a while but later had the opportunity of moving back to Tennessee. Like me, he is amazed at how quickly a Southerner can lose the accent, and such was the case with his lady love. "She came home talkin' like a Yankee," he lamented. "Have you ever heard Yankees talk? They whine! And they talk through their noses – and too fast!" He went on, "I don't like to hear it. When she starts that stuff around me, I tell her to knock it off!" And who said teenagers aren't paying attention to their heritage!

It would probably surprise us to find out just how many non-Southerners secretly admire the southern accent. Last summer, two nicely dressed and very mannerly young men were seen walking down my street in Nashville. Probably two Mormons, I thought. Sure enough, they turned out to be a couple of those fine young men who give two years of their lives evangelizing for their church. Both of them were only nineteen years old, although one of them had been in the field four months longer than the other. From their lingo, it was obvious that they were definitely not from Tennessee. When asked how they liked the South, the enthusiastic answer came almost before the question was finished. "We love it!" The old-timer of the group asked, "Could you tell that I'm not from the South by the way I talk?" Could I? Oh, brother! There was not a hint of southern in his voice, and I answered in the affirmative. With a genuine look of disappointment on his face, he said, "I've already been here six months, and I was hoping that I was picking up some of it."

SOUTHERN BY THE GRACE OF GOD

Notwithstanding all the charm of the southern accent, this silver lining is not without its cloud. A few years ago, a well known news commentator from the north made a plea on his nationwide radio broadcast. "Attention, Southerners! Do posterity a favor. Get a tape recorder and record your older friends and relatives while they're still living, for the southern accent is vanishing from the American scene."

And so it is. With every generation, more of it is lost. Just listen to an older person; then, compare his melodic southern brogue with that of our modern youth. The absence of a regional accent in the latter aptly illustrates how quickly it is being bled out of our dialect. It is more likely than not that Southerners below the age of 50 will not even be able to relate to most of the humorous definitions in the Southern Dictionary which follows these introductory pages.

But what is causing this apparent bleaching of our dialect, and why do we see it at such an accelerated pace nowadays? The answer is manifold, but the major culprit responsible for the rapidity with which it is leaving us is none other than the modern god of *Television*. A dialect is traditionally passed from parent to child, for it is in the home that the child learns his first words, and it is there where he will ultimately copy phrases and inflections from his mother and father. Local association with friends and teachers who speak the same dialect provides reinforcement, and the peculiarities of the language are thus perpetuated for generations. But, enter television, and the game plan changes. Recent surveys have concluded that the average child spends six to eight hours a day in front of the TV. That's more time than he spends in school, or talking to mom and dad, or being with friends. And without exception, you will not hear southern dialect on TV – even in the South.

That ought to tell us something as we hustle about our furiously-paced modern lives, leaving our children to learn their language from Sesame Street and similar syndicated broadcasts originating up north. I've seen that huge pair of thick lips,

40

enlarged about thirty times and completely covering the television screen, urging the children of America to "Repeat after me." The number "10" is repeated over and over: "Tan, tan, tan."

What is this? We don't say "tan" here in the South unless we're talking about lying out in the sun. No, we say "ten" and pronounce it as if it were "tin." At least those of us who pre-date television do!

Then there is the conscious effort on the part of the media who demand that Southerners renounce their southern accents before gaining employment in the field of communication. Their theory holds that the southern accent is equivalent to ignorance, and, should you be caught using it on the air, your background would become suspect and listeners would lose respect for both you and the almighty station who had the moronic idea of hiring you. That's an arrogant presumption if I ever heard one. There is a difference between poor grammar (whether it be from hillbillies or Bostonians) and correct English spoken with a pleasing southern drawl; but, so far, media moguls have not drawn that distinction. The southern accent is taboo in their world.

This narrow view is quite pervasive, affecting even the beauty pageants. I once had a piano student from Elmore City, Oklahoma, who at the age of fifteen had won quite a few beauty pageants across the country. Soon, the Oklahoma City promoters were priming her for a future run at the Miss Oklahoma Pageant and, eventually, the Miss America Pageant. One of the first things she was encouraged to do was to change her southern accent. Although she was an excellent student and spoke perfect English, her accent was unacceptable. They reasoned that her dialect would reveal the fact that she was from a small southern Oklahoma town of only 1500 people – in other words, a rural girl. She must portray an enlightened city girl of mid-America in order to win. After all, she had nearly three years to change her cultural blemish so that she could fool the judges. (I wonder how Miss Mississippi used to win the Miss America Pageants so many times with those awful southern accents!)

There are a lot of things vanishing from our language. One of the customs that I miss the most is the way ladies used to be addressed by their first names, preceded by *Miss* – like Miss Mary. As I remember, it was usually, though not exclusively, applied to unmarried ladies (especially older ones) whom we might refer to as spinsters or old maids, although I never did think either one of those terms sounded very kind. In my daddy's day, it was much more common to address someone in this way. I have heard him speak many times of a favorite school teacher, Miss Leanna. And during the Depression, my parents traded at a country store run by a Miss Lula. When a person "traded out" enough groceries, as my mother called it, they would get a free bowl – one of those milk-colored bowls, kind of thick like ovenware and decorated around the rim with a little band of flowers and a thin gold stripe. Mother got several bowls of different sizes, and she still refers to those dishes as "Miss Lula bowls."

I can remember two elderly, unmarried ladies whom we called Miss Irene and Miss Clifford. Miss Irene, daughter of a Confederate soldier, was a small woman, very thin and just a little bit stooped at the shoulders. She taught piano lessons and wore lots of black, but she always looked neat. Her white hair was always fixed – cut short and curled – and she always wore some kind of dressy shoes, usually black patent. She carried a big patent leather purse because she walked everywhere and needed her pencils, gummed stars, and a few music books with her at all times. She taught wherever she could, mostly at the schoolhouse or the Methodist Church, and she was there in good weather or bad. Miss Irene was a very quiet, unassuming lady who had been born before the turn of the century in Indian Territory Her parents had sent her to the conservatory in Ohio to study music, but by the time I knew her she was back home imparting that knowledge to her students. It never entered my mind that Miss Irene had a last name. All I ever heard was "Miss Irene."

When it came to Miss Clifford, I always thought we were

calling her by her last name because I had never heard of a girl named Clifford. When I was in my twenties she passed away, and I heard a niece refer to her as Aunt Clifford. It was then that I finally learned that her first name was, indeed, Clifford. It had been given to her by her parents who were wanting a boy. Miss Clifford was the Avon lady in my home town. I remember how we liked her. She was very independent and drove an old 1952 Chevrolet and made regular calls on my mother. She was alert and interesting, and we always enjoyed her visits – and my mother always bought something from her. When most older women wore their hair long and rolled up in a little bun, Miss Clifford kept hers cropped short and swept back in sort of a carefree manner. I remember her as a tall, thin lady who wore black high heels and took little quick steps, but what intrigued me most was the way she wore her silk stockings – or were they nylon? – rolled all the way down to her ankles in a neat little roll. I had never seen anyone do that, nor have I seen it since.

I remember people older than me speaking affectionately of two popular school teachers who were sisters, Miss Sallie and Miss Pearl. But those two ladies had retired long before I entered school.

In my school days we called all of our teachers by their last names, although never bothering to pronounce *Mrs.* as "Missus." Even though we knew they were married, it was *Miss* Schafer, *Miss* Holland, and *Miss* Williams. I guess it was a holdover from the first-name days, and I think it's still much that way all over the South today. For one thing, it's just takes too much effort to say "Missus," and, besides, it sounds a little pretentious. I can remember a few occasions when one of our classmates would come up all of a sudden saying "Missus," as if she knew something that the rest of us didn't. It usually didn't last too long, though. Maybe someone told her how prissy it sounded. I don't know. About the only time I can ever remember *Mrs.* being pronounced in that manner is when someone was being announced from a rostrum at some dignified event.

I also recollect hearing people speak of an unmarried seamstress named Miss Gertrude; and I can remember hearing of a Miss Debbie, although Miss Debbie was a widow, not an old maid. (I still don't like that term.) And then there was Miss Jane, who always brought the Sunday School lesson on television every Sunday morning.

It seems too bad to let such a nice southern peculiarity go. A few years ago, it was encouraging to hear an older gentleman at the county courthouse in Hernando, Mississippi, address one of his younger employees as Miss Debbie, and it made me wish every place was like that courthouse and every man was like that gentleman.

Another peculiarity of the southern language is the old practice of naming children, especially girls, after cities and states in the South. Savannah is one of the most popular names that comes to mind. We used to have a lady at our church named Savannah and another one named Florida. That state gave us Miami, a name frequently heard among southern girls, and the state of Texas has supplied us with a couple of popular names – Houston for boys and Dallas for both boys and girls. My great grandmother was actually named after the state itself. She was Texas Adeline Wyatt.

Among states, I suppose Virginia gets passed around more than any other, and well it should. It is a beautiful name, for a state or a girl, and it's been cherished among southern families for generations. I have a cousin named Sharon Virginia Burkes, who was named for her aunt, Virginia Holland. Sharon has passed the name down to her daughter, Virginia Ruth, perpetuating a tradition born out of the lovely name of an old southern state. A classmate of mine loves to tell people her full name because her middle name is Tennessee. And who can forget the famous playwright, Tennessee Williams?

Of course, North and South Carolina have been the inspiration for numerous Carolines through the years. And what southern family doesn't have its Georgia? The aunt of a friend of mine goes by the name of Aunt Sippi, which is short for her real name, Mississippi. And then, of course, there's that universal southern name that heads everybody's list: Dixie. I've known dozens of people who go by the beautiful name of Dixie.

The abundance of state pride in the southern states surely gets some of the credit for this quaint practice, but more than that I think that Southerners seek beauty in life, and it is my opinion that there is a natural inclination to use the beautiful state names, along with a realization that state pride does play at least a part in the choice of names. The names of all of the southern states fall with a pleasing lilt upon the ear, most of them flowing in a musical cadence of four syllables. Somehow, I just can't imagine a girl named Connecticut or New Jersey.

It's a pleasant custom among us, an intrinsically southern tradition that sets us apart from other cultures; but, like our dialect, it seems to be much less prevalent than before, and like a vapor, it soon may vanish into the mist of our forgotten heritage.

For several years, we've been living in a one-world warp that promotes the strange nation that regional and provincial differences are somehow inherently evil, or at very best, unintentionally offensive. Southerners, who have always been steeped in tradition, are the first to suffer when cultures are required to give up their identifying marks – and our dialect is an easy target. It's getting tough nowadays to know the players without a scorecard. In the Miss America Pageant, Miss Louisiana sounds like Miss California, and Miss Florida sounds like Miss Ohio. Charles Kuralt, who claims a southern background, sounds like Walter Cronkite on the evening news.

And what has happened to our Congressmen? Many of them don't have the slightest trace of a southern accent. Might as well be listening to a senator from Minnesota. As a matter of fact, if you live in poor old Virginia now, you *are* listening to a senator from Minnesota. One of Virginia's two U.S. senators was born in St. Paul, Minnesota, and the other was born in Indiana. Another price we pay for losing the war. Too many Yankees who don't want to live in crime-ridden Washington, D.C. They've flooded into northern Virginia, and all hope for saving the southern brogue was washed away in the tide.

I don't know if it's possible to stop the disappearance of our pleasant regional dialect or not, but I do believe that it will take a conscious effort by each individual if it stands a chance at all; and that's something we've never had to do because our accent has always been such an involuntary action.

We can take heart, however – or as Brother Dave Gardner used to say, "Rejoice, Dear Hearts!" -- in knowing that some Southerners who have to spend great periods of time outside the South still take great pride in being and speaking Southern. The enormously popular country-rock group, *Alabama*, introduced themselves to the world with a song entitled *My Home's in Alabama*, in which they proudly advertised their southern accent.

> I'll speak my southern English
> Just as natural as I please;
> I'm in the Heart of Dixie —
> Dixie's in the heart of me. [1]

Recently, I read some remarks made by one of the South's most successful business women, Dolly Parton, in a new southern magazine. She spends more time in the hills of Hollywood nowadays than she does in the hills of Tennessee, but, unlike so many entertainers who hail from the South, she refuses to play down her southern attributes. "I have a lot of southern pride. . . . I've never changed my accent. I've never tried to. I've always been proud of the South. It's a pity when people are ashamed of who they are and where they're from." [2]

Another magazine, *Southern Partisan*, is obviously in agreement with Miss Parton, and even optimistically envisions a turn of events in our favor. Commenting recently on Ted Turner's amazingly successful Cable News Network, which, believe it or not, is based in Atlanta, the magazine wittily remarked, "After watching CNN we can lean back, close our eyes, and dream of a day when we will finally have stolen all the people, all the money, and all the technology from the Northeast. At that point, people in Boston and New York will be huddled around their television sets every night – eyes wide, mouths closed – listening to the anchor men on all three networks begin the evening news by saying: "Evenin'. How y'all doin'?"[3] But, sadly, the ship sailed the other way, and CNN is no more southern than Atlanta. Someone recently quipped, "Where is Sherman now that we need him?"

While we wait for someone to ride in on a white horse and save our terribly neglected dialect, we can take solace in knowing that at least one of our southern attributes is alive and well: the ability to laugh at ourselves. Now that is not to be taken lightly. There are people, even whole races of people, who cannot laugh at themselves. They take offense at stereotypes, and yet it is stereotypical humor that makes people laugh. We don't get offended at hillbilly jokes, nor are we resentful when our southern accent is mimicked to exaggeration. The Texan, known somewhat for his bragging, is the butt of a lot of jokes, but he laughs right along with the crowd. Southerners have always had an abiding sense of humor. We've been able to laugh through the good times as well as the hard times. Had we not possessed this sustaining quality we might not have been so successful in withstanding the nightmare of Reconstruction when there was precious little in our world at which to laugh.

Having survived as we did, however, and realizing that Yankees still flock south to spend their money (which vastly enhances our ability to laugh) we good-naturedly offer the following guide to understanding us, just in case some Yankee gets hold of this book. We even include some hillbilly terms for those who always seem to get lost in east Tennessee or southeastern Oklahoma. Yes, some of it is a bit exaggerated for the sake of humor, but any reader above the age of 50 will undoubtedly be able to relate – and smile.

SOUTHERN DICTIONARY

abode: a flat piece of wood.

addle: to bother or annoy. (Let that snake alone! Don't *addle* it, or we'll both get bit.); also, nervous confusion. (You talk so much you get me *addled*.)

ah: the 18th letter of the alphabet.

airish: cool or drafty. (Shut the windows. It's gettin' a little *airish* in here.)

ain't: a little critter that lives in an ain't bed and carries a powerful sting; also used to address the wives of your uncles. (Uncle Clyde and *Ain't* Ruth); also, a contraction you *ain't* supposed to use.

all: what you put in your car that has to be changed too often. (My car is low on *all*.)

argy: to bicker. (You'd *argy* with a brick wall.)

arn: a hot piece of equipment used for pressing clothes.

awf: opposite of on. (Cut *awf* the stove.)

bad awf: sick, or financially distressed. (He's real *bad awf*.)

bag: to plead. (I won't *bag* nobody for a handout.)

bails: things that go ding-dong.

bob: a sharp-pointed object. (Watch out for that *bob*-war fence.)

bone: the way you arrive in this world, regardless of what the stork says.

bub: Thomas Edison invented this gadget. (That light *bub* is plum burnt out.)

bud: a little animal that flies.

burnt: overly done. (Mama has done *burnt* up the roast again.) This is sometimes confused with the Yankee word *burned*.

carpetbagger: along with the boll weevil, one of the worst pests ever to hit the South.

carry: to take someone somewhere. (Can you *carry* me to the grocery store?)

cheer: a thing you sit in.

chitlins: Don't eat 'em!

clock: the first name of the movie star who played Rhett Butler.

commence: to begin. Emphasis is placed on the first syllable, such as in the word *comments*. (She commence a-talkin' the inute she come through the door.)

cut off: to turn off. (*Cut off* the lights.)

cyclone: a tornado.

daintz: a Saturday night social.

dawg: the correct pronunciation of *dog*.

dead in his tracks: used to describe instant death.

declare: what you have to say every so often if you live in the South. (Well, I *declare!*)

dinner: the noon meal. (Supper is the night meal.)

Dixie: the national anthem.

dock: opposite of light. (I'm afraid of the *dock*.)

doll: the way you used to operate a telephone. (You look up the number, and I'll *doll* it.)

dollin': a term of endearment.

draw up: to shrink. (I told you that shirt would *draw up* if you washed it in hot water.)

dreckly: in a little while. (We'll be along *dreckly*.)

elum: a nice shade tree.

errol: a radio antenna.

faints: a bunch of boards set up end-ways and runnin' around the yard to keep out the dogs.

fanger: one of the things that grow on the end of your hand.

far: The biggest one of these happened in Atlanta.

farred: to be let go from your job.

fawg: the correct pronunciation of *fog*.

fayan: Southern belles hold these up near their faces and swish them right fast to keep cool. You can also buy the ceiling variety.

figger: to study. (I can't *figger* it out.); also, to add. (*Figger* it up, and I'll pay you.)

flare: a bloom, such as a petunia.

49

Fode: They made a real good Model T.

foe: comes after three and before five.

fur: a real handy little preposition. (*Fur* cyrin' out loud!) (What are we havin' *fur* supper?)

fussed: what you win if you're the very best; better than second place.

General Sherman: You might meet him someday if you don't make it through the Pearly Gates.

get-up: what you have worn somewhere when you shouldn't have. (What kind of *get-up* is she wearin'?)

give out: tired. (I'm *give out*. Let's rest a little while.)

good ole boy: This is a term for men, used mostly by men. Used nearly exclusively in the sentence: *He's a good ole boy*. It is a complimentary term, meaning that the man in question is a nice, honest, deep down kind of guy. Even though they don't know what a *good ole boy* is, Northern folks who like to stir up trouble in the South use the term pejoratively. They sneer at *good ole boys*, accusing them of being responsible for whatever is currently irritating the Yankees.

grain: a pretty color; the color some people turn when the neighbors get a new Cadillac.

hail: where bad folks go. It's real hot, and a red man with a pitchfork walks around making sure you don't get any rest.

hard: past tense of *har*. (They *hard* him to work at the sawmill.)

hawg: the correct pronunciation of hog. You Yankees should familiarize yourselves with the different parts of this animal, for you will, most likely, be eatin' jowl, bacon, ham, and cracklins on your stay down here. You want to make dead sure you know what chitlins are!

hep: to give aid. (Hep me out a little. Okay?) School children, smitten by love, used to write this little verse to each other:

The ocean's wide, and I can't step it.

I love you, and I can't *hep* it.

holler: a place between the hills. (They live over in the *holler*.)

holt: to grab onto. (He's got a-*holt* of me and won't let go.)

50

hot: the part of your anatomy that better not stop ticking; sometimes shaped like a valentine.

in a coon's age: a long period of time. (I haven't seen you *in a coon's age*.) Being unfamiliar with the life span of the average coon, I can't tell you how many years are represented by this little phrase. And I have never known the origin of the expression – whether it is one of those considered offenfensive by some, and all that – so I am very careful not to use it around raccoons.

jail: what some food does when it cools off. (Do you think this stuff will *jail*?)

jawja: the correction pronunciation of Georgia. (You Yankees better try to remember not to whistle "Marching Through *Jawja*" while traveling through that state.)

Jefferson Davis: the best President we ever had.

kayan: a metal container.

laig: Most people have two of these, and they can give out on you after a lot of walking.

Law!: A handy little expression that can be used for almost anything: realizing that the person to whom you're not speaking is at the same party, discovering that you have worn the same dress as the hostess, suddenly remembering that you did not put out the cat before you left, breaking a nail, or losing your purse. If you will suddenly slap your chest with the palm of your hand and let out a little gasp as you holler "*Law!*", you can be certain that the person with whom you are riding will immediately slam on his brakes, thinking he has just hit a child. Then, you can tell him that you just cannot possibly go another step without your belongings, and would he be just the sweetest thing alive and kindly turn his car around and take you back to get your l'il old purse? (Yankees would dispense with all that verbiage and simply say, "Turn around. I forgot my purse.")

leaven: the number after ten and before twelve.

let up: to stop or to ease up a bit. (Poor man. She started in on him and never did *let up*.) (*Let up* on that gas pedal. You're goin' too fast.)

line: telling an untruth. (He's *line* like a dog!)

lit: past tense of light. (We *lit* the fire this morning, but it's still chilly in here.)

madge: a state of wedlock that any preacher can put you into but only a lawyer can get you out of. (Their *madge* didn't last.)

make out: to see clearly. (There's the sign. Can you *make out* what it says?); also, to pretend. (*Make out* like you're sick.)

mall: a measurement of distance. (We live about a *mall* down the road.)

marms: your own two arms. (*Marms* are about give out from so much plowin'.)

mayan: a male human being. (Leave my *mayan* alone!)

mere: a lookin' glass.

minners: live bait

mock: what you make with a crayola or pencil; also the writer of the second gospel. (Matthew, *Mock*, Luke, and John.)

moonshine: This has nothing to do with the night sky.

mow: opposite of less. (I'd like some *mow* grits, please.)

naw: another way to say "no."

okry: what we called okra before we got so bloomin' educated. The name change didn't hurt the taste a bit, though.

own: opposite of "off."

paint: heavy breathing. (He's *paintin'* like a dog.)

paints: They come in pairs, and you put them on one leg at a time.

pank: light red.

pick up your room: Mothers use this phrase. It is a command, meaning you better pick up your toys, make your bed, clean up your room, and hang your clothes up where they belong. (You boys *pick up your room*, and do it now. We've got company comin'.)

plum: all the way. (You go *plum* down to the end of the road.)

po: down and out; also, the first word of *"po* white trash."

poor l'il ole thang: a real pitiful mess. It has to be said with much sympathy. (*Poor l'il ole thang.* I'll bet she never had a date in her whole miserable life.)

poplar: a person with lots of friends. (That young man is a real *poplar* boy.)

rang: something you wear on your finger.

reckon: This is one of our basic, fundamental words here in the South. We use it every day, especially when we are puzzled about something. (Now, what do you *reckon* he's up to? Now, why do you *reckon* he did that?) Yankees might assume that it is equivalent to their word, "think," but we use that word, too, sometimes. *Reckon* means more than to think. It means to think and figure all at the same time. That takes a little more effort than just mere thinking. If you say, "I *reckon* I'll be goin' along," it means that you are thinking and figuring and studying about leaving, but you still have an open mind about it and, well, an invitation to stay over for supper just might change your mind.

redneck: This is thought to be the white equivalent for the black word which nobody in the whole wide world is allowed to say. People in the liberal media love to say *redneck*, but they would cut out their tongues before they would say the "n" word. In fact, they will cut out your tongue if you say it. Liberal cartoonists draw rednecks with cowboy hats, boots, and blue jeans. They are always riding in a pickup or dancing at a honky-tonk, and they're usually drinking beer or chewing on a straw from a haystack. The average liberal, however, isn't so particular, labeling anyone who looks, sounds, or acts like a white Southerner as a redneck.

Robert E. Lee: the finest gentleman who ever drew breath. [4]

rot: opposite of left.

ruint: just plum no account any more – sometimes confused with the Yankee word "ruined."

scallywag: one of the three worst names you can call someone in the South. The other two are carpetbagger and Yankee.

Shivalay: a shiny car that lots of people drive instead of a Ford.

shore: certain. (*Shore*, we'll be there.)

sprang: the time of year when flowers bloom and birds sing.

stow: a place of business. (Let's go to the grocery *stow*.)

strang: twine. (You get a *strang*, and I'll get a pole, and we'll go down to the crawdad hole.)

swell up: to get mad and pout. (Now, don't you go *swellin'* up on me, or I'll spank you.)

tacky: One of the most useful words in a woman's vocabulary. (That dress is *tacky*. That's the *tackiest* hat I ever saw.)

tail: to relate a story. (*Tail* me a story, Uncle Remus.)

tal: a large, soft cloth made out of cotton. (Hand me that *tal* so I can dry off.) I think Sherman must have been frightened by a *tal* when he was a child, because that old scoundrel burnt up all the places that made them when he visited Georgia.

tar: what your car rolls on. Sometimes they go flat, but usually only on the bottom.

tar out: to become fatigued. (He sure does *tar out* fast.)

tarred: fatigued; plum tuckered out.

thang: an object. (That *thang* is turned too loud. Cut it down a little bit.)

thank: to use your brain.

that child: This expression is used in reference to any child from toddler to age fifty-five. (*That child* is bound for trouble.) (*That child* worked all her life, put her husband through college, and raised his kids. Now she doesn't have a penny to show for it!)

that poor child: Now this phrase is used for someone who really has got a problem. Again, this can be the real child or the child of fifty. (Now *that poor child* just never did have a chanct. She came from the wrong side of the tracks to start with.) *Chanct* is sometimes confused with the northern word "chance."

tho: to pitch something. (*Tho* me the ball.)

thud: after second and before fourth.

tin: the number after nine and before eleven.

to up and do something: Much, much worse that merely doing something. *To up and do something* suggests malice and aforethought. Someone who up and does something is a low-down clod. (After all these years, he just *up and left her!*)

uppity: If you throw your voice around and appear to be arrogant, they'll say "She's so *uppity.*"

up the road a piece: If you travel in the South often, you will have to ask directions. If you are close to your destination, you will probably hear that it is just *up the road a piece,* which is nice to know unless your gas gauge is sitting on empty, because *up the road a piece* may mean anything from a quarter of a mile to ten miles. The main comfort in this bit of advice is that you are on the right road, but it is small consolation if your destination just happens to be the next gas station.

wail: opposite of sick.

waller: to roll around in something, such as a pig in a mud hole.

war: spun metal. (Hand me that piece of *war,* and we'll *war* this door shut.)

whiz: a question you ask when you're looking for something. (*Whiz* the phone book?)

win: fast air. (My, that *win* sure has been blowing today!)

yale: to holler. (The Rebel *yale* scared those Yankees so bad they turned tail and ran.)

y'all: the handiest l'il old pronoun in the South; used when addressing more than one person.

yo: another l'il old pronoun. (That's none of *yo* business.)

DE LAN' O' COTTON.

III

Pickin' Cotton

Cotton. Identified with the South as much or more than any other subject, idea, or theme. It made the South the richest section of the country before the war and gave the small farmer his quickest return after the war. That's why they called it a "cash crop." As soon as it was ripe, the farmer could pick it, load it into a wagon, take it to town, and come back home with cash.

I never picked cotton. I was a city boy, growing up in the 1950s, and city boys did not pick cotton, even though my "city" was a small town of only 2500 people. But nearly everyone older than me who had grown up on a farm during the 1920s and 1930s – and even in the 1940s – had picked a lot of it. So, in preparation for this chapter, I turned to my dad and a few of the older generations so that I could learn enough about it to explain it to people who have never picked cotton and never will. Gone are the days when it was picked by hand, so before the details of those times have left the memory of everyone alive today, let's go back and find out all about the way it used to be.

My dad grew up on a farm in eastern Oklahoma during the 1920s. Of course, I wasn't around back then, but I had cousins who were growing up in the 1950s on the same farm, living along the same road, and attending the same country school that had been home to my parents in the 1920s and 1930s. Even though thirty years separated the two generations, the method of raising and picking cotton was still the same. I can remember going up to that little country community, which consisted of widely scattered farms about six miles southwest of Wetumka, Oklahoma. The only community property was the Fairview School House, a large brick building of classrooms and an auditorium, which sat just north of a gymnasium, built of brick and native stone, where the rural students played that sport so essential to all country schools – basketball. It was the same school my mother and daddy had attended, the same school where they graduated in 1931.

When I visited in July, my cousins were in school. I thought it strange that anyone would have to sit in a hot schoolroom in July and August, when temperatures frequently hit 100 degrees or more. There was no air-conditioning back then, and you could pretty well count on hot, humid days that averaged 90-95 degrees *inside* the schoolhouse.

Daddy told me it was the same in his day. All country schools had summer school because everyone raised cotton and needed all able-bodied souls in the field when it came time to pick, that time being around late August and early September. For about three weeks or more, depending upon the cooperation of the weather, school was dismissed throughout the rural South while children laid down their school books and picked up their cotton sacks. Spending September in the cotton meant August in the classroom. One of my uncles, who now lives in California and is glad to be as far away from a cotton field as he can get, said that most schools, like the one he attended in rural eastern Oklahoma, also turned out in May for what was called "chopping cotton." That's where you go down the row and thin out the plants by about the width of a hoe blade. A vacant school in May meant a full house in July, for country children were required to spend the same number of days in school as were those attending

Cotton wagons lined up in Wynnewood, Oklahoma, in the fall of 1896. At the end of the street is the Alliance Cotton Yard. When a farmer brought his raw cotton into town, a buyer would inspect it and offer him a price for it. If the price of cotton was low at the time, he could go ahead and have it compressed into 500-pound bales and pay to have it stored in warehouses until the price was better. In this picture, the wagons are loaded with cotton already baled.

schools in town. Thus, the rural summer school.

Cotton was the dominant southern crop. It was aptly called *King Cotton*, for the entire southern economy was linked to it. The cotton fields provided employment, railroads provided transportation, ships took it to foreign markets, mills made cloth from cotton, manufacturers made clothes from the cloth, stores sold cotton goods, and scores of related industries did millions of dollars in business. When cotton prices were good, car dealers and furniture stores did well; when prices were bad, commercial activity was slow all along the line.

According to the old-timers in my hometown, "Everybody

grew cotton. The fields around Wynnewood were white as far as the eye could see."

At one time, that small Oklahoma town was a cotton hub, boasting five cotton gins, a compress, a cotton oil mill, and five huge warehouses, all strung out along the railroad which ran through the town. The Santa Fe Railroad, building north from Texas, had come through in 1887, giving Wynnewood ready access to shipping points south, Gainesville, Dallas, and Houston being three of the most important. Two years later, in the great "land run," Oklahoma City was settled seventy miles to the north and was thus connected via rail with the Texas markets and all points in between.

With markets to the north and markets to the south, the little town buzzed with activity and prospered for nearly 80 years from the endless fields of fluffy white. But a general decline set in sometime in the 1960s, due in part to the new popularity of synthetic fibers and polyester clothing. As the demand for cotton decreased, former fields of white were being supplanted by pastures of green, and ranching took the place of the former cotton kingdom. In addition to the downturn in cotton prices, another section of the country was competing for what was left of the South's cotton production – all due to the development of new irrigation equipment.

How well I remember those first great tubes that stretched out across the fields like giant silver snakes. They were made in long sections of lightweight aluminum, giving them the advantage of being easily moved from one field to another. In large fields, some were mounted upon great spoke wheels and could simply be rolled into the desired positions. If you had enough pipe, you could tap into a water supply – a river or a lake – and pull your crops through a drought. If you had a deep well, you could set a pump and draw out underground water. Either way, the significance to the South was that irrigation now meant watering the dry, arid regions of the west, thus giving southern growers a damaging dose of competition.

A cotton compress. Raw cotton being compressed into 500-pound bales. The compressed cotton was wrapped in burlap and held together with metal straps.

The cotton belt, that area producing the major portion of the country's cotton, had always been centered in the mid-South states of Alabama, Mississippi, and Arkansas, with all of the surrounding states producing large quantities of cotton, as well. But the irrigation systems which opened up fertile lands in west Texas, New Mexico, Arizona, and southern California, have resulted in a westward shift in the cotton belt, which today centers around the flat plains of far west Texas.

As the small cotton farms around Wynnewood gave way to the vast new holdings in the west and the cotton fields became pasture for cattle, gins began disappearing. I can remember the town's two remaining cotton gins, but I can't remember if they were still ginning cotton or had already become empty shells, mere reminders of a unique period in the history of the

South. I have an early and vague recollection of the cyclone that blew the cottonseed oil mill away, but I remember somewhat more clearly the demise of one of those last two gins in the mid-1950s because my dad and his brother bought that old gin, dismantling it to make way for their new trucking terminal and headquarters.

Today, like many small towns that used to depend upon the cotton industry, none of Wynnewood's five gins remain. The last one was adapted for use in a feed and fertilizer business until it was dismantled, and all but one of the 130-year-old warehouses have collapsed from neglect. Because most people today have no idea of the significance of that last cotton warehouse, there is virtually no visible sign of the booming cotton industry which not only stabilized the infant community but undergirded its economy as well during the first 80 years of its existence.

The story is the same all over the Southland – a cotton kingdom from the earliest days of Whitney's cotton gin to a diversified economy where industry, cattle, oil, and scores of cash crops compete with cotton for a share of the economic landscape of the modern South. Yes, cotton is still raised, but it is now produced primarily by growers who operate on a grand scale. The old forty-acre cotton patch has given way to sprawling corporate plantations comprising thousands of acres.

With the passing of the small cotton farmer, a little-heralded but nevertheless important phase of southern culture died – the art of picking cotton *by hand*. It left us with so little ceremony, and even less regret, and in such a small space of time that few souls there were who even took notice of the demise of that once-common chore on most southern farms. Al Thomas, who grew up in north Alabama, reminisced about the introduction of the mechanical cotton-picker, the invention that spelled the end of the laborious process of picking cotton by hand.

"It probably came into limited use sometime in the fifties, but most of us were still picking by hand. The growers with lots of land and money could afford them. It really wouldn't have

Cotton wagons around a county courthouse or perhaps the city hall of some town, probably in Texas. The cotton has already been compressed into 500-pound bales. The old wagon in the picture holds 1500 pounds of cotton.

been profitable for a small grower to spend thousands of dollars on a mechanical picker for forty acres or less. So, for a short while, there were both people and machines picking cotton."

I can remember seeing the first few mechanical pickers rumbling out across the cotton fields. I was just a kid, but my mother and dad had grown up picking cotton and were naturally interested in this monster that was making life a lot easier than it had been for them. It seems like they pointed one out every time we passed a field being gathered by one of those "new-fangled machines." As I listened to my grandparents discussing the pros and cons of the new order, I sensed that something revolutionary was happening. I don't remember any headlines – and I doubt there were any – but I can remember many conversations about those new pickers. I was one city boy who sat up and took notice.

When we compared notes, Al and I both laughed at the similarity of remarks he heard in Alabama and the conversations

I remembered in Oklahoma.

"It'll never work. It leaves too much cotton behind."

"Just look at that field. Why, you can't even tell that it's been picked."

"The thing wastes too much cotton. It leaves as much behind as it picks."

It was true. The thing did leave a lot of cotton behind. Still does. But it was here to stay. By 1960, according to Al's calculations and my own dim recollections, the mechanical cotton picker was in general use. All large growers had them, and small farmers who had forty acres or less in cotton began paying the large planter to come over and run his mechanical picker over their fields. There was no longer a need for people to pick by hand, and there was no profit in it. With what seemed like the rapidity of a mid-summer night's dream, the era of picking cotton passed into the shadows of another time. Like the veterans of some old war, the ranks of those who have harvested the South's trademark crop with their own hands are fast growing thin.

It was this new-fangled machine that put lots of people out of work, and the great migration into the cities began. Those who had picked cotton on the plantations, then picked it for hire after the war, were suddenly out of an occupation. Knowing not what to do, they fled to the cities, only to discover that there was no work there, either.

Facing the prospect of a lost art – yes, there was an art in picking cotton – I interviewed some of my older family members who had picked the nice, white, fluffy stuff earlier in their lives. The first thing I confirmed was a long-held suspicion that no one did it for the sake of pure enjoyment.

My dad: "No, I didn't like it." (This statement could be better appreciated if one could here his tone of voice, in which there was a hint of when-do-we-get-to-the-serious-questions?)

My uncle: "You see why I'm in California, don't you?"

My aunt: (also safe in California) "I've done all of that old

A familiar scene in an Alabama cotton field. William Elisha McLendon and his sons, Will D., James, and Benny, are picking cotton in Pike County, Alabama, probably about 1912. (Photo courtesy of Marty McLendon)

hard work, too. I don't want any more of it!"

My cousin: "I was only twelve years old when I quit picking!"

In fact, it was generally an accepted fact that no one liked picking cotton; but my mother, who also disliked picking cotton, tried to put a little better face on it by saying,

"What I hated more was stacking peanuts higher than my head while all of that dirt ran down through my hair and clothes."

Then, to be fair to the little white plant, I must report that Al Thomas truthfully answered,

"I didn't like it, nor did I dislike it. We just picked it because it was there." He also added that he actually liked the smell of cotton.

"Cotton has a clean, crisp, country smell. It was a good

smell – as good as the smell of hay after a cutting. And, being down there in the cotton patch all day gave me a chance to day-dream. I daydreamed all the time. I used to imagine our cotton going to a gin, then to a mill somewhere to be woven into cloth, then to a clothes factory, and eventually maybe to New York, where some woman would be walking down the street in a dress made from the cotton I was picking right off our own little farm in north Alabama."

It must be noted, however, that Al never did say that he liked picking cotton. In all my growing up days, and all of the days since, I've never heard anyone admit liking it – except my grandmother. And she *loved* it! Yes, I know that most of my cotton-pickin' readers are questioning my credibility at this point, but it is true. I have heard my grandmother say with her own mouth that she *loved* to pick cotton.

I can tell you the year, the month, and almost the day that I first heard her profession of love for harvesting that little plant – a remark that didn't set too well with my daddy, seeing as how he had often regaled me with tales of the drudgery of farm life. The year was 2960, the month was December, and it was a few days before Christmas. We were driving through Arizona, trying to make it to my aunt's house by Christmas. It was one of those delightfully warm Christmases, warm when we left Oklahoma and warmer yet when we arrived in Phoenix. As we sped on towards Phoenix in our 1956 Mercury, it was easy to see the mi-raculous effects of irrigation, and we continued to marvel over mile after mile of cotton fields in what we called the desert.

There were seven of us packed into that car – my cousin, my parents, my brother, my grandparents, and me – and we all heard my grandmother as she looked wistfully out of that back seat window and sighed,

"Just look at all that cotton. How I'd love to be out there pickin' it." I couldn't believe my ears. I had always heard that there was nothing worse than picking cotton; so I asked for a repeat.

"Oh, yes, Honey. I loved it. I'd like to be out there right now."

"Oh, Mama!" was my daddy's response, at which point she gave us another little testimonial about the joys of picking cotton. My daddy launched into his standard how-I-hated-picking-cotton speech, afraid, I suppose, that I might lapse back into my youthful let's-move-to-the-country chant; but it was too late. The cat was out of the bag. There was someone sitting right next to me – someone whose integrity was beyond reproach – saying that she *loved* to pick cotton. After that, I always had a sneaking suspicion that there just might be something pleasant about life on the farm after all, in spite of Daddy's vociferous protestations.

Now that I'm grown and not likely to move myself out into the country, my dad admits that his mother really did like picking cotton. Taking advantage of his new willingness to talk about life on the farm, the good and the bad, I persuaded him to start at the beginning and tell me all about picking cotton. I told him I would like to include some humor in my narrative, asking him to relate any amusing stories he could remember, but Daddy's primary experience in the cotton field had come during his adolescent years, and I could readily see that he didn't think there was anything funny about it.

Daddy says that cotton requires a long growing season – at least 200 days. That's why they don't grow cotton in the north. Too many late freezes in the spring and too many early freezes in the fall. Sometime after January, a cotton grower had to go over his field with a stalk cutter, cutting up the old cotton stalks, sunflowers, cockleburs, and other weeds that grow so well where you don't want them. By February or early March, this operation needed to be complete so a farmer could turn the stalks under as soon as the ground was dry enough to plow. In the 1920s, when my dad worked in the cotton fields, stalks were usually turned under by a twelve-inch turning plow drawn by two mules. Walking behind the plow, a person was doing good if he broke two acres a day.

"Nowadays, a tractor can break a hundred acres a day," says Daddy, "but all we had was mules back then. Where some folks used horses, Papa used mules because mules are tougher. I've seen Papa work horses to death. They just couldn't go as far as Papa wanted 'em to go. He drove 'em awful hard."

A cotton grower liked to get his land turned over early because a good freeze pulverized the ground and crumbled the clods into fine dirt. Then, he could drag a harrow over it and have a smooth field ready for planting. If, on the other hand, it was a wet year, making it impossible to get into the field with a plow until after the weather had quit freezing, the ground would be like a rock.

"You'd turn over big old clods that you never could bust up. And you'd have a hard time covering up your seed."

Next, you laid off your rows with a cultivator. Pulled by a mule, it had two sharp-pointed sweeps or "buzzard wings," which opened up a trench for your seed as you rode along behind it. As soon as the cultivator made its trench, another mule came long pulling a planter, which dropped the seed and covered it up.

"You couldn't plant cotton seed deep like corn or peanuts. You just barely covered it up because it didn't have much pushing power. If you got it planted and then got a toad-strangler that packed it down, it wouldn't ever get out of there. Cotton comes up with its neck folded over, and it would break its neck trying to push up the packed earth."

(Perhaps I should interpret a bit for some of the younger folks. A toad-strangler is a big rain.)

There was a riding two-row planter that could plant two rows at a time, but, like the cultivator, it took two mules to pull.

"I liked the little walking planter, even though it only planted one row at a time. I could control it better, see that all my seed dropped, and get a better stand of cotton with it."

There was also the sulky, a two-wheeled riding plow, but it required three mules to pull the weight of the extra machinery and the rider.

Due to the need for a long growing season, cotton had to be planted in April, or at least not later than the first of May. After it came up – sometime in May – everyone headed for the fields to chop cotton. That meant men, women, and children. Country schools usually let out in May, freeing up an important source of labor, and soon the fields were teeming with entire families busily hoeing out the weeds and thinning the cotton plants to about the width of a hoe blade. That's what they called "chopping cotton." Then, throughout the summer, as weeds reappeared among the rows, it was necessary to go back into the fields to remove the new weeds. This was called simply "hoeing cotton."

A cotton grower hoped for blooms, or at least squares, by July 4. The bud, which preceded the bloom, was called a square, having a square-like shape across the top of it.

"If you had some blooms by the Fourth, you knew you were right on the money. If not, you were going to have late cotton, and you might not get as good a pickin' as you'd wanted."

As soon as the bloom falls off, a little boll begins developing. As the boll swells, cotton fibers grow inside, reaching maturity in six to eight weeks, at which point the boll begins to dry and break open, exposing the soft, white cotton. And that's when the picking starts.

Depending upon the weather, which could throw a farmer off schedule by a couple of weeks sometimes, it was generally expected that the first picking would be ready anywhere from mid-August to the first of September. As the cotton plant kept on blooming for six to eight weeks, it would keep producing cotton at different intervals, and it was necessary to go back into the field several times.

According to Daddy, "The second pickin' came about three weeks after the first one – say around the last of September or first of October. Then, we tried to get that third pickin' as late as we could before a frost. That might be in late October. Then, if a frost hit it before we got to it, we'd pull bolls."

"Pull bolls?" I had heard that term all of my life and always thought it was another word for picking cotton.

"Oh, no," says my dad. "They're two different things. Pickin' cotton is when you grab hold of those locks and pull them out of the bur. Pullin' bolls is when you take a-hold of the whole thing and pull it off the plant and throw it all into your sack."

"Why would you pick sometimes and pull bolls at other times?"

"You always picked when you could," he continued, "because that's how you got good, clean cotton. You didn't want leaves, stems, or any of that bur in your cotton because you wouldn't get as good a price. But if a freeze comes and stops the boll from opening up, you have to go down through your rows pulling off the whole boll. They'd grade you on your cotton, and your bolls wouldn't bring near as much as fresh, long locks of cotton. We usually got two pickin's and a boll-pullin', and we were out of the field by late October or early November."

I wanted to know what was so bad about picking cotton – I mean, why did everyone dread it so?

"Well, for one thing, it would just eat your fingers up. When that l'il ole boll dries and opens up, it lays back and lets the locks stick out. There are either four or five locks of cotton stickin' up out of that boll, and you open up your hand just like you're gonna pick up a baseball. Then, you put your hand down over the whole boll and mash your fingers together between the dried petals of the bur – or boll – and pull the cotton out. Those five little petals are dry and as sharp as a needle right on the end. They'd stick your fingers till they made 'em bleed, so Mama made us little stalls to wear."

This city boy needed an interpretation.

"Stalls are little coverings for the finger just like the fingers of a glove," Daddy explained. "Mama made 'em out of cloth and sewed two strings on 'em. When a finger got sore and started bleeding, you'd put a stall on it and tie the strings around your wrist to keep it on."

Al had mentioned something about bleeding fingers. He had also said that wasps – those big old red ones that really pack a wallop – were down inside the locks looking for that last drop of dew about the same time of morning that he and his fellow pickers started going down the rows. With stinger up, the unnoticed wasp often struck the palm of your hand like a bullet just as you reached for a handful of cotton. Al said it was often that you'd hear someone cry out across the field, "Daddy, I've been stung!" As cool as a cucumber, his dad would start out to meet the injured picker, take some snuff from his mouth, and slap it down on the sting.

Then, continued Al, "As soon as you got back to your row, the snuff was dry. You dusted it off, the stinger fell out, and you were ready to go again."

I was beginning to get the picture. The idea of picking cotton was fast losing its glamour.

My mother reminded me that it wasn't a lot of fun to drag that old cotton sack along behind you out in an Oklahoma cotton field under a blistering August sun.

"If the cotton was tall enough, you could stand up to pick it if your back hadn't give out from bending over. Sometimes, we crawled along the ground, wearing knee pads to keep from wearing out our knees."

"Where did you get your cotton sacks?" I asked.

"We made 'em," said Mother. "You could buy cotton sack material at the store, and they'd roll it off the bolt just like they did print material. The standard length of a cotton sack was eight feet, and the material was a tan color. You could make them any size you wanted, but an eight-foot sack was what most people made."

"Sometimes, we'd make ten-foot sacks, " Daddy put in. "It was easier to pull if more of it lay on the ground, especially if you were standin' up to pick."

"And you'd make smaller sacks for children, according to

their size," said Mother. "Mama made a wide strap so it wouldn't cut into your shoulder."

"Mama sewed a layer of cotton in ours," Daddy added.

Al had told me about the hot sun and dry weather – ideal conditions for picking cotton. That meant that you stayed out there and picked, no matter what. He had an older brother who would get up on a stump and imitate his father, a Baptist preacher, by preaching a sermon and praying. But it wasn't for souls that he prayed – it was for rain, because he had a date for Saturday night.

"Sometimes, the rest of us prayed for rain because there was a carnival in town. If praying didn't do it, there was still a chance if you could kill a snake and hang it over a fence post. That was supposed to bring on a rain. And there were plenty of snakes in an Alabama cotton field!"

My mother wasn't known for picking the most cotton, nor was she known as the fastest picker. In fact, Daddy has always teased her about being the last with the least when it came to weighing up. She described the old yellow cotton spiders that built huge webs between plants and sometimes between rows. Their black and yellow bodies were as big as a half-dollar, and the length of their long legs made them about the size of the palm of man's hand.

"If you didn't see the web, you'd run into it and get it all over you, and you wouldn't know if the spider was on you or in your hair. Then, you'd find snakes every so often up under a plant or slithering across the ground. So you can see why I couldn't pick as much cotton – I had to watch for things!"

So, when that first picking came – in late August – who all went to the field?

"Everybody went to the field." As if to emphasize the truth that the cotton field was no respecter of persons, Daddy added, "Men women, and children – we all went. That's why they turned school out. You had to get in there and get out your crops. Mama would get up and cook us a good breakfast, then we'd all

Mule-drawn wagons full of freshly picked cotton at the cotton gin in Perkins, Oklahoma, in 1910. Part of the gin can be seen in the background.

head for the field. If we were close to the house, we'd come back for dinner. She'd get that old skillet out and fix us up something to eat so we'd have enough strength for the rest of the day. If we were away over in another field, we'd just have to take something with us."

My mother said that her mother stayed at home in the morning, getting a nice big dinner ready. At twelve o'clock, everyone came in from the fields, ate a big dinner, laid down for a short nap, and then went back for the rest of the afternoon. This time, my grandmother went with them. Her husband, my granddaddy, had died when she was only thirty-five, and she was raising seven children alone, six of whom were girls. But it didn't matter – everyone went to the fields.

But what about babies – and little kids?

"I'll tell you what my mother did, " says a friend of mine who now works for the welfare department and has seen as many freeloaders as he ever wants to see. "When I was a baby, my mother laid me on the end of the cotton sack and pulled me along with her. When I got hungry, she'd stop and let me nurse. Then she'd lay me back on that sack and start picking cotton again." He added, "I have no sympathy whatsoever with these women nowadays who want us to provide them with child care, so they can watch soap operas and enroll in a few courses at a community college. They ought to have to come up like my mother did!"

To be sure, there was not a single word of sympathy for those child care promoters among all of the former cotton pickers I interviewed. In fact, there seems to be a well-founded resentment among these hard-working families of the field against air-conditioned mamas who constantly squeeze us for more tax dollars.

Daddy says, "Mama took Avis down to the field and laid her on the cotton sack. As soon as she had a little cotton picked, she'd shake it down to the end of the sack and form it up into a little lump, and that would keep Avis from fallin' off."

My cousin, Janice, remembers a pallet of quilts that was spread under a big pecan tree at the edge of the field. It was the only place you could get relief from the sweltering heat, and it was there that they put the children who were too old to ride the cotton sack but too young to pick. It would be the job of the oldest one on the pallet to watch after the others.

Uncle Hallie also remembers the pallet.

"One day my uncle came along and really fixed me up. I was just a little boy and Mama was out in the field somewhere. My uncle had heard that axle grease would keep the chiggers off, so he got a big handful of that old thick black grease off one of the wagon wheels and put it around my wrist, my ankles, and my neck."

I asked Uncle Hallie if it worked.

"Oh, yes, it worked. It kept the chiggers off, but then Mama couldn't get the axle grease off of me." I guess we could say the cure was worse than the disease!"

I heard about a young man whose wife had died early,

leaving him with five little children. There was certainly no governmental child care program for him. In those days, you took care of your own. One day, this lonely father had his two youngest down in the field with him. Ralph was little more than a year old, and Thomas was between three and four. While the father plowed behind an old mule, Thomas was left to look after little Ralph on the quilt under a large shade tree. No sooner had the man reached the far side of the field than both boys let out piercing screams, followed by loud, fearful crying. Dropping the reins immediately, the long-legged farmer, his red hair flying in the breeze like a flag of distress, ran and jumped his new furrows for what seemed like an eternity, trying desperately to reach his boys in time to save them from whatever danger threatened. His mind was racing far ahead of him, but at length his feet finally brought his trembling body to the quilt as he shouted at Thomas,

"What's wrong?!"

"I don't know," answered Thomas, as the excited father grabbed for little Ralph, who was still screaming wildly. Upon inspection, the man found a grasshopper that had crawled up under Ralph's little dress and frightened him. Taking it out and successfully calming Ralph down, the puzzled father turned to Thomas and asked,

"Well, why are you crying?"

"I don't know," replied Thomas. "I just always cry when Ralph does."

Most children started picking when they were five. Families were larger than they are today, and most families could take care of their own cotton. My dad said,

"Papa didn't go too heavy on cotton. We might have twenty acres, and we could usually take care of that without hiring help. Now, sometimes, we'd hire out to help people, and then hire people to help us till we got our cotton out of the field. Folks helped one another out back in those days."

"And then there was Brother Brothers," said Mother. "He was a preacher, and his last name was Brothers. He preached for

75

the Methodist Church in Yeager, but they didn't get much, if anything, for preaching back in those days, and he was always looking for cotton to pick."

"He was sure a good feller," said Daddy. "I felt sorry for them. They really were poor. He wouldn't weigh a hundred pounds, and his wife wouldn't weigh much more. But they had four children to raise, and they were all willin' to pick. They really needed the money and were glad to get a job."

All this time, I'd been wondering what it paid and how much a man could earn in a day. Daddy quickly let me know that it wasn't enough to keep him on the farm after he graduated from that little country school. In fact, most people left the farm as soon as they could, because of hard work and low pay.

"A man could make $2.50 a day if he really was a good cotton picker. You got paid about a penny a pound for what you picked, and it took a real picker to pick 250 pounds. Most people did well to pick 200 pounds a day. I imagine the average was below that. Your mother did well to get a hundred while she was lookin' out for spiders and snakes."

I listened while my parents explained how the cotton was weighed. They told about the wagon that was parked out in the field and how they'd drag their cotton sacks over to it every once in a while when it came time to weigh up. One of the men, usually the owner of the patch, would stop picking and go over to the wagon. At that point, all of the pickers would bring their sacks over for weighing, which was done on a simple little device called cotton scales. It was a long bar, equipped with a hook and a pea, all of which were hung on the end of the wagon tongue, the tongue having been propped high up in the air by putting the neck yoke under it for a brace. By squeezing a boll or some cotton into the bottom corner of his sack, a picker could wrap a wire tightly around the lump that it made and hang the bottom of the sack on the hook of the scales. Then, the shoulder strap would be used to hoist the other end of the sack up off the ground. With both ends of the sack hanging on the hook, the

Weighing cotton. The cotton scale in this picture is hanging from a tripod instead of a propped-up wagon tongue. Since the only wagon in the picture is full, they are probably dumping the cotton on the ground until another wagon is available.

cotton was weighed by sliding that pea along the bar until it balanced, and the weigher would holler out the weight. Supposing your sack weighed forty-seven pounds, he'd say, "Forty-seven pounds, sack and all. Knock off three pounds for the sack!" According to my folks, that was the standard phraseology.

Once the cotton was weighed, the picker dragged his or her sack over to the side of the wagon and pushed it up over the tall side boards while someone up in the wagon pulled it over and dumped it. Then, it was back to those endless rows, where fluffy puffs of white awaited sore fingers and scarlet drops of red.

When that particular picking was over, whether it was the first, second, or third, it was time to hitch up the horses – or mules – and drive the wagon to town where you hoped you could get a good price. Since everyone was picking at the same time, cotton wagons filled the streets of small cotton towns.

Cotton farmers with their wagons full of freshly picked cotton, lining up around the old bandstand on Main Street in Wetumka, Oklahoma, probably about 1915.

Buyers, who were local men with enough money to gamble on the price of cotton, climbed up on top of each wagon, which was sometimes six feet deep with cotton, and dug around through it to a depth of about a foot.

"Turner McCoy's daddy was a buyer there in Wetumka," said Daddy. "He'd be there on the corner by the Meadors Hotel, and he'd go through the top of Papa's load, pulling up samples. When he was satisfied, he'd look at Papa and say, 'It looks good, Fred. Is all of it that pretty?' Papa would tell him it was, and then McCoy would offer him a price for it – maybe five cents a pound."

If the price was good enough, a cotton grower would make a deal on the spot. As soon as the buyer paid him, the grower drove his team around to the gin, where a long suction tube drew the cotton up out of the wagon. The cotton went immediately into the gin where it was separated from the seed. If there was enough cotton to make a five hundred-pound bale, it was compressed into a bale at the end of the ginning, and the buyer would take it to his warehouse. If there wasn't enough to make a bale, the buyer would have to wait for another load of cotton or take the ginned cotton to his warehouse and store it in a bin. Either way, it was the buyer's responsibility from that point on. He made his money by selling bales when the price was right.

So what happened to the cotton seed?

"Papa always kept his seed. As soon as the cotton was sucked up out of his wagon, he'd drive around under a big chute. The seed ends up away up high, and all they have to do is open the chute and put it right in your wagon. We took it home, saved enough for next year's plantin', and fed the rest to our cows. It made 'em give good, rich cream."

Some farmers sold their seed to the buyer or the gin, who in turn, sold it to a cotton oil mill. The mill cleaned the lint off the seed and pressed the seed to squeeze out an oil which was sold for cooking purposes. That left a hull and a kernel, both of which were adapted for use by thrifty Southerners. Hulls were heated and pressed into little cottonseed cakes, which were sold as a winter food for cows. What was left of the kernel at the end of this whole operation was known as cottonseed meal, a tasty treat for horses and cows. Spreading it over oats, corn, and hay made a farmer's stock eat better.

From my interviews with these knowledgeable cotton pickers of the forgotten past, who were, after all remembering things that had not been brought to mind for more than sixty years in most cases, I learned that most of the weight of raw cotton was due to the seed. It took 1500 pounds of unprocessed cotton to make a 500-pound bale, so one can easily see the availability of seed for the cotton oil mill industry.

The image of an old quilt flashed through my mind – then, another, and another. Quilts that my grandmother had made, all carefully stitched by hand and filled with cushiony cotton. I could see all kinds of old-timey patterns: Flower Garden, Lone Star, Double Bit Axe, Dresden Plate, Double Wedding Ring – that's the one my grandmother made for Mother and Daddy

Memphis was one of the major shipping points for cotton. The building to the left of the arch made of cotton bales is The Cotton Exchange, located on Second Street. The banner reads: MEMPHIS COTTON LOADING DISTRICT FOR BREMEN, CAPACITY 28,565 BALES. The cotton is being shipped directly to Bremen, Germany. This picture postcard was made about 1907.

when they married in 1939. There were bright colors in some of them, especially red. My grandmother once told me that red was her favorite color. But most of the old quilts, which looked to me like works of art, were made of little pieces of tiny print – tiny flower patterns – carefully sewn together by loving hands. I slept under those quilts on cold winter nights at her house and at ours, as she had given us many of those now priceless heirlooms, keepsakes that now repose in the old quilt box that Papa had someone make for her after they married in 1906.

I wondered if the cotton she sewed in between the tops and bottoms had come off her own place. Somehow, it seemed important to know if she had not only sewn and quilted those pieces with her own hands but had actually picked the cotton herself.

"Yes," said Daddy. "Papa would always bring back some of the cotton that rolled off the gin so Mama could quilt with it." I was satisfied then that I had the perfect heirloom from a grand-mother I loved dearly.

My grandfather had two kinds of cotton that had proven the best for him – *Mebane* and *Big Boll Rowden*. That's why he brought his own seed home. Both of those cottons produced long locks, or staples, and one of the measures by which good cotton was determined was the length of its staple. Another thing that determined the price a grower got for his cotton was the clean-liness of it. A buyer would grade your cotton by the samples he took, and my grandfather tried to have the cleanest cotton pos-sible. He was awfully particular about picking it clean, but my grandmother was just as careless as he was particular. I've heard my dad tell how Mama picked cotton.

"She'd take only one row at a time – not two – and she'd go down through there just like a machine. I've never seen anybody, man or woman, who could outpick her, and there never was any-body who could bring a bigger sack of cotton to the scales than she could. Mama was a go-getter! But what she liked was pullin' bolls. She wanted to keep on moving, and it took some time to pick that cotton out of the boll. Sometimes it would stick, and you'd have to go back after the same lock twice. Now, Mama wouldn't do that. She'd go along there grabbin', and what came off in her hand went into her sack. If the whole boll came off, into the sack it went. If a limb came off, it went in the sack."

"Papa was goin' down through there pickin' it clean, and Mama would get 'way ahead of him and turn around and holler, 'Hey, Fred, are you asleep? Come on! Let's get up and get this cotton out!" Then, when it came time to empty the sacks, Papa climbed up into the wagon and started dumpin' them. When he came to Mama's sack, he'd have to go through all of her cotton, pickin' out sticks, bolls, and leaves."

Daddy then reports this frequent exchange between them. Of course, they loved each other dearly and were completely de-voted to each other, but my grandmother loved to tease Papa about being slower to pick than she was.

"Come on, Fred! No use goin' through that. We've got to get this cotton out!"

"Well, Ider, (Her name was Ida, but I never heard him say it without an *r*.) I can't sell this."

"That's what them gins are for!" she would holler back as he picked through all that trash she'd thrown in her sack.

"Ider, you know good and well you've ruined my sample, and that costs us money!"

It was the same every year. My grandmother threw everything in her sack, and Papa picked it out. She loved the third picking because it was boll-pulling time, and it was okay then to put the whole boll in the sack.

There were other pickers who didn't pick clean. Sometimes, a farmer would hire a picker who left lots of stubborn cotton sticking in the boll. Rather than go after it, the careless picker would go on to the next boll, leaving a lot of good cotton behind. An unhappy farmer could see, as he looked out across his field, that the picker was white-bollin' it. This type of picker, known as a "white boller," found it difficult, as his reputation spread, to get a job picking cotton.

There were still a couple of things I wanted to know, one being what a farmer did with his cotton if the buyer didn't offer him an acceptable price when he brought his raw cotton into town. According to my ever-patient source,

"You could go over to the gin and have it ginned and pressed into a bale, and then you could load it on your wagon and bring it home, waiting for the price of cotton to go up."

My other question was: "How long did y'all stay in the field each day?"

"From can till can't!" that was Daddy's answer – short and simple.

My mother answered, "Well, we didn't work that hard, but I can remember being glad to see that sun gettin' low in the west because it meant we'd be goin' in."

Al Thomas added, "During plantin' and pickin' time, we

Cotton bales, ready to be shipped out by train from Macon, Georgia. This post card view of Second Street dates back to about 1902.

worked from daylight till dark. My mother got up at four o'clock and put on something for dinner if we were coming back to the house. Then she made us a big breakfast, and we all headed for the cotton patch. I was one of the lucky ones. I got to quit the field about five o'clock in the afternoon to gather eggs, slop the hogs, feed the mule, and milk the cows."

He continued, "I realize now that Mother worked harder than anybody. She was the first one up in the morning and the last to go to bed at night. In addition to cooking and cleaning and working in the field, she had my grandmother to care for. The victim of a stroke, my grandmother was helpless and required the same attention as a baby. I remember staying home on Mondays to help Mother wash all those diapers and sheets, as well as everything else that was dirty. It took us all day long. Mother washed everything and fed it through the ringer to me, then I rinsed each piece through two tubs of water."

There was one standard that was observed throughout the entire South. Nobody picked cotton on Sunday – nobody!

"Even if someone might have wanted to, he didn't dare do it," said Al. "That was just something you didn't do."

My other sources agreed with Al, telling me that your only chores on Sunday were those of necessity, mainly those involving taking care of the animals.

I had forgotten to ask how much cotton a farmer could produce per acre, so I put that question to these heroes of the cotton patch who were so willingly helping me preserve a bit of history for the future sons and daughters of the South. They all stated that the universal goal of the planter was to get a bale to the acre.

My parents said, "If you were gettin' a bale to the acre you were really doin' good. That was if everything worked for you and you got enough rain – and if the boll weevils didn't get you."

Oh, those pesky boll weevils! The most destructive insect in the South! In the old plantation days, there was no such varmint in the country; but by 1892, they were crossing the Rio Grande and infesting the huge Texas market. An old gentleman in my hometown once told me that they "hit Wynnewood in 1919 and wiped everyone out." They attack at two different times and places. First, they sting the square, causing the bloom to fall off without opening up. If they miss some of the blooms, they sometimes come back and attack the tender little boll by puncturing it with their snout and laying eggs that will hatch out inside the boll where the larvae feed on the developing cotton. In those early years, there wasn't a thing anyone could do to stop them.

"I've seen them get into a field and ruin a whole crop," said my dad, "and there wasn't a thing you could do but stand there and watch." Even today, with modern equipment and pesticides, the boll weevil ruins the equivalent of one out of every eleven bales of cotton produced in this country.

Finally, I asked Al, who had experienced the rigors of the cotton field while growing up in the fifties, if any contrast could be drawn between his picking days and my father's. As it turned out, there was little distinction between the two.

"I suppose the main difference involved the coming of the

An average load of cotton brought to New Orleans by the Mississippi River steamboat "ROBERTA." This post card was mailed May 13, 1914

tractor as a replacement for the mule. You could break more land with a tractor, and it enabled you to do so much more. We sprayed our crops from the tractor. There was a tank which held the poison, and there were two long arms with little sprayers that could stretch out over six rows of cotton at one time. We sprayed the crops once and dusted them twice, all from the tractor. And since it had lights we plowed and planted after dark if it looked like a storm was coming. Sometimes, we worked in shifts all night long."

Al's father was an evangelist – a preacher who went about the country holding revivals for small Baptist churches, for little or no pay. At times, he consented to pastoring a small church if they were in dire need of a preacher, but even then there was little pay. Sometimes, a monthly collection of as much as $30 could be gotten up, and he could always count on a good Sunday dinner for his whole family at the humble home of some poor old church member. And that was no small thing.

"There were nine of us kids, my mother, my daddy, my

A steamboat on the Mississippi River. Loaded from stem to stern, this flat-bottom steamer is carrying thousands of cotton bales, each bale weighing approximately 500 pounds. This photograph appeared on a postcard shortly after the turn-of-the-century.

aunt, my uncle, and my invalid grandmother," said, Al. "You can see why we had to farm. Daddy always put in from forty to sixty acres of cotton, and we worked hard. But I never saw my daddy complain; in fact, he was always trying to help other people. If there were problems or heartaches, we children never knew it, as problems were never discussed in front of us. We were happy-go-lucky!"

As to picking cotton in the fifties, it was done in the same old way, bleeding fingers included.

"I just couldn't pick with gloves of any kind on my hands, but it sure was hard to go down and get those goose locks, as Daddy called them, in the bottom of the boll. Those old burs stuck you like needles."

And of course the weather was still the same, just as hot as it had always been in north Alabama.

"We might feel a little breeze float across the field every so often, and we'd all stand up, wipe the sweat out of our eyes, and try to enjoy as much of it as we could because it wouldn't last over a minute or two. You might not get another one for days."

"We dragged the same old kind of sacks they had been using for thirty or forty years – or more. We weighed up the cotton in the same old way, and I think the price was about the same! We got about a cent and a half for each pound. My brother slipped his little dog in the sack just before weighing up, because he was a slow picker and never seemed to have as much cotton as the rest of us."

Al's generation, the last to go into the fields, was phased out by the mechanical picker, if such an abrupt end can be described as a phase-out. Nowadays, a giant air-conditioned machine lumbers out across the cotton field, sometimes as late as December or January, gulping down great globs of cotton, leaves, limbs, and bolls. In its wake, fragments of white stick here and there on leftover stalks, and hunks of fluff lie carelessly strewn across the dusty ground, causing an old cotton picker of the past to reflect upon a time when it would have been a disgrace to leave anyone's field in such a ragged condition.

In a pensive mood, Al remarked, "You know, that was a very nice time in my life. Even though I wouldn't want to go back, I'm glad I grew up on a farm and was made to work. It taught me how to treat other people. We were honest and so were our neighbors, and everybody helped everybody out back then. I didn't have to be told right from wrong; I learned it by imitating my mother and father. I know that everything I am today is a result of what I learned on the farm."

And what did my own daddy have to say?

"I'll tell you one thing. If all these young kids were brought up in a cotton field, we'd have a different world today!"

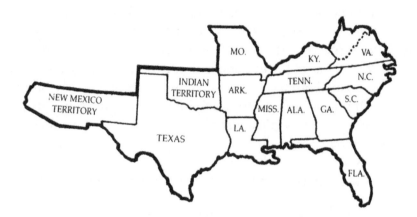

THE CONFEDERACY IN 1861

In its first year, the Confederacy included the southern half of the two future states of New Mexico and Arizona, and the entire state of Virginia, whose western counties would become the Union state of West Virginia in 1863. Although Kentucky and Missouri did not secede, there were Confederate governments set up in each state in opposition to the Union governments there. The five Indian nations in Indian Territory became the only official allies the Confederacy ever had.

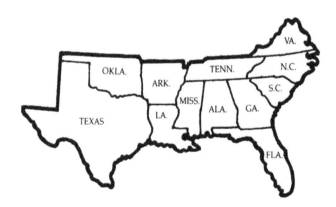

THE SOUTH TODAY

Most current political maps do not include Kentucky and Missouri, although there are many loyal southerners in both states who, due to their history more than their geography, consider themselves southern.

IV

The Hallmarks of Our Confederate Experience

Oddly enough, the idea of secession was not born in the South. As a practical solution to a problem of antithetical interests, it was first considered in December, 1814, by a group of New England states who were disgruntled by taxes and the War of 1812 and who generally held an anti-Southern sentiment toward President Madison, a native Virginian. Ironically, it was a large group of southern states who, forty-nine years later, translated that theory into resolute action, withdrawing from the old union of states and joining together under a new compact called the Confederate States of America.

After all, the union of states known as the United States was only 61 years old when the South first began considering secession in 1850. Even that initial attempt at unified government which began in 1789 was viewed differently by North and South. Southerners saw it as an honest experiment with results yet unknown while northerners were satisfied that it was a binding contract for all eternity. By 1861, Southerners viewed it as a 71-year-old experiment that had failed – and they wanted out.

Unfortunately, the South was the North's cash cow, and the North was unwilling to let the richest section of the country chart its own destiny if that meant losing a penny in the divorce; consequently, the South was shackled with the burden of trying to form a government under the guns of a relentless war. Even so, the Confederacy endured for four courageous years. When the sound of battle died, the South was left with only a memory of its experiment in independence, surrounded by the tangible relics that had survived. As the years wore on, those visible connections to what soon became known as the South's lamented Lost Cause took on a virtual sacred aura.

Two southern cities are significantly symbolic of the Confederacy's fleeting existence: Montgomery and Richmond. Both served as capitals of the Confederacy, and today people make pilgrimages to those cities in order to savor their unique connection to the Confederate governments that existed there. Within those two cities are the executive mansions used by President Jefferson Davis, miraculous survivors of an incendiary war and latter-day iconoclasts who despise all things southern; nevertheless, the Confederate White Houses have become shrines to a great man and a noble struggle for southern independence.

Many homes across the South are an important part of the Confederate legacy, due to their connection with the great leaders of the struggle for liberty. Birthplaces of virtually every hero are marked, and their graves are veritable shrines. The green lawns of southern courthouses are picturesque showcases of the permanent symbols of the South, the granite and marble monuments that tell the story of our unique movement and its battlefield heroes.

One obvious and most interesting emblem of the new nation was a practical item: Confederate money. Most of it was in currency, as opposed to coin. This new and immediate token of the Confederacy touched the lives of everyone and was destined to become a lasting memento of a nation born of necessity under a rising cloud of northern aggression.

The physical appearance of the currency was striking. It was quite handsomely designed, carrying elaborate artwork from earlier U.S. issues and local bank notes. There were pastoral scenes of slaves picking cotton and idyllic scenes of American Indians. Railroad images appeared on some issues, while one bill carried the picture of an artillery unit from the Mexican War. Subjects from classic mythology were utilized, and many public buildings of Greek Revival architecture in the antebellum South appeared as centerpieces, set amidst flowing script which set forth the denomination, terms of the note, and other pertinent details. The first bills were printed in New York and smuggled south, but most of the Confederate currency was eventually printed in Richmond, Columbia, and Augusta. As production moved south, the money began to feature portraits of early southern heroes such as Calhoun, Washington, and Jackson, with subsequent printings honoring contemporary Confederate heroes, including Jefferson Davis and Stonewall Jackson. One interesting note carried the likeness of Lucy Holcomb Pickens, wife of South Carolina's Governor Pickens. Variously known as the Sweetheart of the Confederacy and the Queen of the Confederacy, she was said to be very beautiful. Mrs. Pickens has the distinction of being the only woman to have her image appear on American currency.

Confederate currency was strong at the beginning, but towards the end it had shrunk in value to nearly nothing. It took 1,200 Confederate dollars to equal one Yankee dollar in the closing days of the war. I grew up hearing exaggerated stories about people who papered their houses with the worthless bills and of the man who supposedly said, "I used to go to the store with my money in my hand and come home with a bushel basket of bread; now, I go to the store with a bushel of money and come home with a loaf of bread in my hand."

Such thoughts, among other ruminations, must have been on the melancholy mind of Major S.A. Jones, one of General Stephen D. Lee's staff officers, in 1865. The Confederate army had

surrendered in April, and he was making arrangements to return to his home in Mississippi when he penned these words, appropriately enough, on the unprinted back of a $500 Confederate bill.

LINES ON A CONFEDERATE NOTE

Representing nothing on God's earth now,
    And naught in the waters below it,
As the pledge of a nation that's dead and gone,
    Keep it, dear friend, and show it.

Show it to those who will lend an ear
    To the tale that this trifle can tell
Of Liberty born of the patriot's dream,
    Of a storm-cradled nation that fell.

Too poor to possess the precious ores,
    And too much of a stranger to borrow,
We issued today our promise to pay,
    And hoped to redeem on the morrow.

The days rolled by and weeks became years,
    But our coffers were empty still;
Coin was so rare that the treasury'd quake
    If a dollar should drop in the till.

But the faith that was in us was strong, indeed,
    And our poverty well we discerned,
And this little check represented the pay
    That our suffering veterans earned.

We knew it had hardly a value in gold,
    Yet as gold each soldier received it;
It gazed in our eyes with a promise to pay,
    And each Southern patriot believed it.

But our boys thought little of price or of pay,
　　Or of bills that were overdue;
We knew if it brought us our bread today,
　　'Twas the best our poor country could do.

Keep it, it tells all our history o'er,
　　From the birth of our dream to its last;
Modest, and born of the Angel Hope,
　　Like our hope of success, it passed.

Those Confederate bills were printed on a hand-operated printing press and cut on a manual cutting board. Every bill was signed by hand at the Confederate Treasury Department. They were printed on what was called rag paper, meaning paper made from cotton fibre. Unlike paper made from wood pulp, which will yellow with age and eventually disintegrate, rag paper contains no acid. That's the reason our Confederate money is still with us.

"Save your Confederate money, boys! The South shall rise again!" I've heard that expression all my life, and I've always sort of hoped that it would someday come true; however, I was a sixteen-year-old boy before I ever even saw a real Confederate bill and realized that people were actually saving them. Good reason. They're worth more than Yankee money nowadays. They're handled by coin dealers in the South, and even though they're thin and fragile I've bought a few, just in case. . . .

Without a doubt, the two most enduring symbols of the Confederacy are the Confederate flag, and the song, *Dixie*. Both of them have grown from the popular emblems of the Confederacy into hallmarks of the South of today. Unlike Confederate money, the flag and our song have maintained a utilitarian purpose throughout the years – at least up until most recently, as already noted in the introduction to the 21st-century edition of this book. They symbolize our fierce loyalty, our love for independence, and our reckless courage in demanding it – our indomitable will, if you please. Without them we have no fire, no zeal, no enthusiasm for who we are and where we've been. Our enemies know that, and that's why they continually work at banning the display of our flag and the singing of our of celebrated song.

Non-southerners find it difficult to understand our attachment to emblems of a defeated nation, finding in it too much of a paradox in that we simultaneously hold dear the symbols of the United States. Is it contradictory that we should respect our past loyalties and hold as steadfastly to them as we do our present ones? Perhaps the average person with a vanilla perspective would, indeed, see the incongruity; but then that's just part of being Southern, and we don't expect anyone else to completely understand – in fact, just for the record, we don't care whether anyone else understands it or not. I am reminded of one of William Faulkner's characters who, in answer to a similarly perplexing question from his northern roommate at college, told him that no one could really explain the South to him – that he would just have to have been born here.

The familiar red flag with its blue bars and white stars, universally recognized as the flag of the South, is known by various names, including the *Battle Flag*, the *Southern Cross*, and simply the *Confederate Flag*. It is surprising to many that this popular flag was not the official flag of state of the Confederate government, although it was carried on the field of battle as the ensign of the Confederacy and is today regarded as the bona fide Confederate flag.

There were three official flags of state adopted by the Confederate Congress, even though the battle flag was not one of them. The very first flag was known as the *Stars and Bars*. It featured two broad red stripes, or bars, with a broad white stripe between them. There was a blue union in the upper left hand corner carrying seven white stars in a circle, representing the seven original states of the Confederacy. When you hear Aunt

Sally exclaim, "My stars and bars," this is the flag about which she is shrieking, although she probably doesn't know it. This flag was first raised at Montgomery on March 4, 1861, by Miss Letitia Tyler, granddaughter of former President John Tyler. A fine flag it was, and Southerners were as proud of it as they were of their brand new republic; however, it soon proved to be fatally flawed. Through the smoke and haze at the Battle of Manassas, it was mistaken for the U.S. flag more than once, creating dangerous confusion. It was decided, largely by the military, that a different emblem would have to be devised.

Enter the Confederate Battle Flag. Shortly after the battle, successful though our forces were, General P.G.T Beauregard, then commanding part of the Confederate forces in northern Virginia, proposed a new flag, consisting of a blue St. Andrew's Cross emblazoned with thirteen white stars, resting on a red background. The flag was entirely symmetrical, perfectly square, and bordered by a narrow band of white. Due to its magnificent appearance and partially to the popularity of General Beauregard, it was immediately accepted for use in the field by the armies and the navy. The first actual battle flags were made by three of Richmond's leading belles, the Misses Cary – Constance, Hettie, and Jennie – and formally accepted by Generals Beauregard, Johnston, and Van Dorn in ceremonies before massed troops at Centreville, Virginia. The date was October, 1861.

The Battle Flag became wildly popular, and by 1862 General Beauregard had introduced it into the western armies. The Army of Tennessee used both square and rectangular versions, as did many outfits outside of northern Virginia. Still, the official flag of the government was the Stars and Bars. It flew over the capitol and other government buildings throughout the Confederacy, and occasionally was still to be found among some military units in the field, along with the Battle Flag.

THE STARS AND BARS

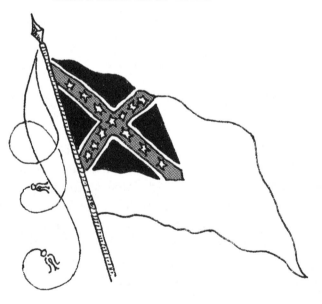

THE STAINLESS BANNER

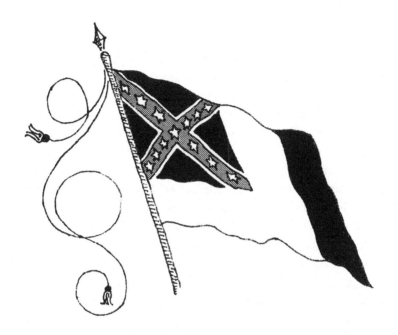

THE LAST OFFICIAL CONFEDERATE FLAG

BATTLE FLAG

Popular acceptance of the Battle Flag contributed to the adoption of a second official flag for the Confederacy, this time a solid white flag with a small Battle Flag design appearing in the top left-hand corner. It was a handsome flag called the *Stainless Banner*, but when carried onto the field and hanging limp from the flagpole it resembled a white flag of truce; consequently, the Battle Flag retained its preeminence upon the battlefield.

The Stainless Banner was official from May 1, 1863, until Congress corrected its "flag of truce" appearance on March 4, 1865, by adding a broad red bar across the end of it. The action came a little too late to be of any practical use. Little more than a month later, on April 9, 1865, General Lee began the first of many surrenders which culminated in the capitulation of General Stand Watie and most of the Indian Territory, some 1500 miles to the southwest, on June 23, 1865. The official flag of the Confederacy never made it onto the battlefield; consequently, the flag that was surrendered over and over in scenes of wretched despair was the same flag under which brave soldiers had marched for four arduous years – the Confederate Battle Flag.

A dream was dying; a nation was dead; and nothing remained but a tattered symbol of immense significance. Thousands of brave souls who had spilled their lifeblood under its banner were absent from the dwindling ranks who now had the solemn duty of retiring the proud emblem from the field. Many strong hearts in war-weakened, undernourished bodies wept over the final furling of the banner they had so gallantly defended. Soldiers, young and old, gazed upon it and strove to touch it for the last time, bitter tears streaming down their furrowed faces as the scenes were reenacted time and again across the late land of cotton.

How it must have hurt to give that flag into hands that hated it, to see it carried off by men who had cursed it, reviled, spat upon it! Reduced to the status of cheap souvenir in the hands of Yankees, many a war-torn Confederate flag was carried off by the conquerors only to end up as a curiosity in a northern courthouse, state capitol, or museum. A few brave men stuffed them inside their shirts rather than have them surrendered. General Joe Shelby, out in the Trans-Mississippi Department, took his men south into Texas rather than surrender, and as they crossed over into Mexico, he ordered that all flags be buried in the waters of the Rio Grande. Only one flag is known to have survived that crossing. One soldier, grabbing a flag from the water, hid it inside his shirt.

Shortly after Robert E. Lee's surrender, the young poet-soldier, Abram Joseph Ryan, sat down and penned what is often called "The Requiem of The Lost Cause." Expressing his anguish over the furling of the last flag and the unbearable significance of it, he verbalized the thoughts of a grief-stricken people.

THE CONQUERED BANNER

> Furl that Banner, for 'tis weary:
> Round its staff 'tis drooping dreary;
>   Furl it, fold it, it is best;
> For there's not a man to wave it,
> And there's not a sword to save it,
> And there's not one left to lave it
> In the blood which heroes gave it;
> And its foes now scorn and brave it;
>   Furl it, hide it — let it rest!

> Take that Banner down! 'tis tattered;
> Broken is its staff and shattered;
> And the valiant hosts are scattered;
>   Over whom it floated high.
> Oh! 'tis hard for us to fold it;
> Hard to think there's none to hold it;
> Hard that those who once unrolled it
>   Now must furl it with a sigh.

SOUTHERN BY THE GRACE OF GOD

Furl that Banner! furl it sadly!
Once then thousands hailed it gladly,
And ten thousands wildly, madly,
    Swore it should forever wave;
Swore that foeman's sword should never
Hearts like theirs entwined dissever,
Till that flag should float forever
    O'er their freedom or their grave!

Furl it! for the hands that grasped it,
And the hearts that fondly clasped it,
    Cold and dead are lying low;
And that Banner — it is trailing!
While around it sounds the wailing
    Of its people in their woe.

For, though conquered, they adore it!
Love the cold, dead hands that bore it!
Weep for those who fell before it!
Pardon those who trailed and tore it!
    But, oh! wildly they deplored it!
    Now who furl and fold it so.

Furl that Banner! True, 'tis gory,
Yet, 'tis wreathed around with glory,
And 'twill live in song and story,
    Though its folds are in the dust;
For its fame on brightest pages,
Penned by poets and by sages,
Shall go sounding down the ages —
    Furl its folds though now we must.

Furl that Banner, softly slowly!
Treat it gently — it is holy —
    For it droops above the dead.

SOUTHERN BY THE GRACE OF GOD

Touch it not — unfold it never,
Let it droop there, furled forever,
   For its people's hopes are dead!

SOUTHERN BY THE GRACE OF GOD

Noble sentiments, to be sure, and fairly universal in the South, but just as time works its merciful duty of healing the heart, so did it slowly soften the shock of defeat, ultimately transforming it into a nostalgic desire to see that flag wave once again over the conquered land. It was an Englishman, Sir Henry Houghton, who advised Southerners to rise above their grief and unfurl their gloried banner. His own England, though much in sympathy with the Confederacy, never officially recognized her, and he alludes to that regret in a few lines of his poem.

A REPLY TO THE CONQUERED BANNER

Gallant nation, foiled by numbers!
　　Say not that your hopes are fled;
Keep that glorious flag which slumbers,
　　One day to avenge your dead.
Keep it widowed, sonless mothers!
Keep it, sisters, mourning brothers!
Furl it now but keep it still —
　　Think not that its work is done.
Keep it till your children take it,
Once again to hall and make it,
All their sires have bled and fought for;
All their noble hearts have sought for —
　　Bled and fought for all alone,
All alone! ay, shame the story!
　　Millions here deplore the stain;
Shame, alas! for England's glory,
Freedom called, and called in vain!
Furl that banner sadly, slowly,
Treat it gently, for 'tis holy;
Till that day — yes, furl it sadly;
Then once more unfurl it gladly —
　　Conquered banner! keep it still!

SALUTE TO THE CONFEDERATE FLAG

"I salute the Confederate flag with affection, love, and undying remembrance."

This salute is used by the United Daughters of the Confederacy. Another version, used by the Sons of Confederate Veterans, is:

"I salute the Confederate flag with affection, reverence, and undying devotion to the Cause for which it stands."

SOUTHERN BY THE GRACE OF GOD

We haven't always enjoyed the freedom of flying the Confederate flag. Soon after the war's tragic end, the dark days of Reconstruction descended upon the South like a vulture upon its prey. A period of persecution which lasted three times as long as the war in many parts of the South, it robbed the people of everything except their pride. As the hated Yankee flag continued to shelter the carpetbag governments shackling the South, our furled banner became even more dear to Southerners; consequently, the Reconstruction despots forbade public display of the Confederate flag.

In 1877, when the South finally succeeded in overthrowing the carpetbag regimes, the veterans of the Confederate army began to emerge with a new enthusiasm for their heroic past. The now-famous reunions were initiated as soldiers began to hold mass gatherings on county, state, and South-wide levels, always displaying their recently unfurled banner.

As time thinned the ranks of the old soldiers, a grateful South resolved to honor them by erecting monuments and protecting the flag. Remembering the relative ease with which the flag was banned under carpetbag rule, the state of Mississippi cleverly ensured its perpetuity by incorporating the Confederate flag into the design of a new state flag in 1894. Sadly, however, as this book goes to press in 2020, it must be noted that the state's Republican governor arbitrarily removed the Confederate emblem from the state flag after promising voters never to do that.

Two other states gave similar honor to the Confederate flag by using the flag's principle feature, the St. Andrew's Cross, in their official state ensigns – Alabama in 1895 and Florida in 1899. And as late as 1956, the state of Georgia hoisted what is arguably this country's most handsome state flag, one-third of which contains the state seal while the other two-thirds depicts the Confederate Battle Flag. In this age of neglected values when Southerners regrettably fail to display the Confederate flag, it is most inspiring to travel across Georgia and see their state flag playing in the southern breeze. With the battle flag as the prominent part of its design, the sight of it is at once happily reminiscent of by-gone days when the actual Confederate flag flew in all its glory stop schools, courthouses, and city halls.

It is with bitter regret that this 21st century edition of *Southern By the Grace of God* is forced to recognize the fact that a scallywag Republican governor of Georgia managed to remove the Confederate emblem from the state flag a few years ago. How things can change in such a short time! Not only is the beautiful Georgia flag nothing but a fond memory, it is possible, even likely, to drive across the entire breadth of the South to-day without seeing a single Confederate flag against the sweet southern sky. Our blameless flag, the emblem of its people, has fallen victim to malicious attacks by evil people in the media, the government schools, and the black-power crowd, all of whom accuse us of something sinister in our affection for the flag of our forefathers. Even worse, our accommodating southern nature has caused us to compromise our convictions and haul down the flag, when standing tall against those accusatory troublemakers would have served us well. Acquiescence to falsehood casts a cloud of suspicion upon the innocent and lends credibility to the liar. The way to refute lies about the Confederate flag is for responsible southern citizens to fly the flag more – not less.

It's probably a blessing that the old veterans who followed that flag through the din of battle are not around to see the vacant flagpoles. It would, no doubt, remind them of the Reconstruction ban. There is, however, a ray of hope shining through the darkness of the present distress, and as usual, it comes not through officialdom but rather from the spontaneity of the same class of people who gave it birth on the battlefield – the common Southerner. Notwithstanding constant diatribes and scathing denunciations of the Confederate flag from the radical social justice warriors who have a strangle hold on most of the editorial functions of our southern newspapers, a significant portion of the general populace continues to resist the brainwashing. In a recent poll conducted by one of the most powerful of these arch

SOUTHERN BY THE GRACE OF GOD

ALABAMA   **(Adopted in 1895)**

FLORIDA   **(Adopted in 1899)**

SOUTHERN BY THE GRACE OF GOD

MISSISSIPPI   **(Adopted in 1894)**

GEORGIA   **(Adopted in 1956)**

enemies of the flag, it was found that 88% of the southern citizenry highly regard the Confederate flag and approve of its official display. It is not the fault of the average Southerner that official display of the flag is lagging. That shame belongs to the malcontents of the media and dishonorable public officials who see themselves as our overseers rather than our elected public servants.

Though absent from official display in near totality, the flag goes forth on the highways and byways of the nation, thanks to truckers and teenagers, bless 'em! That's where you'll see the flag. Antenna flags, bumper-stickers, mud-flaps, decals, radiator shields, car tags, T-shirts, ball caps, key chains. I wish there were as many flags flying from homes and businesses as are to be found on the bedroom walls of our Southern teenagers. The flag companies would have to put on extra shifts.

So it is that the flag may have to be carried by those *real* Southerners until our leaders recover from their timidity. Perhaps residential streets ablaze with Confederate flags would give our feckless public officials the courage to face down black political operatives who are bent on removing every vestige of southern culture. We can fly the Confederate flag from our homes in the same manner that we fly the U.S. flag. Flying the U.S. flag sends one clear message: *I'm American and proud of it.* Flying the Confederate flag sends an additional message: *I'm Southern and proud of it.*

Even amidst that kind of optimism, however, we are faced with the reality that the outrageous attacks upon our culture has worked to convince the major flag companies to cease production of Confederate flags; consequently, it has become terribly difficult to find a flag. Sometimes, a flag can be found at roadside stands, although most of those flags are made overseas and are of inferior quality. Perhaps someone will begin production again soon.

EMBATTLED EMBLEM

O hated flag, I hold you high
  To shine as beacon light
To all the weak in foreign lands
  Who battle for the right.
For once you waved above our land —
  The South, in all her might —
And gave us cheer when days were drear —
  A widow's lamp by night.

Ah, but that was years ago,
  Cry those who loathe our Cause.
Forget, repent, and cease your praise
  Of men who brought you loss.
Should we despise that loss of life,
  Or even loss of Cause?
Far greater man once took a stand
  That led Him to a cross.

They curse, revile, and burn you
  In perverted zealotry,
While those who feel the despot's heel
  Hymn well your liberty.
O sacred flag, O rebel flag,
  O battle flag of Lee —
May all my days be filled with praise
  Of Southland, God, and thee!

— Michael Andrew Grissom

SOUTHERN BY THE GRACE OF GOD

If there is another single feature of our southern culture capable of eliciting the same kind of emotion produced by the Confederate flag, it would have to be the wild, throbbing strains of *Dixie* – the unofficial "national anthem of the South."

It has been said that America has no martial music like the countries of Europe, but that if this country has one song which can excite the people it would have to be *Dixie*. Why does this one song inspire Southerners so? How is it that this modest tune with its simple, whimsical words can create absolute pandemonium in two short bars? How does it yank us up out of our seats and force us to shriek and yell as if we had suddenly reverted to an aboriginal state? As it is, the *how* and *why* are lost somewhere in the succession of years that formed our culture. All we know is that it does. We can only demonstrate the fact and leave the reason to philosophers.

A pianist by trade, I am frequently called upon to provide that rather soft, dull type of repertoire we call dinner music while people sit and talk to one another rather than listen to the piano. I always manage to work *Dixie* in at least once, whether it be banquet, party, or reception, and the result is always the same. The conversation stops; all eyes are on the piano; and, if it is not inappropriate to the event, the crowd gathers around the piano as quickly as summer storm clouds, singing and clapping their hands in time to the music. And then, as regular as rain, the last note of the song brings on a chorus of Rebel yells.

A typical scene depicting the marvelous chaos generated by the sounds of *Dixie* is played out each year at the annual reunion of the Sons of Confederate Veterans. The three-day affair culminates in the Cotillion Ball, a delightful vignette of the Old South. Ladies with their hair done up in ringlets are attired in hoop-skirted ball gowns, while the gentlemen strut around in brilliant Confederate uniforms and dazzling tuxedoes. After presentation of the debutantes, who lead the cotillion in the opening dance, the orchestra plays traditional dance music for the elegantly garbed Southerners. Decorum is preserved, quite

112

naturally, until the orchestra strikes up *Dixie*. Then, notwithstanding hoop skirts, tuxedoes, and aristocratic pageantry, pandemonium breaks loose. It is difficult to hear the orchestra – or a freight train – over the Rebel yells and clapping of hands. And to think that all of this wonderful delirium was brought on by one l'il ole plantation walk-around!

There is no real agreement as to the origin of the word itself, though "Dixie" has been used to designate the Southland since long before the War for Southern Independence. Some think it may be a derivative of the Mason-Dixon Line, while others believe it came from a French ten-dollar bill called a "Dix," the French word for ten. The latter theory is interesting and somewhat plausible. In Louisiana, where the French language was common, bank notes carried the word "Dix" in each corner, and people referred to their money as their "Dixies." Eventually, the entire lower South became known as the land of Dixies, or Dixieland.

The song has been credited to Daniel Decatur Emmett, although there is uncertainty as to its absolute origin. The melody, according to Emmett, was inspired by part of a tune his mother had sung to him as a child, while others think that a similar tune had been sung around plantations and the big river for several generations. There is also the belief that the original words were written by a Southerner named William Shakespeare Hays. A report of its having been taught to music students at La Grange, Tennessee in 1858, further clouds its origin. What we do know is that this song of the sunny South was first written down and set to music in New York on a cold, rainy day in 1859. Emmett, composer of *Old Dan Tucker*, was asked to write a "plantation walkaround" for Bryant's Minstrels, and *Dixieland* was the result. Over the years, the title was shortened by general usage to *Dixie*. Confusion also surrounds Emmett's feelings about the adoption of the song as the southern anthem. Some have reported that this Ohio native was pro-southern; others say that he was sorry he

113

DIXIE

D. D. E.

Con Spirito

DAN D. EMMETT

An old copy of *Dixie,* the "national anthem of the South." Several versions have been sung through the years, but the words appearing here are the ones most frequently sung in the South. The tune has always remained the same.

had written the song, for in his mind it had become a symbol of treason. Whatever the origin of *Dixie*, it didn't seem to matter to Southerners. In 1860, it was heard in New Orleans amidst apprehension that the North was goading the South into war, and the song electrified its southern audience. For people in the South it was love at first sight – or sound, as the case may be. It immediately became the rallying cry of Southerners, and only a few months later this brand new song was given the official nod when it was played at the inauguration of President Davis on February 18, 1861, in Montgomery, Alabama. A Montgomery music teacher became the first person to orchestrate the number for band, and thus it was played all day and into the night by bands gathered for the inaugural occasion. The President's escort, soldiers of the First Alabama Infantry, became the first men to march to the strains of *Dixie*.

As a gesture of respect, it has always been our custom to stand whenever *Dixie* is played. Besides, who can sit still while that magnificent tune is blaring? Even so, the same spectre that haunts our flag now threatens our music as well; consequently, our people, especially our youth, are deprived of the opportunity of experiencing the excitement of *Dixie* by mere fiat of short-sighted school administrators who have banned its playing even though the lyrics are so innocuous as not to offend even the most hard-bitten Yankee or any other peculiar group of people. As a result, we're raising generations of young Southerners who never get to feel the exhilaration or learn the protocol.

A humorous, though pertinent illustration comes to mind. A few years ago we had a particularly obnoxious governor in Oklahoma who was literally swept back into office for a second term on a rock-hard pledge of "No new taxes!" Then, in an apparent abrogation of all principle, the man besieged the legislature with a proposal for the most massive property tax increase in state history. The heavy tax burden culminated in a statewide tax revolt at about the time the governor was taking office for his second term.

SOUTHERN BY THE GRACE OF GOD

A friend of mine became co-chairman of the tax revolt, and, as such, had occasion to receive insults from the governor's machine. She is a Jewish lady, formerly of Shreveport, Louisiana, and she was married to a doctor in my hometown. Shortly after the tax revolt had run its course, Marilyn was attending a doctor's convention near Tulsa, an annual event which gives her a chance each year to visit with a longtime girlfriend whose husband is also a doctor. As luck would have it, the selfsame governor was there for the evening gala and upon being introduced received the customary standing ovation from everyone – except Marilyn. Her friend, quite obviously embarrassed, looked down and said, "Marilyn, what are you doing sitting down?" To which Marilyn replied, "He is not a man deserving of an ovation, and it would be hypocritical of me to accord him one, especially after the way he treated us." Later in the program, after the audience was once again comfortably seated, the band struck up *Dixie*, and to Marilyn's dismay, not a single soul was standing – except Marilyn. Her friend, further embarrassed, looked up and said, "Marilyn, what are you doing standing up?" As straight as a soldier, Marilyn looked down at her and calmly answered, "They're playing *Dixie*. What are you doing sitting down?"

Failure to train and educate the present generation in regard to the significance of our traditions, symbols, and icons, is one problem, but compounding the neglect are the deliberate attempts to discredit our embattled emblems and force their removal from public use. At first, most of the deliberate efforts, although quite successful in many cases, had been localized attacks. In early 1987, a frightening new phase emerged in the form of a nationwide effort to ban the Confederate flag from official display anywhere in the country. It began with a resolution by the NAACP, and it slowly gained traction until the media, the government schools, perfidious politicians, and, sadly, too many churches took up the offensive assault upon our people and our heritage.

Its radical design was no less than a blueprint for ethnic

cleansing of the type that occurred when the Soviet Union occupied most of eastern Europe after World War II, forcing conquered nation states to divest themselves of all national pride and cultural attachments and become "soviet" in word, thought, and deed. Names of streets, schools, parks, highways – all are being renamed as the purge continues. They redefine the symbols of the Old South and re-write its history, labeling anyone who holds onto truth as "racist."

Our Confederate state holidays stand as a yearly reminder of the uniqueness of our southern culture, and yet these most obvious symbols of the South were taken for granted as I began this book in 1987. I thought they were safe. Then, I read a strange statement concerning Abraham Lincoln that gave me pause.

In a recent essay about the South, there appeared an odd observation that Southerners truly believe Lincoln to be one of the greatest presidents ever. The author of that rather presumptuous statement, a well-known figure in America who was purportedly speaking for the South, claims a southern background by virtue of having spent his childhood here, although to my knowledge he has lived his entire adult life in the north. He went on to opine that Robert E. Lee was no longer perceived as a hero in the South, and in a bold assertion that smacked of New-South propaganda – or ignorance – he mused that this new rejection of Lee "was probably good."

My first impression was that the new author was simply out of touch. I knew he wasn't in touch with the Southerners I know, because Lee is synonymous with heroism in the South and unquestionably the most popular hero of the late war. As to Lincoln's popularity, the errant writer is understandably afflicted with the common misperceptions about Lincoln that cause misinformed individuals to accept the carefully contrived notions of his fatherly, harmless, kind, deeply religious, ever-suffering image. Even southern ministers are notorious for accepting these myths at face value, quoting Lincoln with wild abandon while unsuspecting of his irreverent character, his agnosticism, and his refusal to make any profession of faith during his lifetime. It is not my desire nor my purpose, however, to fault ministers of the gospel for studying their Bibles rather than their history books, but rather to encourage those of us who seek truth to insist upon accuracy in history as well as in the pulpit.

However slanted those histories may be, it is still a stretch of the imagination to pretend that Honest Abe has become the consummate *southern* hero. Granting even the concession that Southerners are now educated primarily by books, essays, and saccharine documentaries produced by northerners, there are enough contemporary accounts of the character of Mr. Lincoln to prohibit an embracing acceptance of him among the people of the South. In her wartime diary, Mary Boykin Chesnut repeats a comment by Mrs. Scott, describing Lincoln as "the kind who are always at corner stores sitting on boxes, whittling sticks, and telling stories as funny as they are vulgar." [1]

Lincoln's propensity for vulgar stories was commonly known during his lifetime. Mrs. Chesnut tells of a report from a Mrs. Gibson, formerly Miss Ayer of Philadelphia, who had married south and although she was residing in Richmond was not in sympathy with the Confederacy. "Oh, yes, his best friends say the Yankee President is just the ugliest, the most uncouth, the nastiest joker, etc."[2] Mrs. Chesnut herself responded to another person who had tried to quote one of Lincoln's more decent statements. "I was very glad to hear it, to hear something from the President of the United States which was not merely a vulgar joke, and usually a joke so vulgar that you are ashamed to laugh – funny as it is!" [3]

Several years ago, I read a description of Lincoln that has yet to dislodge itself from my memory. Written by the editor of a Richmond newspaper, shortly after Lincoln's election, it depicted him as a candidate of "scanty political record – a Western lawyer, with the characteristics of that profession – acuteness, slang, and a large stock of jokes – and who had peculiar claims to vulgar and demagogical popularity, in the circumstances that he was once a captain of volunteers in one of the Indian wars, and at some anterior period of his life had been employed, as report differently said, in splitting rails, or in rowing a flat-boat." [4]

Has the rail-splitter from Illinois eclipsed General Lee in the admiration of Southerners over the past one hundred and fifty years? I decided that it might prove worthy of my time to make a survey of the southern states in regard to their holidays, reasoning that a fairly accurate gauge of public opinion might thus be ascertained.

I knew that Oklahoma had no holiday in honor of Honest Abe, and I was not surprised to find that ten of the eleven former Confederate states also disregarded his birthday as worthy of note. The real surprise came from Florida, the southernmost state of the South, where the birthday of Lincoln is a state holiday! As to how this aberration occurred, I can only offer conjecture that perhaps Florida has become the retirement haven of several million more displaced Yankees than Floridians had bargained for. Concerning the thesis that Robert E. Lee was no longer a hero, the results showed a resounding *not so!* Lee's birthday is an official holiday in nine of the eleven Confederate states. In addition, the border state of Kentucky, obliged to honor Lincoln only because of the incident of his birth in that state, more than compensates by having a state holiday on the day of General Lee's birth and another state holiday, called Confederate Memorial Day, on the 3rd of June, birthday of Jefferson Davis.

It was due to the aforementioned essay and the resulting survey which awakened in me a greater appreciation for the fundamental premise upon which Southerners bestow honor. Southerners have always resisted the might-makes-right psychosis which causes otherwise intelligent people to forsake principle and just "go with the winner." How easy it would have been to forget the defeated soldiers of the Lost Cause and accept the heroes of the victorious power in Washington. The Southland could have been strewn with monuments of Lincoln, Grant, and Sherman, paid for, most likely, with federal funds. The poverty-stricken women of the South, with homes destroyed and farms ruined, could have dispensed with their bake sales, ice cream suppers, little home talent plays, and bazaars, with which they laboriously gathered in their nickels and dimes that would one day build the magnificent monuments to men who had lost a war.

But, the easy road wasn't taken, and we who are their posterity are all the richer for it. The conquered boys in gray came home to a hero's welcome, while the women of the South looked upon the gargantuan memorials being constructed in the north and resolved that there would be ample memorials throughout Dixie, monuments which might even rival the appearance of those to the north and would, without a doubt, surpass them in sentiment. "There is no holier spot of ground than where defeated valor lies."[5] In the same vein came the official holidays honoring the heroes of the Confederacy.

In researching the Confederate holidays by state, it was disappointing to find no such honor given in Tennessee, the state who gave so many volunteers to the Confederacy; in Oklahoma, the last holdout of the Confederacy; in Missouri, for whom one of the stars was placed upon the Confederate flag; and in Louisiana, which suffered so much at the hands of the invader during the war and in Reconstruction. It wasn't always so in Louisiana. In the 1960s, Louisiana observed the birthday of Jefferson Davis, but with the passing of time and the election of more liberals and black activists, Louisiana eliminated the Jefferson Davis birthday. At one time, nearly all the southern states observed Robert E. Lee's birthday, but that noble man's birthday has been replaced in most states by the observance of the birthday of Martin Luther King. Several states, including Georgia, Florida, and Arkansas have abandoned all Confederate holidays. Not only has Florida rejected Confederate holidays, it has found room to celebrate Susan B. Anthony, 19th-century social justice warrior from New York.

But be not deceived. The removal of your Confederate holidays are never done by popular vote. These removals are done by your governors and legislative bodies in an effort to reel in the black vote. Republicans are trying to get it, while Democrats are trying to keep it. The overriding interest of politicians is perpetuating themselves in office, and southern heritage is often sacrificed upon the altar of political expediency.

At least, Alabama and Mississippi have held true, both states recognizing Confederate Memorial Day and the birthdays of Robert E. Lee and Jefferson Davis as state holidays. North Carolina still recognizes Confederate Memorial Day, as does South Carolina, and Texas has a state holiday called Confederate Heroes Day. Kentucky still celebrates Robert E. Lee's birthday and a holiday on June 3 that combines Confederate Memorial Day and the birthday of Jefferson Davis. In Virginia, the birthdays of Robert E. Lee and Stonewall Jackson are observed on the third Monday in January.

And even though the slippage is evident, the silver lining to this cloud is that good ol' Honest Abe still has no state holiday in ten of the original eleven Confederate states. Only Florida has succumbed. Oh, but you might say, we celebrate Lincoln on Presidents' Day in February. That, dear reader, is a *federal* holiday, which used to be celebrated as the birthday of George Washington – a Southerner – until Congress decided to "back door" a Lincoln holiday into the South.

INAUGURATION OF MR. DAVIS AS PRESIDENT AT MONTGOMERY, ALA.

V

The War

Granny, in a delightful episode of TV's *Beverly Hillbillies*, was trying to educate somebody – probably Jethro – about The War Between the States. In only one sentence, she explained the whole thing. "It was when the North invaded America!"

That's the best description I've ever heard. And it's just about the way we Southerners feel about it. The real spirit of America – independence, individual liberty, a readiness to defend America's honor – seems to spring from southern soil. The conservative South has always been the bulwark against liberalism and socialism when it seemed that northerners were allowing the country to drift in that direction. Southerners are the ones who can always be counted on to dig in and say "no" to radical change. After all, we've always felt a bit motherly towards the Constitution and the principles connected with that great document and the early days of this republic. We're usually the last to be convinced, if at all, that change is needed in that noble charter, and we are not in the habit of questioning the intent or the wisdom of those statesment of two hundred years ago who produced it and gave us our first taste of liberty.

SOUTHERN BY THE GRACE OF GOD

Not to diminish the heroic efforts of northern colonists, such as Benjamin Franklin, Samuel Adams, Nathan Hale, and Paul Revere, Southerners, nevertheless, have always regarded the institution of self-rule in this country as a fundamentally southern enterprise, and with good reason. Names like George Washington, Patrick Henry, George Mason, James Madison, Thomas Jefferson, James Monroe, the Lees and the Randolphs, all belong to Virginia. Jefferson wrote the Declaration of Independence, Henry initiated the call to arms, Washington commanded the armies that gave us our independence, Randolph presided over the Constitutional Convention, and Madison is known as the "Father of the Constitution." Nine of our first twelve presidents were southern-born, six of them from Virginia alone.

In light of the nation's early history, it's not too difficult to understand Granny's perception of the conflict, and one can but imagine the shock and outrage at the thought of northern troops invading the virtual footstool of Liberty. Southerners, who had no intention of invading anyone, stood aghast as northern plans became more evident. Robert E. Lee was the most notable of many southern military men who were asked by an upstart president named Lincoln to take up arms and invade their native states, an invasion that meant Lee would have to attack Virginia, the home of his father, Revolutionary hero Light-Horse Harry Lee. Such propositions would have been thought ludicrous had they not been urged with such diabolical solemnity.

It was a collision of two different worlds, and perhaps the course had been set for some time. Southerners were, no doubt, expecting confrontation of some kind. After all, there had been strife between gentlemen in the halls of Congress for years, but an *armed invasion* was certainly not anticipated by the populace in general. Southerners considered secession a peaceful and constitutional solution, and notwithstanding exhortations to military preparedness by some of their farsighted leaders, they were caught woefully unprepared for a prolonged defense of their borders when the invasion materialized.

More than 125,000 volumes have been written about the war, and there seems to be no final chapter that satisfies the thirst of those who study the conflict. This lone chapter, or even this one book, can but whet the appetite for further information about that cataclysmic event; consequently, a suggested reading list is furnished in the last chapter of this text for those who wish to delve into the wealth of material existing in America's libraries and bookstores. The recommended works are primarily those written by Southerners, on the assumption that Southerners write from something akin to a first-hand account, owing largely to the fact that the war happened to us in our own backyards. Indeed, in the case of many of the suggested volumes, the accounts are written by actual survivors who give vivid details of the calamity of that war. The emphasis upon reading southern literature is guided by the same reasoning that prompts us to look at the Jews for the most credible reports concerning the gas chambers and concentration camps of the Holocaust rather than to the voices of the Nazis for their feeble defense and glorification of those heinous crimes.

If most readers are like me, they will make only a small dent in the tons of information available to us today. To expedite the acquisition of a fundament grasp of the war, the following three works are recommended as a must, especially for interested readers who consider themselves beginners in studying the most fascinating war in the annals of history.

Edward A. Pollard's *Southern History of the War* was written as the war actually happened, year by year, although it is not in the form of a diary. Pollard was the editor of the *Richmond Examiner*, and as such, had a forum in which he could – and did – vent his wrath against the Confederate government, especially leveling harsh criticism at Jefferson Davis, blaming him with many of the government's problems.

Mary Boykin Chesnut's *Diary From Dixie* is precisely what the title indicates – a diary. It covers every topic under the sun from 1861 through 1865 and is considered the best-kept diary of the war, becoming a history bestseller in 1981. Incidentally, Mrs. Chesnut provides a happy balance against Pollard's anti-Davis stance with her unflagging support of the man through his trials as president of a vanishing nation.

The third book, entitled *Gray Fox*, is enjoying a new popularity in the 1981 reprint of Burke Davis's splendid work about Robert E. Lee. Not only does it bring Lee to life for the reader, it contains a wealth of information about the fighting in Virginia, a major theater of the war.

There have been many names given to that conflict of 150 years ago, including *The War for Southern Independence*, *The War Against Northern Aggression*, *The War of the Rebellion*, and a few facetious names, among them *The Late Unpleasantness*. Over one hundred designations have been assigned to that war, the two most frequently employed, of course, being *The Civil War* (used chiefly by northerners and those Southerners who are unaware of the technical inaccuracy of it) and *The War Between the States* (used almost exclusively by Southerners and those who understand that it was a war between the United States and the Confederate States).

The term *Civil War* has always been opposed by Southerners on the grounds that it was not, as Lincoln tried for four years to imagine, an internal war among citizens of the same country. In true ostrich fashion, he pretended that the Confederate States of America did not exist upon Planet Earth. For all his buffoonery, though, Lincoln, surprisingly enough, was a master of political manipulation and deceit, and in this case his objective was to convince the world that there were simply a few uprisings in several of the states of his protectorate, thereby giving him some perceived moral right to a military invasion of those states. Southerners, on the other hand, cited the Constitution and the rights of sovereign states to disengage themselves from each other as readily as they had chosen to engage in the first place. The new nation formed by the withdrawing states necessarily precluded the use of the term *civil war*, and Southerners viewed it as a war between a nation of southern states and a nation of northern states, hence the term *War Between the States*.

Today, the average person uses the term *Civil War* without making a distinction between the two terms, not in a conscious effort to defend Lincoln's carefully crafted argument, but because he is more familiar with the concise expression, *Civil War*. One event that paved the way for Southerners to accept *Civil War* into their vocabulary occurred in 1961, the beginning year of the centennial commemoration of the war. Every state that was involved in the conflict, north and south, was encouraged to create a centennial commission which would cooperate with the National Civil War Centennial Commission for the purpose of coordinating commemorative events throughout the four-year observance. After some resistance, the southern states grudgingly agreed to use the term *Civil War* for the sake of uniformity. Even so, Southerners who understand the war's ramifications usually defer to the wisdom of the past and continue to speak of *The War Between the States*.

Generally speaking, a specific label isn't even required, for Southerners simply talk about "the war," as if there had never been another armed conflict since '65. Everything in the South is dated by the war. "That was before the war". . . "My folks were ruined by the war". . . "I reckon it happened about fifty years after the war." That war, that catastrophe of monumental proportions, was enough to cause everything since to pale in comparison. Coupled with the black years of persecution called Reconstruction, the war did become a milestone, or perhaps we should say *the* milestone of southern history. An entire civilization was turned upside down and dared by ruthless watchdogs, who wielded bayonets over a disarmed southern citizenry, to pick itself up. Not just any civilization. Not by any means. This society was arguably the most highly-developed in the world. It was a nation of people endowed by nature and in love

127

with the arts. A highly refined agricultural class of people, tillers of nature's soil, the southern culture reflected a people at peace with nature and with one another. The war that demolished that proud civilization is, then, truly the South's point of reference, for the halcyon world that existed before is no more than a fond memory.

Time heals all wounds, so they say, and today North and South are much more tolerant of the differences which exist between them, differences which will always be there to some degree, but which are becoming remarkably less all the time. That feeling of good will is much to be desired, although the very unity that promotes the harmonious relations has a way of exacting its toll, and it is increasingly apparent that the toll thus exacted is the incremental loss of our southern identity and recognition as a distinct section of the country. The quaint, provincial charm that once was ours has given way to the rule of Wall Street, and the same fast-food strips that feed our northern neighbors have blighted every one of our once-alluring southern cities. Atlanta's skyline could be Detroit's or Pittsburgh's. In the prosperous South of the 1980s, we are stampeding toward anonymity and boring conformity to a way of life which is only a carbon copy of another civilization. That's the price we pay. If we could achieve the better relations and at the same time retain the uniqueness of our own culture, it would be the better course.

Each year, as we move further away from the scenes of the war, the very years themselves diminish the bitterness, the acute feelings, and the personal involvement with the issues of the conflict. We laugh at our North-South jokes and cooperate in sports, music, and leisure time activities in an overall spirit of congeniality, quite unlike the days preceding and immediately following the war. But do we really want to reduce our grasp of the War Between the States to a Blue-Gray football game in Montgomery? I think not.

There is virtue in remembering. Not all memories are pleasant ones by any means. Some are quite odious. The survivors of

Hitler's concentration camps know this better than anyone. If, however, we refuse to remember, we fall victim to our own carelessness and fulfill the old saying, "Those who ignore the mistakes of the past are doomed to repeat them." The Jews will never forget the Holocaust, and Southerners must not forget the War.

The invasion of the South was so senseless, so unnecessary. The burning of homes, destruction of entire communities, pillaging, looting, killing, violation of southern women, torture, summary executions – all so uncalled for. Gentlemen should have been able to bid each other farewell and part company without firing a shot. To the credit of the leadership in the South let it be said that this course of action was pursued vigorously, and to the credit of many in the North it was equally promoted. At first, even the influential Horace Greely, in his *New York Tribune*, proclaimed, "Wayward Sisters, Depart in Peace!" Unfortunately, the constant drumbeat of Abe Lincoln and the fanatic abolitionists who raised him from obscurity to sudden power drowned out the voices of reason and, once the War was enjoined, transformed many of the former peacemakers into war hawks.

In her diary, Mrs. Chesnut noted the war hysteria sweeping the North.

> The New York Tribune is so unfair. It began howling to get rid of us. We were so wicked. Now that we are so willing to leave them to their over-righteous self-consciousness, they cry "crush our enemy or they will subjugate us." The idea, that we want to invade or to subjugate! We would only be too grateful to be let alone. Only let us alone. We ask no more, of Gods or men. [1]

Such absolute perfidy reigned throughout the Lincoln regime that any early hopes of peace were dashed to pieces by pure deceit. Lincoln needed a war. His political back was against the wall, and war seemed the only way out. For his relentless manipulation of events which precipitated the awful conflict, he earned the dubious distinction of creating one of the most widely used contemporary terms for the calamity: *Mr. Lincoln's War.*

Lincoln was the tragic figure of the war, if indeed, anyone can be more tragic than the southern victims of the war. But, in a literary sense, such as a character in a novel, Lincoln was truly the tragic figure. A rough-cut backwoods creature who claimed he had educated himself, he was always running for some kind of public office and, just as often, failing to win the contest. A tall, gangling, awkward fellow of questionable parentage and with crude manners, he literally stumbled into the presidency by a quirk of Fate. His only base of support was the abolitionist Republican party, the fanatic element of the day, whose leaders kept its followers worked into a constant frenzy. His campaign rhetoric had inflamed and frightened the southern states so thoroughly that seven of them seceded upon the mere news of his election, and thus his presidency became the first sectional administration in the history of the Union. He lost a son during the war; his wife became mentally unbalanced; and he was nearly defeated in the election of 1864 due to the unpopularity of his war. He was inexperienced and virtually unqualified to guide the nation in its moment of crisis but ended up with the job that would send over 360,000 northern boys to an early death. And then somebody shot him.

Mr. Lincoln was keenly aware that his chances for the unlikely prospect of winning the presidency rested solely with the abolitionist Republicans' extremely sectional appeal to nor-therners. He had no delusions of support in the South; in fact, most southern states didn't even put Lincoln's name on the ballot. By promising the North every plum of victory, including that one item that lay at the bottom of the eternal division, a high tariff on imported goods which would force the South to buy manufactured items in the North at inflated price, Honest Abe served warning to Southerners as to what his election held in store for them. The Democrats split into factions with four men running in the same party, an unfortunate schism which virtually assured the election of the partisan Lincoln.

In December, 1860, when the results were known, South Carolina called for a state convention which first met at the Baptist Church in Columbia, then, due to a smallpox epidemic, removed itself to Charleston, where, on December 20, the delegates voted unanimously to sever South Carolina's ties with the United States. Years of fighting those same issues that Lincoln now championed had come to a head, and Southerners who had very deliberately considered their options for several years, met in state conventions throughout the lower South and systematically voted to secede from the Union. Forty-three days after South Carolina's brave lead, all seven states of the Deep South had removed themselves from the clutches of the new Lincoln administration.

Meeting in Montgomery, Alabama, in February, 1861, the seven seceded states formed the Confederate States of America and selected Jefferson Davis as provisional president. They immediately set about organizing a government similar to the one their ancestors had fashioned for the United States, adopting the same Constitution with minor changes that clarified the doctrine of states' rights once and for all. Limited military preparations were begun as a precaution, though there were many voices, North and South, advocating peaceful coexistence. Wishing to avoid what might turn into a ruinous war, an event which would hinder the complicated, urgent task of instituting a complex new government, to say nothing of the prospective loss of life and property that such a war would visit upon the people, the Confederacy sent a peace commission to Washington for the purpose of securing peace with the United States, negotiating removal of Federal troops from Fort Sumter and other Federal institutions in the South, and settling all claims of public property.

The embassy, composed of Martin J. Crawford of Georgia,

Alfred B. Roman of Louisiana, and John Forsyth of Alabama, traveled to Washington and requested a meeting with Lincoln's Secretary of State, William H. Seward, on March 12, exactly one month to the day before the Battle of Fort Sumter would launch the two nations into actual war. Tension was in the air, a tension heightened by the puzzling tenacity with which Mr. Lincoln doggedly held on to two military bases in the Confederacy while abandoning scores of others without a great deal of obvious reluctance.

From the beginning, there was an air of mystery and lack of protocol surrounding the treatment of the peace commissioners in Washington. The president, refusing to see them, never officially recognized them, and Secretary of State Seward would communicate with the commissioners only through Supreme Court Justice John A. Campbell. President Davis, in Montgomery, was baffled over the lack of information received from the peace ambassadors, who in turn were puzzled by the stalling efforts on the part of Mr. Lincoln.

The Confederacy was asking that Federal troops be removed from Fort Pickens, Florida, and from Fort Sumter, which lies in the harbor at Charleston, South Carolina. The underlying question: What was Mr. Lincoln's purpose for forcing two garrisons of northern soldiers to remain in disputed territory? His cabinet, even though made up of rabid abolitionists, advised him to evacuate Fort Sumter, as did his General of the Army, Winfield Scott. All kinds of peace proposals were flying throughout the northern states, and southern peace commissioners were on the steps of the capitol in Washington. Still, Mr. Lincoln refused even so much as to convene Congress until as late as July, 1861, long after the guns of war had decided the issue. James David Altman, historical analyst from Charleston, South Carolina, recently wrote, "Faced with a delicate situation of such national importance as he was in the spring and summer of that year, it seems odd that Lincoln did not desire the aid of Congress to search for a peaceful solution during those turbulent months."[2]

Fort Sumter is an island fortress. It didn't take long for the Federal troops to exhaust their food supplies after South Carolina seceded from the Union. Since January 20, the governor of the state had been supplying food to the garrison, which consisted of about 130 military personnel, while patiently anticipating their removal by the U.S. government. But as the month of March dragged on, even Justice Campbell could get little out of Lincoln or Seward as to the future of the men stranded down at Fort Sumter. Occasionally, he reported to the peace ambassadors from Dixie that Seward had assured him of the president's intention to evacuate the fort, but the commissioners were noticing a suspicious increase in military activity in Washington. The capitol was taking on the look of a fortified city. Soldiers were arriving in droves; the Mediterranean squadron was ordered home, as were other forces; and several ships were being outfitted in New York for a journey somewhere.

Altman writes, "Was it Lincoln's intention for war to begin at Fort Sumter? Historical evidence seems to point to that conclusion. There were many people in the North who were opposed to coercing the southern states back into the Union. Certainly there was little groundswell support for an overly aggressive policy on the part of the United States. Lincoln knew this, and yet he was also aware that should it appear that it was the Southern Confederacy that began hostilities, the Northern people would feel themselves symbolically injured and would rally to he flag."[3]

Rose O'Neal Greenhow, the Confederate spy who moved in the best of Washington's social circles, confronted Oregon's Senator Edward D. Baker, a close advisor of Lincoln, on the issue of Fort Sumter. His reply was revealing. "It is true, a great many lives may be lost, and we may not succeed in reinforcing Fort Sumter. But the President was elected by a Northern majority, and they are now becoming dissatisfied; and the President owes it to them to strike some blow by which he will make a unified

133

Rose O'Neal Greenhow

This fearless lady stayed in Washington after the southern states seceded so that she could send valuable information south to President Davis and the military leaders of the new Confederacy.

Northern party."[4]

During March, while both countries waited for some kind of solution, Lincoln sent two of his political cronies on separate visits to Charleston to determine the attitude of the people of Charleston toward the Union and the secession movement. Of course, he found that Charlestonians were solidly opposed to the old Union and would look upon an effort to send military provisions to the soldiers at Fort Sumter as an act of war. As a cover for the subterfuge, his second agent, Ward Lamon, paid a visit to Governor Pickens, declaring he was there for the purpose of arranging the removal of the garrison. Even the fort's commander, Major Anderson, having already advised the president that it was too late to provision the fort, was of the opinion that he and all of his troops would soon be sent home.

Thus it was a tremendous shock when suddenly, on the 8th of April, the Lincoln government rebuffed the Confederate peace ambassadors and informed Governor Pickens that twelve vessels with an aggregate force of 285 guns and 2400 men had already sailed for Fort Sumter!

Confusion reigned supreme. Major Anderson, inside the fort, wrote to Washington, "I ought to have been informed that this expedition was to come. Colonel Lamon's remarks convinced me that the idea, merely hinted at to me by Captain Fox, would not be carried out. We shall strive to do our duty, though I frankly say that my heart is not in the war which I see is thus to be commenced. That God will still avert it, and cause us to resort to pacific measures to maintain our rights, is my ardent prayer." [5]

In Montgomery, President Davis and his cabinet, alarmed at the prospect of armed troops headed for South Carolina, hurriedly tried to come to some kind of decision before the heavily armed fleet reached Charleston. Their dilemma: If the Confederacy demanded surrender before the fleet arrived – which would surely be rejected by Major Anderson – and then had to take the fort by force, history would blame the South for firing the first shot in a terrible war that would likely be thus commenced; if, on the other hand, no action were taken until the fort was strengthened by a massive fleet, countless lives would be lost in an extensive battle. Lincoln's debating days, in which he had mastered the technique of placing his opponent in a dilemma, were serving him well in this situation, even though the interest of peace was ill-served by his political machinations.

Weighing the matter heavily, President Davis opted for the plan which might avoid the effusion of blood and correspondingly ordered General Beauregard to take the fort as soon as possible. General Beauregard, following instructions, sent a letter to the commander of the fort on April 11.

> SIR: The Government of the Confederate States
> has hitherto forborne from any hostile demonstration

against Fort Sumter, in the hope that the Government of the United States, with a view to the amicable adjustment of all questions between the two Governments, and to avert the calamities of war, would voluntarily evacuate it.

There was reason at one time to believe that such would be the course pursued by the Government of the United States, and under that impression my Government has refrained from making any demand for the surrender of the fort. But the Confederate States can no longer delay assuming actual possession of a fortification commanding the entrance of one of their harbors, and necessary to its defense and security.

I am ordered by the Government of the Confederate States to demand the evacuation of Fort Sumter. My aides, Colonel Chesnut and Captain Lee, are authorized to make such demand of you. All proper facilities will be afforded for the removal of yourself and command, together with company arms and property, to any post in the United States which you may select. The flag which you have upheld so long and with so much fortitude, under the most trying circumstances, may be saluted by you on taking it down.

I am, sir, very respectfully, your obedient servant,

G.T. BEAUREGARD,
Brigadier General, Commanding

Major Anderson replied that he could not surrender; whereupon, General Beauregard sent word that he would open fire in one hour. As luck would have it, the Confederates, racing to reduce the fortress before reinforcements arrived, were aided by a storm at sea and a mixup in orders which resulted in delay of the expected entry into Charleston Harbor of the expedition fleet. The battle erupted with the simultaneous appearance of some of the ships which had reached their rendezvous point in the offing of the harbor but too late and not close enough to support Major Anderson's response to General Beauregard's attack. Though the battle raged from 4:20 a.m., April 12, until 1:30 p.m., April 13, the Union fleet made not one move from its observation position in the offing, even when the fort caught fire at two separate times. General Beauregard, seeing the flames, sent an offer to help in extinguishing the second conflagration; whereupon, Major Anderson took advantage of the opportunity afforded by the temporary truce and made the surrender he had rejected nearly two days earlier.

There had been no casualties, and General Beauregard's terms were lenient. He allowed Major Anderson to keep his surrendered sword and lower his flag with ceremony, guaranteeing him safe passage out of the harbor. During the gun salute to the flag, an accidental explosion killed one man and mortally wounded another, the only casualties of the entire affair. As the troops were being ferried out of Charleston harbor, bound for New York on the steamer *Isabel*, they passed by the Confederate batteries on Cummings Point, where the Southern soldiers stood in silence with uncovered heads, paying tribute to the reluctant warriors who had so gallantly defended themselves.

The first major battle was now history. What had begun as a gentlemen's war would end exactly four years later as a holocaust, punctuated by deeds of savagery against the inhabitants of a brutally invaded South. Infamy would follow Generals Sheridan, Wilson, "Beast" Butler, Sherman, and a host of other Yankees, in their safari-like expeditions through the fabled land of cotton. Brevet Major George W. Nichols, officer on General Sherman's staff, chronicled his experiences on the abominable "march to the sea" in a diary he would shamelessly publish after the war.

The solemn truth is, that the Southern people have never had any conception of the National Idea. They do not know what it is to be an American. . . .

Our work has been the next thing to annihilation. . . . . [General Sherman said] "There is a class of people at the South who must be exterminated before there can be peace in the land.". . .

Nearly all these places are deserted, although here and there we find children, whom it is difficult to persuade that they are not at once to be murdered. . .

It may be for the good of future generations that this Rebel horde should be swept from the earth. . . .

In the record of great wars we read of vast armies marching through an enemy's country, carrying death and destruction in their path; of villages burned, cities pillaged, a tribe or a nation swept out of existence. . . . History, however, will be searched in vain for a parallel to the scathing and destructive effect of the Invasion of the Carolinas.[6]

History is replete with wars, and it is too often true that war, in all its ghastly array, is inaugurated for political advantage rather than to right some moral wrong. For the 20th-century student of American history, it has always been difficult to ascertain the truth pertaining to the war's commencement because assassination tends to deify a character, whether prince or scoundrel, as it certainly did in the case of Lincoln. True to form, the assassin's bullet worked its mysterious magic and seemed for almost a century to have absolved Lincoln of even the capability of ulterior motive. School children all across the land have memorized Lincoln's Gettysburg Address as if it were Scripture from the Bible, and most people in America were trained to believe that "Lincoln saved the Union," when in actuality he destroyed it. But in the hindsight of 150 years, a stronger light has been cast upon the character of Lincoln. Emotional analysis has given way in some impartial quarters to factual study, and modern historians are not so timid in accusing Mr. Lincoln of a deliberate political plot to prevent peaceable relations between the Confederacy and the United States. Small wonder then that it has increasingly been labeled "Mr. Lincoln's War."

The scheme to maneuver the South into firing the first shot seems to have originated with Lincoln himself, but the development of the ominous plot was done in consort with his Secretary of State, William H. Seward, and a political crony named Gustavus V. Fox, all Republicans. Lincoln's election was the first victory for the new Republican party, and already seven states had bolted the old Union – a disastrous beginning for a new administration. Northern Democrats were furious, calling for peace, not war. One can but imagine the scenarios conjured up by the Republicans as they surveyed the dismal situation: possible impeachment of the new president, likely defeat in the Congressional elections of 1862, a reputation as the party that split the nation – or all three. Out of such desperate minds the plot was hatched. If the South could only be made to fire upon the flag, public opinion in the North would most likely crystallize in favor of the new president.

An observant English editor wrote of Lincoln, "He has thought that a political object was to be obtained by putting the Southerners in the wrong, if they could be maneuvered into firing the first shot."[7] His Secretary of the Navy, Gideon Welles, wrote, "It was very important that the Rebels strike the first blow in the conflict."[8] Lincoln's confidant, G.V. Fox, outlined the plan: "I simply propose three tugs convoyed by light-draft men-of-war. . . the first tug to lead in empty, to open their fire."[9]

Not waiting for Mr. Fox's grand scheme, of course, the reluctant Confederacy fired upon Fort Sumter, playing directly into the hands of the plotting president. The helplessness felt by southern diplomats was noted by E.A. Pollard, "Nothing was left but to accept the distinct challenge of the Lincoln government to arms."[10]

On May 1, 1861, after the commencement of war was a *fait accompli,* Lincoln explained to Fox, who was disappointed that the ships had arrived too late to have participated as he had envisioned, "I sincerely regret that the failure of the attempt to provision Fort Sumter should be the source of annoyance to you. . . . You and I both anticipated that the cause of the country would be advanced by making the attempt to provision Fort Sumter, even if it should fail; and it is no small consolation now to feel that our anticipation is justified by the result."[11]

The action at Fort Sumter had the desired effect. There arose the predictable outcry, and Lincoln, satisfied in the extreme, accordingly called for 75,000 volunteers to "put down the rebellion." The seven states of the Confederacy – Alabama, Florida, Georgia, Louisiana, Mississippi, South Carolina, and Texas – were soon joined by four more southern states. Virginia was immediate in her action, seceding four days after Fort Sumter. By June 8, Arkansas, North Carolina, and Tennessee had joined their southern neighbors. In the Indian Territory, each of the Five Civilized Tribes – Cherokee, Chickasaw, Choctaw, Creek, and Seminole – seceded in separate actions and, joining the Confederacy, became its only official allies.

Though Maryland was populated to a large extent by Southerners, the reins of government were quickly seized by the authoritarian regime of Lincoln. Members of the state legislature were arrested and thrown into prison, thereby preventing secession of that small state which encircles Washington, D.C. Many of Maryland's sons went south and joined regiments from other southern states, while some managed to organize a few Maryland units to fight for the South. Missouri and Kentucky found themselves in similar situations, although southern sympathizers in those large states were numerous enough to contribute significant numbers of soldiers and sums of money to the Confederacy. In recognition, the South determined that the two extra stars in the Confederate Battle Flag should stand for Kentucky and Missouri.

In the far west, Arizona Territory was claimed by the Confederacy, the southern half of the territory being reinforced by Confederate military units early in the war. Arizona Territory was comprised of what eventually became the two present-day states of Arizona and New Mexico and stayed in Confederate hands for about a year. Then, in the Battle of Glorieta Pass on March 28, 1862, Confederate forces, after winning a victory, had to fall back to Sante Fe because of the loss of their supply wagons, resulting in a gradual and complete withdrawal from the entire Arizona Territory.

There were certainly peculiarities dividing North and South long before the war, but it was the collision of the two cultures that provided the kind of close encounters that further defined and sharpened those differences. Each side viewed the other with corresponding contempt. An amusing, though earnest, illustration comes from Lee's march into Yankee territory just before the Battle of Gettysburg. As the Confederates entered Chambersburg, Pennsylvania, Mr. Hoke, an observant merchant in that city, believed that the Confederates were awe-struck with "the rich and beautiful country," and bragged that "the evident superiority of the country north of the Potomac to that south of it . . . exercised a discouraging effect upon the soldiers."[12]

They were stricken alright, but it wasn't with awe. Writing from the same city at the same time, a Confederate soldier, Captain Blackford, wrote to his wife in Virginia. "We are now in the Cumberland Valley, and a fine country it is – that is, as yankees count fineness – small farms divided into fields no larger than our garden, and barns much larger than the houses in which live their owners, their families and laborers. The land is rich and highly cultivated, much more highly than the men who own it. . . . While I note physical comfort, I see no signs of social refinement. All seem to be on a dead level, like a lot of fat cattle in a clover field. . . . You never saw a country so densely popu--lated. . . . Never in my life have I seen as many ugly women since coming to this place."[13]

Captain Blackford would not long have to look at ugly women, however, for this was the last of only two times that General Lee took his troops north. Outside of some cavalry dashes into the lower regions of the North by General Jubal Early, General John Hunt Morgan, Colonel John S. Mosby, and a few other daring cavaliers, the war was fought exclusively in the South.

The armies were as different as night and day in nearly every conceivable aspect. One look at them, and the difference was apparent. Northern armies were always dressed according to regulation in an endless supply of new uniforms. As they penetrated deeper into the South, long supply lines stretched behind them, assuring them of abundant food, medicine, toiletries, and items necessary to a comfortable life in the military. Yankee soldiers could crawl into tents at night and listen to the bands playing their favorite tunes. An endless supply of overcoats and blankets kept them warm during the cold winters, and none had to go barefooted.

Ammunition was no problem in the Federal army. The great northern factories turned out armaments of war faster than the Yankees could use them, and, eventually, the introduction of the repeating Spencer rifle gave them an advantage that was tantamount to victory. While Confederate soldiers had to drop back and load their old muskets after every single round, Yankees could fire in rapid succession, decimating ranks of re-loading Southerners.

The ever-increasing cavalry units rode on the finest horses, outfitted with the best saddles to be found anywhere in the world. There were adequate numbers of doctors and nurses attending the Union army, with an ample number of ambulance wagons to transport the wounded behind the lines for treatment. In all, it was a well-heeled army and a well-oiled operation.

It was a different story in the South. When uniforms were available, many of the men would resemble one another in their Confederate gray, but often it was a mixture of homespun outfits

Private William J. Owen in 1863. This young man served in
Co. D, 31st Alabama Infantry. Dressed in anything they could
find, our boys went forth into battle against a superbly outfitted U.S. Army, sometimes outnumbering our forces three to
one. The only thing new about Private Owen's outfit is his
ammunition belt and his Enfield rifle. (Photograph courtesy
of Hunter Phillips)

that merely tried to differentiate the soldier from the Yankee
blue. The most common homemade uniform consisted of a pair
of pants and a shirt or coat dyed with the hulls of the butternut,
or walnut, tree. After several months, uniforms could be more
truthfully described as rags, with little hope of replacing them at
frequent intervals.

The shoe supply was a matter even more serious. In 1862,
the First South Carolina reported 100 of its 300 men barefooted in
northern Virginia, where General Alexander said, "The lack of

In a familiar scene across the South, ladies cut their draperies and curtains into blankets for their ill-clothed Confederate soldiers. This scene is a still shot from a documentary movie, called *Dixie*, produced in 1924 by Yale University. (Photo from December 1924 issue of *Confederate Veteran* magazine.)

shoes is deplorable, and barefooted men with bleeding feet were no uncommon sight. . . . For rations, we were indebted mostly to the fields of roasting ears, and to the apple orchards."[14] On November 15, 1862, General Longstreet's men started on a long march to Fredericksburg, about 3,500 of them without shoes. Lack of shoes was a continual problem, made worse for the soldiers of Stonewall Jackson, who took his acclaimed infantry on so many of those famous rapid flanking marches that they were referred to as "Jackson's foot cavalry." It was said that Jackson's scantily shod forces were easily tracked in the snow by the blood from their feet.

Food was meager at best. Meat was scarce, and sometimes a biscuit would be one day's rations. Just before the end, General

Wise complained to General Lee that his men had not had a bite for more than a week; whereupon, General Lee searched until he found a small portion of food to divide among them. His own breakfast that very day had been a cup of tea from the kindness of a nearby home. It was often that men would go two or three days without a meal, and many times that meal came from whatever was growing along the road. A few kernels of corn could be carried in the pocket until the army stopped long enough for it to be parched. General Lee once said that he had lost more men from lack of proper food than to enemy bullets.

How this southern army stayed in the field for four years under the conditions with which it was faced has not yet been fully answered. Small wonder that the Confederate soldier has often been called the "Eighth Wonder of the World." As Burke Davis once wrote, "No one had ever seen such an army." [15]

Many of these soldiers were men from plantations, sons of wealthy and educated figures in southern society, now living in trenches with not a tent over their heads, suffering from scurvy, dysentery, and lice. Starvation was their lot; yet, when a shipment of bacon made it through the blockade from Nassau and was offered to Lee's troops, some regiments voluntarily turned over their food to the poor in Richmond who were as destitute as the lowly soldier.

In late June, 1863, as Lee's men were passing through Chambersburg, a citizen of that northern community described them. "The Confederate infantry . . . presented a solid front. They came in close marching order . . . their dress consisted of every imaginable color and style, the butternut predominating. . . . Hats, or the skeletons of what once had been hats, surmounted their partly covered heads. Many were ragged, shoeless, and filthy . . ." though "well armed and under perfect discipline. They seemed to move as one vast machine." [16]

There were few factories in the South to manufacture the needs of war. The 4,000 miles of southern coastline had been blockaded by U.S. ships, and the northern borders of the

Confederacy were lined with Yankee troops. Lacking an effective navy, the South lay isolated from Europe's supplies. The South was a virtual island, unprepared to sustain itself apart from world commerce.

At the end of four toilsome years, General Gordon, surrounded by his affectionate men just after Lee's surrender, looked over his beleaguered boys in gray and shouted to them, "Soldiers of the Second Army Corps. No mathematician con compute the odds against which you have contended"[17] Those odds included having to scramble around the battlefield after a fight, picking up bullets left by Yankees so they would have ammunition enough for the next scrap.

The fundamental perception of war, itself, was no less a contrast between the two countries than the physical condition of their armies. The unwarranted wreckage strewn across the Southland was not merely that of military significance and was perceived by southern soldiers as barbaric. The infamous northern general, W.T. Sherman, unabashedly declared war on the civilian population of the South, proclaiming that women and children must be made to feel the war as heavily as the soldier in the field. In her diary, Mrs. Chesnut called him a nightmare, a ghoul, a hyena. Needlessly, he burned virtually everything in his meandering path from Atlanta to the sea, a distance of approximately 300 miles. His army, spread out over a width of sixty miles, destroyed homes, schools, churches, and entire communities. The heart of Georgia was cut out. Then, he turned northward and destroyed the center of the fine old state of South Carolina, home of many Revolutionary War heroes. All that remained in his wicked path were chimneys surrounded by the smoking ruins of what once were family dwellings.

On March 5, 1865, writing from a refuge in Lincolnton, North Carolina, a town, incidentally, not named for the U.S. president, Mrs. Chesnut had just gotten word from a Catholic priest of the destruction of Columbia.

Sherman's men had burned the convent. Mrs. Munroe had pinned her faith to Sherman, because he was a Catholic, and now! Father O'Connell saw the fire. The nuns and girls marched to the old Hampton house and saved it. They walked between files of soldiers. Men were rolling tar barrels and lighting torches to fling over the house when the nuns came. Columbia is but dust and ashes, burned to the ground. Men, women, and children are left there, houseless, homeless, without a particle of food. They are picking up the corn left by Sherman's horses in their picket ground and parching it to stay their hunger. [18]

There were, of course, men in U.S. uniform who were participating in the invasion of the South out of some vague sense of duty or who had been drafted against their will and were repulsed at the wanton attacks upon southern civilization. It is unfortunate, however, to have to realize that such men of principle probably constituted the minority of this alien force. The incursion of the South, which bore the novelty and sensation now associated with the excessive buffalo hunts of the western plains, was executed with a "soldier of fortune" abandon fostered by a widely held conviction in the North that Southerners were the dregs of humanity and, therefore, legitimate prey. The imagined aboriginal state of Southerners seemed to assuage the guilt of violating the southern home and basic human rights.

Mrs. L.S. Hall, wife of a state legislator from Wetzel County, in the western part of Virginia, was forced to walk the streets of New Martinsville, her clothes tied in a bundle over her head. After being submitted to a terrible outrage, her home was burned to the ground.

William Gilmore Simms, noted poet and author whom Edgar Allan Poe called "the best novelist America ever produced," wrote from eyewitness perspective about the scores of negro women who were molested by regiments of Yankees in successive relays. He told of a negro woman who was viciously assaulted in Columbia by northern soldiers, who then drowned her in a mud puddle. White women, likewise, were left to the mercy of unbridled Yankee soldiers, while their husbands, fathers, and sons were dying on the front lines. Yankees imprisoned women for the mere infraction of waving their handkerchiefs at passing southern prisoners and then subjected them to indignities in their incarceration.

In the mountains of Virginia where partisan rangers or guerilla fighters were sometimes the only effective resistance to the looting and burning, a ranger shot one fleeing bluecoat in the head and stopped to search his body. From a burning home, this Yankee had stolen women's clothing, wine, two bolts of cloth, sheets, curtains, and lace – all tied to his saddle. In his pockets were found jewelry and a letter from a northern girl who begged him to send her stolen things from some of the "rebel" homes he passed.

The beautiful Shenandoah Valley was blackened from one end to the other by soldiers under the command of various officers, the most notorious being General Phil Sheridan, a heartless creature of diminutive stature who seemed to have an obsession with fire. At times, he burned people out for simply having a gun in the house. Sometimes, he entertained himself by burning every fifth home. Upon occasion, he selected his target by accusing the occupants of sending a signal by lantern to Confederate guerillas on some hill, when in reality it had been only a grieving mother and father who had lit a lamp in the dark to read a message of death from the front. Sheridan decreed that any person who aided a partisan ranger in any way would be burned out immediately, the mere suspicion of which caused numberless burnings. After the war, Little Phil, as they called him, went out west and fed his inferiority complex by wiping out the Indians.

The Union officers, from Grant on down, were as guilty as

those who committed the brutal acts, for in their hands rested the power to prevent the atrocities; but, rather than forestall, they issued orders to wreak havoc. Grant, in particular, was responsible for goading Sheridan into pursuing his barbarity in the Shenandoah Valley, one of the richest and most beautiful sections of Virginia. As columns of smoke swirled skyward day after day, Sheridan was acquiring one of the vilest reputations of the war. With great alacrity he received Grant's brutal orders to hang any of Colonel Mosby's men they could find, *without trial*, and to abduct all of the families of Mosby's Rangers, taking them to Fort McHenry as hostages. In August of 1864, Sheridan rather boastfully sent a message back to Grant. "Mosby has annoyed me and captured a few wagons. We hung one and shot six of his men yesterday. I have burned all wheat and hay, and have brought off all stock, sheep, cattle, horses, etc. south of Winchester."[19]

Much of the blame for these barbaric escapades rests squarely at the top. Mr. Lincoln was under constant criticism for what had become a lengthy war, a war with no end in sight. The election of 1864 was at hand, and the Democrats had chosen their candidate: George B. McClellan, a former general whom Lincoln had removed from command in 1862 and, more importantly, a peace candidate. Even Lincoln's closest friends confided that he probably had no chance of being reelected. Always the politician, however, Lincoln bore down upon his already relentless pressure on his generals for more victories – victories at any cost – and for an increasingly harsh prosecution of the war in general. Sherman's obliging devastation of Georgia delighted the president and rallied the voters, who provided the ten percent margin by which he was reelected – a political victory bought with blood.

An officer attached to Sherman's command wrote of his disgust in a letter. "I tell you the truth when I say we are about as mean a mob as ever walked the face of the earth. It is perfectly frightful. If I lived in this country, I never would lay down my arms while a 'Yankee' remained on the soil. I do not blame

149

"I tell you the truth when I say we are about as mean a mob as ever walked the face of the earth." – a Yankee officer attached to Sherman's command. (photo from *Pictorial History of the Civil War*.)

Southerners for being secessionists now. I could relate many things that would be laughable if they were not so horribly disgraceful."[20]

Athens, Alabama was invaded in 1862 by one of Lincoln's arsonist generals, Russian-born John B. Turchin, who told his troops that he would shut his eyes for an hour while they "stopped" in Athens. After a while he noticed that all was relatively peaceful, so he inquired of his adjutant as to the expected torching of the city. No arson had been reported. The general then said to inform the men that he would close his eyes for an hour and a half this time. Finally, the soldiers took the hint and fell to work looting, plundering, and burning Athens. In a rare show of discipline and conscience, his superiors had General Turchin court-martialed and dismissed from the service; however, when Lincoln got wind of it, he rewarded the Russian beast by restoring his command and handing him a promotion!

Nothing was sacred. On their way into Virginia, prior to the first large land battle of the war, Yankees had entered Bethel Church where they scrawled on holy walls, "Death to the traitors!" and "Down with the Rebels![21] Even though battle had not yet occurred on Virginia soil, Colonel Daniel Hill had to send out a company to rout a bunch of Federal soldiers who were already plundering a house. William Gilmore Simms reported incidents of Yankees digging up fresh graves in search of jewelry buried with the dead.

Northern civilians seemed equally as determined to shed their civility. On the retreat from Gettysburg, a rapid flight to avoid being overtaken by the victorious Federal army, terribly wounded and dying soldiers had to be jostled along rough, rocky roads, all the while screaming in their death agony for help. General Imboden's cavalry rode ahead of the cumbersome, slow-moving wagons carrying the pitifully maimed men, most of whom hadn't even had a morsel of food in thirty-six hours. At Greencastle, Pennsylvania, after the vanguard had passed through the town, leaving the wagons unprotected for a long stretch, about fifty citizens of the community rushed from their houses, and, wielding great axes, hacked the wheels of the wagons, collapsing them in the road. General Imboden furiously raced back to the town, rounded up all the guilty citizens he could find, and held them as prisoners of war. Several wagons had to be abandoned and the sick crowded into wagons that were still operable.

Without a doubt, the most senseless acts were those involving the torture of helpless prisoners in northern prisons. There was simply nothing to be gained from tormenting incarcerated soldiers who had neither money nor valuables to satisfy the Yankee thieves, yet torture was administered. Only one instance of such contemptible behavior is sufficient to illustrate the horror. Taken from E.A. Pollard' *Southern History of the War*, it is best told in Pollard's own poignant narrative.

This statement was taken from the lips of Captain Calvin C. Morgan, a brother of the famous General Morgan.

Captain Morgan was among those of his brother's expedition who, in last July, were incarcerated in the penitentiary of Ohio. On entering this infamous abode, Captain Morgan and his companions were stripped in a reception room and their naked bodies examined there. They were again stripped in the interior of the prison, and washed in tubs by negro convicts; their hair cut close to the scalp, the brutal warden, who was standing by, exhorting the negro barber to "cut off every lock of their rebel hair." After these ceremonies, the officers were locked up in cells, the dimensions of which were thirty-eight inches in width, six and a-half feet in length, and about the same in height. In these narrow abodes our brave soldiers were left to pine, branded as felons, goaded by "convict-drivers," and insulted by speeches which constantly reminded them of the weak and cruel neglect of that government, on whose behalf, after imperiling their lives, they were now suffering a fate worse than death. But even these sufferings were nothing to what was reserved for them in another invention of cruelty without a parallel, unless in the secrets of the infernal.

It appears that, after General Morgan's escape, suspicion alighted on the warden, a certain Captain Merion, who, it was thought, might have been corrupted. To alleviate the suspicion (for which there were really no grounds whatsoever), the brute commenced a system of devilish persecution of the unfortunate Confederate prisoners who remained in his hands. One part of this system was solitary confinement in dungeons. These dungeons were close cells, a false door being drawn over the grating, so as to exclude light and air. The food allowed the occupants of these dark and noisome places, was three ounces of bread and half a pint of water per day. The four walls were bare of everything but a water-bucket for the necessities of nature, which was left for days to poison the air the prisoner breathed. He was denied a blanket; deprived of his overcoat, if he had one, and left standing or stretched with four dark, cold walls around him, with not room enough to walk in to keep up the circulation of his blood, stagnated with the cold, and the silent and unutterable horrors of his abode.

Confinement in these dungeons was the warden's sentence for the most trivial offences. On one occasion one of our prisoners was thus immured because he refused to tell Merion which one of his companions had *whistled contrary to the prison rules*. But the most terrible visitation of this demon's displeasure remains to be told.

Some knives had been discovered in the prisoners' cells, and Merion accused the occupants of meditating their escape. Seven of them, all officers, were taken to the west end of the building and put in the dark cells there. They were not allowed a blanket or overcoat, and *the thermometer was below zero*. There was no room to pace. Each prisoner had to struggle for life, as the cold benumbed him, by stamping his feet, beating the walls, now catching a few minutes of horrible sleep on the cold floor, and then starting up to continue, in the dark, his wrestle for life.

"I had been suffering from heart disease," says Captain Morgan, speaking of his own solitary confinement on another occasion. "It was terribly aggravated by the cold and horror of the dungeon in which

I was placed. I had a wet towel, one end of which I pressed to my side; the other would freeze, and I had to put its frozen holds on my naked skin. I stood this way all night, pressing the frozen towel to my side and keeping my feet going up and down. I felt I was struggling for my life."

Captain Morgan endured this confinement for eighteen hours, and was taken out barely alive. The other prisoners endured it for *sixteen days and nights.* In this time they were visited at different periods by the physician of the penitentiary – Dr. Loring – who felt their pulses and examined their condition, to ascertain how long life might hold out under the exacting torture. It was awful, this ceremony of torture, this medical examination of the victims. The tramp of the prisoners' feet, up and down (there was no room to walk), as they thus worked for life, was incessantly going on. This black tread-mill of the dungeon could be heard all through the cold and dreary hours of the night. Dr. Loring, who was comparatively a humane person, besought Merion to release the unhappy men; said they had already been taxed to the point of death. The wretch replied, "They did not talk right yet." He wished them to humble themselves to him. He went into the cell of one of them, Major Webber, to taunt him. "Sir," said the officer, "I defy you. You can kill me, but you can add nothing to the sufferings you have already inflicted. Proceed to kill me; it makes not the slightest difference."

At the expiration of sixteen days the men were released from the dungeons. Merion said "he would take them out this time alive, but next time they offended, they would be taken out feet foremost." Their appearance was frightful; they could no longer be recognized by their companions. With their bodies swollen and discolored, with their minds bordering on childishness, tottering, some of them talking foolishly, these wretched men seemed to agree but in one thing – a ravenous desire for food.

"I had known Captain Coles," says Captain Morgan, "as well as my brother. When he came out of his dungeon, I swear to you I did not know him. His face had swollen to two or three times its ordinary size, and he tottered so that I had to catch him from falling. Captain Barton was in an awful state. His face was swollen and the blood was bursting from the skin. All of them had to be watched, so as to check them in eating, as they had been starved so long."

We had had in this war many examples of Yankee cruelty. But the statement given above may be said to take precedence of all that had ever yet been narrated of the atrocities of the enemy; and it is so remarkable, both on account of its matter and the credit that must naturally attach to its authorship that we doubt whether the so-called civilized world of this generation has produced anywhere any well-authenticated story of equal horror. [22]

War, in all its destructive force, is horrible enough without barbaric deeds and crimes against humanity, but it was precisely this excessive wickedness that generated the bitterness, hatred, and mistrust toward the northern people that lasted so long. The very term *Yankee* is, to this day, one of the most offensive words in the southern vocabulary, although it is four letters shorter nowadays than it used to be.

Southern society had difficulty comprehending such inhumanity. Chivalry was still observed in the South. The southern code certainly did not allow for the depravity of hanging a

David Owen Dodd, too young to join the army, was executed for writing down information about the Union forces occupying his hometown of Little Rock, Arkansas.

teenager whose only fault lay in having written down the locations of Federal positions within his hometown of Little Rock, Arkansas, which was at that time under Yankee occupation. Accused of being a spy, David Dodd was intimidated and hanged, and in a scene reminiscent of the young Sam Davis in Tennessee, he would not implicate another human being, saying "I will not betray a friend." His youthful body, frail and lean, was not heavy enough to choke him, so the officer in charge of the ghoulish scene ordered two privates to jump up and hang on to his legs until he died. All this, while an unarmed Little Rock citizenry looked on in horror, voicing an outcry that went mercilessly unheeded. In stark contrast to southern sensitivies, Lieutenant James Munns, Jr., a Yankee officer from Iowa, illustrated the utter contempt Union soldiers had for the inhabitants of the South when he wrote in a letter back home, "I was pleased to have the satisfaction of seeing a double-dyed traitor, who was arrested as a 'spy,' hung by the neck until life departed."

Not only did General Frederick Steele, commanding the unwelcome forces in Little Rock, order the execution, he forbade any spoken words or music at what passed for a funeral of the poor teenager, and he forbade David's parents, who lived south of Little Rock at Camden, Arkansas, to attend the austere service and bury their son. In fact, the only people in Little Rock who were allowed to be at the stilted, government-dictated service, were two of David's aunts and their husbands. David's father, Andrew Dodd, never well again after losing his only son in such gruesome manner, called the New York-born Steele a murderer and disgrace to humanity.

Remove all the trappings of war – military authority, military discipline, political prejudice – and what it boils down to is this: A 45-year-old New York man murdered a 17-year-old Arkansas boy. Andrew's father was right on both counts.

General Lee's prosecution of the war depicted the southern idea of what's fair in war and what isn't, procedures which were essentially embodied in the Geneva Convention of 1949 with additions of protection added in 1977. These were agreements between nations to insure humane treatment of prisoners of war, the sick, and the wounded. In addition, Lee's chivalric code forbade injustices against civilians and set the standard for Confederate military officers. His orders were published and read to his troops: "It must be remembered that we make war only upon armed men, and that we cannot take vengeance for the wrongs our people have suffered without lowering ourselves in the eyes of all whose abhorrence has been excited by the atrocities of our enemies, and offending against Him to whom vengeance belongeth."[23]

Lee took 75,000 men into Pennsylvania, clashing with the Federal army at the little village of Gettysburg. Behind them, their own homes lay in ashes, yet, according to historian Clifford

Dowdey, they did not burn a single house in the enemy's land. Strict orders were issued against plundering, and foraging was to be done under supervision of officers. A British observer made note of the good behavior of the southern troops, writing that he saw none of the inhabitants disturbed or annoyed by the soldiers.

General Ewell had been the first to pass through the country, requisitioning provisions for his troops. When General Lee came upon the fertile Pennsylvania farmlands, a lady of the area visited him with the story that some citizens were starving because of General Ewell's recent visit. Lee replied, "We requisitioned to provide food for our troops, so that the men could be kept from coming into your houses themselves. God help you if I permitted them to enter your houses.[24] Always magnanimous, though, he told her to send a miller to the commissary officers, and he would see that they were provided with adequate flour.

There were Southerners, true enough, who, out of sheer anger and desperation, would have retaliated against Yankee civilian property; but they represented the minority while most Southerners chose the high road taken by General Lee. Edward Pollard, however, was a voice for the minority opinion which held that retaliatory destruction of northern civilian property might serve to shorten the war, which, incidentally, was the exact excuse precisely used by the Yankee government to justify their depredations. Pollard, editor of the *Richmond Examiner*, was critical of Confederate reluctance to retaliate.

> The fertile acres of the Pennsylvania valley were untouched by violent hands; all requisitions for supplies were paid for in Confederate money; and a protection was given to the private property of the enemy, which had never been afforded even to that of our own citizens. So far as the orders of Gen. Lee on these subjects restrained pillage and private outrage, they were sustained by public sentiment in the South, which, in fact, never desired that we should

retaliate upon the Yankees by a precise imitation of their enormities and crimes. . . . Such a return for the outrages which the South had suffered from invading hordes of the Yankees, would in fact have been short of justice . . . . But Gen. Lee was resolved on more excessive magnanimity; and at the time the Yankee armies, particularly in the Southwestern portion of the Confederacy, were enacting outrages which recalled the darkest days of medieval warfare, our forces in the Pennsylvania valley were protecting the private property of Yankees, composing their alarm, and making a display of stilted chivalry." [25]

Whether stilted or not, it was definitely chivalry. The officers of the Confederate Army, to a large degree, had come directly off the plantation, where an honor code was an integral part of the system. General Zollicoffer, upon entering Kentucky, announced that every citizen of that state, regardless of political allegiance, was to receive protection from the men of his command, an exact duplicate of General Lee's offer to the people of Maryland when he penetrated that northern state. Out in Missouri, General Sterling Price received the sword of the defeated Yankee, Colonel Mulligan, then promptly returned it to him, making Mulligan and his wife guests at his own headquarters while the colonel awaited exchange. General Price put his personal carriage at their disposal and offered them every courtesy.

These men were cavaliers. They were dashing, daring, and debonair. They captured the fancy of many women, North and South. These captivating courtiers, the last of the world's knightly warriors, were given to tipping their hats, serenading their ladies, and forever bowing. One impetuous Confederate officer, in all his glory, dashed into a Yankee town, trying to catch up with Lee's troops headed for Gettysburg. Having ridden through the familiar, friendly country of North Carolina and

159

Virginia, he didn't realize how conspicuous his gray uniform had become as he crossed into enemy territory. When he rode straight into the village of Greencastle, Pennsylvania, hostile townspeople made him suddenly aware of the danger he faced, at which point he covered his mortal fear by lifting his hat and bowing profusely to the startled villagers until he had literally bowed out of town.

A Yankee colonel gave a long account of the "soft-mannered Rebels" when he encountered Jeb Stuart's cavalry at Chambersburg. This was newsworthy stuff, as it wasn't often that northerners felt the presence of Rebels upon their own turf. He described their "politeness" and how they thanked him for his candor when informing them that he was a Republican. He further related that these Southerners "politely" asked him for food, and he commented as to how one private soldier bowed to him and asked for a few coals to light a fire.

Not to be forgotten, however, was the terrible fire with which Jeb Stuart could strike. And strike he did! The raid of October 9 and 10, 1862, wasn't all bowing and manners. He wrecked military stores, telegraph lines, and railroads used for carrying Yankee soldiers south; but, true to his chivalric instincts, he left private property unspoiled.

The North, while resting on full bellies, had continuously destroyed the South's food supply until Lee's troops were literally starving at Appomattox; yet, they naïvely tried to believe that the swollen population of Andersonville prison, which numbered 35,000 (more men than were present for duty in many Confederate armies), were somehow to be fed like princes. In fact, the Confederate Congress had enacted a law allowing prisoners the same rations as soldiers in the field, the problem being that there was little food for either.

In an attempt to rectify this appalling situation, President Davis and the Confederate Congress tried, throughout the war, to exchange prisoners with the Lincoln government, but met with little success. In the early phases of the war, there were exchanges, but it became an elemental part of Lincoln's war strategy to keep all of the southern soldiers locked up in northern prisons, thereby preventing them from returning to the desperately thin ranks of their armies. Upon occasion he would publicly voice regret at the callousness of his chosen method, but with some common little fable he would attempt to mollify northern mothers who cried for release of their captive sons.

These mothers provided a large proportion of the opposition in the North to Mr. Lincoln's war. By late 1862, the war had dragged on for nearly two years with little success on the battlefield. Support for the war was flagging. Searching for a way to infuse the effort with new vigor, Lincoln embraced the idea, advocated by the fanatic abolitionists, of freeing the slaves. It was a slick political move in that it would rally to his side those radical one-issue demagogues who had provided the margin of his presidential victory but who had increasingly become disenchanted with him for his silence about slavery. Many of these extremists, their passions aflame, were bordering on lunacy. One of their leaders in particular, William Lloyd Garrison, celebrated the 4th of July by publicly burning a copy of the U.S. Constitution, calling it an "agreement with Hell." Still, Lincoln needed their support, and the Emancipation Proclamation did the trick, even though the document was purely academic, for it did not free one slave in those states still in the Union, yet somehow sought to order the freeing of slaves in the Confederacy, which was not even within the purview of Honest Abe.

After the interjection of the slave issue in 1863, confusion abounded as to the purpose of the war, with many soldiers under the impression that they were suddenly fighting to free the slaves from something or someone, while others contended they were opposing the southern theory of states' rights. Still others were merely serving out the tedious terms of their drafts and were aggravated by the idea that they had spent two years slogging through the hot, humid South only to free the slaves. Even earlier, due to the constant agitation of the abolitionists before and during the war, the main objective of the war was unclear.

When the Federals occupied Nashville in 1862, they announced that they were there to preserve the Union, *not to free the slaves*. And yet, the *Richmond Daily Dispatch* published a letter found on the battlefield after the Battle of Murfreesboro. It was from a northern girl to her brother in the Federal army, and it laid the blame for the war squarely upon the idea of emancipation.

> But poor boy, you are not out of this horrid war yet. If you had married and settled down, instead of going to war, it would have been better for you. Look at the slaughtering that has been done, and the negro is still not free yet. There have been enough white men killed to have paid for the infernal negro fifty times over, and you will never conquer the South until you have killed the last man of them – There is too much grit there. They have been wronged, and they know it, and will die rather than give up. [26]

There was a rudimentary misconception among northerners about slavery and the negro in general. Fiercely believing that slaves were an unhappy lot just waiting for a chance to escape, northern abolitionists promoted the idea of slave rebellions and uprisings against their masters. Underground newsletters circulated, and secret agents were sent south to foment rebellion. One of their few successes, if murder can be called a success, occurred in Virginia in 1831 when former slave Nat Turner led several slaves on a brutal killing spree in the dead of night. Before he and his black butchers were caught, over sixty white people had been viciously murdered by decapitation and other abhorrent means, including amputation of arms and legs by meat cleaver. Family members were forced to look upon their hideous handwork as the meat cleavers chopped.

Old John Brown, an abolitionist who roamed the country, reveled in such gory activity. In May, 1856, he led a similar raid near Osawatomi, Kansas, massacring five settlers in the dead of night. He next appeared in the public eye when, in 1859, he started south with a band of abolitionists intent upon instigating a large-scale servile revolt. Heavily armed, his band entered Harper's Ferry, Virginia, where they seized the Federal arsenal and captured a locomotive roundhouse. They killed the town's mayor and took forty citizens hostage, but the first victim of this madman was a free negro named Heyward Shepherd, whom John Brown killed in a rage when the negro refused to join the insurrection. On October 10, 1931, the United Daughters of the Confederacy dedicated a monument to all of the faithful slaves of the South, placing it at Harper's Ferry in memory of Heyward Shepherd.

During the war, as Yankees plundered their way south-ward, they were dismayed at finding no interest among the slave population for an insurrection against their masters. Indeed, not-withstanding the many tales of the "underground railroad," whose glories and numbers mysteriously continue to grow with each new textbook, Yankees found, much to their surprise, a widespread loyalty among the slaves which they encountered. One Yankee soldier, perplexed at not being able to persuade a slave in Columbia to leave his master, remarked, "If you want to stay so bad, he must have been good to you."[27] That, of course, is stating the obvious, but it was a revelation to this "visiting" Yankee.

Mrs. Chesnut included in her diary a vignette which illustrates the harmony that often existed between slave and owner. Dr. Gibbes had been visiting a particular country home in Virginia when a Yankee soldier who had lost his way came in and asked for brandy. When the lady of the house brought it, he declined it, saying that he thought it might be poisoned.

> She, naturally, was enraged. "Sir, I am a Virginia woman. Do you think I could be as base as that? Here Tom! Bill! Disarm this man! He is our prisoner." The negroes came running in, and the man surrendered

without more ado. Another Federal was drinking at the well. A negro girl said: "You go in and see Missus." The man went in, and she followed crying triumphantly: "Look here, Missus, I got a prisoner too!". . . Now, if slavery is as disagreeable as we think it, why don't they all march over the border where they would be received with open arms? [28]

Federal troops soon tired of the negroes, especially those who were left homeless by the burning of their plantations, for they followed the armies begging for food and the proverbial promise of "forty acres and a mule." Those who could be persuaded to go into the Yankee army were organized into colored regiments, but they were unaware of the real intent of their recruitment. In the most deceitful fashion, they were placed in the front ranks of a charge when a particularly murderous fire was expected. Sometimes, a colored company was sent in to "test the fire of the other side." If it resulted in heavy casualties, the regular troops would make other plans.

Lincoln's Emancipation Proclamation may have thrilled the abolitionists, but it solidified the opinion among Union soldiers that if the war was now an effort to free the slaves, then the negro ought to do the fighting. Charles G. Halpine, an Irish immigrant and staff officer, expressed that sentiment in a popular poem titled *Sambo's Right to Be Kilt.* Writing under the pseudonym of Miles O'Reilly, and in an Irish brogue, Halpine opined, "The right to be kilt we'll divide wid him, and give him the largest half!" Sergeant Cyrus B. Boyd, of the 15th Iowa Infantry, said, "If any African will stand between me and a rebel bullet, he is welcome to the honor and the bullet, too." Colonel Edward H. Ripley, of the 9th Vermont, declared that it was "better to sacrifice niggers than white men." Moreover, this feeling was not confined to soldiers in the field. Governor Samuel J. Kirkwood, of Iowa, said, "When this war is over and we have summed up the entire loss of life . . . I shall not have any regrets if it is found that a part of the dead are niggers and that all are not white men." [29]

At the end of the war, there was little semblance of law and order under the boot heel of the occupying Federal forces. A story came out of Richmond about the fat, rather dirty, negro barber who was one of those who thought he would be glad to see the dawning of Yankee rule. Apparently too affectionate, he threw his arms around a Yankee officer who freed himself from the negro, drew his pistol, and shot him dead on the sidewalk, declaring that it was time to stop that kind of nonsense.

In this unusual war, it was common for officers and men of wealth on both sides to have body servants attending them. Northerners had the strange notion that the body servants of southern men were eagerly awaiting an opportunity to flee. In *Death of a Nation*, Clifford Dowdey reports the following incident.

> George Wills, the North Carolina preacher's son, had one of these personal servants, who acted as chef, valet, and forager. This Wash was one of the negroes whom well-intentioned Pennsylvania housewives tried to induce to steal away from their masters. One woman, trying to get at Wash's loyalties, asked him if he were treated well. "I live as I wish," he replied politely, "and if I did not, I think I couldn't better myself by stopping here. This is a beautiful country, but it doesn't come up to home in my eyes." [30]

Today, the northern view of southern slavery is about as foggy as ever, due primarily to a constant input of false information and political narrative. Rather than delve into historical narrative on the subject, it is much easier and more entertaining to derive a notion of slavery from the prurient, profane world of TV. The disconcerting thing is that more and more *Southerners* are falling victim to the inflammatory propaganda of *North & South*, *Roots*, and other fictional works. In a day and age of imagination run wild, we Southerners would do well to consult the works of scholars like Ulrich Phillips, the foremost authority on slavery. His classic treatise, *Life and Labor in the Old South*, was the result of three decades of research and has been the standard work on slavery since its publication in 1929.

Had it not been for the political considerations leading to Lincoln's insertion of emancipation into the war effort, slavery would have undoubtedly been relegated to its rightful place as a peripheral issue of the conflict. It still amazes some to discover that, out of six million Southerners, less than 400,000 owned a slave. In other words, only seven percent of the southern population were slaveholders in even the strictest sense of the word. The number of practical slaveholders, those holding large numbers of slaves, varies from 2,200 to 10,000, depending upon the researcher, the study, and the criteria, but, at any rate, it is in the neighborhood of only one-tenth of one percent. Another surprise to modern readers is that more than two percent of the free black population were slaveholders. As early as 1830, there were approximately 175,000 free negroes, of whom 3,690 owned 12,601 other blacks.

Among the relatively small number of large slaveholders one could find those who did not like the "peculiar institution" but considered it a problem with no immediate solution. Mary Boykin Chesnut was one of them. From a family of large slaveholders, she surmised that she was probably the biggest abolitionist of them all, stating flatly, "I hate slavery."[31] She stated that she was a woman who would gladly have given up her house servants for the privacy which she said the northern women enjoyed.

The average southern soldier was not fighting to preserve slavery – he had no direct connection with it. In simple terms, he fought because honor called and called and called. There was a crying need for soldiers at the front as men in gray fell by the hundreds, and sometimes thousands, in each battle. The small southern population couldn't replenish the ranks, even when it had to turn to young boys of thirteen and old men of seventy-three. Upon rare occasion were Confederate forces equal to the number of Yankees opposing them. Most of the time they were outnumbered by at least a third. The last two years of the war would find southern forces outnumbered by two to one and three to one in nearly every major military action. Pursued by well over 200,000 men, General Lee was finally forced to surrender his effective force of only 8,000, most of them unarmed and out of ammunition. Fearless heroes, they were a loyal group of patriots among whom not one man was found who favored surrender, even under such circumstances, but rather would have fought on with rifle butts and doubled fists if General Lee would have but allowed it.

But don't think that the saintly Robert E. Lee, for whom untold numbers of southern boys would be named over the next hundred years, was going to be held accountable for having to succumb to such overwhelming odds. No, Sir. Southern women would see to that.

Years ago, I was invited to dinner at the home of Laura Youngblood, a charming octogenarian who lived in what is known around Davis, Oklahoma, as the Youngblood Mansion. It isn't really a mansion, but it is a large, three-story Victorian home looking much as it did when built by Laura's father, Dr. Thomas Howell, in 1899. The Howells were from Mississippi, and, as I remember, were related to Jefferson Davis's second wife, Varina Howell, of Natchez, Mississippi. The Youngblood home is situated at the end of a winding gravel road a few miles west of Davis.

There were about eight of us, including a Georgia cousin named Madeline Howell, a very colorful lady, also in her eighties, who was dressed that evening quite elegantly in a light green floor-length evening gown. Seated around the Victorian dining table under a crystal chandelier, we were a motley crew of young and old, representing various interests endemic to our disparate generations, and were therefore engaged in nothing more than light, frivolous conversation. When a lull came in the discourse, the silence was broken by the elderly Madeline who, in her heavy Georgia drawl that had not changed in over seventy years of living in Oklahoma, turned to me as if there were no ears but mine within the sound of her voice, and asked in a proud and serious tone, "Do you know what General Grant said to General Lee?"

Now I know quite a bit of what Grant said to Lee, but Madeline asked it as if it had happened within the past week, so I sat dumbfounded, and replied, "No." Not even half-way cognizant that all eyes and ears were now on her, awaiting this profound answer, she looked straight at me as if she herself hadn't yet surrendered and stated, "He said, 'General Lee, I have not out-generaled you; I have just out-numbered you.' "

To be honest, I had never heard that remark, but every Southerner subscribes to the sentiment in Madeline's defense of General Lee. No one has ever out-generaled Robert E. Lee, and likely never will. There has never been a more capable assembly of generals in recorded history than those of the Confederacy. Even Mr. Lincoln once remarked that the problem was that all of the good generals were on the other side.

Those overwhelming numbers have always been a source of regret to Southerners, causing us to accept the fact that we had to make up in quality what we lacked in quantity – and still lost that war. Even while growing up in the 1950s, I frequently heard the old brag that "any Rebel can whip five Yankees," sometimes the number being as high as ten, depending upon the virility of the braggart.

Much fun has been poked at the inept, blundering amateurs out of which Lincoln tried to make generals. To oppose Lee in Virginia, he went through seven generals in four years, one of whom was John Pope, a pompous, bombastic individual who was replacing the timid General McClellan, an officer who cautiously dug in and set up elaborate headquarters, awaiting the most opportune circumstances before engaging Lee in battle.

General Pope, upon assuming command, announced to his troops that he had come from the western theater where he followed his enemy, attacking him where found, and that the policy of taking strong positions and holding them was over. His headquarters were to be in the field and his troops on the move. In theory he was right, but his pomposity gave amusement to Lee's magnificent Army of Northern Virginia, and the story that made the rounds was that Pope had shouted, "My head-quarters are in the saddle!" Lee's army laughed over Stonewall Jackson's purported retort, "I can whip any man who doesn't know his headquarters from his hindquarters."[32] Before General Pope could differentiate between the two, Stonewall Jackson's boys had indeed whipped him. Two months after Pope's blustering, Jackson and Lee rolled him up at the Second Battle of Manassas, and he was through.

There were many victories on the battlefield for the boys who wore the gray. The First Battle of Manassas and the Second Battle of Manassas were Confederate victories on the same field of battle only thirteen months apart. At the Second Battle Lee's 48,500 Confederate troops faced 75,000 Yankees, yet won an astounding victory. At the Seven Days Battles around Richmond in June of 1862, Lee's army of only 80,000 drove 115,000 enemy soldiers back upon the James River. On a cold December day of the same year, 78,000 Rebels routed 110,000 Yankees in a stunning victory at Fredericksburg, Virginia. In May of the following year, they defeated the Yankees once again at Fredericksburg.

The Second Battle of Fredericksburg was a one-day event, part of the four-day Battle of Chancellorsville, in which Lee delivered to the enemy what was probably their most decisive defeat. It was tactical perfection. With only 57,000 men, Lee and Jackson divided the army and attacked a Federal army of 134,000 men, scattering them like seed and driving them back towards the Rappahannock River. Lee spent the fifth day planning for an attack which would have annihilated the huge Federal army, but as he cautiously felt his way toward them, he found that they had slipped across the river on pontoons during the night and were in full retreat.

The fact that Lee's tactics at Chancellorsville have been studied the world over is a monument to his military genius; but the battle was too dearly won, for the South was plunged into deep mourning by the death of Lee's right-hand man. The beloved Stonewall had been accidentally shot by his own men during the second evening of the battle and died eight days later. It was a tragic personal loss for Lee and a strategic loss for the military. There is a popular school of thought among historians that had Stonewall Jackson lived the South would likely have won the war.

By 1864, as the Confederate army continued to shrink with each battle, Union numbers were swelling. At the Wilderness, 63,000 Confederates successfully resisted 141,000 of the enemy, but Grant could now afford to divide his army in the style of Lee, forcing General Lee to send troops he actually couldn't spare to counter the separate moves of the Federal masses. Still, Lee's embattled Confederates thwarted every attempt Grant made on Richmond, soundly thrashing him with a force of only 60,000 men at Cold Harbor on June 1, 2, and 3. Grant, who had 117,000 present for duty that day, later regretted having even attempted the charge at Cold Harbor. He lost 7,000 men in one hour alone. Total losses for the three days were 12,000 men for the Federals and about 1,500 for the Confederates.

Out in the west, as the Kentucky-Tennessee-Mississippi region was called, General Albert Sidney Johnston's Army of The Mississippi won the field on the first day of the Battle of Shiloh on April 6, 1862, but it came with a price: the death of General Johnston. General Beauregard assumed command and was preparing to push the Yankees back into the Tennessee River when he learned that General Earl Van Dorn's Army of the Trans-Mississippi could not arrive in time to offset the 20,000 addition Federal troops who had arrived by steamboat during the night, so the Confederate army began a slow withdrawal to Corinth,

Mississippi, while managing, however, to inflict heavy damages upon the Federals during the withdrawal.

On July 13, 1862, General Nathan Bedford's cavalry made a dash into Murfreesboro, Tennessee, surprising the Union forces and breaking their occupation of the city. On June 10, 1864, General Nathan Bedford's cavalry of 3,500 men routed a Yankee force of 8,500 at the Battle of Brice's Crossroads in north Mississippi. These actions, typical of the Union defeats at his hand, were repeated time and again. Forrest was a military genius, even though completely untrained in the art of war. When Robert E. Lee was asked to name his greatest general, he purportedly answered, "A man I have never met. His name is Forrest."[33]

If there had been several Nathan Bedford Forrests, the outcome of the war might well have been different, but as hard as Forrest worked to make the South victorious, the tide in the Kentucky-Tennessee-Mississippi theater was turning. The fall of Vicksburg on July 4, 1863 was only the precursor of things to come. On September 19 and 20, the Battle of Chickamauga, even though somewhat successful, failed to keep the enemy out of Chattanooga, thus setting the stage for a long Confederate retreat into Atlanta.

With the burning of Atlanta by Sherman's forces on November 15, 1864, the outlook was abysmal. General John Bell Hood, who was expected to follow and harass Sherman, turned north instead, heading for Nashville, mistakenly thinking that Sherman would turn and pursue him. Instead, Sherman headed for Savannah in his infamous "march to the sea" with virtually no one to impede his destructive advance. Two weeks later, Hood was defeated at Franklin, Tennessee, in a headlong charge that killed 55 regimental commanders and six Confederate generals, including General Patrick Cleburne, the best division commander in the Army of Tennessee. The total losses were horrific, 1,750 killed and 3,800 wounded. The Union forces retreated into Nashville and prepared for another Confederate

Captain Tod Carter joined the Army of Tennessee in 1861 and was captured at Chattanooga in November, 1863. The young soldier escaped in late 1864, rejoining his command only a few days before the fierce Battle of Franklin, which swirled around his family's home. He was wounded only 200 yards from the house, where his family huddled in the basement during the battle. Found on the field after the battle, he was brought home and died within forty-eight hours.

attack, which was not long in coming.

On December 15, Hood's remaining force of 30,000 exhausted men faced an overwhelming army of more than 55,000. After two days of hard battle, Hood's once-famous Army of Tennessee fled south and would have been annihilated by the pursuing Yankees but for the rear-guard action of Forrest's cavalry. Many of the soldiers of the defeated and disbanded

Army of Tennessee made their way to North Carolina to join up with General Joseph E. Johnston only to be surrendered with his army in April. It was a bitter end to a valiant, heroic attempt at independence.

Looking back over the battles of the late war, both victories and defeats, perhaps one of the most interesting and consequential battles was the Battle of Manassas, later termed the Battle of First Manassas due to the occurrence of another battle there. Yankees called it the Battle of Bull Run. (They were always lost, so they named battles after whatever river or stream was nearby.)

For one thing, it was the first major land battle of the war. The troops on both sides were untested, and the first battle could be expected to give indication of things to come. The atmosphere in Richmond was indicative of the general mood of the South – wary and apprehensive. The Confederate capitol had been moved to Richmond, and Congress was scheduled to begin its first session on July 20. Declaring that the "Rebel Congress" should not be allowed to convene, northern newspapers, led by the shrieking *New York Tribune*, had toiled for over a month to inflame public sentiment with their truculent cries of "On to Richmond! Forward to Richmond!" For the new Confederacy, it was victory on the battlefield or annihilation in Richmond. The Confederate capitol, primary target of the invasion, lay only 100 miles south of Washington, D.C., and a cautious Confederate army was setting up a line of defense in northern Virginia.

Amid the hysteria of howling politicians and the constant drumbeat of the northern press, newly assembled Union troops, reflecting the cocksure attitude of the North, pranced out of Washington on July 16, crossing the Potomac onto Virginia soil, gayly outfitted in the newest of dark blue uniforms complete with brass buttons and trappings that fairly sparkled in the summer sun. The big battle loomed just five days ahead and would take place only twenty miles from Washington, D.C., but the fancy Union soldiers were cautiously feeling their way along, somewhat uncertain as to just where they would run upon those "Rebels." By the time they reached Manassas Junction where the Confederates were waiting, they had already run afoul of some of them at a crossing of the Bull Run. A Federal detachment on reconnaissance had run into some of General Longstreet's Confederates who promptly repulsed them, capturing twenty prisoners, 175 stands of arms, and a large number of blankets and accoutrements. Sixty-four dead bodies were found and buried by the Confederates.

An amusing incident occurred which further deflated the ego of the brand new Yanks. If spit and polish were to win the war, it certainly didn't show when a company of Union soldiers became divided by a thick growth of tall shrubs as they marched ever onward to crush the "foolish Rebels" and "take Richmond." It's not clear as to just who first noticed those glistening rifles and bayonets of the enemy, but there they were, bobbing up and down, as the Rebels apparently and unknowingly marched alongside their foes. Someone gave the order to turn and fire, and a barrage of lead was unleashed upon the tall hedgerow. On the other side, having been suddenly attacked, the supposed Rebels, who were in reality only a separated line of the same Federal outfit, dropped down and fired back into the hedgerow, thinking they had been caught by Rebel fire. How the shooting stopped is not known, but someone evidently discovered the mistake, and the Union troops marched on, arriving upon the Manassas battlefield rather nonplussed, having already fought their own men.

The intrepid Mrs. Greenhow, working behind the scenes in Washington, sent word to General Beauregard that the Yankees were advancing for an attack upon his position, which lay along the south side of Bull Run for a distance of about eight miles. In Washington, you would have thought it was Mardi Gras for all the festivities and excitement. Carriages were actually being loaded with picnic lunches, and overly confident politicians were ticketing their luggage for Richmond.

The grand army of Lincoln was facing the hastily assembled, volunteer army of the South across Bull Run, a creek that feeds into the Occoquan River. Union generals had orders to advance on Sunday, July 21. "The movement was generally known in Washington; Congress had adjourned for the purpose of affording its members an opportunity to attend the battle, and as the crowds of followers and spectators, consisting of politicians, fashionable women, idlers, sensation-hunters, editors, etc., hurried in carriages, omnibuses, gigs, and every conceivable style of vehicle across the Potomac in the direction of the army, the constant and unfailing jest was, that they were going on a visit to Richmond." [34]

It had all the trappings of a collegiate football game. "The idea of the defeat of the Grand Army . . . seems never to have crossed the minds of the politicians who went prepared with carriage-loads of champagne for festal celebration of the victory that was to be won, or of the fair dames who were equipped with opera glasses to entertain themselves with the novel scenes of a battle and the inevitable rout of 'rebels'. . . [Such was the] revolting spectacle of the indecent and bedizened rabble that watched from a hill in the rear of the army the dim outline of the battle and enjoyed the nervous emotions of the thunders of its artillery."[35]

The two armies faced each other and lay in parallel lines like two toothpicks, separated by Bull Run, a stream which had several fords and a strong bridge. The battle plan for the Confederates was to swing their right flank against the Federal left. Meanwhile, the Federal commander, General McDowell, had decided to swing his right flank against the Confederate left. A simultaneous charge could have resulted in both armies going in a circle, but the Yankees opened their attack first, having sent 13,000 men south and west around the extreme left end of the Confederate line during the night. Early on the morning of July 21, the Union artillery opened fire in front of the line while waiting for the infantry column that had swung around the

Confederate left to attack. Delayed by several things, the boys in blue lost the element of surprise, and the boys in gray were waiting for them, though in greatly reduced numbers, a result of their long thin line.

In the meantime, General Beauregard's planned attack on the Federal left had not happened yet, and, from the sound of battle, he began to suspect that his own left was in trouble. And, indeed, it was. The overwhelming Yankee force was pushing General Barnard Bee's left flank back upon the Confederate center, and his inferiority in numbers had resulted in losing some high ground to the oncoming foe. His men were trying to retreat and at the same time cover themselves from a devastating fire of enemy bullets, when five regiments under General Thomas J. Jackson arrived in the nick of time. It was General Bee who rallied his troops and simultaneously gave General Jackson his famous sobriquet when he called out: "See, there is Jackson standing like a stone wall. Rally on the Virginians!" [36]

It was an effective rally. The Southerners turned upon the Yankees, gradually pushing them back, but General Bee was mortally wounded in the charge. It was the habit of southern officers to be near the van of the charges they ordered, leading their men into battle, but it would cost the South many able leaders.

The Yankees, numbering about 37,000, had pushed across to the south side of Bull Run, where they were looking in a downward direction upon the readjusting lines of Confederates. They had extended their right flank very widely around the Confederate left, when, suddenly, in the distance there could be seen more troops headed towards the Confederate left. As it happily turned out, the troops were those of General E. Kirby Smith, who had just arrived on the Manassas Gap Railroad from the Army of The Shenandoah. General Johnston, senior commander of the southern forces, ordered Smith's 1,700 infantry and Beckham's artillery battery to fall upon the Federal right. At that point, General Beauregard seized the opportunity of having fresh reinforcements on his left and attacked the Federal center.

With a combined force of about 35,000 now, the Southerners dismantled the Grand Army of the Republic. Up and down the line, southern soldiers began to yell, thrilled beyond their wildest expectations at seeing the backs of the much-ballyhooed army of the invincible North. The wild high-pitched screams probably began as an instinctive response, but it soon swept the entire line in wave after wave, having such a de-moralizing effect upon the fleeing Yankees that the famous Rebel Yell, born here in a spontaneous instant, would be ad-vantageously used in many a future battle.

Firing directly into the Union lines, yelling and running at the fleeing mass of humanity, the formerly untested southern army had before them the grandest spectacle of chaos and hor-ror that would be seen during the whole war. Throwing off every item that might slow their desperate departure, the Yankee sol-diers left behind them miles of litter, including guns, canteens, jackets, hats, horses, artillery pieces, knapsacks, and a host of items necessary to war.

"The retreat, the panic, the heedless, headlong confusion was soon beyond a hope. Officers with leaves and eagles on their shoulder straps, majors and colonels who had deserted their comrades, passed, galloping as if for dear life. Not a field officer seemed to have remembered his duty. The flying teams and wagons confused and dismembered every corps. . . . Army wagons, sutler's teams, and private carriages choked the passage, tumbling against each other amid clouds of dust and sickening sights and sounds. Hacks containing unlucky spectators of the late affray were smashed like glass, and the occupants were lost sight of in the debris. Horses, flying wildly from the battlefield, many of them in death agony, galloped at random forward, joining in the stampede. Those on foot who could catch them rode them bareback, as much to save themselves from being run over as to make quick time." [37]

At the outset of the rout, a shell from the Confederate artillery blew up a wagon on the Cub Run Bridge on the main retreat route through the little town of Centreville, so it was sheer pandemonium upon that road, with men getting across that stream as best they could, leaving artillery and other weapons in the hands of exultant, screaming Rebels who turned the artillery around and further added to the panic by firing over the terrorized, unorganized mass of fleeing humanity. It must have been a thrilling sight, indeed, to view the backsides of Yankees who, only hours before had bragged that they would whip those Rebels in one day and with little effort! It was sweet chaos.

The frightened, running swirl of civilians, soldiers, and ladies in full society regalia didn't stop at Centerville, in spite of the reserve that had earlier been posted there. Straight into Washington they fled with no looking back, for it was generally feared that the Confederates were right on their coattails and would soon be in Washington to capture the capital city. Nor were many content to stop in Washington. People were evacuating by every road out of the city, and a guard had to be placed at the depot to keep the panic-stricken soldiers from getting aboard the outbound trains. The army was disorganized, and the city quaked for days, expecting the terrible fighting force of the Confederacy to descend upon it forthwith. What a remarkable difference a day had made!

Why that follow-up was not made has been debated ever since that fateful day. President Davis had arrived upon the battlefield in time to witness the victory, and in the evening met with Generals Johnston and Beauregard concerning an advance upon Washington. Many historians believe that if the southern troops, tired though they were, would have gone on into the Yankee capital and captured it the war would have come to a decisive end then and there, resulting in a treaty of peace between two American nations, thereby precluding four hard years of anguish, pain, and death. Two friendly nations. No more squabbles over tariffs, taxes, railroads, states' rights, settlement of western lands, representation in Congress. Nothing. Two divergent nations, separated along lines of natural differences that were there from the beginning. No more war.

But we have to deal with what was, not what could have been. Mr. Lincoln, having been spared the humiliation of an occupied capital, though evidently stung by the embarrassment of the rout, tried for four years to humble the Confederate president in the same fashion. Disastrously unsuccessful and visibly flustered, he once asked General Winfield Scott,

"Why is it that you were once able to take the City of Mexico in three months with five thousand men, and we have been unable to take Richmond with one hundred thousand men?" [38]

"I will tell you, Sir, " replied General Scott. "The men who took us into the City of Mexico then are the same men who are keeping us out of Richmond now." [39]

Finally, though, the end came, and Richmond was simply evacuated. It had withstood every malicious design against it, for its protectors were Robert E. Lee and his marvelous men in gray.

Lee's remaining army of only 35,000 was no larger than the first band of patriots who had marched out to do battle with the enemy at Manassas almost four years earlier. They were now stretched out for thirty-six miles, from north of Richmond to Dinwiddie Court House, southwest of Petersburg, in a very vulnerable thin line of defense. The Yankee hordes were multiplying like rabbits and swarming like bees. Every day seemed to bring more of them into the Federal ranks as they continuously assaulted that defensive line Lee had been guarding for nine long months.

Cut off from food and ammunition supplies on all sides except to the west, General Lee and President Davis had discussed the nearly foregone conclusion that Richmond would have to be given up soon. On April 2, General Lee notified President Davis that he was abandoning the Petersburg line and that Richmond should be evacuated immediately. Lee headed west toward Amelia Court House where food and supplies were supposedly awaiting him, hoping that he might make a successful stand or link up with General Johnston's army to the south. Nothing was there. No food. No ammunition. So Lee headed west out across the hills toward Lynchburg, all the time being raided and slashed by the Yankee cavalry who burned his wagon train and captured General Ewell and his troops.

With only 28,000 men left, of whom only 8,000 were now armed, General Lee was virtually surrounded by 200,000 men under Ulysses Grant. It seemed uncanny that the whole Federal army had at last divined Lee's plans and had so effortlessly countered his escape where they had failed in four years to anticipate his moves. In truth, what had happened was an unfortunate blunder upon the part of the fleeing Confederate government. Confederate officials there had required General Lee to advise them in writing of his plan of withdrawal in the event that Richmond had to be evacuated. In their haste to escape with their lives, the departing officials had left details of Lee's proposed route in the abandoned city, and Grant had but to follow a map!

Against the pleas and supplications of his proud warriors, General Lee, nevertheless, assumed the entire dishonor which falls upon a great army when it surrenders, and entered into negotiations with General Grant. He reasoned that his little band of starving patriots could not save the South at any cost now and that any further spilling of blood would be futile. It was all over.

General Joshua Chamberlain, a Union general from Maine, who would later become governor of that state, recorded what he saw of the heartbreaking surrender. He was most impressed by the men's devotion to the Confederate flags they were giving up. He didn't know it, but many of those flags disappeared from their staffs before the surrender, hidden inside the shirts of disillusioned, heartbroken soldiers of the Lost Cause.

And now they move. The dusky swarms forge
forward into gray column of march. On they come,

with the old swinging route step and swaying battle flags. In the van, the proud Confederate ensign, the great field of white with a canton of star-strewn cross of blue on a field of red, the regimental battle flags . . . following on . . . the whole column seemed crowned with red.

Before us in proud humiliation stood . . . men whom neither toils and sufferings, nor the fact of death, nor disaster could bend from their resolve; standing before us now, thin, worn and famished, but erect, and with eyes looking level into ours. . . . On our part not a sound . . . but an awed stillness . . . as if it were the passing of the dead.

As each . . . division halts, the men face inward towards us across the road, twelve feet away; then carefully dress their line . . . worn and half-starved as they were . . . they fix bayonets, stack arms; then, hesitatingly remove cartridge boxes and lay them down. Lastly – reluctantly, with agony of expression – they tenderly fold the flags, battle-worn and torn, blood-stained, heart-holding colors, and lay them down: some frenziedly rushing from the ranks, kneeling over them, cling to them, pressing them to their lips with burning tears." [40]

Soldiers tried to touch "Marse Lee" as he rode among his troops, knowing that they would probably never see him again this side of Heaven. Then, each man, many without shoes, simply walked towards home.

A.C. Jones, of the 3rd Arkansas Regiment, said, "This was our hour of intense humiliation. So long as we carried our guns we felt something of the dignity of soldiers; but when we tramped away leaving these behind, we felt like a lot of hoboes stranded upon an alien shore."

The war was over; but what awaited the defenseless

Southland now that it had lost its noble experiment in freedom? As both armies lay poised at each other in the hours before the portentous meeting between Lee and Grant, some of the officers in Lee's presence began to wonder aloud what the world would think of surrendering such an army as this? Would it not be better to die?

With a remark foreboding gruesome days that perhaps few but Lee foresaw, he sadly answered, "How easily I could be rid of this, and be at rest! I have only to ride along the line and all will be over. But, it is our duty to live. What will become of the women and children of the South if we are not here to protect them?" [41]

In this faded old water-stained photograph, we see a young soldier, typical of those brave young men who volunteered early in the war. This is Daniel D. Phillips, born near Nashville on December 29, 1842. He enlisted as a private in the First Tennessee Artillery. Private Phillips was made lieutenant in this noted artillery unit but would soon be captured at Island No. 10 on the Mississippi River. After being exchanged, he was captured at Port Hudson, this time confined until February 1865. When exchanged at Richmond, he set about reorganizing his command, but there was such chaos near the end of the war that his efforts proved futile.

A CARPETBAG LEGISLATURE

The reek of vile cigars and stale whiskey, mingled with the odour of perspiring negroes was overwhelming. . . . The space behind the seats of the members was strewn with corks, broken glass, stale crusts, greasy pieces of paper, and picked bones. The hall was packed with negroes, smoking, chewing, jabbering, pushing, perspiring. . . . Every negro type was there, from the genteel butler to the clodhopper from the cotton and rice fields. Some had on second-hand seedy frock coats their old master had given them before the war, glossy and threadbare. Old stovepipe hats, of every style in vogue since Noah came out of the ark, were placed conspicuously on the desks or cocked on the backs of the heads of the honourable members. Some wore the coarse clothes of the field, stained with red mud. . . . Each member had his name painted in enormous gold letters on his desk, and had placed beside it a sixty-dollar French imported spittoon. . . . The uproar was deafening. From four to six negroes were trying to speak at the same time. . . . The most of them were munching peanuts, and the crush of hulls under heavy feet added a subnote to the confusion like the crackle of a prairie fire. . . . The speaker was drowned   in a storm of contending yells.

— THOMAS DIXON , 1904

VI

Reconstruction — A Southern Nightmare

"Their felonious fingers were made long enough to reach into the pockets of posterity. They coined the industry of future generations into cash and snatched the inheritance from children whose fathers are unborn. A conflagration, sweeping over the state from one end to the other, and destroying every building and every article of personal property, would have been a visitation of mercy in comparison to the curse of such a government." [1]

The dark days of Reconstruction encompass a period of ten wicked years, from 1867 to 1877. The war had ended in 1865, and Southerners who had been driven from their homes all over the tortured land, returned, along with newly paroled soldiers, to scenes of destruction and desolation unknown before or since on the North American continent. They didn't cross bridges, for there were no bridges. Those were primary targets of war and had long since been burned. They didn't ride horses, for horses

185

went first to the Confederate army, and if any were left, the Yankees stole what they wanted and killed the rest. And rarely did they ride in a wagon. When they did, it was a dilapidated remnant of war pulled by a bone spavined old mule. Railroads were nothing more than a fond remembrance, so in the end war-weary feet carried war-ravaged bodies slowly across the trails and dirt byways of the South, each turning off to his former home, or whatever was left of it, along the way.

From 1865 until 1867, when Reconstruction got under way in dreadful earnest, the Southerner was solely occupied with physically rebuilding the South, with little time to entertain political thoughts. A Confederate general plowed fields with a broken down old plow in the same way as his neighbor who might have been the lowly private. Men of former means sat in the midst of demolished cities, cleaning mortar off bricks which could be used to construct a new building, when and if the money could be found to erect a new structure. In 1904, Dunbar Rowland, quoting Bishop Charles B. Galloway, wrote, "How those brave men, the sons of affluence, addressed themselves to the grinding conditions of sudden and humiliating poverty can never be described by mortal tongue or pen."[2]

There were virtually no fences left, the rails having been burned for firewood. Even if there had been fences, cattle had long ago been driven off and eaten by invading Yankees. Where once had been miles of lovely homes, neatly framed by well-kept yards and gardens, only tall, blackened chimneys now stood. Alabama, Georgia, Mississippi, South Carolina, and North Carolina had been thoroughly sacked and burned, and hardly a cotton gin stood anywhere in Dixie. Homes that weren't burned to the ground were systematically looted with the passing of every Union army. When Reconstruction visited its venomous presence upon the South, the Southerner, beset with seemingly insurmountable physical tasks, had no interest in an academic debate as to the right or wrong of military rule by the name of Reconstruction or any other name. He instinctively knew it was wrong and was interested only in stopping it. That, in itself, though, would take nearly ten long years, for there was no longer a southern army to face the foe. It was now a matter of an unarmed southern populace pitted against the largest army ever assembled on the continent.

The epoch of Reconstruction is not a pleasant study, and the story isn't easy to tell. Not only is it politically complicated, as would be almost any given ten-year period of history, but it is almost inconceivable that political situations could be allowed to deteriorate to such a degree as to permit the kind of degradation that occurred in that fateful decade.

On June 3, 1903, Galloway, in a speech at the dedication of Mississippi's new captiol, said, "No proud people ever suffered such indignities, or endured such humiliation and degradation. More heartless than the robber bands that infested Germany after the Thirty Years' War were the hordes of plunderers and vultures who fed and fattened upon the disarmed and de-fenseless South. Their ferocious greed knew no satiety, and their shameless rapacity sought to strip us to the skin." [3]

It is difficult to find books and accounts which want to deal with the subject in its shocking truth, many authors having written from the peripheral viewpoint of their prejudicial northern background, a handicap which often causes them to try, without success nonetheless, to put a pretty face upon that ugly era. Their works, in most cases, attempt to find redemp-tion among the hideous political crimes of the times while at the same time ignoring the sufferings sustained by the actual southern citizens who bore the indignities. In fact, as recently as this year, a New York revisionist, billed as an authority on Reconstruction, wrote in an opinion piece for the *New York Times* that the era was "a remarkable moment in the history of American democracy."

It has been my experience that the most significant gleanings are to be found in the many community and county libraries across the Southland, where locally written narratives give vivid first-hand accounts of that period. One work which did attain wide acceptance and is oft quoted by honest historians is Myrta Lockett Avary's *Dixie After the War*, published in 1906. In addition, there is the newly discovered autobiography of the novelist Thomas Dixon, a work entitled *Southern Horizons*.

Admittedly a subject both complicated and unpleasant, Reconstruction is, nevertheless, considered here because it shows the true mettle of our southern ancestors in their patient endurance and eventual triumph over outrageous persecution, and I would be remiss if I withheld its saga in a text on southern heritage. As Galloway so fittingly observed, "No brave people ever endured oppression and poverty with such calm dignity and splendid restraint." [4]

Some background is in order. First, it must be understood that the present day Republican and Democrat parties are not mirror reflections of their 1870s counterparts, of whom we will be compelled to speak often in the following pages. To the contrary, the two political parties have, over the past one hundred and fifty years, become somewhat alike, so that the Democrats of today hold the same negative attitude towards the South that the Republicans of the Reconstruction era embraced, while the Republicans of today still find themselves closely aligned with the cultural negativity of the Republicans of the 1870s, hence the bipartisan assaults upon our Confederate icons.

The negro vote of the 1870s, of which one hundred per-cent belonged to the Republicans, now belongs in its entirety to the modern Democrats, a switch that has caused a 21st century swing in the southern white vote to the Republicans. Not-withstanding the shift in the white vote, it remains true that a significant number of white Southerners, although often voting Republican, are still registered as Democrats, due largely to the memory of Republican Reconstruction, even though modern white Southerners may only vaguely comprehend the connection that was so apparent to those of two and three generations back.

Secondly, we need to take a brief look at the socio-political conditions then existing in the North for a better understanding as to how Reconstruction could have happened at the hands of a society calling itself civilized. Their cities were gleaming, untouched by the cruel hand of war, and their factory output was at unprecedented levels as the war machine ground on at full speed. They lived safely in cities and towns where all the comforts of life were afforded them, taking no thought of losing their homes or their liberties.

But sometimes those who wage war suffer at their own hands as surely as their victims are made to endure the horrors of the oppressors. A war of aggression tends to brutalize – to bring out the worst in the aggressor. Incessant railings by northern abolitionists, both before and during the war, began to take their toll upon the better part of the northern character. A representative denunciation of the time was found in an abolition pamphlet of 1863, entitled *Interesting Debate*. It contained part of a speech made in the Pennsylvania State Senate.

> I said that I would arm the negro – that I would place him in the front of battle – and that I would invite his rebel master with his stolen arms to shoot his stolen ammunition into his stolen property at the rate of a thousand dollars a shot. I said further, that were I commander-in-chief, by virtue of the war power and in obedience to the customs of civilized nations, and in accordance with the laws of civilized nations, I would confiscate every rebel's property, whether upon two legs or four and that I would give to the slave who would bring me his mater's disloyal scalp one hundred and sixty acres of his master's plantation; nor would I be at all exacting as to where the scalp was taken off, so that it was at some point between the bottom of the ears and the top of the loins. [5]

This continuous type of inflammatory rhetoric fostered abhorrent actions by the northern military forces who so often went unchecked in their trek across Dixie. Personal hatred for the planter of the South ran deep among northern civilians and their soldiers. One of their favorite indignities was to subject the white populace to insults from former slaves whenever they could manage to arrange it. One example, among thousands, is drawn from the activities of General wild, a Yankee whose disposition matched his name.

In North Carolina, burned plantations had resulted in roaming bands of negro bandits. In the northeastern part of that state, the crimes perpetrated by these hoodlums were particularly outrageous. They raided the unprotected countryside, burning houses and looting with near impunity. They entered the homes of defenseless ladies, forced them to entertain at the piano, cursed them, robbed them, stripped them of their clothing, and subjected them to indignities better left unprinted.

This kind of activity characterized the reign of General Wild, who commanded a force of "free" negroes. When his army invaded northeastern North Carolina, he found only local militia volunteers trying to protect the country. Calling these citizens "guerillas," he urged the negro bandits and white scoundrels traversing the area to step up their depredations against the white population. The governor of the state had granted a citizen named Daniel Bright permission to raise a small unit for local defense, but Bright was unable to accomplish it and retired to his farm. General Wild's soldiers hunted him down, hung him at the side of the public road near his farm, and hung a placard upon his body.

With no one to restrain them, Wild's soldiers plundered ceaselessly. Upon one occasion, however, two of his negroes were captured; whereupon, the infuriated general took two "hostages" in retaliation. They were two of the most respectable married ladies in the area, Mrs. Phoebe Munden, wife of Lt. W.J. Munden, and Mrs. Elizabeth Weeks, wife of Pvt. Pender Weeks.

190

Both husbands were away in the service of the Confederate army. Mrs. Munden was at home with her three young children.

Mrs. Munden seemed to have fallen victim to the larger portion of General Wild's wrath. Arrested by his soldiers on a cold December day, the lady watched her home laid in ashes. In delicate health, she was allowed to save nothing except what she wore. Taken to Elizabeth City, she was bound hand and foot and confined in a room with several male prisoners, having no fire, bed, or bedding. The next day, Mrs. Weeks was thrown into the same room. Neither of the women were allowed to leave the room except for the most necessary duty, and then only under the constant guard of an armed negro soldier. After several days, they were removed to Norfolk Virginia, with General Wild permitting a negro to hold the rope by which Mrs. Munden was bound so tightly that her wrists were bleeding. Thus they were led into Norfolk.

Wild's despicable, cowardly deeds were matched throughout the battered land of Dixie by countless other soldiers who, hardened by war and accustomed to brutality, would go home at war's end to vote, influence public opinion, hold public office, and elect to office those who would shortly promulgate a vindictive, vengeful Reconstruction upon a prostate South.

Did the perverted prosecution of this war breed corruption among the northern politicians at home, or was it the degeneracy of the people at home that fueled the depravity at the war front? Whatever the answer, the situation began feeding upon itself, and the North did not escape the backfire of its own rage.

Unlike the South, which had unity of purpose, mainly to protect its homes and firesides from ruthless marauders, the North was a mixing bowl of internal turmoil even amid the safety and comfort of their shining cities. There were many factions, most of whom opposed the war or some aspect of it, especially as they saw their sons daily fed into the sausage grinder of a seemingly unending pursuit of some political objective. In fact, the abolitionists and the increasingly fanatical

Republicans were about the only ones in favor of a war. But even they were dissatisfied with what they perceived to be a hesitation upon the part of the president to turn the war into a fight to free the slaves. About the only point of agreement – and even this was disputed in the southernmost parts of Illinois, Ohio, and Indiana, as well as the border states which stayed in the Union – was the unmitigated hatred of the people of the South.

The president had doggedly dragged the nation into a war that soon lost its novelty and patriotic fervor. In an attempt to squelch the growing opposition, he assumed the duties of a dictator and operated as if the entire North were under martial law. Newspapers were suppressed, editors were arrested, and unreasonable searches and seizures were made in direct violation of Constitutional rights. In Kentucky's elections of 1863, the Democrats offered a ticket of candidates who ran on a platform calling for an end to the war and restoration of the Union. Mr. Lincoln's government arrested the candidates for Congress in two congressional districts and one candidate for the state legislature from Lyon and Livingston counties. On July 31, General Burnside declared martial law in Kentucky, and soldiers, already occupying the state, were empowered with even more authority.

The government had instituted in every city and town in the state a Board of Trade which regulated shipments of goods into the interior of the state. To receive a permit for his business, an individual was required to demonstrate his loyalty, each board having the right to make up its own loyalty test. Usually, this test took the form of requiring a "loyal" (Republican) vote in an election, thus the 1863 electorate was blackmailed into retaining the Lincoln Republicans in office.

Historian James Ramage points out the shift in allegiance toward the end of the war. Even though Kentucky had stayed within the Union, the Lincoln government in Kentucky was so oppressive that Kentuckians became increasingly pro-southern and, most likely, would have gone with the Confederacy if they had it all to do over. Ramage noted that after the war, when Kentucky began its program of marking significant sites and events in that state, people's requests for historical markers bore out the dramatic shift in loyalties. The overwhelming majority of requests came for events and places connected with Confederate General John Hunt Morgan, leaving Honest Abe – who was born in Kentucky – and even Daniel Boone to a distant second and third place.

Lincoln's obsession was subjugation of the South, constitutional or not. On September 24, 1862, he suspended the most basic of democratic rights, that of *habeas corpus*, the right of an individual to be brought before a judge or court upon restraint of his liberty. Borrowed from English law, it is intended to protect a person from illegal imprisonment. In its place, Lincoln instituted martial law, with military tribunals making arbitrary arrests and handing out summary punishments in lieu of civil courts of law.

General Burnside, after his defeats upon the battlefield, had assumed command of the military district of Ohio, Indiana, and Illinois. Issuing orders that he would not tolerate free speech when it meant declaring sympathy with the South, he arrested former U.S. Representative Clement L. Vallandigham, of Ohio, who had expressed his dismay at the loss of civil liberties in the Unites States under Honest Abe. Denied access to civil courts, Vallandigham was tried and convicted by a panel of eight army officers, then sentenced to imprisonment in Massachusetts. Fearful that political repercussions would follow his incarceration, Lincoln had him banished to the Confederacy.

Lincoln was witnessing near revolt in the Midwest. Burnside had sent troops to occupy the offices of the *Chicago Times* to prevent its publication; whereupon, the president prudently rescinded the occupation after 20,000 northerners held angry demonstrations.

The Supreme Court closed its eyes during the dark days of Lincoln's war, adding to the growing despotism of the administration. Vallandigham's arrest in 1863 had resulted in a challenge by him to the suspension of *habeas corpus*. Working its way through the courts, it reached the Supreme Court in 1864 only to find that the court would decline to assert jurisdiction over Lincoln's military tribunals.

In 1862, Democrats gained control of the Indiana and Illinois state legislatures. Governor Morton, the Republican governor of Indiana, blocked the assembling of the legislature by persuading the Republican minority to boycott the sessions, thereby preventing a quorum. Illinois Governor Yates, also a Republican, seized upon a technicality and adjourned the legislature in his state for two years, a tyrannical action which resulted in a mass rally by 40,000 angry Democrats in Lincoln's hometown of Springfield.

In early 1863, more newspapers were suppressed in Pennsylvania, Ohio, and Iowa. The lights of freedom were going out all over the United States, which now had not the moderating influence of the states' rights advocates of the South to temper the traditional recklessness with which northern politicians were prone to trample civil liberties under foot. Just how close America's experiment in democracy came to failing under Lincoln and the Republicans of the 1860s and 1870s would shock modern Americans were it fully known.

Lincoln's Secretary of War, Edwin M. Stanton, was a malevolent enemy of freedom. After his confirmation, Stanton assumed the duties of his office, relishing the role of keeping the Union safe from those he considered treasonous individuals. In a chilling preview of twentieth-century totalitarianism, he once told a visitor to his office, when pointing out an object on his desk, "If I tap that little bell, I can send you to a place where you will never hear the dogs bark." Official records indicate he rang his little bell often enough, with 15,535 citizens arrested and sent to military prisons during his term as Secretary of War.[6] His military tribunals were responsible for the arrest and imprisonment of approximately 38,000 citizens during the War Between the States.

With elections held at the point of the bayonet and liberties of the press, speech, and public meetings curtailed, it was only natural that parallels were being drawn between Russia and the United States. In New York Harbor, at a lavish banquet given to a Russian fleet, northern orators proclaimed that the day had come for the "twin civilizations" to unite in dominating the world as partners in the manifest destiny of the nineteenth century. While the United States was destroying the South, Russia was sub-jugating the Poles. "Russia and the United States" said a French writer of the time, "proclaim the liberty of the serf and the emancipation of the slave, but in return both seek to reduce to slavery all who defend liberty and independence." [7]

Lincoln's attempts at replacing the old republic, to which northerners had grown accustomed, with one of despotic rule caused frequent public outrage. These frequent backlashes assumed their most violent form when directed at the military draft. Instituted in 1863, the draft was an abomination to many northerners, and extreme opposition surfaced throughout the North. Particularly offensive was the provision that allowed the rich to escape military duty by either paying a substitute to go to war or by simply paying $300 to the government. Approximately 203,000 northern men avoided the draft by virtue of the ill-conceived provision.

The most violent reaction erupted in New York City on July 13, when a riot broke out and raged for three days in what historian Burke Davis called "the nearest approach to revolution" during the entire war. Mobs surged through the streets, burning buildings and destroying the drum from which the names of 1200 New Yorkers had been drawn for military service. Due to the concentration of all available troops at Gettysburg, there were no soldiers to check the violence. Policemen and militia units, woefully inadequate for the task, had to face the rioters alone.

Angry mobs burned fine homes, business buildings, the draft office, a Methodist church, a negro orphanage, and sundry other buildings. One negro was hung, then burned as people danced around the burning body. More than thirty negroes were killed – shot, hung, or trampled to death.

The mobs grew to an estimated strength of between 50,000 and 70,000. For three days they swarmed through the streets, setting up barricades on First, Second, and Eighth Avenues, where sometimes a force of only 300 policemen would have to face 10,000 attackers at a time. Some troops eventually filtered into the town; whereupon, the crowds took to alleys and rooftops where they killed soldiers with bricks and guns. The gangs caught the colonel of a militia unit, stomping and beating him to death. After dragging him to his home, men, women, and children demonically danced around his body.

Eventually, enough troops arrived to put an end to the rioting. Casualties were heavy. Nearly 2,000 people were dead from the melee. An embarrassed Lincoln government tried to affix blame to certain political foes, including New York's Governor Seymour, a Democrat, and Fernando Wood, former mayor of the city. Still, nothing swayed Lincoln from his grim determination to pursue the war to its bitter end.

Chaotic conditions in the North were in sharp contrast to those in the beleaguered South where one might have expected the exigencies of war to necessitate periodic curtailment of basic privileges, yet, to the credit of President Davis, never was the *writ of habeas corpus* suspended during the lifetime of the Confederacy.

Alarmed at the despotic rule of the Lincoln government, northern Democrats met at their national convention in Chicago on August 29, 1864, to lay plans for dismantling the Republican administration, although chances were slim that the minority Democratic party could do so. Calling the convention to order, August Belmont intoned, "Four years of misrule by a sectional, fanatical, and corrupt party has brought our country to the verge of ruin." [8]

The temporary chairman, former Pennsylvania Governor Bigler, said, "The termination of democratic rule in this country was the end of the peaceful relations between the States and the people. The men now in authority, through a feud which they have long maintained with violent and unwise men at the South . . . are utterly incapable of adopting the proper means to rescue our country from its present lamentable condition." [9]

So desperate was the situation of the country that the permanent chairman of the Democrat National Convention, Governor Horatio Seymour, of New York, was willing to adopt a conciliatory demeanor toward the South. Inveighing acridly against Lincoln and the Republicans, he said, "They were animated by intolerance and fanaticism, and blinded by an ignorance of the spirit of our institutions, the character of our people, and the condition of our land . . . they will not have the Union restored unless upon conditions unknown to the Constitution. They will not let the shedding of blood cease, even for a little time, to see if Christian charity, or the wisdom of statesmanship, may not work out a method to save our country. . . . This administration cannot save the Union. We can. We demand no conditions for the restoration of the Union. We are shackled with no hates, no prejudices, no passions. We wish for fraternal relations with the people of the South. We demand for them what we demand for ourselves, the full recognition of the rights of the States." [10]

What a pity the Democrats were denied victory! With it might have come the end of the war with no ensuing nightmare of Reconstruction. But Lincoln's oft-used and well-timed victories upon the battlefield secured for him once again the presidency. Even though General George B. McClellan had been favored in some pre-election soundings, victories in the Shenandoah, on the coast, and in Missouri had stifled some of Lincoln's opposition. The capture of Atlanta shortly before the election – result of much prodding by the embattled president – virtually secured his re-election on November 8, 1864.

Against this toxic backdrop the black night of Reconstruction fell upon the South.

Lincoln had succeeded in holding enough captured territory in Arkansas and Louisiana to set up *de facto* governments in both states in 1864, a year before the war ended, claiming that ten percent of the population had taken an oath of loyalty to the United States. That was his requirement for bringing the "wayward sisters" back into the fold – that, plus a demand that each state agree to emancipation. Though the vast majority in Arkansas and Louisiana remained true to the Confederacy, the Lincoln governments in both states promptly elected scallywag members to the U.S. Congress; but the Republican Congress, in its first clash with the president over his procedure for "reconstructing" a state, refused to seat them.

The contention was that the South must be punished, not merely readmitted, to full fellowship and good will without a little bloodletting. It was also of supreme importance to Republicans that they maintain their voting majority in Congress. The war had propelled this embryonic political party into a position of control for the first time, and they jealously contended for preservation of that power. If Lincoln allowed the southern states to rejoin the Union with so little requisite corrective action, how could Republicans prevent the return to power of the southern Democrats who would be taking their old seats in Congress again? Therein lay the challenge.

Whether Lincoln would have succeeded in his relatively lenient plan for reunification will never be known, for he was assassinated on April 14, 1865, only five days after the surrender of Robert E. Lee. Vice-President Andrew Johnson, a Democrat who had been chosen by Lincoln to siphon off Democratic votes in the 1864 presidential election, ascended to a presidency that would collide head-on with the increasingly vicious, vituperative Republican Congress.

Like Lincoln, Andrew Johnson assumed that it was the duty of the president – not Congress – to reconstruct the states of the Confederacy. He also held the same fatuous notion as Lincoln that the southern states had never really left the Union after all, insisting, therefore, that only a simple, quick formula of his invention would suffice.

In May, 1865, he recognized the governments of Arkansas, Louisiana, Virginia, and Tennessee as legitimately reconstituted under Lincoln's plan, and he granted amnesty to Confederate citizens who took a loyalty oath, providing they did not own taxable property worth more than $20,000. As to the other seven Confederate states, he outlined his plan of four steps: (1) abolish slavery, (2) repudiate the Confederate debt, (3) rescind the ordinances of secession, and (4) ratify the Thirteenth Amendment, which the Republican Congress had passed in January, 1865. The Thirteenth Amendment abolished slavery. It would become the first of only three amendments to the venerable Constitution which were ratified under pressure tantamount to political blackmail.

By December, 1865, all of the southern states except Texas had fulfilled President Johnson's requirements. Texas did so in April, 1866, and all of the southern states subsequently elected members to Congress.

Congress was full of radicals, but two men particularly stood out as leaders of the mob: Thaddeus Stevens in the House of Representatives, and Charles Sumner in the Senate. Stevens represented a Pennsylvania district and was a hotheaded politician who drove Republicans with an iron hand. Bald since his youth, he wore a wig which sometimes rearranged itself when he was vigorously railing against Southerners in his House speeches. He was extremely caustic, and thus a perfect ally for Senator Sumner, who had been a senator from Massachusetts for several years. Sumner was dogmatic and uncompromising, and he held a special hatred for Southerners in general, an attitude made more intense by an incident in 1856 in the Senate. During a Senate speech, he launched a vicious personal attack upon Southerners, and more specifically upon the aged Senator Butler from South Carolina. Two days later, Senator Butler's nephew, Preston Brooks, who himself was a Congressman, caught Sumner alone in the Senate chamber and avenged his uncle by mercilessly beating Sumner with a gutta percha cane, leaving the senator an invalid for three years.

The hatred for Southerners that consumed both men boded ill for a defeated, defenseless South. Republicans who followed their lead were soon referred to as *Radical Republicans,* or *Black Republicans,* and they would soon live up to their names. As early as 1865, Thaddeus Stevens had left no doubt as to his plans for the South in a speech delivered before the House of Representatives. Burning with a deep-seated envy of the wealthy planters, he envisioned the South as a mirror image of the North and its small farms.

> The whole fabric of southern society *must* be changed and never can it be done if this opportunity is lost. Without this, this Government can never be, as it has never been, a true republic. Heretofore, it had more the features of aristocracy than of democracy. The southern States have been despotisms, not governments of the people. It is impossible that any practical equality of rights can exist where a few thousand men monopolize the whole landed property. The larger the number of small proprietors the more safe and stable the government. If the South is ever to be made a safe republic let her land be cultivated by the toil of the owners or the free labor of intelligent citizens. This must be done though it drive her nobility into exile. If they go, all the better. [11]

The first item of business was to deny Southerners their seats in Congress, giving Republicans time to bolster their strength in the fall elections of 1866. In the meantime, they created a congressional committee to investigate and report on "southern representation" in Congress. They had already established the Freedmen's Bureau in 1865 to aid negroes in the South, but in 1866 Congress gave it new powers, including authority to hold military trials for people suspected of denying rights to negroes, as well as the authority to intervene in any dispute concerning labor contracts between white land owners and the negroes hired by them.

After the war, freedmen aimlessly roamed the countryside with little purpose or direction. The North had freed them, promising to take the white man's land away, divide it up, and give each freedman the proverbial "forty acres and a mule." But freedom, in reality, brought poverty, hunger, and homelessness. Many former slaves tried to stay on their plantations or tried to return after a brief excursion into the elusive world of freedom, and just as many former slave owners tried to hold their planation families together; but the North had done away with the system and destroyed the land. Most of the planters were in a shape similar to former Confederate Major General M.C. Butler. At home in South Carolina, he was twenty-nine years old, had lost a leg in the war, had a debt of $15,000, three children and a wife to support, seventy freed slaves, and only one dollar and seventy-five cents in cash.

It was generally suspected by those who had owned slaves that the freedmen would not work under wage arrangements unless they were compelled to do so. Their suspicions were confirmed to a large degree by the growing concentrations of freedmen around army camps, near towns, and in their own shanty towns along the highways where they existed on hand-outs from the Freedmen's Bureau and sympathetic whites. To get them back into the fields and give them supervision once again, southern legislatures enacted Black Codes, which primarily set forth the terms of labor contracts between freedmen and land owners. It was stipulated that freedmen would have to take proper care of their employer's tools, animals, and property; and, to insure against wandering off the job, the codes required the freedman to honor his yearly contract for the full year or forfeit all of his wages earned up to the time of abandonment.

201

In the absence of any definition from Washington, the Black Codes attempted to define the status of the freedman, who was neither a slave nor a citizen. Though they varied from state to state, the codes conferred upon the negro certain rights to own property, make contracts, sue in court, and enter into legal marriage. Restrictions were placed upon him in certain areas, especially those pertaining to social convention and bearing of arms.

The freedmen paid little attention to the work contracts, as is graphically illustrated in a diary kept by Mrs. Mary E. Rives. Widowed by war, she and her three children tried to proceed with business on their plantation a few miles from Shreveport, Louisiana. On June 26, 1865, she wrote, "Some are willing to stay and work a little and be fed, clothed and doctored as I have always done, but all are unsettled in their minds and hardly know what to do."[12] She continued,

> 4th of July, 1865. Well, this Day of Independence is celebrated in grand style by the Yankees. . . . I fear even the next 4th will not be so gay. . . .
>
> 4th of August. . . . All the freedmen's work lost this week . . . there is neither profit nor pleasure living with them now. They will not work. They do not average five hours a day work. They do not feel free when they are at work. . . .
>
> August 22 – The freedmen are idling away nearly all their time. They have been threshing wheat and have not done as much in four days as they should have done in one. . . .
>
> Sept. 9 – I am getting very anxious to leave my home. There is no pleasure living where no one is willing to do their part. My horses are not fed and watered as they used to be. The corn is pulled and left on the ground for four or five days. . . . My fine mare was stolen last night by a Freedman. [13]

On November 9, Mrs. Rives moved into Shreveport where she lived with Mr. & Mrs. M.H. Estner. The scene was a familiar one. To the simple-minded slave, through no fault of his own, freedom simply meant that he would never have to work again; consequently, there was precious little white people could do to convince him to go back to work, and, with no one to help with the crops, many former plantations fell into ruin.

Northerners, always unable to understand anything outside their field of expertise – whatever that might be – viewed the Black Codes as an effort by Southerners to retain the use of negro labor and, in a sense, ignore the abolition of slavery. They were also incensed by the sight of ex-Confederate statesmen elected to Congress and waiting to take their seats in the new session. Georgia had elected former Vice-President of the Confederacy, Alexander H. Stephens, to the United States Senate, an action that both vexed and confounded the general northern citizenry.

The northern mind has never understood the southern heart, and this was a prime example of the great gulf existing then and even now between the two peoples. Deluded by way of the old adage that "might makes right," northerners thought that Southerners would somehow turn against principle and reject Confederate leaders simply because of their military defeat. Many good causes fail, but failure doesn't define the rightness or wrongness of the cause. Southerners did not feel that they had done wrong in their pursuit of independence, nor do they feel guilt today. It was a brave attempt at securing states' rights that failed, and Fate's decree was accepted; but to dishonor southern heroes? Never.

Major R.E. Wilson, formerly of the 1st North Carolina Battalion of Sharpshooters, spoke the southern mind when he said, "If I ever disown, repudiate, or apologize for the cause for which Lee fought and Jackson died, let the lightnings of Heaven rend me, and the scorn of all good men and true women be my portion. Sun, moon, stars, all fall on me when I cease to love the Confederacy. 'Tis the cause, not the fate of the cause, that is glorious!" [14]

Unable to grasp the mood of the South – or unwilling to accept it – northerners saw Reconstruction as a Heaven-sent opportunity to remake the South in the image of the North. But, as a recent college history text states, "Reconstruction represents the most extreme example in our history of an attempt by the majority to impose a social concept upon a minority that did not wish to be changed." [15]

While southern Congressmen, denied their seats in Congress, waited for the next move, Congress lost no time in designing a plan to disfranchise southern whites and give exclusively to the negro the right to vote. There were nearly 4,000,000 negroes in Dixie, most of whom could neither read nor write. Most of them had no comprehension of matters beyond the boundaries of their own plantation, this ignorance of affairs presenting a golden opportunity for the Republicans to instruct them how to vote. Forbid white people to vote, then negroes could be manipulated into sending Republicans to Congress from every southern state. It was a gift on a golden platter.

First, however, the negro had to be given citizenship, so Congress passed a Civil Rights Act in April, 1866, bestowing citizenship upon everyone except Indians. The government was busy killing Indians out west, so it would never do to include the Indians. The legislation, which only granted citizenship – not the right to vote – to the freed slaves, was so badly written that even some Radical Republicans doubted its constitutionality, causing them to press Congress to incorporate its provisions into an amendment to the Constitution in order to protect it from action by the courts. This Fourteenth Amendment also prevented most prominent Southerners from holding office, thereby eliminating most of the newly-elected Southern Congressmen.

President Johnson opposed the amendment, and battle lines were drawn. The mid-term elections of 1866 were upon the country and both sides vied for support. President Johnson traveled across the North urging the election of Democrats to defeat the Radicals' harsh programs, including the Fourteenth Amendment. The Radicals campaigned for passage of the citizenship amendment but concealed their bizarre plan to force negro suffrage upon the South; instead, they diverted attention to emotional issues, storming across the northern states, reminding voters of the late war and the soldiers who had been killed at the hands of southern armies, all the time equating Southerners with Democrats. This operation was called "waving the bloody shirt." Radical Republicans would become quite adept at it, employing it in many successful elections to come.

Having many agents in the South, operating behind the facade of the Freedman's Bureau, the Radicals possessed the machinery for instigating race riots at opportune times. With a little prodding, the illiterate negro masses could be worked into a frenzy at most any time. It seemed more than coincidence that several riots broke out in several southern cities right before the election. In Memphis and New Orleans, large riots occurred in which many negroes were killed, the events playing directly into the hands of the Radicals who screamed for more troops, more money, and more discipline of the white population in the South.

A third element that worked to the advantage of the Radical Republicans was the political recalcitrance of Andrew Johnson. He was a stubborn Democrat faced with a vengeful Republican Congress, and he opposed nearly everything the Radicals tried to ram through. Like Lincoln, he had the rough, vulgar language of the back country from which he sprang, and when heckled at his speeches throughout the Midwest he lost more support than he gained by his uncouth expression and intemperate remarks. Johnson was a political outcast. He was neither southern nor northern. Southern by virtue of residence only, he denounced his home state of Tennessee when she seceded and declined to resign his seat in the U.S. Senate. He had never liked the planter society of the South, but, on the other hand, he didn't care for the majority of northerners, either. When portions of Tennessee came under military rule during the war, his reward for being the most prominent Southern to desert the South was an appointment as military governor of the state, a move that greatly displeased the people of Tennessee. And then, by a quirk of Fate, this tailor from East Tennessee was propelled into the highest office in the land and, almost as quickly, thrown into the political battle of his life.

The Radicals won an overwhelming victory in the mid-term elections of 1866. The makeup of the new Senate would be 42 Republicans and 11 Democrats, while the new House of Representatives would pit 143 Republicans against only 49 Democrats. Thus mandated, their machine rolled on over the constant veto of President Johnson. In March, 1867, the first Reconstruction Act was passed, dividing the ten unreconstructed states into five military districts. Each district was under command of an army general, and thousands of troops were spread throughout southern towns and villages to do the bidding of those commanders. Tennessee was spared military occupation since it had been the only southern state to ratify the Fourteenth Amendment, the other ten having refused to do so.

Declaring their contention that the states had indeed left the Union, unlike the position that Lincoln and Johnson had taken, the Radicals announced that they would treat them as conquered provinces. The very sons and daughters of those men who framed the revered old Constitution that the Radicals were effacing with their meddlesome amendments were now to be treated as nothing more than barefoot aborigines.

Every southern state was required to rewrite its constitution in a constitutional convention of delegates chosen in a statewide election of all adult males, *except those with disqualifications*. This meant that many ex-Confederates could not vote, and it meant that negroes, even though they were not yet citizens, could vote. To insure that enough whites were disbarred so that the convention would be composed of a manageable group of pro-Republican delegates, the Radicals installed registrars armed with enormous powers. Each voter had to step before the registrar and swear a complicated loyalty oath which was offensive to native Southerners. Even if a southern white man could bring himself to make an oath of allegiance to such a despotic government, the registrar was empowered to reject the oath if he deemed it made in bad faith. In this way, the registrars in every community could reject enough white votes to guarantee a safe Republican majority. As a result, they registered 703,000 negroes and only 627,000 white men in the South.

State constitutions, framed by noble sires and men of letters, would thus be relegated to the trash in favor of cheap pamphlets produced by inferior minds pretending to be duly elected delegates to these co-called "constitutional conventions." Typical of the self-serving arrangements incorporated into the new constitutions was Article 99 of the Louisiana Constitution of 1868, which embodied the Recantation Oath, a provision which effectively disfranchised white voters. A man had to swear that he had never of his own free will served the Confederacy in a military or civil capacity, voted for secession, or "acting in advocacy of treason, wrote or published newspaper articles or preached sermons." [16] No honorable man could bring himself to declare such a falsehood, and the records of Caddo Parish are indicative of the disastrous effects the oath had upon the entire state. In 1868, no white men in the parish took the recantation oath. The 3,586 registered voters in Caddo Parish were mostly negroes who voted the Republican ticket just as the Radicals had instructed them to do.

Amid all this turmoil, the disfranchised people of the South had to contend with the worst troublemaker Satan could have supplied – the carpetbagger, so-called because he came South carrying all of his belongings in one small suitcase made in the fashion of the day from a piece of floral, carpet-like material. It said one of two things of him: firstly, that he was either a man of no means – a financial failure – and could, therefore, carry all of his belongings in such a bag; or secondly, that he was so seized of greed that his haste necessitated packing so lightly. In either case,

207

THE CARPETBAGGER
An 1872 caricature by cartoonist Thomas Nast.

one thing is absolutely certain: he proceeded to prey upon a disconsolate people with no pangs of guilt and no sense of remorse.

His southern counterpart, the scalawag – or scallywag – was even more revolting. A southern white man turned traitor for betterment of his financial lot, he forsook the plight of his own people and welcomed the carpetbagger with open arms. Together with the benighted negro, they comprised the triumvirate that would carry out a reign of terror over the broken South for more than ten years.

The loathsome carpetbaggers descended upon the South like a swarm of locusts, devouring land, homes, and anything of value they could wrench from the hands of financially distressed Southerners. With the help of the negroes and scallywags, they got themselves elected to county offices and judgeships, where they had the power to levy outrageous taxes upon the property of native Southerners who, due to the disastrous effects of the war, were unable to pay the levies. Foreclosures were rampant, and carpetbaggers made themselves rich upon the misfortunes of grandsons of men who had fought and won the American Revolution. Scandalous, revolting, contemptible. There are no words that can begin to do justice to the foul, evil deeds perpetrated by these northern vultures who swarmed in to pick the carcass of the defeated South. They were leeches, parasites upon a defenseless people under the brutal occupation of an army that allowed such creatures to rob a prostrate South in its hour of profound humiliation.

And now with Andrew Johnson's Reconstruction plan completely scrapped, the Radicals' hand greatly strengthened by the 1866 elections, Congress laid out the rest of its plan. In addition to writing a new constitution, each state had to guarantee negroes the right to vote and ratify the Fourteenth Amendment. By requiring *conquered provinces*, the term Republicans now used for states which were out of the Union, to ratify a constitutional amendment, this haphazard, vindictive Congress cast a legal cloud upon an already cumbersome amendment – a flaw still unresolved by Constitutional scholars of today. If the requirements were met, Congress reserved the right to scrutinize the constitution of each "province," and, if that new constitution met the qualifications of their diabolical scheme, to readmit the province to the Union as a state. Congress would then "consider" removing Federal troops from that state. In other words, the Republican Congress would be glad to have the state back in the Union if it was firmly under their control.

Congress had all bases covered. Subsequent Reconstruction acts increased its control over southern politics. One especially odious act was extremely useful to the Radicals. It empowered military commanders to remove elected state officials who displeased the regime and appoint officials more to their liking. There were plenty of carpetbaggers waiting in the wings.

Constitutional law and order had taken a holiday, and Congress was determined that nothing should stop their radical move toward centralized government. President Johnson was next on their list. His opposition to their machinations was a source of irritation, and the Radicals had been plotting to impeach him at their earliest convenience. Two pieces of legislation had been cooked up to trap him and, at the same time, diminish the power of the presidency. The first act required him to issue all military orders through General Grant, a Radical Republican. The second act prohibited him from removing any of his Senate-confirmed officials without permission of the Senate.

Their golden opportunity arrived when Johnson deliberately removed Secretary of War Stanton from his cabinet without the consent of the Senate. The House of Representatives promptly passed articles of impeachment against him, and on March 13, 1868, the Senate began the trial – the first impeachment action ever taken against a president. It was a shameful episode in the history of the United States, but considering the evil that emanated from the bowels of the Radical Republicans, it is not surprising. What is surprising is that seven Republicans voted against removing Johnson from office, thereby saving him from conviction by one lone vote.

In the same infamous year, Congress attempted to silence the Supreme Court. In this black endeavor, they were more successful. The Supreme Court had already become a problem for them and their schemes. In 1866, in the case of *Ex parte Milligan*, it had ruled that Lincoln had been acting unconstitutionally when he did away with civil courts, replacing them with military tribunals. In 1868, the Supreme Court agreed to hear the case of *Ex, Parte McCardle*, a challenge to the constitutionality of the first Reconstruction Act. Before the court could hear that case, Congress passed an act withdrawing appellate jurisdiction of the Supreme Court in cases of this type. In addition, it sought to essentially do away with the court by stipulating that if a Justice died or resigned he was not to be replaced. Under this decree, the Supreme Court dwindled to only six members.

The assaults upon the executive and judicial branches were evidence that Congress was purposely creating an imbalance in the American system. They intended to make the legislative branch supreme. Suffering from a viral anti-South psychosis, the Radical Congress saw itself as a revolutionary body, architects of a new order that would replace the American idea of checks and balances with a totalitarian regime committed to a new social order in the South.

The year of 1868 also brought a long-awaited presidential election. The unmanageable Andrew Johnson was dumped by the Democrats in favor of Horatio Seymour, while the Radicals gleefully nominated the popular, cigar-chomping General of the Army, Ulysses S. Grant. In retrospect, Grant has been perceived by most historians not so much as a vicious Radical like his colleagues in Congress, but as a weak official who, given to much drink, was easily manipulated by a strong-willed Congress, jealous of its powers. Influenced by persuasive politicians and dominated by Congress, Grant acquired the distinction of having the most corrupt administration of any U.S. president.

His election was secured by the carpetbag governments in the South who gave military protection to thousands of negroes and instructed them to vote Republican. Realizing more fully the importance of the negro vote to perpetuating the Radical Republican agenda, Congress lost little time in drawing up another of its "pressure amendments." This one, the Fifteenth Amendment, made sure that the negro's right to vote was protected everywhere, even in the North, where Ohio, Michigan, Kansas, and Minnesota had balked at incorporating negro suffrage in their state constitutions. To offset possible rejection of the amendment by some northern states, Congress once again made ratification of an amendment a requirement for readmission of the states still out of the Union – Mississippi, Texas, Georgia, and Virginia.

By 1870, all of the southern states were back in the Union, but carpetbaggers were still at work. It was a swindler's dream.

211

THE CARPETBAGGERS
A painting by N.C. Wyeth

Southerners owned the land and could, therefore, be taxed to support a corrupt government in which they were not allowed to participate. Scalawags, carpetbaggers, and negroes elected each other to the statehouses of every southern state where their proceedings were a travesty of justice.

In South Carolina, out of 155 state legislators 144 were Radical Republicans. Of those, 98 were negroes, of whom only 22 could read and write. The State Treasurer and Secretary of State were negroes, and the Governor was a carpetbagger. Voting unto themselves gold watches, horses, carriages, champagne, and other outlandish things, they quickly bankrupted South Carolina, the state debt rising from $7,000,000 to $29,000,000 in a brief period of time. South Carolina would go well into the 20th century before overcoming the effects of carpetbag plunder.

The negroes were interested in social services to be paid for by the southern taxpayer. Coached by the wily carpetbagger, who made sure he received his share of the revenue, the negro in the legislature was responsible for raising the Louisiana tax rate by 400% in four years. Throughout the South, carpetbag tax assessors took delight in humbling landowners by demanding higher taxes in scenes reminiscent of *Gone With the Wind's* white trash character, Jonas Wilkerson, who, elevated to stature of tax collector, demanded that Miss Scarlett fork over $200 or lose *Tara*.

In *The March of Democracy*, James Truslow Adams wrote, "The political trash, white and black, grew rich selling franchises, public property, and political favors for any price they could to get money for themselves. One carpetbag governor cleaned up a half million dollars in his term."[17] That governor was H.C. Warmoth, of Louisiana, who built his private fortune from public money. He smugly insisted that corruption was the fashion.

It was not the first time Louisianans had dealt with enemy occupation and the corruption that that entailed. New Orleans had fallen to the enemy early in the war. In 1862, the city was placed under the command of U.S. General Benjamin F. Butler, who to this day is still referred to as "Beast Butler," a name he earned early in his stay in the Crescent City. One of his first evil deeds was to execute the handsome 42-year-old William Mumford, even amidst pleas from Mumford's wife to spare her husband and father of their children. His crime? Climbing to the top of a pole and pulling down a U.S. flag which had been hastily hoisted by a detachment of marines who had rushed ashore and pulled down the Louisiana state flag before the city had surrendered.

Then, Butler began systematically looting the city and potions of the state. He controlled all of the operations of food procurement, sales, and distribution to the poor, making thousands of dollars "under the table" on the operation. Along with

"Beast" Butler
This photograph was made in New Orleans
while he was ransacking the city.
(photo courtesy of Glen C. Cangelosi)

his brother, Col. Andrew J. Butler, he amassed great wealth from his illegal enterprises during the year of his reign in New Orleans. Butler confiscated $60,000 worth of sugar, loaded it onto a Federal warship, and sent it to Boston where he intended to sell it for $160,000. He banished over 4,000 Louisiana farmers and seized their cotton, which was brought into New Orleans and put up for auction at ridiculously low prices, where Andrew was often the prime buyer. The Butler consortium then sold it at premium prices, making thousands of dollars each time. In another theft, Butler seized $800,000 from the Dutch consul in New Orleans, pocketing every cent. For stealing costly furniture and vast amounts of silverware from the homes of New Orleans citizens, Butler gained an additional nickname of "Spoons Butler." At the time of Butler's death in 1893, the Massachusetts general's worth was 7 million dollars, and much of it came from New Orleans. It was estimated that his brother, Andrew, came away from New Orleans with two million dollars.

And now Louisiana was going to be fleeced again.

A sketch of Reconstruction in Louisiana is representative of the situation that existed throughout the South, and though we can recite the events of those troublesome times in a book, it is impossible for those of us living in this age to grasp the horror that stalked the lives of our ancestors for nearly twelve years.

The events in northwestern Louisiana are especially illustrative, owing partly to the fact that Shreveport was the wartime state capital after Federal forces occupied southern Louisiana. In addition, the *Shreveport Times*, newly organized in 1871, became the leading voice for Louisianans during Reconstruction.

With the South, once the richest and most beautiful area of the country, lying in ruins and the Confederate government dismantled by the troglodytes who laid the South in ruins, there was no civil authority to protect the people from the wandering bands of former slaves. No sheriff. No chief of police. No police force. No nothing. Governor Allen, in his farewell letter, optimistically said, "I would advise that you form yourselves into companies and squads for the purpose of protecting your families from outrage and insults and your property from spoilation. . . . Within a short while the United States authorities will no doubt send you an armed force to any part of the State where you may require it for your protection." [18] He had no way of knowing that the United States would send a huge force of negro troops to garrison Shreveport for two long years. The troops were undisciplined, arrogant, and resentful of the white people of Louisiana. The people of Shreveport were unwilling hosts to these former slaves who took great pleasure and delight in lording it over the white man. They humiliated the citizens with every kind of insult imaginable while their Radical political leaders, black and white, systematically looted the state.

The governor of the occupied state, J. Madison Wells, called for an election to be held in November, 1865. The Democrats, who at this time could still vote, nominated him for governor, and he won the election. Fearing Radical reprisals, however, the people of Caddo Parish, in April, 1867, submitted resolutions of cooperation with the Union to the military commander of the state, who happened to be the notorious Phil Sheridan. Notwithstanding expressions of accommodation from the citizens, General Sheridan, who had violently destroyed the Shenandoah Valley of Virginia, removed Governor Wells from office and appointed a man more in tune with the Radicals.

With enough Radical Republicans in the legislature, Louisiana constructed a constitution containing the infamous Recantation Oath; consequently, in 1868, white loyal Southerners were disfranchised. As a result, Henry Clay Warmoth, the corrupt Republican, and Oscar Dunn, a Republican negro, were elected governor and lieutenant governor respectively. Warmoth presided over a legislature composed of scalawags, carpetbaggers, and newly-freed negroes who spent the state into ruin.

With a police force in Shreveport composed only of negro troops who cared little for the safety of white citizens, white men organized the Knights of the White Camellia. The Knights in Caddo parish, declaring "a white man's government or no government," made night rides breaking up incendiary political meetings in which scalawags and carpetbaggers were instructing and inflaming the gullible freedmen.

In 1868, two race riot broke out in Bossier parish, resulting in the death of 150 negroes. A negro leader from Arkansas was reportedly the instigator, but further evidence involving previous uprisings pointed to the Freedman's Bureau and its carpetbag supporters.

By 1870, the Knights of the White Camellia had been so successful in Caddo parish that Governor Warmoth threatened to send his state militia there to protect the negroes in the fall elections. But this was the same year that saw the expiration of the hated Recantation Oath from the state constitution; consequently, Southerners were once again among the voting population of their homeland, and the Knights accordingly disbanded.

In late 1871, these determined citizens acquired the public voice of their resistance in the form of the *Shreveport Times*, a brand new daily newspaper which set the state ablaze with its bold criticisms of the Reconstruction hoodlums. On June 1, 1872, it defiantly called for an end to carpetbag rule in Louisiana, and a mysterious organization soon appeared.

The organization was preceded by a continuing series of disturbing events. John McEnery was the Democratic candidate for governor in 1872, and Shreveport businessmen solidly pledged that they would not advance money or supplies for the coming year to any planter who rented land or gave employment to any laborer who voted the Republican ticket in the forthcoming election. Although the election was rife with fraud, McEnery was the winner at the ballot box. But that didn't last long. The Radical Returning Board simply declared Republican William Pitt Kellog the winner. He was inaugurated on January 14, 1873, ushering in a reign of constant lawlessness and political turmoil as yet unmatched in the state.

Virtually controlled by negroes who were goaded by carpetbaggers, the Radical state government had organized the Metropolitan Brigade, a semi-military organization composed generally of negroes and commanded by former Confederate General Longstreet. A brooding individual of uneven temperament, Longstreet had already fallen out of favor with his brothers-in-arms for his refusal at Gettysburg to follow Lee's orders to attack, the result of which was the deadly Pickett's

Charge and entire defeat of the Confederate forces at Gettysburg. And now, here he was in charge of the Metropolitan Brigade, complete with a gunboat fashioned after the steamboat *Ozark*, in which he could land his troops at any port in the state where white people were attempting to assert their rights.

By the spring of 1873, the stage was set for the organization of the White League. Colonel James Hollingsworth, of Shreveport, called a meeting of several like-minded individuals, to whom he explained the plan. A White League would be set up in every parish and would consist primarily of a political club, but with an auxiliary rifle club which would be composed entirely of former Confederate soldiers. Hollingsworth further explained that the political club would be open to every white man who would join and that it would serve as a camouflage for the inner workings of the association. The men sitting before him were asked to be the secret inner circle. They were each to find eight loyal men to aid them; but, in order to keep Radicals from infiltrating the group, the membership of this executive committee would not be increased.

The purpose of the rifle club was to oppose the Metropolitan Brigade, but the inner circle was commissioned with a broader goal. Rallying the entire White League membership behind its efforts, the executive committee was to try to stop the killing of negroes when the carpetbaggers instigated a race riot. Hollingsworth pointed out that the negroes of Louisiana were ordinarily a harmless people who committed outrages only when stirred up by the carpetbaggers, and that the death of a negro was fuel for the fire of the corrupt government. Instead, Hollingsworth proposed that no carpetbagger be allowed to escape alive from any future race riot. The *Shreveport Times* immediately concurred when, in 1873, it declared "Their career is ended; we are determined to tolerate them no longer. If they care for their infamous necks, they had better stop their work right now and look for a safer field of rascality. If a single battle gun is fired between the whites and blacks, every carpetbagger and scalawag that can be caught will in twelve hours be hanging from a limb"[19]

Just as the White League was forming itself, the Radicals incited a bloody riot in Colfax, where about 300 negroes were killed. The riot probably helped swell the membership of the League in those parts, for the *Minden Democrat* estimated that northwestern Louisiana had 10,000 who were ready to ride.

In response to the White League, the Radicals further incited the negroes, forming them into Union Leagues. In June and July, large shipments of arms arrived from New Orleans and were delivered to negroes along the rivers between Natchitoches and Shreveport. Fearing more uprisings and massacres, the parishes of Caddo, De Soto, and Bossier petitioned the state of Texas for annexation. Resolutions of sympathy were made by the people of Texas, but the proposition was squelched by the Radical government in Louisiana.

The *Shreveport Times*, always in the vanguard, called for a convention of the white people of Louisiana to assemble at Alexandria on September 1, 1874; instead, however, the state Democrats, convinced that the time was ripe, assumed charge of the effort and scheduled a meeting in Baton Rouge a week earlier.

In the midst of this encouraging political activity, a Radical and two of his negro henchmen threw the state into turmoil by killing two white pickets who were posted on the road leading into Coushatta. The town of Coushatta immediately called for help, and men began assembling in Shreveport the next day. Dispatches arrived from the Texas cities of Marshall, Longview, and Jefferson, promising help if needed.

Before the Shreveport contingent could move south, word came that a Coushatta posse had captured several white Radicals and some negroes who were responsible for the crime; therefore, the men from Caddo parish stayed home. Unaware of the arrests, however, were about a thousand men from other parishes and Texas. Their presence in Coushatta frightened the daylights out of the white prisoners who, accordingly, offered to resign their carpetbag offices and leave the state. Their offer was gladly accepted and they were started, under guard, toward Shreveport, which is about forty-five miles north of Coushatta. But seventeen miles south of Shreveport, the party encountered a group of men who murdered the prisoners.

On September 2, Governor Kellog, alarmed at the growing resistance to his carpetbag regime, wired President Grant for military intervention, a request which, surprisingly enough, Grant denied. The next day Governor Kellog declared martial law in Louisiana. Two days later, Grant changed his mind and ordered massive bodies of troops into the state. Once more Louisiana was under strict military occupation, and carpet-baggers seemed to breathe more easily.

But this was 1874, and the people of Louisiana were growing impatient and much bolder. In August, Natchitoches parish had succeeded in running off its tax collector, judge, district judge, and police jury. Two weeks after the riot at Coushatta, there was a bloody upheaval in New Orleans, where the White League overthrew Governor Kellog's administration and installed the Democratic officials who were the rightful winners of the 1872 election. Several parishes in northwestern Louisiana followed suit and set up their own *de facto* governments after forcing the Radicals to flee.

Known as the Battle of Liberty Place, the confrontation on September 14, 1874, in New Orleans occurred when several thousand white Louisianans stormed the state house, which had been moved by the U.S. army from Baton Rouge to New Orleans after the southern half of the state came under occupation by Union troops in 1862. The determined citizens, their leaders making a statement to negroes in Louisiana that their rights and property would not be harmed, defeated General Longstreet's Metropolitan Brigade which had showed up with rifles and a cannon. Capturing the cannon, the angry citizens routed the Brigade, Longstreet escaping only by riding through a city building on horseback. Having already forsaken the South in its distress, he further alienated his fellow veterans by firing upon the crowd, many of whom were former Confederate soldiers. After the war, veterans refused to sit by Longstreet or even acknowledge him at their reunions.

The White League installed Governor McEnery and all the officials legitimately elected in 1872, but Grant, ever accommodating to his scurrilous friends, ordered the *de facto* governments to disperse within five days. Additional troops and warships were sent to the state, and, by September 19, Kellog had forced his way back into the governor's chair. A few days later, the *Shreveport Times* declared, "The President's soldiers may reinstate there the officials of fraud, but the moment the troops retire Mr. Kellog will be expelled or killed." [20]

Going on, it commented about the expected demise of the *de facto* governments in other parishes. "If the federal government again strikes them down, then let the infamy of the deed rest upon the shameless Northern people, beneath whose withering influence no sentiment of liberty can survive; under whose policy of meanness, cowardice, and hate, every community that does not worship it must be trampled in the dust and every civilization that does not pay tribute to it blasted by its curse."

On October 16, a Federal posse began a march through four northwestern Louisiana parishes, arresting large groups of men without warrants and on charges of conspiracy and intimidation in the murder of the white prisoners south of Shreveport. In De Soto parish, the men of the White League escaped to the woods, but in Caddo parish, about seventy-five men were arrested, including the organizer of the White League, Colonel Hollingsworth.

A virtual state of war existed in Louisiana for the next two years, and various atrocities occurred throughout the entire period. In 1876, the White League supported a Confederate war hero, Francis Nicholls, for governor, while the Radicals put up Stephen Packard as their candidate. True to form, the Radical

Returning Board threw out enough ballots to declare Packard the winner. The votes in eight parishes were completely thrown out as punishment for the Colfax and Coushatta affairs of 1874.

Like most southern states, Louisiana had about decided that the words of Patrick Henry were as true as they had been a hundred years earlier. Life was not so dear, nor was peace so sweet, "as to be purhcased at the price of chains and slavery." As the carpetbagger Packard was inaugurated, the southern men of the state defiantly swore Nicholls in as governor and helped him establish a legislature made up of men elected by the legitimate white citizens of the state. Parish and city governments across the state rebuffed the Packard government and recognized the authority of Nicholls A new Supreme Court was appointed by Nicholls, and the state taxes were deposited into the treasury of his government.

On March 24, 1877, Nicholls boldly announced that his government was complete and invited the newly-elected President, Rutherford B. Hayes, to inspect the situation. On April 20, President Hayes ordered all troops out of the State House, and Governor Nicholls moved in. Louisiana's nightmare was over, and Southerners could once again enjoy their lovely old Deep South state of majestic oaks and Spanish moss. Paradise regained.

Not only had the people of Louisiana resolved to do or die, President Hayes was making good on a promise he had made in securing his election. In 1873, a severe financial panic had hit the United States, giving the Democrats an issue in the 1874 congressional elections. The corruption of Grant's presidency, coupled with the panic, had swept the Democrats to victory, making them the majority party in the House of Representatives for the first time since 1858. This new power was to play a significant role in the disputed presidential election of 1876.

The Democrats chose Samuel Tilden as their candidate and preached reform, while the Republicans chose Hayes and "waved the bloody shirt" once again. The returns were in dispute in Oregon and the three southern states still occupied by Union troops: Louisiana, Florida, and South Carolina. An electoral commission, consisting of eight Republicans and seven Democrats, was created by Congress for the purpose of recommending a winner. Voting along party lines, the commission selected Hayes. The Democrats, who held a vast majority in the House, agreed to the decision with the stipulation that *all troops still protecting the carpetbag governments in the South be withdrawn.* Although the other eight southern states had in one way or another regained home rule, a Republican machine still existed in each state, representing a continuous threat as long as the Republicans in Washington had the authority to send troops back into the South. Without a doubt, the compromise in the House was the most important agreement ever to affect the South, for with the departure of the last Union soldier went everything that had made life unbearable for twelve long years.

The withdrawal of the troops put an immediate end to the carpetbag governments. Radical Republican rule had made a two-party system in the South impossible for more than a hundred years to come. Not a phase of southern life escaped the scrutiny of these Republican tyrants. Even the old gray woolen jackets worn home from the war were called a uniform and summarily forbidden to be worn. Many who had nothing else to break the winter cold sewed gray bits of cloth over the brass buttons in an effort to declassify the old garments lest a guard find him plowing the field in a "criminal's coat."

There were three requisite conditions for Republican power in the South: the negro vote, Republican control of the national government, and Federal troops. Should any one of these supports be weakened or removed, Republican rule would collapse in the same fashion as a three-legged stool. The Southerner had little control over troops or national politics, having himself been barred from voting, so he turned his efforts to the local scene. There, in the shadows of the night, secret societies began to spring up in an effort to stop negro voting and, in the process, run the carpetbaggers out of the South.

This unidentified Confederate officer poses before the camera in the studio of C.R. Rees & Company in Richmond, Virginia, in 1869, four years after the war. During Reconstruction, it was illegal to wear a Confederate uniform, so this soldier had to be sure and change before leaving the studio. Henry Kyd Douglas, an officer on the staff of General Stonewall Jackson, had his picture made, but in his haste to get back home wore his uniform out on the street. He was arrested, convicted by a military tribunal, and thrown into prison.

The romance of the period, with its night rides, daring plots of retribution, and scenes of southern women sewing costumes by day that southern men would wear by night, has been captured in the several works of Thomas Dixon. For a true sampling of the tenor of the times, the reader would do well to obtain a copy of Dixon's 1905 classic, *The Clansman*, which was the inspiration for D.W. Griffith's motion picture epic, *The Birth of a*

Nation. The silent movie, which portrays the classic struggle between the carpetbag regime and the Ku Klux Klan, was despised by the liberal press because, as in the novel, white people overcome their black oppressors. So controversial did the media make it that Dixon and Griffith enlisted the aid of United States Chief Justice Edward Douglass White in overcoming would-be censors who would have kept the story of white deliverance from black rule forever buried. Fortunately, it has passed into our literary lexicon as a masterpiece of American drama, described by President Woodrow Wilson, who held a White House screening of the movie, as "history written with lightning." [21]

The clandestine organizations which proliferated across Dixie were called by different names, including the Knights of the White Camellia, the Red Shirts, the White League, and the White Brotherhood; but the association which attracted the most attention was the Ku Klux Klan. Not to be confused with the Ku Klux Klan of the present day, the original Klan was organized for the same reason as the White League of Louisiana – to rid the land of the curse of carpetbag tyranny. Formed in Pulaski, Tennessee, in 1866, the Ku Klux Klan quickly spread across the South. The members wore robes and hoods of symbolic, mysterious designs, while frightening negroes and whipping scalawags and carpetbaggers. An alarmed Radical Congress passed two acts, one in 1870 and another in 1871, aimed at suppressing the Klan, but, due to the secrecy of its organization, Congressional efforts to stop it were futile. By 1877, with troops finally withdrawn from the beleaguered South, assuring home rule once again, there was no more need for secret societies, so the last units of the Klan disbanded.

In her memoirs, May Winston Caldwell, who lived on the Franklin Pike, not far from downtown Nashville, described the Ku Klux Klan she remembered from her youth.

The thing that struck terror into us children more
than the Battle of Nashville was the Ku Klux Klan

225

that had its meetings in the then abandoned Fort Negley. When twilight came or in the misty moonlight these figures of ill-omen would sally forth. The appearance of one of the Klan caused consternation; and after seeing one, it was days before we got back to normal.

Each member of the Klan was required to provide himself with a costume. There was a white mask for the face, with openings for the eyes and mouth. A tall cardboard hat was so constructed as to make the wearer appear much taller than he was. A long robe concealed the entire person, and there was also a covering for the horses and some sort of muffling for their feet. Each member also carried a small whistle with which, by means of signals agreed upon, they communicated with each other. Being near Fort Negley, where they held their midnight meetings, our street was a frequent rendezvous for these riders of the night.

We now realize that this mysterious organization was a chivalrous knighthood whose task was to rescue our helpless people from the terrors of the carpetbaggers and the reconstruction regime from which we suffered for years after the war.

Without the secret societies and rifle clubs, it is doubtful that home rule would have returned before the end of the century. After years of persecution, Southerners were left with no other choice. They had to take matters into their own hands if ever they hoped to live again as free men and women.

Violence in Hamburg, South Carolina, on July 4, 1876, gave birth to the Red Shirts, who rode through hill and dale with the same fervor of Paul Revere who had ridden a century earlier for the sake of freedom. Coarse language and insults were the daily fare from the foul mouths of freedmen, and womanhood was imperiled in the state. Former Confederate Generals M.C. Butler and M.W. Gary advocated what they called the "straight-out" system, declaring that nothing but a straight-out fight could now succeed in overthrowing the corrupt government. In response to an order forbidding him to interfere in the election of 1876 in his native state, Gary responded, "You could put a soldier in front of every cottage in the State and could not prevent the return of South Carolina to her own people."[22] Adopting as their uniform the red flannel shirt, in derision of the cheap sensational Radical practice of "waving the bloody shirt," they moved as swiftly as the minutemen of old in ridding the state of the unwanted thugs who had become leaches upon southern society.

Out in Indian Territory, which 40 years later became the state of Oklahoma, the hammer fell hard. Troops, under the command of Gen. Phil Sheridan, who was fond of saying the only good Indians he ever saw were dead ones, occupied the entire area. For their allegiance to the Confederacy, the Creeks, Cherokees, Choctaws, Chickasaws, Seminoles, and smaller tribes were being intimidated with threats by the Republican Congress to colonize former slaves from the entire South on lands belonging to the Indians. Although this didn't come to pass, the idea of "forty acres and a mule" was so seriously and widely projected, it had the effect of enticing ex-slaves from Texas, Arkansas, and Missouri to pour into the Territory, where they squatted on Indian lands and raided the corn cribs and smokehouses of Indian citizens. To make matters worse, the Radicals proposed to give the former slaves of the Indians all of the rights held by Indians plus an equal share in tribal annuities, lands, and other benefits, some of which came to pass in the resulting harsh Reconstruction treaties forced upon the tribes. Eventually, the government took away one-half of Indian Territory and gave it to the plains Indians of the far west who frequently attacked the Five Civilized Tribes.

Conditions in Indian Territory were already among the worst in the old Confederacy. A full twenty-five percent of the population was dead from the effects of the war, and almost every home and village was destroyed from the constant raiding. Today, hardly an antebellum structure is to be found within the state of Oklahoma, mute testimony to the war's virtual destruction of Indian Territory.

The grinding poverty was worsened by the freedmen who stole chickens, hogs, horses, and cattle. The Federal armies of occupation were there to protect the negro, not the Indian, so the Five Civilized Tribes resorted to vigilante committees to restore order and check the thievery of the freedmen. The Choctaws and Chickasaws were the first to form their mounted patrols. They met secretly, devising signals and determining punishment for violators of the vigilante code. They maintained secret communication channels and made night rides to intimidate freedmen, who usually congregated together in shanty towns. If, after having been warned, a negro was found outside his community, he would be whipped by these Indian patrols. If, when caught, he was in possession of a hog, cow, or horse, the freedman was executed on the spot. The success of the Choctaw and Chickasaw vigilante committees led to the formation of similar groups among the Creeks, Seminoles, and Cherokees, and some semblance of order returned.

Reconstruction was a nightmare, and its effects left deep scars. Thomas Dixon spent his childhood in an occupied North Carolina, consequently devoting his life to telling its awful story. The recognized authority on slavery, Ulrich B. Phillips, was born in Georgia during the last year of Reconstruction. In 1889, at the age of twelve, he persuaded his parents to rename him Ulrich. At birth, he had been christened Ulysses, but he had seen enough to know that he did not want to share the name of anyone who had played such a role in defeating and humiliating his homeland. Former Confederate Secretary of War, Robert Toombs, another Georgian who remembered Reconstruction, was said to have gloated over the great Chicago fire of 1871. Even today, Reconstruction's memories evoke indignation among Southerners. In

1987, a Tennessee state senator succeeded in having a huge portrait of "Parson" Brownlow removed from the state capitol. The oil painting, depicting the unpopular Reconstruction governor ostentatiously pointing towards the U.S. flag, was placed in the basement museum across the street where, as one Nashville attorney told me, it is hanging at eye level so that visitors can see the tobacco juice stains made by the spitting of ex-Confederates upon the image of the governor who denied them the right to vote.

Southern Partisan magazine recently remarked, "Many Americans today, in this age of historical amnesia, would disbelieve that one part of their country was once put under military occupation by another part, that heinous crimes went unpunished, that summary arrests and summary executions were common, that courts were subverted, legislatures corrupted, and the majority of the electorate disfranchised – all at the instance of the federal government." [23]

Indeed, some wish to cover it up – or worse, to rewrite it into a distortion of the facts. Even the Board of Education in the state of South Carolina decided, in 1985, to rewrite the textbooks in such a fashion that Reconstruction would be characterized as a *milestone in social progress.* Even a carpetbagger knows the folly of such an absurd idea. Albion W. Tourgee, an Ohio-born carpetbagger who, along with many other carpetbaggers, descended upon North Carolina shortly after the war, knew it for what it was. It wasn't social progress, and, writing of its abject failure in his novel of 1879 called *A Fools' Errand,* he admitted, "We tried to superimpose the civilization, the idea of the North, upon the South at a moment's warning. We presumed that, by the suppression of rebellion, the Southern white man had become identical with he Caucasian of the North in thought and sentiment; and that the slave, by emancipation, had become a saint and a Solomon at once. So we tried to build up communities there which should be identical in thought, sentiment, growth, and development, with those of the North. It was *A Fool's*

229

Errand." [24]

Corporal Sam R. Watkins, of Columbia, Tennessee, was living proof that Reconstruction had failed to diminish devotion to the Lost Cause. Writing in 1881, he said, "Secession may have been wrong in the abstract, and has been tried and settled by the arbitrament of the sword and bayonet, but I am as firm in my convictions today of the right of secession as I was in 1861. The South is our country, the North is the country of those who live there. We are an agricultural people; they are a manufacturing people. They are the descendants of the good old Puritan Plymouth Rock stock, and we of the South from the proud and aristocratic stock of Cavaliers. We believe in the doctrine of State rights, they in the doctrine of centralization. John C. Calhoun, Patrick Henry, and Randolph, of Roanoke, saw the venom under their wings, and warned the North of the consequences, but they laughed at them. We only fought for our State rights, they for Union and power. The South fell battling under the banner of State rights, but yet grand and glorious even in death."[25]

Let none among us disparage our Southern ancestors. Let us only hope that even a droplet of the revolutionary blood that flowed in their veins has trickled down to us. It is ironic that the very code of honor which the Yankees thought four years of cruel war had washed out of our souls was the same standard that steadily sustained us through Reconstruction. It's that implacable faith and inexorable resilience, particularly southern in nature, that makes us what we are – *Southern By the Grace of God.*

The original Ku Klux Klan (1866-1877) played a vital role in ridding the postwar South of brutal carpetbag rule. This 1921 poster is an advertisement of the classic silent movie, *The Birth of a Nation*, based upon *The Clansman*, Thomas Dixon's popular novel about the Ku Klux Klan.

Beautiful Dixieland

WORDS AND MUSIC BY
ERNEST SUTTON

New York

VII

A Portrait of Dixie

Within the next several pages, the magic of the camera will introduce us to Southerners of the past, some who experienced the war, some who survived Reconstruction, and others who came along shortly thereafter. Here are the faces and places of the beautiful Old South as it was before the war and as it was after arising, like the phoenix, from the ashes.

Most of the photographs before the war are of the faces rather than the places, for photography was in its infancy during the years before the war, and most photographs were taken in the studio

Photography began in 1839 in Paris, France. It was brought to America by Samuel F.B. Morse, developer of the Morse Code. The first images were on silver plated copper and were called daguer-reotypes, after the developer Louis Daguerre. By 1852, a similar type of image on glass was being produced and called an am-brotype. Daguerreotypes were made between 1839 and 1860, while ambrotypes were in vogue between 1852 and 1880.

In the 1860s, many photographs were developed on sensitized pieces of thin, enameled iron. Called tintypes, these odd little metal photographs were popular through the 1890s. They were cut in many irregular shapes, and the images were usually rather dim and gray-looking without sharp contrasts.

By far the most popular medium was paper. Pictures were developed on photographic paper and glued to pieces of cardboard called studio cards. Known as cabinet prints, they were widely used from 1868 through 1914. A smaller version, measuring approximately 2 3/8" x 4" and in many cases featuring only the head or head and shoulders of a person, was called a *carte de visite*, or CDV, and was used at times as a calling card. The *carte de visite* was popular from 1859 through 1905.

Cameras were large and cumbersome in the 19th century, so a 35-year-old entrepreneur named George Eastman invented a small camera for personal use, naming it the Kodak. It was introduced in 1888 with a pre-loaded roll of film with 100 exposures. Kodak's slogan was "You press the button; we do the rest." After the roll of film was exposed, the camera was sent to the company. The film was developed and sent back to the customer. In 1889, Eastman invented a flexible type of film that could be rolled into the camera, and by the 1890s people were taking millions of "snapshots."

In this chapter, old pictures from all these modes of photography, plus a few old postcard views, will be presented. The reproduction of photos in this paperback version of *Southern By the Grace of God* will not appear nearly as bright and clear as they were in the original hardback version. In the hardback edition, all of the photographs were printed on enamel stock, the type of glossy paper upon which school yearbooks are printed. Paperback books are printed on a soft, porous type of paper than soaks up the ink and allows it to spread, thus dulling the detail. Still, we have worked to get the best quality possible.

With the exception of a few Confederate Veterans Reunions of the 1920s, and a handful of pertinent photos from the 1960s, all of these photographs date backward from the World War I era and are intended to depict southern life in the magical way that only the photographer could capture it. Most of the images have never been published before and, although some of them are of generals and persons of great fame, most of the photos are representative of the average citizen of the South, someone who might have been an ancestor of folks like you and me.

Included here are photographs from all eleven of the former Confederate states plus the border states of Kentucky and Missouri, as well as the state of Oklahoma, formerly Indian Territory, the only ally the Confederacy ever had. The majority of the photographs are from my own collection, augmented by loans from friends and several archival agencies.

My ever-expanding archives is largely the result of purchases at antique stores and flea markets, where it is not only surprising, but sad, indeed, to find wonderful old family photographs that have been relegated to such indiscriminate, impersonal disposal.

When found, many of these neglected photos are of inferior quality, faded, worn, damaged, or printed on poor stock. But it must be remembered that after War and Reconstruction, the South lagged far behind the rest of the country in having disposable funds for such luxuries as photography. We are ever indebted to those of our ancestors who pinched that penny tightly enough to be able to afford the few photographs that we do have.

OLD PHOTOGRAPHS NEED SPECIAL CARE. THEY FADE WHEN EXPOSED TO THE LIGHT. KEEP THEM IN A BOX OR DRAWER. NEVER FRAME AND HANG THEM ON THE WALL. IF YOU WANT TO DISPLAY AN OLD PHOTOGRAPH, HAVE IT COPIED, THEN FRAME THE COPY. STORE ORIGINAL PHOTOS IN A DARK PLACE. HANDLE PHOTOS BY THE EDGES ONLY. FINGERS LEAVE OILY PRINTS THAT CAN DAMAGE THE IMAGE.

RALEIGH, NORTH CAROLINA, ca. 1890. Four beautiful little Southern girls, whose pretty faces give indication that they are probably sisters. This photo was made at the Wharton & Moore Studio in Raleigh.

WHITESBORO, TEXAS, ca. 1919. Decorated for the parade, an old car, representing the firm of McMahan-Foster, is ready to roll. (Photo courtesy of Dr. William F. King)

GAINESVILLE, TEXAS, ca. 1896.
Frank S. Gates

LOUISVILLE, KENTUCKY
ca. 1880

MONTGOMERY, ALABAMA, ca. 1890. Oh, those nicknames! B.F. Goolsby, "The Pretty Boy"; George Preiss, "The Gentleman,"; George McAdam, "The Good Thing"; James Hawkins, "The Irish Sport"; J.D.Carney, "Too Young."

237

FRANKLIN, TENNESSEE, January 15, 1921. Surviving members of Co. B, 1st Tennessee Regiment, in front of the Pension Office. The United States, dividing up our tax money, paid huge monthly pensions to Union veterans while refusing these old men a penny because, sixty years earlier, they had fought on the "wrong side." Small wonder that Yankees were often called "sore winners." The women of the South never wavered in supporting these old veterans. Eventually, they convinced every southern state legislature to provide Confederate pensions to fill the gap left by an obdurate U.S. government. (Photo courtesy of Carter House & Museum)

SOUTH CAROLINA, ca. 1930. Spanish moss, gray and mysterious, festoons giant live oak trees, lending an air of romance to the coastal regions of the Deep South. An epiphytic plant, the moss grows best where humidity is high. It can be found growing naturally as far inland as 225 miles, the area around Shreveport, Louisiana being a good example. Although it will grow on various types of trees, or even on a fence post, its favorite host is the live oak tree. In contrast to a parasite, Spanish moss derives its nutrients from the atmosphere alone. This view is from Brookgreen Gardens, just south of Murrells Inlet.

Moss-draped trees on Pomegranate Street in Sebring, Florida in 1921.

239

SHAWNEE, OKLAHOMA, ca. 1907. This photo was made by the Streeter Studio in Shawnee.

TENNESSEE, ca. 1862. William Brimage Bate, shown here during his service in the Confederate army. When the Mexican War broke out in 1846, Bate enlisted in a Louisiana unit. During the War Between the States, he enlisted as a private in 1861 but soon became colonel of the 2nd Tennessee Infantry. In 1862, Bate became brigadier general, CSA. After the war, Bate served as governor of Tennessee from 1882 to until his appointment as U.S. Senator in 1887. On March 4, 1905, while attending the inauguration of President Teddy Roosevelt, Bate caught cold and died five days later of pneumonia.

Rolling cotton bales up the ramp and onto this steamboat, part of the New Orleans-Vicksburg Packet Company. This photograph might have been taken at Vicksburg or any of several other points served by the packet company, and it may date as far back as the turn-of-the-century or as late as the 1930s.

OKLAHOMA, ca. 1910. Wheat harvest workers at the home of John Skinner.

This photograph was in a collection of Kentucky pictures, but nothing is known about this picture except the names, all written on the back of the photo: Ray Jesse, Roy Gabbert, James McKinney, Sterman Lancaster, Preston Haden, and Charlie Duncan. Seated is Frank Zinsz. The little boy is not named.

CAMDEN, TENNESSEE, ca. 1900

WYNNEWOOD, INDIAN TERRITORY, ca. 1900. The two young men standing are Penn Rabb and Bob Mitchell. Seated, left to right, are Ed Strange, Ed Mitchell, and Thornton Shirley. Since the men are all dressed alike, it is evident that they are part of some event. If the occasion is a wedding, it might be the wedding of Thornton Shirley, who married Rushie Lael on November 11, 1900. The photograph was taken at Martin Brothers Studio in Wynnewood.

243

FORT WORTH, TEXAS, January 17, 1897. "From Penn to Bob." Penn Rabb, attending school at Polytechnic College in Fort Worth, mailed this photograph to his friend, Bob Mitchell in Wynnewood, Indian Territory. All four of these clowns have cigarettes hanging from their mouths, while Penn is the one holding the gun.

DALLAS, TEXAS, 1925. Silas C. Buck holds the flag of the 16th Confederate Cavalry, a unit made up partly in Mississippi and partly in Alabama. On April 12, 1865, he hid this flag from his captors at the Battle of Mobile. Years later, he wrote of the incident. "The colors were the last which ever floated over a Confederate line of battle east of the Mississippi. I bore these colors in the fight, of which fact I feel proud. Throwing away the staff, I hid the colors and thus saved them from surrender. Just before we separated, I gave the colors to Col. Spence who has had them ever since. He brought them to Dallas and kindly allowed me to bring them home to show my family. Precious relics. I feel as if my child had come home after years of absence. I was seventeen when we, not the colors, were surrendered, and I am inclined to believe I was one of the youngest, if not the youngest, color bearer in the Confederate army." This photograph was made at the UCV Reunion in Dallas. (Photo courtesy of the Kentucky Historical Society)

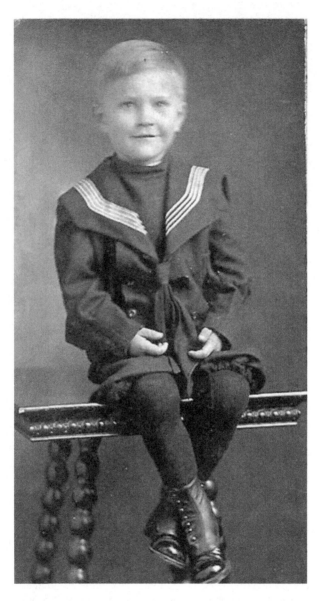

ROGERS, ARKANSAS, ca. 1904. This photograph was made in the Bingham Studio in Rogers. A message on the back reads: "Merry Xmas to LeRoy from Kenneth."

CARROLL COUNTY, VIRGINIA
ca. 1910.
Cora Farmer's daughter.
(Photo courtesy Larry Alderman)

ALEXANDER, ARKANSAS
ca. 1895
This photograph was made
in the studio of Henry Holland.

DALLAS, TEXAS, ca. 1895.

CLIFTON FORGE, VA.   S. S. GRIFFITH & CO.
PHOTOGRAPHERS.

CLIFTON FORGE, VIRGINIA, ca. 1890. In this photograph, these two men display a copy of *Compendium of Cookery and Reliable Recipes*, which was published in 1890. At first, it was thought that they might be the authors, but the book was compiled by two ladies and Dr. S.H. Hughes, a chemist in Boston, so the connection between these two Virginia men and the book is not known.

249

SHREVEPORT, LOUISIANA, June, 1865. A rare find, this is believed to be the last Confederate photograph of the war. On May 26, 1865, General Buckner, at that time in New Orleans and acting for General E. Kirby Smith, accepted terms for surrendering the forces of the Trans-Mississippi Department. On June 2, General Smith approved the terms from Galveston, terms which immediately paroled soldiers and officers and freed them to go home. Wishing to record for posterity a remembrance of their gallant efforts and long association with the Confederate cause, these officers gathered in Shreveport for one last photograph, donning clean, unworn uniforms which were probably carefully preserved in anticipation of celebrating a Confederate victory rather than the loss that brought them to this Shreveport studio. Standing, from left to right, are David French Boyd; unidentified man; D.C. Proctor, First Louisiana Engineers; and William Freret, Major of Engineers. Seated, are Octave Hopkins, First Louisiana Engineers; H.T. Douglas, Colonel of Engineers; and Richard M. Venable. (Photo courtesy of University of the South)

MISSOURI, ca. 1912. Four of the Kimberlin brothers: I.J., W.G., P.S., and J.N. The younger brother, J.N. relates an incident of the war. (Story and photo from *Confederate Veteran*, November, 1912)

My father and four brothers went out early in the defense of the South. I was too young at that time, but remained at home and did all that I was able to do for Quantrill. Father was severely wounded, which disabled him for active service, and he came back home to nurse his wounds. . . . The Federal Commander, Colonel Pennock, by some means learned that Father was at home suffering from wounds, and at once began a scheme to capture him. We had a neighbor named Massey, who was a sympathizer with the Federal army. He and Father had been for years close friends. Pennock, having gained this information, at once sought out Massey and had him go to my father and pretend great friendship for him and advise that if my father would come in and surrender and take the oath of allegiance he could then return home and remain under the protection of the United States flag.

After considering the proposition made by Pennock through the lying, deceptive Massey, my father accepted the offer, and in company with Massey went direct to the colonel's quarters. Immediately upon my father's being introduced, Pennock turned to one of his guards and said: "Put this old devil in jail." On the following morning, Father was sent under guard out home, where he was brutally hanged in his own barn amid the cries and pleadings of my heartbroken mother and her helpless children.

This was September 2, 1862. The home was then stripped of its contents and burned to the ground. The barn, having a great deal of feedstuff stored therein, was not burned at that time; but about two weeks later, after hauling all the feed away, the barn was burned. Not content with what they had already done, they set fire to the rail fence around the farm and burned it to the ground.

About one month after the brutal murder of my father, these same robbers captured old man Sanders and another old gentleman named Crawford and brought them to where my mother then lived and killed them both in our yard. Mr. Sanders was about seventy-three years old and Mr. Crawford was about three years younger.

STAUNTON, VIRGINIA, ca. 1902. An attractive Virginia family. Southerners are a handsome race of people with classic, refined features, the result of nearly 300 years of a delicate blending of Europe's old world nationalities. The most commonly found bloodlines among Southerners are French, German, Dutch, English, Scotch, and Scotch-Irish, with an occasional trace of American Indian.

BEAUMONT, TEXAS, ca. 1900. Made by Holland's Studio. Message on the back reads: *Margaret and Mr. Landis in a decorated trap in the floral parade in Beaumont.*

LEBANON, TENNESSEE, 1909. Mary Sue Davis, a beautiful Southern girl in her graduation picture at Cumberland University in Lebanon.

This publicity photo of Will Rogers (opposite page) was made sometime between 1900 and 1904. Known as "Oklahoma's Favorite Son," Will was born in 1879 in the Cherokee Nation to parents who were part Cherokee. His father, Clement Van Rogers, had served under Confederate General Stand Watie as a cavalry officer in the Cherokee Mounted Rifles. Will was named after William Penn Adair, a Cherokee leader and colonel who also served under Stand Watie.

Will began his performing career with Texas Jack's Wild West Circus in South Africa, later joining Wirth Brothers Circus in Australia. Returning to the United States in 1904, he appeared at the World's Fair where he emphasized his roping tricks and gained wide notice by the entertaining industry. Before his career ended in an airplane crash in Alaska in 1935, he was part of the famous Ziegfeld Follies, had made 71 movies (50 silent films and 21 "talkies"), had written more than 4,000 syndicated columns, and was the highest paid actor in Hollywood.

Best remembered for his good-humored quips, in which he poked fun at nearly everyone in politics, he was once asked by a reporter if he belonged to any organized political party. "No," Will answered, "I'm a Democrat."

GAINESVILLE, GEORGIA, 1912. Miss Etta Hardeman holds the flag she gave to the Georgia Brigade of Cavalry. Maid of Honor for the brigade at Rome, she noticed that they had no flag and determined that they would have one before the Macon Reunion. A few months later, thanks to Miss Etta, they carried a proud new flag in the parade at Macon. (*Confederate Veteran*, November, 1912)

WILLIAM PENN ADAIR

This photograph was probably made between 1860 and 1870. William Penn Adair, for whom Will Rogers was named, was born in 1830 in Georgia. In 1838, as a child, he made the removal to Indian Territory on what the Indians called their "Trail of Tears." Adair became a lawyer, serving in political office both before and after the War Between the States and on the Supreme Court of the Cherokees. During the war, he served in the First Cherokee Mounted Volunteers under General Stand Watie. After being promoted to the rank of colonel, Penn organized the Second Cherokee Mounted Volunteers. After the war, as the government began punishing the Cherokees for their Confederate participation, he represented his people in Washington. While there, he died on October 23, 1880, and was interred in Arlington National Cemetery. Soon, thereafter, the Cherokees brought his body back to the city cemetery in Tahlequah, Oklahoma.

DAVIS, OKLAHOMA, ca. 1920s. Turner Falls, 77 feet high, is located in the heart of the Arbuckle Mountains in south central Oklahoma. It is named for Mazeppa Turner, a Confederate veteran who served in the 2nd Tennessee Cavalry under General Nathan Bedford Forrest. The falls were discovered in 1878 when Turner built a cabin on Honey Creek. Instead of eroding the mountain, the water deposits travertine as it rushes over the rocks, building the falls ever outward. It is now the center of a 1500-acre recreational area.

NASHVILLE, TENNESSEE, 1903. While attending the last reunion of the surviving Confederate generals, General Fitzhugh Lee (left) and General William Hicks Jackson were photographed at *Belle Meade*, the home of General Jackson.

257

LITTLE ROCK, ARKANSAS, 1910. The interior of a radiator shop. Although it is difficult to discern in this photograph, reduced in size to fit the page, the calendar on the wall is turned to March, 1910.

HOT SPRINGS, ARKANSAS, ca. 1912

ASHEVILLE, NORTH CAROLINA, ca. 1906
This photograph was made in
the Lewis Studio of Asheville.

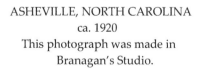

ASHEVILLE, NORTH CAROLINA
ca. 1920
This photograph was made in
Branagan's Studio.

MARGARET MITCHELL
1941

Margaret Mitchell, one of the most famous women in America, was born in Atlanta on November 8, 1900. Both of her grandfathers had served in the army of the Confederacy, so Margaret grew up eagerly listening to her grandparents and elderly relatives relate stories of the War for Southern Independence, the details of which would provide the backdrop for her classic novel, *Gone With the Wind*, the most widely read novel of all time. "I heard so much when I was little about the fighting and the hard times after the war that I firmly believed Mother and Father had been through it all instead of being born long afterward."[1] So immersed was Margaret in the Confederate legacy, that she once quipped that she was ten years old before she knew the South had lost the war. Her older brother, Stephens Mitchell, said of Atlanta, "The city was a Confederate town. That was its history. This was still conquered territory, and you could feel it. And it never would get out of your bones."[2]

She began writing *Gone With the Wind* in 1926. Ten years later, it was published to wide acclaim, second only to the Bible in popularity. Even though it was awarded the Pulitzer Prize, the author steadfastly refused requests to write a sequel. Translated into 70 languages, it has sold more than 30 million copies.

In 1939, it was made into what the Guiness Book of World Records calls "the most successful film in cinema history." It broke all records, selling over 200 million tickets in the United States and Canada.

While walking across the street in Atlanta, Margaret Mitchell was struck by a drunk driver on August 11, 1949, dying on August 16 at the age of only 48.

ATLANTA, GEORGIA, 1898. A magnificent photograph of six Confederate veterans. These old soldiers, some of them maimed by war, served as Miss Winnie Davis's last escort at the Confederate Reunion in Atlanta in 1898. The *Daughter of the Confederacy* died later that year at the age of 34. From the United Confederate Veterans camp # 435, they are W.M. Dunbar, W.I. Delph, F.E. Eve, W.A. Gibbes, W.J. Steed, and George P. Bush.

BRINKLEY, ARKANSAS, ca. 1901. This photograph of a lovely young girl was found in a box of discarded photographs in an antique mall. It is a shame that formerly cherished family photos often end up this way.

MOBILE, ALABAMA, ca. 1895. Another discarded photo found in an antique store. This handsome Alabama boy meant something to someone years ago. He even left his name on the back: H.E. Flagger.

TULSA, INDIAN TERRITORY, ca. 1900. All that is known about this unusual photograph is that it was made by the Hubbert Studio of Tulsa. Notice that all of the men are holding what appears to be advertisements for a shoe company. Was this perhaps a group of well-known people – maybe entertainers – who are endorsing a particular brand of footwear? The picture appears to have been taken on a stage somewhere. Could the presence of the young boy and the little girl indicate that this may have been a popular family act? Or, could this be a family shoe enterprise? Perhaps this is a photograph of the father, his sons, and daughter advertising their line of footwear. One of the men is showing off a pair of high lace-up leather boots. The young boy is wearing a new pair of leather shoes, and the little girl has a pair of button-up shoes. The older man has a pair of high-topped, lace-up boots underneath the legs of his trousers, while the man in the center of the picture is wearing some loose-top boots (waders?) in which he has stuffed some of those mysterious papers.

PIKE COUNTY, ALABAMA, ca. 1895. It's early fall, and men are bringing their wagons full of freshly-picked cotton to John McLendon's gin. John was a private in Company I, 15th Alabama Infantry when they charged up Little Round Top at Gettysburg. He served until surrendered with Robert E. Lee at Appomattox. (Photo courtesy Marty McLendon)

PASS CHRISTIAN, MISSISSIPPI, ca. 1913. Mrs. John Ayer, owner of *Beaulieu*, offered her home to President Woodrow Wilson as a winter retreat, thus the name, Dixie White House. It was heavily damaged by Hurricane Camille in 1969 and was demolished shortly afterwards.

Charleston, S. C. Calhoun Monument - Marion Square.

CHARLESTON, SOUTH CAROLINA, ca. 1908. A postcard view of the impressive monument to John C. Calhoun, the South's preeminent statesman of the 19th century. Beginning his career in the House of Representatives, Calhoun served as Secretary of War under President Monroe, Vice-President under Presidents John Quincy Adams and Andrew Jackson, Secretary of State under President Tyler, and U.S. Senator from South Carolina, a position he held until his death in 1850. Calhoun defined and made practical application of the great constitutional principle of state's rights, a cherished doctrine of lovers of freedom the world over, the basis of which supported the South in her quest for independence during the 1860s as well as her defense against forced integration in the 1960s. In his last piece of correspondence, ten years before the North and South went to war, Calhoun wrote that it was "difficult to see how two peoples so different and hostile can exist together in one common Union." Calhoun has been labeled the best orator America ever produced, yet this magnificent monument has repeatedly been vandalized by those who seek to eradicate every aspect of the culture of the white South.

266

DALLAS, TEXAS, ca. 1908. An old postcard view of the Confederate War Memorial in Pioneer Park Cemetery in downtown Dallas. It was designed by Frank Teich, a German-born American sculptor who was responsible for at least one third of all the Confederate monuments in Texas. The cornerstone for this elaborate monument was laid in 1896. It was dedicated by the United Daughters of the Confederacy on April 29, 1897, in a ceremony which drew thousands, including hundreds of Confederate veterans. The monument was originally located at City Park but was moved to the cemetery because of the construction of a freeway. Still, seedy politicians and black operatives are calling for the complete destruction of this magnificent work of art – a memorial to Texas soldiers.

267

ST. LOUIS, MISSOURI, ca. 1895. Many a Southern boy attended military school in the South's numerous military academies. This handsome young cadet had his picture made in the studio of F.W. Guerin, located at 409 North Broadway in St. Louis.

PEWEE VALLEY, KENTUCKY, ca. 1904. Confederate veterans while away the hours in the comfortable sitting room of the Confederate Home, founded in 1902 to take care of Kentucky's aging soldiers. (Photo courtesy of the Kentucky Historical Society)

KENTUCKY, ca. 1910. A family with their buggy and team -- probably more reliable than one of those newfangled horseless carriages.

ST. BERNARD PARISH, LOUISIANA, ca. 1907. Variously known as Four Oaks and Three Oaks, this magnificent plantation home was built in 1831 for Sylvain Peyroux, a successful sugar planter. A local landmark for years, it was one of the largest homes south of New Orleans. Unfortunately, it became the property of American Sugar Refining Company, which suddenly, without prior warning, demolished the house in 1966. Even though the loss was devastating, the destruction of this beautiful place galvanized Louisianans into being more aggressive in saving what few old plantation homes still exist.

The picture above is a post-card view. The picture to the right was taken sometime before the house was demolished in 1966. Neglect has led to the sad demise of many of these old Louisiana plantation homes, but sugar refineries, railroads, and oil refineries account for much of the needless destruction.

270

WESTWEGO, LOUISIANA, 1923. A stately antebellum home called Seven Oaks, across the river south of New Orleans. Built in 1840, it is shown here crumbling to ruins, surrounded by big black oil tanks, neglected by its railroad company owners. This wonderful home no longer exists.

WILKINSON COUNTY, GEORGIA, April 24, 1866. It had been two years since William Green Lewis had enlisted in the army, and it had been one year since the end of the war, but William was so proud of his Confederate uniform that he got married in it. That's the day this ambrotype was made. It mattered little to William that the uniform was too big. After all, he was only 15 when he joined Company D of the 8th regiment of Georgia Militia. What mattered to William was his love for the Confederacy and that uniform, a feeling shared by his descendants today. (Photo courtesy of Miriam Brown)

VIRGINIA, July, 1861. These are the confident faces of the Southern army shortly before it virtually annihilated the blustering, pompous Army of the United States in the first battle at Manassas Junction. Had our young heroes in gray been able to foresee the years of tribulation awaiting the South, they surely would have marched on, tired though they were, into Washington, taking the city and ending the war within the space of a few days.

273

COLUMBIA, SOUTH CAROLINA, ca. 1910. The fire department with their fire engine. (Photo courtesy of South Caroliniana Library)

McALESTER, INDIAN TERRITORY, June 14, 1906. (opposite page) These are the retiring officers of the Christian Endeavor in Indian Territory at their 16th annual convention. An inter-denominational organization, Christian Endeavor was founded in 1881 for youth in their teenage years. Members of all churches were welcomed as members. The lady in the front row, second person from the left, has a ribbon that says "First Christian Church." The 20-year-old man on the back row is J.Y. Wheeler, who belonged to the Methodist Church. The only other identifiable person in the picture is Dr. Mott. He is the first person on the left, sitting in the front row. (Photo courtesy of Margaret Wheeler)

BOWLING GREEN, KENTUCKY, November 20, 1884. A handsome Kentucky boy, Leonard Phebus, at the age of seventeen.

ATLANTA, GEORGIA, ca. 1885. On the back of this nice cabinet print, produced by the T. E. Hudson Studio of Atlanta, this pretty Georgia belle wrote, "To my darling sweetheart, with fondest love." The only thing she left out was her name.

Oh, those wonderful new Kodaks! They were so popular in the early 1900s. In the top photo, a young man named George tries to sell a No. 2 Flexo Kodak to a man in a store thought to be in Texas. The photograph below shows several new owners trying out their Kodaks. The Spanish moss and live oak trees indicate a location in the lower South.

ATLANTA, GEORGIA, ca. 1885. This handsome man posed for his picture in the C.W. Motes Studio, located at 34 Whitehall Street. The Motes Studio won a gold medal at the International Cotton Exposition in 1881.

This unidentified soldier – only a teenager – rushed to the front to protect his family and home. The Yankees were on their way, murdering, burning homes, and violating women. The front lines made men out of boys overnight. Thousands would never even return home. This young soldier was one of the heroes for whom the South built everlasting memorials, and yet today's lazy, drug-ridden, disgusting generation of spoiled brats, some in their 20s, 30s, and 40s, run around the country vandalizing the monuments we erected to the memory of young men like the one in this picture. (Photo courtesy of Paige Sawyer)

Belle Boyd, born in 1844 in Virginia, was educated at Mount Washington Female College, then went on to become a debutante in Washington, D.C., at the age of 17, shortly before the war broke out. Becoming a spy for the Confederacy, Belle was arrested many times, once spending five months in a Yankee prison. In 1862, she endangered her life by rushing onto the field, bullets tearing holes in her dress, to advise Stonewall Jackson of the Yankee strength at Front Royal, information which allowed him to destroy the command of General Banks two days later at Winchester.

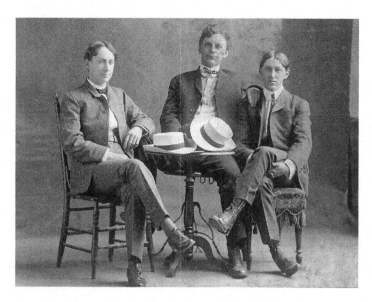

OWENSBORO, KENTUCKY, ca. 1900. Posing for the camera in Smither's Studio are Preston Haden, Tobe Phipps, and Will Coleman.

KENTUCKY, ca. 1910. This is one of those photographs made into a postcard, popular in the first two decades of the 20th century. It was an easy way to send family pictures to relatives.

PENSACOLA, FLORIDA, 1861. A Confederate camp at the Warrington Navy Yard. Bands of Southerners like these, with very little in the way of uniforms and only the weapons they brought from home, kept a huge Yankee army at bay for four years. They were often called "The Eighth Wonder of the World."

FREDERICK, OKLAHOMA, ca. 1920. (Courtesy of James Redeker)

ST. LOUIS, MISSOURI, ca. 1897.
This fashionable lady had her picture made
at the Smith Studio in St. Louis.

283

NASHVILLE, TENNESSEE, ca. 1899. Like so many old family photos, this one ended up in a cardboard box in an antique mall. First published in *When the South Was Southern*, nothing was known about it. Then, one of my readers identified this pretty lady as Josephine Austin of Nashville. The picture was probably made about the time of Josephine's marriage to James Alexander Wemyss on June 21, 1899. (Information courtesy of Ken Thomson)

284

SHREVEPORT, LOUISIANA, ca. 1920. A little boy named Edwin pretending to crank somebody's automobile.

RICHMOND, VIRGINIA, ca. 1910. This is an old postcard view of the White House of the Confederacy, occupied by President Davis from 1861 through 1865. From here he directed the day to day affairs of government in our quest for Southern independence – our late, lamented Lost Cause.

285

Soldiers' Monument, Eufaula, Ala.

EUFAULA, ALABAMA, 1910. The South was riven by four years of brutal war and scarred by twelve more years of oppressive occupation by enemy forces. Poor though it was, it was determined to build monuments to its soldiers, once boys and young men but now aging veterans. Ladies of the South raised the money by bake sales, bazaars, and little home plays until they had enough to build impressive memorials that rivaled the famous monuments of France. This one in Eufaula is but one example of the thousands that grace the South today.

286

CONFEDERATE MONUMENT, TRAVIS PARK, SAN ANTONIO, TEX.

SAN ANTONIO, TEXAS, ca. 1907. This magnificent Confederate monument was financed by the ladies of the UDC who held bake sales, teas, quilting bees, and bazaars. Designed by Elizabeth Montgomery of Louisiana, it was the first monument in the United States to be designed by a woman. In 1899, the city council, by unanimous vote, gave the United Daughters of the Confederacy perpetual use of the land for the statue. It stood in Travis Park for 118 years, but in 2017 the city council took it over and destroyed it under cover of darkness.

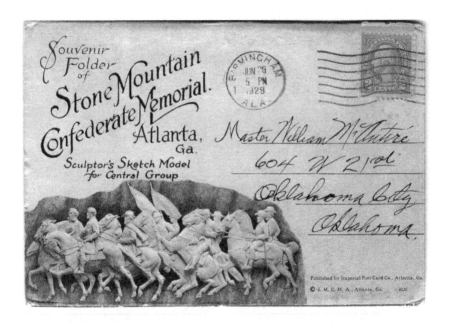

ATLANTA, GEORGIA. This postcard folder was mailed on June 26, 1929. Inside the folder are several pictures of the proposed monument, along with the following presentation:

"Stone Mountain, sixteen miles northeast of Atlanta, Georgia, is the largest solid body of granite in the world. It stands alone in the midst of a plain, nearly 1,000 feet high, seven miles around the base, and a mile to the summit up the sloping side. It is older than the Rocky Mountains, the Appalachian Mountains, the Alps, or the Himalayas. On the north side, which is an almost perpendicular precipice, the greatest monument of all time is now being carved in memory of the soldiers of the Southern Confederacy. It will consist of a central or reviewing group, representing the Confederate leadership of Davis, Lee, and Jackson and groups of infantry, cavalry, and artillery. The equestrian figures in the central group will be as tall as a ten-story building. Below the central group, a great memorial Hall, to be dedicated to the women of the Confederacy, will be carved out of solid granite at the base of the mountain, every architectural detail consisting of solid granite, undetached from the mother lode, so that Memorial Hall will endure as long as the mountain endures."

Carving was supposed to begin in 1916 by Gutzon Borglum, but he was not able to begin work until 1923 because of funding problems and World War I. In 1925 a dispute arose, and Borglum left to carve the famous Mount Rushmore. Augustus Lukeman began carving in 1925, but by 1928 construction was once again halted, and the monument stood untouched for 36 years. In 1958, the state purchased the mountain and the carving was finally completed in 1972.

Davis, Lee, Jackson, and color bearer in master model for central group.

ATLANTA, GEORGIA, July 20, 1925. These men took charge of the sale of the South's share of the Confederate Memorial Half Dollars, the proceeds of which were used to finance the carving. Pictured here are the governors of Florida, South Carolina, Alabama, and Mississippi, and dignitaries representing the governors of Tennessee, Oklahoma, Kentucky, Virginia, Louisiana, and Texas, as well as the Commander-in-Chief of the UCV, and the president and four members of the Stone Mountain Memorial Association.

This is the model for the Memorial Hall that was to be carved into the base of the mountain. An ambitious project for a South still reeling from carpetbag governments, it was difficult to raise enough money to finish the job, so the Memorial Hall with its reflecting pool was never constructed. Tragically, even the carving itself has become the target of political hoodlums, much like Hitler's "brown shirts," who call for blasting it off the mountain. In his frightening novel, *1984*, George Orwell warned of such a perilous turn of events in this country.

290

Home of Confederate Soldiers, Beauvoir, Miss.
Pub. by Martin & O'Neal, Gulfport, Miss. — Made in Germany

BILOXI, MISSISSIPPI, ca. 1907. This old postcard view of *Beauvoir* was made while Confederate soldiers were living in the home. Some of the old soldiers can be seen on the front steps and near one of the live oak trees in the yard. In 1902, thirteen years after President Davis died, his widow, Varina, sold the property to the Mississippi Division of the Sons of Confederate Veterans with the stipulation that it be used as a home for Confederate veterans and later as a memorial to her husband. Barracks and other buildings were constructed on the 52-acre site, and the property served as Mississippi's Confederate Veterans Home until the last soldier died in 1953. Afterwards, the home was restored and eventually turned into the Confederate shrine that we know today. *Beauvoir* is a National Historic Landmark and is still owned by the Mississippi Division of the Sons of Confederate Veterans.

In 1969, *Beauvoir*, located on the beach at Biloxi, survived Hurricane Camille, but on August 19, 2005, Hurricane Katrina almost destroyed the home. Most of the other historic buildings were washed away, but the home stood, even through the 24-foot storm surge that tore through the building. After two long years of painstaking restoration, *Beauvoir* once again opened its doors to the public on June 3, 2008, the 200th anniversary of Jefferson Davis's birth. Now, "The Shrine of the South," as it has been called, is open again for tours on a regular basis.

291

NASHVILLE, TENNESSEE, ca. 1908. The U.S. government steadfastly refused to provide pensions or old age assistance of any kind to Confederate soldiers, even though taxes were extracted from Southerners to pay for fat pensions given to Union veterans. As a result, the southern states dug into their meager reserves and provided pensions, as well as homes, for their aging Confederate veterans. Some of the states, such as Texas and Virginia, built in the cottage style, while others such as Georgia, Oklahoma, and Tennessee, built in the "grand hall" style. The Confederate Home in Tennessee, as shown above, was constructed in 1894 on land originally belonging to Andrew Jackson. The state had bought the remaining 500 acres of Jackson's estate in 1859. Thirty years later, when it proposed using the deteriorating mansion as a home for Confederate veterans, several local women swung into action to oppose the plan. Hurriedly organizing the Ladies' Hermitage Association, they tried to persuade the General Assembly to sell the entire property to them. Under-estimating Tennesseans' devotion to their Confederate soldiers, the women were rebuffed when the Assembly decided to retain 475 acres for construction of a Confederate Home, letting the ladies have the mansion and only 25 acres. For some reason, all of the soldiers were suddenly removed from the home in 1916 and forced into quarters at the Tennessee Industrial School. In 1935, the remaining 475 acres, including the Confederate Home, was transferred to the women operating the *Hermitage*, and they lost no time in demolishing it, using the bricks for their new visitors' center. (Photo courtesy of Bert Jared)

Confederate Home, Ardmore, Okla.

Construction began on Oklahoma's Confederate Home in Ardmore in June, 1910, and opened in July of the next year to full capacity. An additional two buildings were soon constructed to house an overflow of applicants. The postcard view was made about 1911, while the photograph below, showing a newly arrived load of watermelons, was made in 1914. This is the last Confederate Home built in the grand hall style left in the world.

293

NATCHEZ, MISSISSIPPI, ca. 1933. Mississippi's only surviving example of a plantation home with a fully encircling colonnade, *Dunleith* was built about 1855 or shortly thereafter by Charles Dahlgren who would become a Confederate general in the ensuing war. In 1858, Dahlgren sold it to Alfred Vidal Davis, who would also become an officer in the Confederate army.

Natchez sent six generals and more than fifteen military units to the Confederacy, and in later years, with its wealth of antebellum homes, the city would proudly call itself "Natchez , where the Old South still lives" as it invited people to visit the city and tour its elegant old homes. But social justice warriors slinked into the city in the early 1970s and began remaking the city into something it never was. The Old South slogan was changed to "Natchez, a good place to live." The Confederate flag that welcomed folks to Natchez was removed. The beautiful Confederate Pageant that ran at night during Pilgrimage was reinvented and renamed "Natchez Tableau." Then, promoting a false history of the town, these revisionists claim that Natchez had been a Union stronghold because of a handful of wealthy planters who held pro-Union sentiments, even though the sons of several of those planters served in the Confederate army. Today, some of those old homes are still available for tours, but they take a back seat to balloon races, motorcycle rallies, gun and knife shows, and various weekend events that can be found anywhere. Trying to mimic the international scene, these folks showcase Mexican restaurants, French cafes, Italian eateries, and bistros, but you have to cross over into Louisiana if you want fried chicken, gravy, biscuits, cornbread, blackeyed peas, and iced tea.

LEXINGTON, KENTUCKY, ca. 1861. A lady and her little boy in the photographic studio of W.R. Phipps in Lexington.

BROOKFIELD, MISSOURI, ca. 1860s. This young man posed for his picture in the studio of J.C. Gardner in Brooksville.

A LADY OF ARKANSAS, ca. 1863

NEW ORLEANS, LOUISIANA, April, 1923. "The crucial moment was the passing of the aged veterans with their timeworn battle flags. All of a sudden, you would hear a silence descend, and when you looked up you saw this great mass of blood-red flags, held high with their white stars, and a long line of old men shuffling along. And nobody said a word, but tears just flowed down everybody's cheeks. That was your nation that you were crying over, and you knew it."[3]

Every year, the United Confederate Veterans held a grand reunion in some southern city. Every large city wanted to host it, so it was passed around from year to year. Attended by thousands, it was a grand event that lasted for several days. Confederate flags lined the business district, and the red carpet was rolled out all over town for the old soldiers. These were the South's heroes, and every form of hospitality was extended them. The high point of the reunions were the parades, the main attraction of which were the aging old soldiers who walked or rode horses down the center of admiring throngs.

Age was thinning out the ranks, but the old soldiers still showed plenty of spunk. During their business sessions at New Orleans, the membership rejected a suggestion that all future reunions be held in conjunction with Union veterans, denounced those who claimed that the South had rebelled against the Constitution, and railed against the "teaching of false history in the schools."

In the picture above, a small contingent of veterans, the youngest of whom were already in their 70s, steps out into line of march. When it began to rain, a reporter asked one old soldier if he might be afraid of getting wet. "Rain's not botherin' us," he replied. "We're all too well seasoned to get warped."[4]

298

RALEIGH, NORTH CAROLINA, ca. 1910. This impressive Confederate monument, dedicated to the memory of North Carolina soldiers, was unveiled on May 20, 1895. Seventy-five feet tall, it stands in front of the State House. But, like so many other priceless cultural objects in the South's deracinated cities, it has become the target of lazy, restless mobs with subversive names like Smash Racism Raleigh, Young Democratic Socialists of America, and Youth Fighting United States Empire, who vandalize it and threaten its removal "by whatever means necessary." [Addendum. As this book goes to press, the monument was destroyed after the governor, this time a demoniac Democrat, sent word that he wanted it removed. The mob showed up and obliged him.]

299

SUSAN BRADFORD
ca. 1863

Susan Bradford was born March 8, 1846 at Pine Hill Plantation in Leon County, Florida. The plantation was established by her father, Dr. Edward Bradford, and consisted of 3,270 acres north of Tallahassee. Following the war, on November 1, 1866, Susan married a former Confederate officer, Nicholas Ware Eppes, whose father owned a plantation about five miles from Pine Hill. After the war, Nicholas, who was a grandson of Thomas Jefferson, served as County Superintendent of Public Instruction before assuming management of Pine Hill plantation. In 1904, he was brutally murdered. Three blacks stood trial for the murder, and one was executed. The family always believed that corrupt state officials were behind the murder, fearing Nicholas might reveal details of

300

political corruption. After the murder, Susan withdrew from the public eye, but after a period of grieving she resumed her position among Tallahassee's social elite, becoming active in the United Daughters of the Confederacy and the Daughters of the American Revolution. In her later years, Mrs. Eppes wrote a volume of poetry and a number of historical articles, but she is best remembered for her valuable reminiscences of 19th-century life in north Florida. She authored two books, her last a riveting account of antebellum life, the war years, and the ordeals of Reconstruction titled *Through Some Eventful Years*. A few lines of her Reconstruction experience follows.

"Carpetbaggers swarmed down upon the land, sowing the seeds of hate and discord between the whites and blacks. . . . A man who called himself Saunders, and seemed to be able to walk unlimited miles without tiring, made incendiary speeches throughout the county. Gin-houses were fired; many bales of cotton were destroyed; dwelling houses were watched by the occupants thereof, night and day; sometimes torches were found and extinguished before it was too late; and occasionally a dwelling burned to the ground. Life became a horrid nightmare. Crimes, too vile for words, became of frequent occurrence and it came to be, in what had once been considered the center of civilization, that "every man's home was his castle" in reality. Guns and pistols were kept loaded and ready; yes, and the women and children, the larger ones, were taught to use these weapons for their personal protection. . . . The incessant haling of our men and our women as well, before a military tribunal, to be tried and condemned, without the slightest pretense of justice, aroused intense bitterness. We did not know when morning dawned what might befall us ere the sun went down. Insolence from the negroes became more and more frequent. Much of this friction could have been prevented, but feeling ran high on both sides. Then the Freedman's Bureau was established and the carpetbaggers came like unto an army of locusts, seeking what they could devour. If life for the Southerner was hard before, it became almost unendurable under these conditions. Yes, the Old South was slowly but surely dying; that is to say, the Old South was dying politically, financially and socially, but the spirit of the Old South can never die. So long as a loyal son or daughter of the Old South remains, they will recall with pride the glorious deeds of the armies of the Southern Confederacy; they will speak with tenderness of the war work of Southern women; they will *Tell it to the last of times, No Nation rose so fair and white, Nor fell so free of crimes.*" The traditions, the principles, the customs of bygone days will be forever cherished, and we hug to our hearts these comforting lines:

> *Truth crushed to earth will rise again,*
> *The eternal years of God are hers,*
> *While error, wounded, writhes in pain*
> *And dies amid her worshipers.* [5]

301

And so we close this chapter with three photographs of more recent vintage. This postcard was produced by Cypress Gardens in Florida, where the pyramid stunt was performed four times daily. Three people on skis, two people on their shoulders, and the Confederate flag at the top. The South was commemorating the centennial of the War Between the States during the early '60s. It was a time when we were comfortable with who we were. No wringing of the hands over slavery – it was just a relic of the historic past and, like horse and buggy days, gone forever. It was a time before Hollywood fictionalized the South and made it into something it never was. We knew who we were, and we were proud of it.

The picture above was made in Oklahoma during the 1980s. Below is a picture of the majorettes in the Robert E. Lee High School Band of Montgomery, Alabama, holding the state flag, the flag of the school band, and the Confederate flag. It was probably made in the 1960s.

"There stands Jackson like a stone wall. Rally on the Virginians!"

— GENERAL BARNARD BEE, CSA

VIII

Confederate Heroes

The South is a land of heroes, strewn from border to border with thousands of monuments to those who put duty above self and left in their wake a fabulous southern legacy. Their deeds, permanently recorded in granite, marble, and bronze, shine as a beacon to the youth of every generation. Hardly is there a community in the South without its graven memorial to valor, from the simple block of stone in a rural Arkansas town to Richmond's magnificent Monument Row with its overwhelming statues of Lee, Davis, Jackson, and Stuart.

The panorama of southern history, from the earliest days of the Lost Colony of Roanoke and Jamestown, is resplendent with individuals of courage and resolve. Who can match the roll call of southern statesmen during the American Revolution and the first fifty years under the newly acquired republic? Patrick Henry, John Randolph, James Madison, George Washington, Thomas Jefferson, James Monroe, Light-Horse Harry Lee, Daniel Boone, Davy Crockett, Andrew Jackson, John C. Calhoun, John Tyler, Zachary Taylor, James K. Polk – to name but a few. These men are truly national figures, for we share them with a nation who proudly concurs in their achievements.

But it is to the heroes of the Lost Cause that Southerners give more attention, not from any lack of national patriotism, as has been our criticism, but rather from a fuller measure of patriotic honor and vindication. Southerners are raised on hero worship. It's a part of our heritage. We're taught from childhood to emulate the deeds of great men and to revere their memory. Whether the cause succeeds or fails is not the point; if it is right in precept, we accord the honor.

While compiling this book, I visited many commemorative sites in the South, finding one of the most inspiring attractions in Chattanooga, Tennessee. It was there that I encountered a young man who, probably on a vacation trip through the South, had run head-on into the southern emphasis upon paying homage to our Confederate defenders. He seemed quite aggravated by it all when I ran afoul of him. The place was Confederama, a wonderful diorama of the battles around Chattanooga, expertly produced with lights, music, and a taped narrative that leaves no doubt as to which side should have won the war.

As several were milling around the souvenirs in the lobby, I couldn't help but notice the man, who looked to be near thirty, purchasing his ticket for the next narration. The elderly hostess, who was as gracious as she could be, welcomed him with a smile as she handed him the ticket and made change for him. To every-thing she said he grunted impatiently, then began pacing the floor, nervously awaiting the doors to open. Soon, the hostess announced that we could go on in, and we filed into the room as she turned up the music. The sounds of *Dixie* had already raised the hair on my arms, and I followed the man through the audi-torium door, feeling about a foot taller after the music started.

About three feet ahead of me, he abruptly stopped, glanced at the diorama and the displays around the wall, and said to me in a curt, sneering tone, "These people down here take this stuff seriously, don't they?"

I was caught completely off guard, and at first said

306

nothing. *Dixie* was blaring away in the background, and I was mentally unprepared to deal with a man who had paid three dollars for the privilege of scorning a popular patriotic attraction. Recognizing the contempt in his voice, I finally responded, "Well, yes sir, they do, and I'm one of them!"

"Well, I'm not," he said in his clipped brogue. "I'm from Hawaii, and I don't know why you people fought all those wars and why you keep fighting them!" (Now, for the record, he was not one of those tanned-skin, congenial natives.)

"We were invaded by the North. We picked up our guns and shot back. That's why we fought. And I dare say that you would have fought, too, had you been invaded."

"We were invaded," he snapped.

"Not by Yankees, you weren't."

"By the Japanese – in World War II."

"And did you fight back?"

Now here I could see *his* pride showing through. Elevating his chest as would befit a naval midshipman in dress parade, he fairly bristled as he blustered, "Yes, we fought back, and we whipped them, too."

"And did you build monuments to the memory of your military dead there in Pearl Harbor?"

"Of course, we did," he answered, as if I were the one asking foolish questions now.

"Well, sir, now you know why we fought all those wars, as you call them, and why we remember."

That was what I said. I hope it was a little bit of southern manners that kept me from saying what I wanted to say. I would like to have told him that when his funds for the U.S.S. Arizona Memorial in Pearl Harbor were running low it was a *southern* boy by the name of Elvis Presley who came to his rescue!

Sadly, on a later visit to Chattanooga, the withering forces of political correctness had exacted their toll. Confederama had undergone a name change. It is now Battles for Chattanooga Museum. When I expressed my displeasure at the loss of the old name, someone explained, "Well, we have Yankees coming through here, so we have to please both sides." I guess the unhappy man from Hawaii would like it now.

Because we give so much honor to our Confederate heroes we are eternally accused of "still fighting the war" as if we actually enjoy acknowledging the carnage, the destruction, the famine of that holocaust! No, we're not still fighting the war; we're still giving the glory. There is something intangible about a lost cause that specially marks its heroes, and I suppose that only a Southerner – or one who has gone down with a lost cause – can comprehend the peculiar devotion it generates. Henry Timrod captured its essence when, in 1867, he wrote an ode to be sung at the decoration of Confederate graves in Charleston's Magnolia Cemetery. Called the most perfect ode in the English language, here is the last stanza:

> Stoop, angels, hither from the skies,
> There is no holier spot of ground
> Than where defeated valor lies,
> By mourning beauty crowned!

A hero – or heroine – is usually someone who risks life and limb, and certainly a protracted war provides the arena from which the brave are beckoned. The contest for our independence ground on for four long years in the literal yards of our homes, requiring the utmost of every man, woman, and child who except for the exigencies of a home front war would have remained uncalled to heroic deeds.

So, in a sense, everyone became a hero by merely opposing the onslaught. Certainly, the aged man of seventy who marched away to bolster the thinning ranks of gray and face the Yankee soldier of twenty would have to be counted a hero, as well as the teenage boy who, not much more than a child, fell in the front lines, ripped by torturous fire from a thousand enemy guns. Poor George Lamkin, of Winona, Mississippi, was only eleven years old when wounded at the bloody Battle of Shiloh. Every man who shouldered a gun in defense of his home deserves a hero's tribute. Honor, also, to the faithful slave who outwitted the Yankee soldier and saved his master's home from the torch. And the noble woman of the South! Who cried more tears, sewed more socks, read more casualty lists, prayed more prayers, buried more sons? Who could have endured more – and complained less – than the southern woman? Yet, never did she raise her voice to claim her rightful station as heroine of the Lost Cause, but was content, rather, to enshrine the warriors of the battlefield in the temple of a country's praise.

Heroes every one of them, and yet convention dictates that some must rise above others to become the objects of our collective gratitude. Even so, the roll of honor is awesome, and it was exceedingly difficult for this author to have to arbitrarily select from it only a small number for inclusion in this volume. Left unheralded here are the feats of the flamboyant "Cavalier of Dixie," Jeb Stuart, who, with his twelve hundred cavalrymen, rode completely around the Federal army of 115,000 before Richmond; the fearless spy, Belle Boyd, who dashed wildly through an open field in front of the Federal army, waving her bonnet to the Confederates as a sign to advance; the elusive "Gray Ghost," John S. Mosby, who entered enemy lines one night with six men, capturing a Yankee general asleep in his bedroom; the courageous George Pickett and his 15,000 men who had to make the dreadful assault upon Cemetery Ridge; the daring young John Pelham – "the gallant Pelham" – whose two small artillery guns held the entire enemy at bay in Fredericksburg; the enormously brave scout, DeWitt Smith Jobe, who, like Sam Davis, refused to divulge his information and was consequently tortured by his Yankee captors who put out his eyes, cut out his tongue, and strangled him to death with a piece of leather; the intrepid southern spy, Rose O'Neal Greenhow, who was carrying gold and important dispatches from England when she drowned off the North Carolina coast, weighted down by gold coins sewn into her clothes for secrecy; the 247 young cadets from VMI who aided General Breckinridge in defeating the Yankees at New Market, Virginia; and a host of others equally valiant.

> Can the victors give a reason
> Why the men who wore the gray
> From our hearts should march away
> And should pass from us forever
> Like the dreamings of the night?

— Abram Joseph Ryan

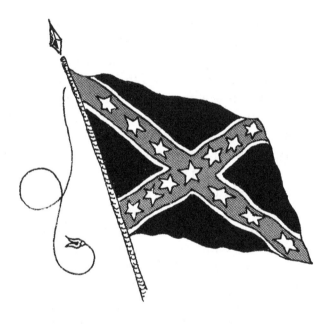

JEFFERSON DAVIS

A biographical sketch cannot begin to do justice to the memory of a man who was arguably the most qualified and distinguished statesman in America by the time of the demise of the three political giants, Calhoun, Clay, and Webster, in the early 1850s. Had it not been for the war that intervened, he might well have been President of the United States, and if his prior accomplishments were a presage of a possible presidency, no doubt he would have ranked with Washington, Jefferson, and Jackson as the best remembered representatives of that office. His name had, in fact, been placed in nomination at the Democratic National Convention in 1860, but he did not seek the position, preferring instead to work for the nomination of John C. Breckinridge.

Such was the pattern of his life. He was not instinctively imbued with political ambition. To the contrary, his biographer, Hudson Strode, observed that history pursued Davis. In nearly every instance of his life, his candidacy or appointment was pressed upon him by his friends, and out of a deep sense of duty he served in public office; but his most contented hours were spent at his plantation on the Mississippi River and later in the balmy, serene environment of *Beauvoir* on the Gulf Coast.

Jefferson Finis Davis was the tenth child of Samuel Davis and Jane Cook. His father, who had fought in the Revolutionary War, was a Georgian of Welsh descent. His mother was a South Carolinian of Scotch ancestry. After the birth of five children, the Davises moved to Kentucky where Jefferson was born on June 3, 1808 in a rural area now known as the village of Fairview. During his infancy, the family moved to Wilkinson County, Mississippi, where young Jefferson grew to manhood in the low country of the Deep South.

In November, 1889, only a month before his death, he dictated a brief autobiography for Belford's Magazine. Concerning his education, he said, "After passing through the county academy I entered Transylvania College, Kentucky, and was advanced as far as the senior class when, at the age of 16, I was appointed to the United States Military Academy at West Point, which I entered in September, 1824. I graduated in 1828, and then, in accordance with the custom of cadets, entered active service with the rank of lieutenant." [1]

At Transylvania, he developed a lifelong friendship with George W. Jones, a boy from Iowa who would later become a general in the U.S. army and U.S. Senator from Iowa. Jones de-

312

scribed Davis at college as "always gay and brimful of buoyant spirits, but without the smallest tendency toward vice or immorality. He had that innate refinement and gentleness that distinguished him through life. He was always a gentleman in the highest sense of the word." [2]

Judge Peters of Mount Sterling, Kentucky, remembered him as a good student who was "always prepared with his lessons, very respectful and polite to the president and professors. I never heard him reprimanded for neglecting his studies or for misconduct of any sort. . . . He was amiable, prudent and kind to all with whom he was associated, and beloved by teachers and students." [3]

At West Point, a fellow cadet described him. "Jefferson Davis was distinguished in the corps for his manly bearing, his high-toned and lofty character. His figure was very soldier-like and rather robust; his step springy, resembling the tread of an Indian 'brave' on the war path." [4]

Davis saw routine duty on the frontier and distinguished himself when, in 1832, his detachment cut off the retreat of Black Hawk, thus ending the Black Hawk War.

It was also in 1832 that Davis evinced his firm belief in the doctrine of states' rights. South Carolina had drawn the wrath of President Jackson over the nullification issue, and it looked for a time as if the regiment to which Davis belonged would be sent into South Carolina. He would later write of the incident.

"By education, by association, and by preference, I was a soldier, then regarding that profession as my vocation for life. Yet, looking the issues squarely in the face, I chose the alternative of abandoning my profession rather than be employed in the subjugation of, or coercion of, a State of the Union, and had fully determined and was prepared to resign my commission immediately."[5] Fortunately, the confrontation never occurred.

In June, 1835, Davis resigned his commission and married Sarah Knox Taylor, daughter of Col. Zachary Taylor, future President of the United States. He then settled into the satisfying life of planter at *Brierfield*, his plantation on the Mississippi River near Vicksburg. But tragedy was waiting in the wings and struck like lightning. Sarah died of malaria only two months after their wedding. Davis, severely depressed, lived in "great seclusion," as he put it, for seven years "on the plantation in the swamps of the Mississippi." [6]

On February 26, 1845, he married Varina Anne Howell, of Natchez, Mississippi. In November, he was elected to the U.S. House of Representatives where he served until June, 1846. At that time, a regiment of Mississippi volunteers was organized at Vicksburg for duty in the Mexican War, and it would have none other than Jefferson Davis as its colonel. Resigning his seat in Congress, Davis and the Mississippians proceeded to Mexico, where he further distinguished himself by bravery and ingenuity at Monterey and Buena Vista, returning to the United States as a hero of the Mexican War. At Monterey, he was one of three commissioners appointed by General Taylor to receive the surrender and carry on negotiations for the capitulation. President Polk attempted to reward Davis for his meritorious war service, but once again, principle and a firm belief in states' rights took precedence. Polk had offered him a commission as brigadier general of volunteers, but Davis refused it on the grounds that only states had the right to appoint officers in the militia.

History continued its pursuit of Jefferson Davis. As soon as he arrived home, the Mississippi legislature appointed him to the unexpired term of U.S. Senator Speight, who had died. After serving Senator Speight's term, Davis was elected for his own six-year term in 1850. The *Macon Telegraph and Messenger* wrote, "The historian, Prescott, pronounced him the most accomplished man in that body when it was full of giants." [7]

His plaudits did not go unnoticed. When the Democratic candidate for governor in Mississippi retired from the race in mid-stream, a call went forth for Davis to replace him in the governor's race. Oddly enough, Davis was not elected to the only state office for which he would ever run, but his mere candidacy had required him to resign the U.S. Senate seat; consequently, in 1852 he retired back to his plantation, although it would prove to be only a brief period of political inactivity. The newly-elected President Franklin Pierce was not content to let talent as that which Davis possessed lie idle on a remote Mississippi plantation. Though he had to work at persuading Davis to accept the position, Pierce finally succeeded and appointed him Secretary of War in 1853.

As Secretary of War, Davis was able to complete some of his previous proposals as Senator. Recognized by most historians as the ablest Secretary of War ever, his accomplishments are far too numerous to enumerate, although a few bear mentioning here. The Smithsonian Institution was established under his authority; he instituted the civil service system; he began the movement to construct a canal across Panama, designating the exact spot where construction began fifty years later; he had three routes surveyed for a transcontinental railroad; he introduced the rifled musket, the Minié ball, and the light infantry; and, he introduced a humanities program at West Point.

When his tenure as Secretary of War was up in 1857, he rejoined the Senate, having been reelected by his home state. By this time, North and South were in a shouting war, and the U.S. Senate was consumed, as was the House, with the constant elements of that controversy.

Northern historians have always delighted in promulgating the idea that Davis was a "hot-headed secessionist," *secessionist* being a bad word in their dream of centralized government. The myth is perpetuated in school textbooks today in an effort to discredit Davis and, in a larger sense, to discredit all who claimed state sovereignty and the right of secession. Notwithstanding their accusations, "Mr. Davis was active and earnest in his efforts to effect a compromise and reach a basis which would permit the Southern States to remain in the Union. He was a member of the committee of the Senate to whom was referred the famous Crittendon Compromise, and avowed himself willing to accept that or any other plan that the opposing factions could agree upon, and that promised any reasonable hope of success. But the Republican members of the committee rejected absolutely everything that the Northern and Southern Democrats and Whigs agreed on and seemed determined not to consent to anything that promised a settlement." [8]

His reticence concerning secession caused his fellow members of the Mississippi congressional delegation to suspect that he might be opposed to secession altogether; however, upon hearing that his state had seceded, he resigned from the Senate and made a farewell speech to his colleagues. In an emotional goodbye, he asserted Mississippi's right to secede, tempering it with an advocacy of peace and friendship between North and South. His illustrious career in Washington, D.C. came to an end as he walked out of the Senate chamber on January 21, 1861. That night, Mrs. Davis overheard him praying for peace.

The Davises went back to *Brierfield*, and Mr. Davis accepted a commission as Major General and was appointed commander-in-chief of all Mississippi volunteers. Though advocating peace, Davis was a prudent man. He recommended immediate military preparations "to meet the war which he believed the Republicans of the North would force upon the South." [9]

While thus engaged in Mississippi, he was not present at the meeting of the Provisional Congress of the Confederate States in Montgomery, Alabama, but on February 9, the delegates unanimously chose Davis as Provisional President of the new Confederacy, and a telegram was dispatched to Vicksburg immediately.

Jefferson Davis was helping Varina prune rose bushes at *Brierfield* on Sunday afternoon, February 10, when a courier arrived from Vicksburg with the telegram. History, in its relentless pursuit, was calling him to his greatest role – a role which he was inwardly reluctant to accept. Though quite humbled to be the recipient of such an offer, Davis had always enjoyed military pursuits and was expecting to aid his new country in that capacity; however, in his characteristic way, he answered the call of his people and made plans to leave for Montgomery.

Without a doubt he was the man for the job. In an interview with the *Baltimore Sun* on the day Davis died, John H. Reagan, U.S. Senator from Texas and former Postmaster-General of the Confederacy, voiced that sentiment.

"Mr. Davis was one of the few men who measured the full force of the war. He from the first contended that it was likely to last a number of years instead of a few months, as many persons predicted. It was at first proposed to enlist an army . . . for six months. Mr. Davis promptly disposed of that suggestion by declaring that it would take at least a year to organize an efficient army, as soldiers could not be made in a few days." [10]

Ironically, it was Davis who, after the complete rout of the Yankees in the first battle of the war, foresaw a chance to end the war at once by a vigorous pursuit of the fleeing enemy into Washington, only to find that he could not persuade his generals to advance.

Davis was under no delusions about an easy beginning for the new republic. His first letter to his wife after reaching Montgomery reveals his keen insight.

> I was inaugurated on Monday, having reached here on Saturday night. The audience was large and brilliant. Upon my weary heart was showered smiles, plaudits, and flowers; but, beyond them, I saw troubles and thorns innumerable.
>
> We are without machinery, without means, and threatened by a powerful opposition; but I do not despond, and will not shrink from the task imposed upon me. [11]

What a monumental task was before him! Within ninety days, he had to form a government and create a navy, an army, a currency, and a postal system. The South had only one rolling mill and one powder mill, and its ports were blockaded; but under his direction the new Confederacy brought forth a fighting unit that held the North at bay for four long years, and victory, except for the hand of Fate, was within its grasp on several occasions.

The victory at Manassas proved the value of his preparations. "At this period his popularity with his people knew no bounds. It was only after disaster came that grumblers arose to criticize and condemn his conduct of affairs; but he always had with him the hearts of an overwhelming majority of the soldiers and the people." [12]

Critics can always be found when reverses occur, and Davis had a very vocal one in the person of Edward Pollard, editor of the *Richmond Examiner*. Corporal Watkins, on the other hand, probably spoke for the average man in the trench, when he wrote, in 1881:

> Hon. Jefferson Davis perhaps made blunders and mistakes, but I honestly believe that he ever did what he thought best for the good of his country. And there never lived on this earth from the days of Hampden to George Washington, a purer patriot or a nobler man than Jefferson Davis; and, like Marius, grand even in ruins. [13]

Recognizing the magnitude of the task before President Davis, and commending him for his efforts, the editor of the *Raleigh News and Observer* wrote, sometime after the war:

> It is profitless to discuss how far any measure of the Confederate government was right or wrong, but as for Mr. Davis, he had the responsibility; he had full knowledge of all the circumstances; he had the general plan of the whole war from Texas to the

Potomac to subserve and watch and to carry out. It is to our glory that there was no Fort Lafayette at the South. It is to the honor of the Confederate government that no Confederate secretary ever could touch a bell and send a citizen to prison. [14]

Asked what he thought was Davis's principal motive behind his participation in the conflict, Senator Reagan, in 1889, said, "To secure a government that should be friendly to the people. He was an intense believer in the doctrine that the States should control absolutely their domestic affairs . . ." [15]

On April 2, 1865, Richmond was evacuated. President Davis and his cabinet started south. On April 9, Robert E. Lee surrendered, followed by the surrender of Joseph E. Johnston on April 26. Davis and some of his cabinet members were threading their way through the occupied parts of Georgia, hoping to slip undetected across the Mississippi and into the Trans-Mississippi South where resistance was still strong, when they were surrounded at Irwinville, Georgia, at a camp in the woods.

Lincoln had been assassinated on April 14, and a wild and crazed North demanded Davis's head. Not unlike today, the northern press fanned the flames until mob psychology took over. Reward posters went out for his arrest. The President of the Confederacy, completely innocent of the assassination, was captured on May 10, transported to Fortress Monroe in Virginia, and chained like an animal in a damp cell. For two years he was tortured and denied many of the most humane rights. He had absolutely no privacy, being placed in an open casemate where guards and the curious were allowed to watch him like a caged lion. A light was kept burning twenty-four hours a day, giving him virtually no rest until after many months his wife was allowed to make him a mask for his eyes. The full account of his suffering can be read in *The Prison Life of Jefferson Davis*, written by a northern physician, Dr. Craven, who was assigned to Davis and who became very attached to his noble patient.

Political forces in the frenzied North trumped up charges of complicity in the assassination, cruelty to prisoners during the war, and treason. Not even a trace of evidence could be found on the first two counts, so the House of Representatives decided to go forward on a count of treason against both Davis and Robert E. Lee. General Grant had Lee's indictment removed, but Davis remained imprisoned for two years, awaiting his trial. On May 11, 1867, Davis was released on bail of $100,000, paid by several prominent northern men. A "packed jury" of twelve blacks and twelve white men awaited a trial which never occurred. Davis, himself, was eager for such a trial so that he could prove that secession was not treason, but on February 15, 1869, the government's attorney informed the court that he would no longer prosecute Davis. Fear that a jury might find Davis innocent and thereby validate the constitutionality of secession lay at the bottom of dropping the case against Jefferson Davis.

In Richmond, thousands were wild with exultation, and soon there was rejoicing throughout Dixie. The hero of the Lost Cause had suffered for them, and the vindication of Davis was the vindication of the South.

After two years of prison Davis's health was seriously impaired, and in an effort to regain a measure of it he spent the next few years traveling, sometimes abroad. He was also without means and had to seek employment. Eventually, he went to Memphis as president of an insurance firm, then on to his final residence on the beautiful Gulf Coast. There, at Biloxi, Mrs. Sarah Dorsey offered him her home, *Beauvoir*, as a refuge where he could write his memoirs. Rather than accept outright charity, he agreed to begin making payments on the property. A year later, Mrs. Dorsey, knowing she was terminally ill, made out a will leaving *Beauvoir*, three small Louisiana plantations, and $50,000 in financial assets to Jefferson Davis and his daughter, Winnie. In 1881, Davis published his *Rise and Fall of the Confederate Government*, accomplishing the monumental work he had envisioned for years.

This photograph was made at *Beauvoir* in 1885, four years after completing his two-volume work, *Rise and Fall of the Confederate Government*.

Though Davis did not often appear in public, he occasionally spoke at various Confederate monument dedications across the South, where he received the adoration of a grateful people. On November 6, 1889, at the age of 81, he made a visit to his *Brierfield* plantation near Vicksburg and suddenly became ill.

He was there for four days but refused to send for a doctor before embarking on his return trip. Meanwhile, some of his servants sent Varina a telegram, whereupon she took a train to New Orleans and then a steamboat upriver, finally reaching the vessel on which her husband was returning. Davis received medical care as two doctors came aboard further south and diagnosed his condition as acute bronchitis complicated by malaria. He made it to the New Orleans home of Judge Fenner, a long time friend. Davis's doctor, Stanford Chaille, was called to his bedside and determined that he was too ill to travel back to *Beauvoir*. For two weeks, he remained bedridden but stable. Then he took a turn for the worse in early December, losing consciousness on December 5. In the presence of several friends, Jefferson Davis passed away early in the morning of December 6 while holding Varina's hand.

Upon hearing of Davis's illness, many friends, including Senator Jones, the intimate comrade from Iowa, made their way towards New Orleans, though most of them arrived too late to see him alive.

As he lay in state in the New Orleans City Hall, which, like every business building in the city was draped in black, a spontaneous movement was underway for a funeral befitting a king. Ten thousand people had already passed his casket on the first day, December 7. The next day, viewing hours were lengthened to 10 p.m. each night. Dignitaries had arrived, plain folks had come, and thousands of dispatches were received from every Confederate state and the Indian Territory.

At noon, December 11, the casket was removed to the porch where the funeral was preached to a sea of people filling every standing space as far as the eye could see. The funeral procession consisted of every organization conceivable, numbering probably 10,000 participants, including the governors of eight southern states. The crowd, numbering over 200,000 people, was the largest ever assembled in the South for a funeral, A shocked North, reeling in astonishment, was finally convinced that the hearts of Southerners would ever belong to Jeff Davis and the Confederacy, notwithstanding their every attempt to discredit the movement and disparage the leaders of the glorious Lost Cause.

This is the funeral procession as it wound its way through the French Quarter. The catafalque can be seen resting on a wagon pulled by six horses, followed by what seemed to be an endless procession of organizations and individuals paying their last respects to the great leader of the South.

Even the *New York Herald* showed a bit of envious longing to be able to claim the legacy of Jefferson Davis, writing, "In the essential element of statesmanship, Davis will be judged as the rival and parallel of Lincoln. When the two men came face to face, as leaders of two mighty forces, bitter was Northern sorrow that Providence had given the South so ripe and rare a leader and the North an uncouth advocate from the woods." [16]

In this old photograph, one can see the masses lining the streets in New Orleans as the funeral procession slowly makes its way through the grieving city.

The *New Orleans Times-Democrat* related a special incident which bears repeating. It is illustrative of the gentle character of the man who had to be tough enough to withstand a war, imprisonment, ill health, and three decades of slander for bearing the cross of the South.

As a result of his gracious dignity, Mr. Davis never came in contact with a menial but that at once they grew devotedly attached to him. More than once have family and friends quizzed him regarding the absorbing love of the porters, servants, and slaves that accident threw his way. Never was a man more loved by those who served him, and this was peculiarly noticeable among the negroes he owned before the war. One of the most affecting incidents connected with the death was the arrival and grief of this old negro, a former slave of Mr. Davis's brother, the late Joe Davis.

For a number of years Miles Cooper, a decrepit colored man, has sent from his present home in Florida, little tokens in the way of fruits raised by his own hands for the hospitable Beauvoir table. Through the local press, Miles heard of Mr. Davis's extreme illness, and, putting every personal interest and comfort aside, hastened to see the master he loved. Unused to traveling, aged and uncertain in his movements, the unselfish servant again and again missed connection in the short trip, was delayed, left behind, and put to every possible annoyance and inconvenience. Finally, he arrived, and full of pleasant anticipations, hurried up to look once more in those kindly eyes and feel the cordial grasp of that genial hand. Reaching the residence, all stilled as it was, surrounded by an atmosphere of death, the servant learned of Mr. Davis's death the night previous. It was more than he could bear, and breaking down with an outburst of deep grief Miles sat crushed and hopeless, only asking the one favor to be admitted to the presence of his master. Everyone, save the family, had been denied entrance, but Mr. Farrar, at Mrs. Davis's request, led the way, and soon the ex-slave stood face to face with the noble dead. It was pitiful to hear the sobs and wails of the old man. He mourned with unaffected grief for the "Mars Jeff" of his youth, and prayed earnestly for the welfare of those he left behind. [17]

While the choir sang *Rock of Ages*, President Davis was temporarily entombed in the Army of Northern Virginia Monument at Metairie Cemetery. Before his death, he had left up to Varina the location of his final resting place. Within a day of his death several cities across the South – among them Memphis, Macon, Louisville, Atlanta, Montgomery, Richmond, Vicksburg, and Jackson, Mississippi – began requesting his remains. In 1891, Varina let it be known that her first choice was Davis's *Brierfield* Plantation in Mississippi, but because she feared flooding she had decided that Richmond, Virginia would be the most appropriate location for his final resting place.

In1893, Jefferson Davis's remains were exhumed and lay in state again for a day at New Orleans. Then, with a continuous cortège accompanying his remains, a special car provided by the Louisville & Nashville Railroad made its way to Richmond, stopping for ceremonies at Mobile, Montgomery, Atlanta, Charlotte, Greensboro, Raleigh, and Danville, Virginia, the "last capital of the Confederacy." At Montgomery and Raleigh, Davis's body lay in state at both capitols. At Richmond, there was another ceremony at the state capitol, followed by his interment in Hollywood Cemetery.

"Thus was broken another cord that bound the living, throbbing heart of the South to the dead but loved and unforgotten past." [18]

PAT CLEBURNE

A life-size figure of a Confederate general proudly watches over throngs of sight-seers in a most unlikely place – New York Harbor. There, in the American Museum of Immigration, located in the basement of the Statue of Liberty, stands the only statue of a general, an inspiration to all immigrants who come to America to better their lot. It is the statue of Patrick Ronayne Cleburne, an Irish immigrant who volunteered for Confederate service as a private, then rose in less than two years to the rank of Major General.

Pat Cleburne, whose name is pronounced as if it were spelled "Clayburn" – except in Texas, where the city named for him is pronounced exactly as it is spelled – was the third child born to Mary Anne Ronayne and Joseph Cleburne of County Cork, Ireland. Named for Patrick Ronayne, his maternal grandfather, little Pat was born March 16, 1828, only one day before St. Patrick's Day, a coincidence that may have served as a good omen for the development of an extraordinary young Irishman.

He was called Ronayne in his Irish youth, though he would come to be admired and loved by the people of the South as General Pat Cleburne. His early education came at the hands of private tutors. At twelve, he was enrolled in an expensive private school for boys, where the discipline was strict and served him well for the role he was to play in commanding a division of Confederate soldiers. After three years at Spedding School, he was forced to withdraw due to the death of his father, who had been a successful physician and who had intended that Pat become a doctor as well.

For three years, Pat was apprenticed to Dr. Thomas H. Justice of Mallow, some twenty miles north of the Cleburne home place. In 1846, he traveled 165 miles to Dublin to take an entrance examination at the medical school there, only to fail the exam. Pat was a very sensitive boy. He was nearly eighteen years old, and having failed the test, he thought he had disgraced his family name. As a result, he decided to lose himself for a while in the military. He joined the British 41st Regiment of Foot, where he would stay for three years and seven months, rising only to the rank of corporal, that rank coming after more than three years of steady service. Pat would be heard to remark many years later that he rejoiced more over his long-awaited promotion to the lowly rank of corporal than his attainment of the rank of Major General.

Heavy taxes, the scourge of civilized societies, brought hardships to the Emerald Isle, sending the Cleburne estate into a precipitous decline. Pat's mother had died when he was an infant, his father when he was fifteen. His stepmother, of whom he was very fond, reluctantly made the decision that the four oldest children, all of whom were over the age of nineteen, should emigrate to the United States.

Pat was twenty-one years old, and having received a small legacy from his real mother's family, he purchased his discharge from the British army on September 22, 1849 for a sum of twenty pounds. With his sister, brother, and stepbrother, he boarded the *Bridgetown*, which set sail from the Port of Cork on November 5, 1849, bound for New Orleans, Louisiana, where it arrived on Christmas Day. A letter of introduction accompanied the young voyagers, but Pat boarded a steamboat for Cincinnati, leaving his brothers and sister to present the letter to Mr. Duncan in New Orleans. Two days later the sister and brothers followed him up the Mississippi, rejoining him in Cincinnati. Within six months, however, Patrick Cleburne would leave Cincinnati forever, bound for Dixie and his destiny.

Cleburne had made a good hand in a Cincinnati drug store and was recommended for an open position at a drug store in Helena, Arkansas, a town of about 600 people on the west bank of the Mississippi River. In June, 1850, he arrived in Helena and accepted the position of manager, a move which resulted in a lifelong friendship with Dr. Nash, one of the owners. For the next eleven years, Cleburne would spend his time among the friendly inhabitants of Helena, the citizens of which accepted the affable young man into its best society.

His physical appearance was described as a man of 150 pounds, five feet nine inches tall, having large gray eyes, thick brown hair, and a muscular build. He possessed great strength and stood erect with a military bearing. In 1856, his health was permanently impaired by a shooting involving a friend named T.C. Hindman, who was to become one of five Confederate generals hailing from Helena. As Hindman and Cleburne walked down a street, some political enemies of Hindman shot them both. Before collapsing, Cleburne shot and mortally wounded his assailant. The bullet which felled Cleburne entered his lower back, and he hovered between life and death for a week while

Dr. Nash desperately tried to pull him through. Cleburne had studied law, and he later complained of the pain which afflicted him during long court room debate and hours of bending over law books in his library. Oddly enough, the military career he would later pursue seemed to improve his condition.

Pat Cleburne was a deeply religious person, having been baptized an Episcopalian at St. Mary's Church in Ireland. In 1852, he became a Mason and also joined the Sons of Temperance, a group of men who advocated abstinence of liquor. He was a regular visitor at the Presbyterian Church, but the outdoor camp meetings in the woods impressed him more than anything else, and he wrote about them to his stepmother in Ireland. He refused to listen to smut, and his dislike of vulgarity was well known. Dr. Nash, who later became his biographer, said that he had never heard Cleburne swear an oath in his life.

Cleburne's interaction with the warm people of Helena, in addition to his study of constitutional law, brought him into perfect alignment with the southern idea. He was as southern as the most native-born, and his patriotism was evident from the beginning. On June 24, 1853, Cleburne gave a public address at a large Masonic celebration in Helena; whereupon, the *Southern Shield*, Helena's newspaper, found this to say in its edition of the following day: "Mr. C., we believe, hails from over the water, but he is thoroughly Americanized. The eloquent bursts of patriotism that fell from his lips on yesterday stamps him as a patriot in the broadest sense of the term." [19]

He was thrilled with antebellum life in Helena, which had more than doubled its population since he had arrived in 1850. By 1860, Cleburne had made several major purchases of land and, like all Southerners, was alarmed at northern fulminations. When the Yell Rifles were formed in the summer of 1860 to protect Phillips County in the event of hostilities, Cleburne volunteered as a private. In January, 1861, he wrote to his half-brother, Robert.

As to my own position, I hope to see the Union preserved by granting to the South the full measure of her constitutional rights. If this cannot be done I hope to see all the Southern States united in a new confederation and that we can effect a peaceable separation. If both of these are denied us I am with Arkansas in weal or in woe. I have been elected and hold the Commission of the State as captain of the volunteer Rifle Company of this place and I can say for my company that if the stars and stripes become the standard of a tyrannical majority, the ensign of a violated league, it will no longer command our love or respect but will command our best efforts to drive it from the State. [20]

On April 27, the Yell Rifles departed for Camp Rector, just north of Memphis. Assembling at the courthouse in Helena on Sunday morning, they marched to the Methodist Church for worship. The yard was full of people who could not get inside, including many of the young ladies of Helena who had presented Captain Cleburne with the Stars and Bars, the first flag of the Confederacy. A Bible was presented to the company, and then the men marched to the landing where hundreds of cheering, crying people bade them farewell.

On May 7, one day after Arkansas seceded by a vote of sixty-nine to one, Cleburne wrote again to Robert.

I am with the South in life or in death, in victory or defeat. I never owned a Negro and care nothing for them, but these people have been my friends and have stood up to me on all occasions. In addition to this, I believe the North is about to wage a brutal and unholy war on a people who have done them no wrong, in violation of the constitution and the fundamental principals of the government. They no longer acknowledge that all government derives its validity from the consent of the governed. They are about to invade our peaceful homes, destroy our property, and inaugurate a servile insurrection, murder our men and dishonor our women. We propose no invasion of the North, no attack on them, and only ask to be let alone. [21]

On May 14, Cleburne was elected colonel of the First Arkansas Regiment, which, on July 23, put itself under the authority of the Confederate Army, joining General Hardee's command. Cleburne's previous training with the British Army and his natural proclivity for military discipline played a role in winning him command of a regiment on October 28. He instilled pride and discipline in his men who, in return, gave him undying devotion and loyalty. His troops were known far and wide as the best-drilled brigade in the army. Pat Cleburne's remarkable qualities were unmistakable, and by March 4, 1862, the Irish immigrant had risen from private volunteer to Brigadier General.

The first battle for Cleburne's men came at Shiloh on April 6 and 7, 1862, where they led the advance of the army and fought in the front line both days, and as Cleburne said in his official report, "were never rested or relieved for a moment."[22]

The first day of the battle was witness to general Cleburne's routing of General Sherman's entire division from their camp. In concert with other units, Cleburne's brigade finally pushed the Yankees from their stronghold at the Hornet's Nest, and by evening the entire Union army was huddled with its back to the Tennessee River.

On December 13, 1862, Cleburne was promoted to the rank of Major General, continuing to distinguish himself throughout the succeeding days of the war. At Chickamauga, Cleburne pushed his division upon the Federal line and drove the enemy back a mile and a half, all the time riding back and forth from brigade to brigade in a fury of effort and speed, cheering them on and directing their attacks upon the reeling Yankees. It was here on September 19, 1863, at Chickamauga that Cleburne earned his sobriquet, "the Stonewall Jackson of the West."

The fighting around Chattanooga, Tennessee included the Battle of Missionary Ridge, fought on November 25, 1863, a day General Sherman wouldn't soon forget, for he suffered defeat again at the hands of Pat Cleburne. The Confederate Army was posted along the top of Missionary Ridge in a long, thin line, a line so thin in the center that it would eventually give way, causing the Confederates to begin a retreat towards Dalton, Georgia. During the battle, Cleburne's division formed the Confederate right on the north end of the ridge where a rail-road tunnel runs through the hill. Sherman attacked straight up the precipitous hill but was repulsed by the determined Confederates who couldn't even get their artillery guns trained down on the bluecoats because of the sharp slope of the ridge. To compensate, the resourceful Rebels rolled boulders down upon the heads of their antagonists, and the artillerymen lit the fuses of their shells and rolled them down the hill like bowling balls. Before Sherman was totally removed from action, a detachment of Confederates rushed through the tunnel from the back side, catching the Federals from the rear and taking a large number of prisoners.

The entire Army of Tennessee numbered about 37,000 men at Missionary Ridge. It was facing 80,000 Yankees under General Grant. Faced with overwhelming odds and having lost the line of defense upon the ridge, General Bragg ordered the army to re-treat as quickly as possible through a break in the Georgia mountains called Ringgold Gap. To Cleburne's fighting division of about 4,000 men was given the task of fortifying this narrow gap and holding off the huge Federal army, which was in hot pursuit of the retreating Army of Tennessee. On the 27th of November, Cleburne did just that, repulsing every attempt of the sprawling Federal monster, buying precious time for Bragg to get the wagons, artillery, and troops safely down the road. His astounding feat received an official resolution of thanks from the Confederate Congress, who recognized that the entire Army of Tennessee might have been annihilated except for Cleburne's actions.

After the fall of Atlanta in September, 1864, General Hood, who had replaced General Bragg, ordered the Army of Tennessee to march back toward Nashville. Cleburne's Division was a thoroughly trained unit, proud of its fame on many a battle-field, and it was difficult for the warriors of those hard fought battles to begin seeing the Confederacy head downhill.

At Powder Springs, Georgia, Cleburne's men serenaded him on the evening of October 2. In response, Cleburne made an address in which he encouraged the men to fight on, ending with his famous statement of devotion to the Confederacy. "If this cause that is so dear to my heart is doomed to fail, I pray heaven may let me fall with it, while my face is toward the enemy and my arm battling for that which I know to be right." [23]

On a Saturday afternoon, November 26, General Cleburne stopped to rest at a little red brick church near the town of Columbia, Tennessee. The ivy-covered Gothic-style church, known as St. John's, rested 'neath a canopy of tall tress which also sheltered the cool graveyard of the church. Perhaps reflecting upon the similarities of this place and old St. Mary's in Ireland where his father was buried, he turned to Captain Hill and said, "It would not be hard to die if one could be buried in such a beautiful spot."[24] Always pensive, the actual danger of the battlefield seemed to weigh heavily upon his mind. Often speaking of death as if he expected it, he was resolutely prepared to meet the Grim Reaper in defense of his country. In his letter to Robert, on May 7, 1861, he warned, "I may die in this conflict."[25] Two days after pausing at St. John's cemetery, Cleburne addressed his troops, vowing that he would never lay down his arms and that he would rather die than surrender.

At Franklin, General Hood ordered a foolhardy frontal

assault against the heavily entrenched Federal army. It was the most foolish advance ever ordered by a Confederate commander, and Hood's generals tried to counsel him against it. Unyielding, however, the impetuous Hood turned to General Cleburne and told him to fix bayonets and take the breastworks at all hazards, to which Cleburne resignedly replied, "General, I will take the works or fall in the attempt." [26]

General Govan, a fellow soldier from Helena, leaned over and remarked to Cleburne that few of them would ever return to Arkansas to tell the tale. Cleburne responded, "Well, Govan, if we are to die, let us die like men." [27]

The charge was made by 15,000 splendid Confederate soldiers. Bands played *Dixie* and *The Bonnie Blue Flag* while the bravest men on earth marched squarely into the jaws of death. General Cleburne was in the thick of the advance and soon had a horse shot from under him. A nineteen-year-old Mississippi boy named James Brandon offered his bay mare to Cleburne, but it, too, was shot out from under the general as he tried to mount it. General Govan later recalled that Cleburne then moved into the deadly smoke and haze of the battle on foot, holding his sword in one hand while waving his cap in the other. Only seconds later, the sharpshooter found his mark, shooting the gallant Pat Cleburne just below the heart. All night long, his brave soldiers lay in the ditch below the breastworks, waiting for orders that never came. In the morning light, an artilleryman found the body lying about forty yards in front of the breastworks.

The casualties were enormous – 6,252 Confederate soldiers killed, wounded, or missing in action. And the figure among general officers was staggering. One general was captured, six were wounded, five were killed, and one was mortally wounded. Never had death claimed as many generals in one battle. The five dead men were Generals Pat Cleburne, S.R. Gist, H.B. Granbury, John Adams, and O.F. Strahl. General John C. Carter died soon after the battle. Four of the bodies were taken to *Carnton*, the plantation home of John McGavock, located just southeast of the battlefield, where they were laid out on the back veranda until arrangements could be made with their families.

Several of the generals and other officers, including Pat Cleburne, were taken to Columbia for funeral and burial in Rose Hill Cemetery, but Chaplain Quintard was greatly bothered by the close proximity of their resting place to graves of Federal soldiers. He immediately arranged for them to be disinterred and buried at St. John's Church, in the little cemetery so admired by Pat Cleburne only a week earlier.

The flood of tributes to this great man are impractical to list here. Howell and Elizabeth Purdue's compilation of eulogies and memorials fill an entire chapter in their definitive work, *Pat Cleburne, Confederate General*.

On April 26, 1870, General Cleburne's body was started on its way home. For twenty-four hours it lay in state in Columbia, where all businesses were closed out of respect. Escorted to the depot in a grand procession, the body was placed aboard the train to Memphis. All of the businesses in Memphis were closed, and the largest crowd that city had ever seen watched the procession that took the body from the depot to the boat landing. Those involved in the procession and solemn ceremony that day were Generals Anderson, Chalmers, Fagan, and Pillow, Bishop Quintard, former Governor Harris, and former President Jefferson Davis. On April 29, Pat Cleburne was finally laid to rest in his hometown of Helena, Arkansas. His grave, in the Confederate section of Evergreen Cemetery, is marked by a marble monument, sixteen feet tall, placed there in 1891 by the ladies of The Phillips County Memorial Association. Funds for the monument came from the rich and the poor, including $2.50 from a negro man who remembered how kind Cleburne had been to him as a little slave boy peddling apples in Helena.

On April 28, 1870, the same day his body arrived in Memphis, the *Memphis Daily Appeal* compared him to Stonewall Jackson.

Two such men have rarely lived in the same age, and that two such faultless soldiers should have risen in the armies of the same government at the same time, and each should have alike commanded the admiration of mankind, of accomplished soldiers, and the undying love of their compatriots, is the chiefest wonder of the late mighty convulsion.

In 1867, in *A Sketch of Maj. Gen. P.R. Cleburne*, General D. H. Hill wrote:

Patrick R. Cleburne deserves a prominent place among the great heroes who have illustrated Southern heroism and Southern history. His name brings a thrill of the heart to every true son of the South, just as his presence brought success wherever he moved on the field of battle. "Cleburne is here!" meant that "all was well." [28]

ROBERT E. LEE

There has never been – nor will there likely ever be – a mortal more admired, more esteemed, or more revered than Robert E. Lee. His enemies were few, his friends legion. By war's end, he was already a legend. He had become the embodiment of the South, and his name synonymous with it. He was the soldier-statesman and the ultimate hero of the Lost Cause. Today, he is, without a doubt, the quintessential southern hero.

Robert Edward Lee was born January 19, 1807, in Westmoreland County, Virginia, at *Stratford Hall*, the ancestral home of the Lees. He was the fifth child of Anne Hill Carter and Henry "Light-Horse Harry" Lee, former governor of Virginia and distinguished cavalry officer of the Revolution. Both the Carters and the Lees were among the foremost families of Virginia.

In 1811, when Robert was four years old, the family was forced to move to Alexandria due to financial troubles. He was educated in the schools of that place, and in 1824 sought appointment to West Point, entering the academy in 1825. The military career of his father, who had died when Robert was only eleven, was an inspiration to him, and it can be said that Robert E. Lee was truly a professional military man. It was the only profession he would know until the last five years of his life, all of which were spent as president of Washington College.

Lee graduated from West Point in 1829, second in his class and without a demerit against his name. Until the outbreak of the War Between the States, he spent thirty-two years in the routine duty of the military, rising from the rank of lieutenant to colonel. He was stationed at various places around the country, from the east coast to the frontiers of Indian Territory and west Texas.

On June 30, 1831, he married Mary Ann Randolph Custis, great-granddaughter of Martha Washington. The wedding was held at the Custis mansion, *Arlington*, an imposing temple-like structure in the classical Greek tradition, which sat high on a Virginia hillside overlooking the capital city of Washington. In 1857, his father-in-law died, leaving the property to Robert E. Lee and his wife, who made it their home until forced to flee in 1861. An unfortunate casualty of the war, *Arlington* was sold for non-payment of taxes while the Lees were in Richmond. Even though Mrs. Lee sent payment for the taxes, the U.S. government, determined that she should never have the house, insisted that she make payment in person. Confined to a wheel chair with crippling arthritis, she could not make the trip. As a result, the U.S. government foreclosed on the mansion and put it up for sale. Not only did the U.S. government, being the high bidder at the auction, take the mansion, the Yankee military buried Union soldiers in the immediate yard, up near the house and in Mrs. Lee's garden, so that the Lees would never want to live in the house again even if they could reclaim the property at some point in the future. Today, the stolen mansion is the focal point of Arlington National Cemetery.

The Yankees denuded the estate's forest and absconded with souvenirs from the mansion. Massive oaks were cut down on the 1,100-acre property, and the hillside was fortified with artillery batteries.

The Mexican War that raged from 1846 through 1848 had provided a virtual dress rehearsal for the War Between the States. Many of the brilliant Confederate generals and statesmen, including Jackson, Lee, Beauregard, and Davis, saw duty in such far away places as Vera Cruz, Buena Vista, and Monterey. At Vera Cruz, Lee's skill was credited for the victory, and for his services in the storming of Chapultepec he was advanced to the rank of colonel.

In 1852, Lee became the superintendent of West Point, making several lasting improvements in the academy, but it wasn't the type of military service most desired by him. With the help of Secretary of War Jefferson Davis, he was transferred in 1855 to the command of a cavalry regiment on the Texas frontier.

Mary Lee had developed chronic arthritis, and it was while Lee was on leave at *Arlington* to tend to her that John Brown raided Harper's Ferry. Lee was ordered to Harper's Ferry in October, 1859, quickly disposing of the troubled Brown and his insurrection army.

Although Robert E. Lee was successful throughout his military career, it was the War Between the States that lionized him. When Abraham Lincoln decided to invade the South, Lee was his first choice to command the Federal army. But, when offered the command, Lee, a Virginian first and foremost, replied, "If the Union is to be dissolved and the Government disrupted, I shall return to my native state and share the miseries of my people, and save in defense will draw my sword on none." [29]

In early April, 1861, while strolling the grounds of *Arlington* with a northern visitor, he pointed towards the Capitol lying across the Potomac. "That beautiful feature of our land-scape," he said, "has ceased to charm me as it once did. I fear the mischief that is brewing there."[30] On April 17, Virginia voted to secede; on April 20, Lee submitted his resignation from the U.S. Army; on April 23, he accepted the appointment as commander of Virginia forces.

This group of officers of the 8th New York Militia are enjoying their unwelcome visit to *Arlington* in June, 1861, shortly after Mrs. Lee was removed from the home. Union General Meigs, an arrogant, vindictive officer who despised Lee and wished him dead, was the architect of the ghoulish plan to shuffle dead soldiers around the property. When Union soldiers were buried a distance away from the house, Meigs ordered them dug up and buried in the yard close to the house so that none of the Lees would ever want to live there again.

Yankee soldiers lolling around *Arlington* in 1864.

Lee immediately set about mobilizing the state volunteers and fortifying the rivers against enemy movements by water. In May, he was commissioned full general in the Confederate army and made advisor to President Davis. First dispatched to western Virginia, Lee stopped a threatened invasion there but was not successful in rallying the pro-Federal citizens to his cause. His next assignment was to make an inspection of the defenses around Charleston, South Carolina and other defensive positions in the southeast. He was there until March, 1862, bolstering the excellent fortifications that General Beauregard had begun. As a result of their work, Charleston held out against heavy bombardments until the very end of the war.

When General Joseph E. Johnston, then commanding the Confederate Army in Virginia, was wounded, President Davis appointed General Lee to take his place. On June 1, 1862, Lee assumed command of these proud volunteers from all over the South. They would soon become legendary as The Army of Northern Virginia.

In the following three years, Lee would at no time have a force comparable to his foes in numbers, artillery, or equipment.

The odds against him were always three to two, and many times three to one. After the war, while considering the idea of writing a history of his campaigns, Lee wrote to his leading officers, "It will be difficult to get the world to appreciate the odds against which we fought."[31]

General McClellan had 100,000 men who had advanced to within seven miles of Richmond, and another 40,000 were on the Rappahannock, marching to reinforce him. Three other Federal forces were threatening Stonewall Jackson in the Shenandoah Valley to the west. Yankees were swarming into Virginia like bees, and Lee had to devise a plan to thwart them.

First, he ordered General Ewell to join Jackson in the valley, where the forces of those two able officers thrashed the Yankees so soundly at Cross Keys and Port Republic that an attack upon Washington was feared, resulting in the expected withdrawal of the Federal army from the Rappahannock.

Next, Lee recalled Stonewall Jackson from the valley and took the offensive against the monstrous army of McClellan, pushing him back to Harrison's Landing by July 1 in a series of engagements known as the Seven Day's Battles. Lee had captured a lot of superior small arms for his men, relieved Richmond, and raised the morale and confidence of the army. His stock began to rise with the people of the South. He was their man.

To the north of Richmond, another huge army was advancing under General Pope. Lee marched his army north to attack Pope, crossing the Rapidan in mid-August. Pope, realizing that Lee's army was on its way, withdrew north of the Rappahannock and was backing up ever closer to Washington, screaming for help from McClellan, who was rapidly loading his men onto transport ships. Lee's plan had worked. Before McClellan's men could be unloaded on the Potomac and marched overland to reinforce Pope, Lee had ordered Jackson to swing around to the northwest of Pope and attack his communications and supplies from the rear. On August 22, General

Jeb Stuart captured Pope's baggage train, papers and all. On August 29, at the same location of the first Battle of Manassas, Pope discovered Jackson and attacked him. The next day he struck again, wrongly thinking that Jackson was retreating. Lee fell upon Pope while he was busily engaged with Jackson. The result was a Federal retreat toward Washington. Once again, northern Virginia was cleared of the dreaded Yankees, this time by a battle known as Second Manassas.

Lee's obvious purpose was to attack the Yankee capital, which lay a little over twenty miles to the east, but McClellan's entire army was entrenched there. Lee then decided to make a strike into the North and headed towards Maryland to destroy the Baltimore and Ohio Railroad. His ultimate target was Harrisburg, Pennsylvania, where he would have been able to cut the other important east-west railroad in the area.

The Army of Northern Virginia advanced to Frederick, Maryland. They were now forty-five miles north of Washington and thirty miles south of Pennsylvania, putting the northern population into a panic. Lee sent five divisions under Jackson southwest to Harper's Ferry, but it was a terribly costly day, for McClellan had happened upon a lost copy of Lee's plans for the Maryland campaign and straightway pushed forward for a surprise attack. As Lee began a withdrawal to South Mountain on September 14, he was attacked all along his line. Withdrawing to Sharpsburg, Lee set up a defensive line west of Antietam Creek, where McClellan again attacked on September 17. At last, Jackson and his famous "foot cavalry" arrived, and the Federal advance was halted after what would become known as the bloodiest single day of the entire war. Although there were more Federal dead than Confederate, Lee's dead, wounded, and missing numbered almost 13,000, and now he would have to retreat into Virginia to save the rest of his army. For some reason, McClellan did not pursue. It was a complete failure, all because of a carelessly dropped Order No. 191, in which Lee informed General D. H. Hill how he planned to divide and distribute his army.

For failing to pursue Lee, McClellan was removed from command, joining what would become a long list of generals who were removed by Lincoln for failing to ensnare Lee. Now it was Burnside's turn. Advancing down the Potomac, General Burnside established headquarters at Aquia Creek then marched a short distance to Fredericksburg, Virginia. He would have to cross the Rappahannock just east of the town and assault Marye's Heights, a formidable hill west of the town. The town lay between the river on the east and the hill on the west, so on the frigid day of December 11 Burnside began shelling it, causing its inhabitants – mostly women, girls, and little children – to flee their homes, trudge through the freezing mud, and huddle in the open fields with only what assistance the Confederate soldiers could provide against the cold winter weather. Lee, who always referred to the Yankees as "those people," looked down from his artillery positions on the hill. "Those people delight to destroy the weak and those who can make no defense; it just suits them!" [32]

Two days later, on December 13, Burnside attacked Lee's entrenched forces directly through the town and, after a terrible day of battling, was driven back with horrible losses. Lee did not follow up the next day, and Burnside was wisely counseled not to renew the attack. On December 15, Burnside withdrew across the Rappahannock, badly beaten and soon to be relieved of command.

Then, along came Joseph Hooker. He had an elaborate plan to cross the Rappahannock above and below Fredericksburg. Lee astonished the world by dividing his army, which was outnumbered two to one, into three pieces, sending General Jubal Early and 9,000 men south towards Fredericksburg to oppose the Federal left and 26,000 men under Stonewall Jackson north to oppose the Federal right near Chancellorsville. Lee remained in front of the main portion of Hookers' great army with only about 13,000 men! From May 1 through May 4, 1863, General

Lee's Army of Northern Virginia proceeded to roll up the Union Army. Jackson had outflanked Hooker, and Lee moved forward. On May 5, Lee spent the day preparing to attack the defeated Federals again, but during that day and the following night, Hooker withdrew towards Washington.

Chancellorsville became Lee's greatest victory. Even today, students of military warfare still study the strategy and tactics of his brilliant victory and the bold division of his forces. But elation soon turned to sorrow. On the second day of the battle, Stonewall Jackson had been mortally wounded. As a sadness swept over the army, it was apparent that he would not survive, and on the 10th of May the great Stonewall was gone. Lee wept bitterly over Jackson's death. Not only had he lost a dear friend, he had lost a partner who could think and act in perfect harmony with the execution of his military plans. Jackson would never be replaced. Lee simply divided Jackson's corps, assigning half to A. P. Hill and the other half to R.S. Ewell.

The absence of Jackson was evident in Lee's last attempt to carry the war to the North. On the 1st, 2nd, and 3rd of July he engaged an enemy superior in number at Gettysburg, making repeated charges which became disjointed and delayed due to subordinates who failed to proceed as directed. General Ewell was slow to advance, giving the Yankees time to become entrenched at Cemetery Ridge, and General Longstreet became obstinate and simply refused to attack, thinking Lee's plans were bad. When he finally did advance, after several admonitions from Lee, it was too little too late. On July 4, Lee's army was forced into a rapid retreat from Pennsylvania. Once again, the Federal Army, this time under a new general named Meade, did not pursue, and the Army of Northern Virginia crossed back into Virginia.

There are always those who search for a flaw in the fabric of a great man. Those who look for such things ironically point to Lee's kindness, forbearance, and great capacity for forgiveness, alleging that it caused him to be negligent in discipline. It is true

346

that he was a kind general, attentive to his men. He shunned offers to headquarter in spacious Virginia homes, choosing instead to pitch a tent among his men and eat the same fare doled out to his soldiers. A South Carolina private described the affection they had for "Marse Lee."

> The men hung around him and seemed satisfied to lay their hands on his gray horse or to touch the bridle, or the stirrup, or the old general's leg – anything that Lee had was sacred to us fellows who had just come back. And the General – he could not help from breaking down . . . tears traced down his cheeks. [33]

Lee seldom reprimanded, even for insubordination. After the defeat at Gettysburg, attributable in considerable measure to the stubbornness of Longstreet, Lee merely looked at him and sorrowfully said, "It is all my fault. I thought my men were invincible."[34]

During the winter of 1863-1864, the Army of Northern Virginia subsisted on a daily ration of a pint of cornmeal and a quarter pound of bacon – when they could get it. The horses were near starvation, hardly able to drag the guns or carry the cavalry, and the army's only equipment consisted of their arms and ammunition. Lee would never be able to take the offensive again. He was reduced to awaiting and countering each move of the superbly outfitted and expanding Federal army.

On May 5th and 6th, 1864, Lee repulsed Grant, now in command of the Federal army, at The Wilderness. On May 7, Grant began to move south, realizing that Lee would have to be beaten by attrition rather than on the field. Through the rest of May and half of June, Grant slashed his way towards Richmond, meeting repulse after repulse, knowing that he could more than replace his lost men, while Lee could not hope to replace a single one.

On June 18, Grant laid siege to Petersburg. Nine months later, Lee was out of supplies and forced to evacuate Petersburg and Richmond. Heading west towards Amelia Court House, expecting stockpiles of food and ammunition, his army found nothing awaiting them. On April 9, 1865, his depleted army of 28,000 men, only 8,000 of whom were armed, found itself surrounded by 200,000 well-fed, well-armed Yankees. Although death seemed preferable, surrender was the only practical course. On February 6, Lee had finally been designated General-in-Chief of all the Confederate armies – and now he was forced to capitulate!

It was all over. There had been 2,154 military actions of one degree or another in Virginia. General Lee had borne the brunt of many a battle, kept the Yankees out of Richmond, prevented invasion of the lower South via Virginia, and led his famished, rag-tag heroes into the legendry of the South. Lee's successes on the field were attributed to his universal comprehension of the art of war. He possessed the ability to analyze his military intelligence, accurately gauge the strength of offensive and defensive bodies of troops, mentally put himself in the place of his opponent, organize his troops to execute his strategy, and overcome his adversary. And yet, it was the great sensitivity of Robert E. Lee that caused him to say that he mourned the loss of every soldier in his command. War was a poor way of life to this sensitive military genius who once remarked that it was probably good that war was so terrible, else men would grow too fond of it.

After the war, Lee was the exemplary statesman. The eyes of a nation were upon him, and scores of lucrative business proposals filled his mail every year, yet he chose to accept an offer from Washington College in Lexington, Virginia, where he could help shape young minds for future service to his beloved Southland. Lee served as president until his untimely death on October 12, 1870. His body and those of his family rest beneath the chapel on the campus. Shortly after his death, the college was renamed Washington and Lee University.

Several years after the war, when some were prone to give in to the old might-makes-right adage, wondering – since the South did not win – if the South had erred in opposing northern political rule and forming its own government, Lee remarked to General Wade Hampton, "We could have pursued no other course without dishonor. And sad as the result has been, if it had all to be done over again, we should be compelled to act in precisely the same manner." [35]

STONEWALL JACKSON

Among serious students of the war, there has long been a school of thought that not only is it a possibility, but a distinct likelihood, that the war could have been won *if only Stonewall Jackson had lived*. It isn't a new idea, just a valid one. Soon after his death, the Army of Northern Virginia suffered a deadly reverse at Gettysburg, and from that time on it was generally believed throughout the South that things would have been different if only Stonewall could have been spared a couple more years. In her diary, Mary Boykin Chesnut, taking note of one calamity after another, wished many times for an Albert Sidney Johnston or a Stonewall Jackson.

> And now that they begin to see that a few years more of Stonewall Jackson would have freed them from the yoke of the hateful Yankee, they deify him. They are proud to have been one of the famous Stonewall Brigade, to have been a brick in that wall. [36]

That's the Stonewall Jackson legacy, carved out in less than twenty-five months in the Confederate army. The very brevity of his service only magnifies his monumental achievements. Any survey of the half-dozen greatest American soldiers invariably includes, and usually starts with, Robert E. Lee and Stonewall Jackson.

Jackson's beginnings were humble. Like many Southerners, he was of Scotch-Irish stock. He was the third child of Julia Beckwith Neale and a lawyer named Jonathan Jackson. His given name was Thomas, but for some reason his parents did not give him a middle name. It was after he was nearly grown that he added the name Jonathan, thus becoming Thomas Jonathan Jackson for the first time. His family had been poor, and his parents died when he was very young, leaving him in the care of a kind bachelor uncle, Cummins E. Jackson. Cummins raised him on a farm in western Virginia, where he could offer him but little education.

From this lowly, obscure background emerged a brilliant military strategist. Jackson entered West Point in 1842, handicapped by his meager education but resolved to dig in and make something of himself. In 1846, he graduated seventeenth in a class of fifty-nine. This was no small accomplishment in a West Point class that would furnish twenty-four generals to the

Confederate and Federal armies between 1861 and 1865.

Sent almost immediately to Mexico, where war with that country was raging, he distinguished himself at Cerro Gordo, Vera Cruz, and Chapultepec, for which actions he was brevetted major. In 1848, he returned to routine duty in the States. In 1851, he accepted a position as professor of artillery and natural philosophy at Virginia Military Institute in Lexington, Virginia, resigning from the army in 1852.

When Virginia seceded, Jackson took charge of the troops that were collecting at Harper's Ferry. A few weeks later, in May of 1861, he was replaced by General Joseph E. Johnston. Ordered to Richmond, he was made brigadier general on June 17 and placed in command of a brigade in Johnston's army.

On July 16, Rose O'Neal Greenhow, the intrepid spy who stayed in Washington after the southern states seceded, sent word that the Federals were advancing towards Centreville and Manassas. On the 17th, President Davis ordered General Johnston, who was covering the Shenandoah Valley, to hurry his army back over the mountains to reinforce General Beauregard at Manassas. The first brigade to arrive was that of General Thomas Jonathan Jackson. At 4 o'clock on the afternoon of the 19th, the astonished Beauregard looked up to see Jackson walking in to report the early arrival of his 2500 men. It would be noon the next day before General Johnston and the rest of his soldiers would finally arrive. Jackson had set a precedent for the swift movement of troops. It would become his trademark, and many an unsuspecting Yankee would turn around to find Jackson suddenly upon him. He moved his infantry around by sudden night marches and over unlikely routes with such lightning speed that his troops became known as "Jackson's foot cavalry."

In the ensuing battle, a Federal column marched around the left flank of the Confederates and began enveloping the left end of the army with heavy fighting. As weakened Confederate troops retreated, they rushed past General Jackson and his troops who were standing steadfastly against the foe. General Barnard

Bee, taking note of the resolute stand of Jackson's men, rallied his shaken Southerners by shouting, "See, there is Jackson standing like a stone wall. Rally on the Virginians!"[37] The boys in gray eventually carried the day, and Bee's exclamation gave Jackson his famous sobriquet of "Stonewall," though Jackson always modestly insisted that General Bee, who tragically fell mortally wounded moments after his famous statement, had intended his comment to apply to his entire brigade rather than to Jackson himself.

In the Valley Campaign of 1862, Jackson made a record for himself and his mighty men by pouncing like a panther upon every force Washington tried to send up the Shenandoah Valley. Jackson, who had been promoted in October, 1861 to the rank of major-general, was in command of the Shenandoah Valley with a force of 17,000. His comparatively small command kept four Federal armies at bay, eventually defeating them one by one, ridding the valley of more than 60,000 bluecoats. His activities there kept Washington busy supplying troops to the valley, thus preventing reinforcements to the operations against Richmond.

When Lee needed help, Stonewall would make one of those lightning marches, much to the consternation of the enemy who thought he was elsewhere. Mary Chesnut alluded to his pervasive reputation in her diary. "Stonewall cannot be everywhere, though he comes near it."[38]

His command was the most efficient and prestigious in the Army of Northern Virginia. Even though he required much of his men, those who thought they could endure it sought a place in his ranks. His brilliant moves and deadly hammer strokes put fear into his opponents, most of whom learned to respect the mere name of Stonewall Jackson. The northern comic writer and lecturer, Artemus Ward, teased his Yankee audiences with the reputation of Jackson's preeminance.

One evening, before a solidly pro-Union audience, he said, "We have among our officers one good general, Stonewall Jackson. . ." At this there was a cry of protest from the audience, which Ward allowed to die down before he concluded his sentence. . . "but he is among our officers a little too often to be pleasant." [39]

Jackson was an absolute master in the art of flanking movements. A prime example of his prowess occurred at the Second Battle of Manassas in August, 1862. Lee's 48,000 men were facing the overwhelming army of General Pope, which numbered more than 75,000. Stonewall took 20,000 men, marched them up and around the right flank of Pope's army and, gaining his rear, destroyed his base of operations. He had marched almost half of Lee's army fifty-one miles in two days! Then Stonewall hit Pope from one direction while Lee struck him from another.

After the death of Jackson, "General Buckner had seen a Yankee cartoon in which angels were sent down from heaven to bear up Stonewall's soul. They could not find it, and flew back sorrowing, but when they got to the Golden Gate above they found that Stonewall, by a rapid flank movement, had already cut a way in." [40]

Jackson and Lee were a perfect combination, each one often able to anticipate the other's thinking. There was no better co-ordination in the Confederate Army. Their ultimate victory came in May, 1863 at Chancellorsville, when together they almost annihilated the huge army of General Hooker, an army of 134,000 splendidly equipped Yankees. Although outnumbered by more than two to one, Lee divided his army of 57,000 into three small forces, sending Jackson with 26,000 men in a circuitous flanking movement around the Federal right. As he wandered through the underbrush of the wilderness, the Federals thought he must be retreating – until he fell upon the rear of the Federal right flank! He routed the entire XI Corps by an attack which started about 6 p.m. that day. Soon, the monstrous Federal army would begin a rapid retreat across the river, once again badly defeated by one of

Stonewall Jackson's famous flanking movements.

In the twilight, returning from an inspection of the front, Jackson and his staff were fired upon by some Confederate pickets who mistook them for the enemy. Jackson was wounded in the arm, which soon had to be amputated, and though he insisted upon staying with the army, he was removed to Guiney's Station for his own safety. He had been wounded on May 2 and probably would have recovered had pneumonia not set in. On May 10, he was gone. Lee sorrowfully refused a request from Jackson's men to go to Richmond and march in his funeral procession because the enemy was making movements directly in front of the army.

Stonewall Jackson's strength of character was one of his greatest attributes. He was fundamentally religious, being a strong adherent of Presbyterianism. Both his first wife, who had died shortly after their marriage, and his second wife, Mary Anna Morrison, were daughters of Presbyterian ministers. At VMI, he had a habit of praying for his cadets every day before instructing them, and it was quite well known that he prayed before going into battle. He once said that he never was so ungrateful as to drink a cup of water without thanking God for it.

In some ways, Jackson was eccentric, as are many men of great stature. Upon occasion, he would hold one arm straight up over his head while riding at the head of his troops, and it has been said that there were no chairs in his study at VMI, where he supposedly stood for hours memorizing his lectures and studying his Bible. One thing is sure: He was independent and knew when to take action. At the first Battle of Manassas, he was wounded in the hand and afterward sought the army surgeon for treatment. The surgeon announced that a finger would have be amputated, but when he turned to pick up his instruments Jackson rode away.

NATHAN BEDFORD FORREST

Robert E. Lee often told an amusing anecdote about a negro cook in the army who came into headquarters one day.

"General Lee," he said, "I been wantin' to see you a long time. I'm a soldier."

"Ah. To what army do you belong?"

"Oh, General, I belongs to your army."

"Well, have you been shot?"

"No, sir. I ain't been shot yet."

"How's that? Nearly all our men get shot."

"Why, General, I ain't been shot 'cause I stays back where the generals stay." [41]

This observant cook was nobody's fool, but he would have been in a heap of trouble had he cooked for the command of Nathan Bedford Forrest out in the west, as they called the Tennessee/Alabama/Mississippi theater of war. Forrest was not a general content to direct actions from the rear. He became so caught up in the charge that he *led* his men into the fray, sustaining the initial impact on the front lines.

While covering the retreat from Shiloh, Forrest launched a smashing charge against enemy cavalry. Well in advance of his men, he penetrated the enemy lines into their reserves, suddenly finding himself surrounded by dozens of blazing enemy rifles. Although he and his horse were severely wounded, he stubbornly grabbed his two Colt revolvers, blasted a hole in the mass of bluecoats, and dashed to safety. It wouldn't be the last time he would charge wildly into the enemy and have to "cut his way out," nor would it be the last time he was wounded. And it wouldn't even come close to being the last time he would have a horse shot out from under him. This was the fourth time – there would be twenty-five more.

All of this because Nathan Bedford Forrest stayed at the front and took it straight to the enemy. But then, the army cook had never met this man Forrest. Even General Lee. when asked who was the greatest soldier in his command, replied that he was a man whom he had never met – a man named Forrest.

This extraordinary daredevil, who came to be called *The Wizard of the Saddle*, was born on July 13, 1821 in Bedford County, Tennessee to William Forrest and Mariam Beck. In 1834, the family moved into Tippah County, Mississippi. William had given up his blacksmithing in Tennessee to try his hand at farming in the north Mississippi lands of the recently displaced Chickasaws, but before he could get his place carved out he died, leaving his wife and eleven children in poverty.

It was 1837, and Nathan Bedford, only sixteen years old, had to become the man of the family. In his veins flowed the thrift and pluck of his Scotch-Irish forefathers, and soon it would be evident that the blood was still there. He provided for his mother and his ten younger brothers and sisters by working first as a farm hand, then as an animal trader. Later, he accepted an offer from an uncle to join his mercantile business in Hernando, Mississippi, where his partnership with his uncle enabled him to amply provide for his family. By 1851 he was able to leave that enterprise to become a real estate broker in Memphis.

Six years earlier, in 1845, he had married Mary Ann Montgomery, a well-bred young lady of plantation society. As the 1850s saw a steady increase in his earnings, Forrest began to buy up land, and upon moving to Memphis became a dealer in slaves. Even though that occupation was frowned upon by most Southerners, Forrest was no ordinary buyer and seller of slaves. He never allowed families to be separated, even doing his best to find the husband or wife if a slave was brought to sale without his or her mate. In addition, he insisted upon washing and dressing his slaves in clean garments. His treatment was so kind that slaves regularly appealed to him to buy them for his own plantations – and eventually he did just that. Closing his slave market, he kept those he had on hand and became a planter on a large scale. By the time the guns of war had sounded, Nathan Bedford Forrest was worth a million and a half dollars – a huge sum of money in those days.

On June 14, 1861, he enlisted at Memphis as a private in Captain Josiah White's Tennessee Mounted Rifles, but prominent citizens of the community knew he was fitted for much more than the rank of private and accordingly called upon Governor Isham Harris and General Leonidas Polk with a request that he be given a commission. The result was authority to raise a battalion of cavalry as well as an appointment to lieutenant colonel in the Confederate army. By October, he had eight companies in his command, having outfitted most of the troops at his own expense. He had paid for over 500 Colt navy pistols, 100 saddles, blankets, and whatever supplies were lacking among the assembled men, who numbered about 650.

Nathan Bedford Forrest was the true swashbuckler of the war – fast moving, hard-riding, apt to dash directly into enemy ranks and battle it out one to one, or in some cases, one to a dozen. He did not believe in waiting to be attacked. He had learned as a lad how effectively he could unbalance an opponent by suddenly throwing himself at the would-be attacker.

At Parker's Cross Roads, he exhibited his ability to bluff, thereby saving most of his command from what could have been a most conclusive defeat. They had driven a Yankee force from two positions and by flanking movements had them nearly surrounded. Forrest and the majority of his command were directly facing the Yankees, who had thrown up white flags and were awaiting their official surrender, when all of a sudden a huge Yankee force surprised Forrest's cavalry and suddenly attacked them from the rear.

Colonel Carroll, with a great deal of haste, dashed up to Forrest. "General Forrest, a heavy line of infantry is right in our rear. We are between two lines of battle. What shall we do?" Forrest replied, "We'll charge them both ways!" [42] Firing right and left, they rushed from between the two lines, squeezing out just in the nick of time. To cover the retreat, Forrest took his escort and another regiment to the rear while most of his command escaped. The Yankees were in hot pursuit, so Forrest halted every man he could reach, ordering them to get in line, turn around, and advance upon the pursuing enemy. Lieutenant Baxter protested, "General, I am entirely unarmed; I have neither gun, pistol, nor sword." Forrest shouted back, "That doesn't make any difference; get in line and advance on the enemy with the rest; I want to make as big a show as possible." [43] Several men were likewise unarmed, but the sudden dash at the enemy checked their advance, and the Confederates escaped.

In April, 1863, Federal forces under Col. Streight tore out through Alabama, headed towards Rome, Georgia to destroy the railroad. After several days of running battle with Forrest, Streight was forced to take a stand. Forrest, who was a brigadier general by this time, captured the entire force of 1700 men by showing Streight, under a flag of truce, that he was facing an overwhelming force. While they were talking, Forrest, by pre-arrangement, had his artillerymen circle the only two cannons he had around the top of a hill to give the impression that more guns were arriving. After Col. Streight thought he had counted fifteen artillery guns alone, he figured the infantry must be in the thousands and, without further delay, surrendered his force to Forrest's command on only 400 men!

General Forrest was as independent a man as there was in the army. At the completely unnecessary surrender of Fort Donelson in early 1862, while Forrest was only a colonel, he became infuriated with Generals Buckner, Floyd, and Pillow, when he happened upon them talking about surrender. The generals feared they were surrounded, but Forrest informed them that he would cut his way out if need be; that he had not come there to surrender; that he had promised his boys' parents to take care of them; that he did not intend to see them die in prison camps that winter; and that he was going out if only one man followed. Forrest waked his cavalry that night and led them out, unopposed, under cover of darkness. The next day General Buckner needlessly surrendered 13,000 Confederate soldiers.

Forrest's cavalry was a part of the Army of Tennessee, commanded by a lackluster general named Braxton Bragg, of whom it has been said that "he could snatch defeat out of the jaws of victory." When Forrest, who had never experienced the defeat of his own command, realized the utter folly of trying to win under the inept General Bragg, he gave Bragg a tongue-lashing and refused to follow him any longer. President Davis, although a personal friend of General Bragg, knew full well that he might lose an able cavalry commander if left under the command of the bumbling Bragg: consequently, he gave Forrest an independent command and promoted him to the rank of major general.

General Sherman put thousands of men on the trail of "that devil Forrest," as he called him. General Sturgis was sent out twice to find Forrest, writing to Sherman after the first expedition, "My little campaign is over, and I regret to say Forrest is still at large. . . . I regret very much that I could not have the pleasure of bringing you his hair." [44]

Sherman ordered Sturgis out again. Leaving Federally-occupied Memphis on June 1, 1864, he caught up with Forrest on June 10 at a little place in Mississippi called Brice's Cross Roads. Sturgis had approximately 8500 men with which he intended to crush the 3500 men of Forrest's cavalry. In what has been called the only perfectly executed battle of the war, Forrest leaped at him from the front, charged both of his flanks, and attacked him from the rear. In the ensuing rout, the bridge on the main road was blocked by an overturned wagon, and Yankees plunged headlong into the water to flee the screaming Rebels. Forrest pursued vigorously, his men scattering bluecoats through the woods and across fields. It had taken Sturgis nine days to march out from Memphis; it took him only sixty-four hours to make the return trip with a Confederate cavalry close on his heels. Confederate losses were 492 kill and wounded, while the Federals lost 2,240. Forrest had captured all the enemy artillery, 176 wagons, supplies, and 1500 prisoners.

Sherman was livid. "I cannot understand how he could defeat Sturgis with eight thousand men. . . . Forrest is the devil, and I think he has got some of our troops under cower. . . . I will order them to make up a force and go out to follow Forrest to the death, if it costs ten thousand lives and breaks the Treasury."[45]

No one ever captured General Forrest. His only defeat came at the end of the war. He was a lieutenant general by then, trying to shore up the defenses of Selma, Alabama against an expected attack from 14,000 Yankee troops. It was April 2, 1865, and the end was obviously near. Richmond was being evacuated that very day, and men were scarce in the lower South. Forrest could find only 3,000 at Selma, including his own cavalry, the militia, old men, and some boys. They withstood the onslaught bravely but were finally forced to cut their way out to avoid capture, heading west towards Marion. On April 15, Forrest concentrated his forces at Gainesville, Alabama, and it was here that he received the dreaded but anticipated news that General Richard Taylor, on May 4, 1865, had surrendered the Department of Alabama and Mississippi, which included the remnant of Forrest's command.

There was talk of heading west into the Trans-Mississippi Department, or even going to Mexico, but Forrest reluctantly accepted the surrender and urged his men to go home and help rebuild the shattered South.

The career of Nathan Bedford Forrest had streaked across the pages of history like a blazing comet across the southern sky. He had deviled the Yankees for four years, captured 31,000 prisoners, come under fire 179 times, and killed thirty Yankees with his own hands. He remarked that the latter feat had made him "one up on them," a reference to their record of having shot twenty-nine horses out from under him. At one time, he had placed artillery batteries on the west bank of the Tennessee River, shelling three gunboats, eleven transports, fifteen barges, warehouses, wagon trains, and scores of Federal soldiers, resulting in the destruction of six million dollars worth of enemy supplies and an entire gunboat fleet.

His reputation as a fierce fighter was universally known. John Allan Wyeth, in his biography of Nathan Bedford Forrest, wrote of an incident bearing this out.

> He often brought a smile to the many friends gathered around him in telling of the incident at Cowan's Station, when he was being hotly pursued through that village by the Federals, and a

fiery Southern dame, not knowing that she was addressing the great General Forrest, shook her fist at him and upbraided him as a coward for not turning about to fight the Yankees. The last words he heard her say as he passed on the roadside were: "Why don't you turn and fight, you cowardly rascal? If old Forrest were here, he'd make you fight." [46]

One of the most famous quotes from the war fell from the lips of Forrest when General John Hunt Morgan once asked him the secret of his many successes on the battlefield. Forrest replied, "To git thar fustest with the mostest!" And of course the controversy still rages as to whether Nathan Bedford's grammar and dialect were so colorfully deviant, though it is well known that his spelling was terrible and that he hung on to many of the old expressions of his backwoods upbringing, such as "fetch" for "bring," "betwixt" for "between," and "thern" for "theirs."

After the war, he successfully developed his plantations and became president of the Selma, Marion, & Memphis Railroad. Although he suffered financial reverses several times, he always managed to rebound.

In December, 1865, several bright young college men in Pulaski, Tennessee organized a secret organization called the Ku Klux Klan. They invented fanciful names, such as kleagle, titan, wizard, and cyclops, in order to make the organization sound even more mysterious. Initially, it was only a social club with the sole purpose of whiling away the dreary post-war days, but it soon occurred to some astute observers that the game of dress-up and clandestine meetings might be the answer to the carpet-bag regime of old Parson Brownlow, Reconstruction governor of Tennessee. Throughout the South, civil law had been suspended in favor of harsh military rule, leaving without protection thousands of orphans and widows of Confederate soldiers. To stop the wanton attacks against defenseless women and children and to thwart many unjust acts of the spurious carpetbag governments, the Ku Klux Klan was soon turned into a vigilante force to restore law and order.

As the rumors of the Klan spread over Tennessee during 1866, General Forrest, quick to see its possibilities, made a trip to Nashville to see his former chief of artillery, Captain John W. Morton, in hopes he could find out more about the clandestine organization. As luck would have it, Morton, still a boyishly young man at the time, was Grand Cyclops of the Nashville "den" of the Klan, and, after explaining the operation to Forrest, swore him in as a member and took him to a meeting that night at the Maxwell House Hotel. It was immediately apparent that Forrest was the perfect choice to lead this daring band, and by 1867 he was named *Grand Wizard of the Invisible Empire*. By 1869, Forrest, concluding that law and order had been reestablished in Tennessee to the extent that people were once again safe in their homes and that robbery and theft were no longer a threat to people and their property, ordered the Ku Klux Klan disbanded, although it continued in other states, sometimes under different names, until each state had reclaimed the peace and safety that had been destroyed by carpetbag rule.

On October 29, 1877, Nathan Bedford Forrest passed away in Memphis at the age of 56. Thousands followed the funeral cortège to Elmwood Cemetery. Many former Confederate officials, including President Davis, rode in the procession. Few people were aware during Forrest's lifetime that he had contributed large amounts of his fortune to the welfare of disabled Confederate soldiers, their widows, and orphans in an effort to fill the gap left by the U.S. government, which steadfastly refused to contribute so much as a dime to alleviate the sufferings of former Confederate soldiers while appropriating millions to Union veterans. After his death, Mrs. Forrest faithfully continued the contributions until she had virtually exhausted the entire estate.

The monuments and memorials to Nathan Bedford Forrest are many. Probably the most impressive memorial is the colossal statue of Forrest astride his horse at Forrest Park in Memphis. Considered one of the three best equestrian monuments in America, it stands upon a huge pedestal, the base of which rests over the graves of the general and Mrs. Forrest, whose remains were removed from Elmwood Cemetery.

As the 21st edition of *Southern By the Grace of God* goes to press in 2020, its is sad to note that black political activists in Memphis, led by a white mayor who hails from Indiana, have finally, after years of obscene, insulting efforts, succeeded in removing the statue and are awaiting the disinterment of the General and Mrs. Forrest.

JOHN HUNT MORGAN

If the knighthood of the Old South could be rolled up into one man as its definition of chivalry, John Hunt Morgan would be the word. He was handsome, perfectly proportioned, worshipped by the ladies, and idolized by the men of his time. While the South was suffering disastrous defeats of its large armies, he was slashing away at the enemy on its own soil, giving new hope to weary southern hearts. Raised in an aristocratic family, he was educated and trained in all the proper graces of the antebellum

366

South. At an early age, he acquired that requisite triumvirate of knighthood – the ability to ride, handle a weapon, and physically protect his honor. Like a knight of old, onto the pages of history he rode, avenging the persecuted peasants of Kentucky, rescuing damsels in distress, and eventually winning the hand of his lady fair in Tennessee.

Born in Alabama on June 1, 1825, to Calvin Morgan and Henrietta Hunt, he was named for his maternal grandfather, John Wesley Hunt, of Lexington, Kentucky, probably the wealthiest man west of the Allegheny Mountains. From the Morgan side of the family, John Hunt Morgan got his dashing, daring, impetuous nature, for the Morgans were highly respected men of their time, esteemed for their valorous deeds. But it was from the Hunts that John inherited his taste for the finer things of life. His blue blood flowed from the rich Hunt vein.

Depressed economic circumstances, brought on by tumbling cotton prices, necessitated a move from north Alabama to Lexington, Kentucky when John was five years old. In Lexington, Henrietta's father was able to include the family in his successful business empire, insuring to them a comfortable life in upper class society.

John's education came from home and a neighborhood school until he was old enough to enter Transylvania University, a prestigious school of higher learning attended by several notables, including the future president of the Confederacy, Jefferson Davis. True to his cavalier instincts and Kentucky custom, John challenged a fellow student to a duel, which, by 1844, had become illegal in that state. Neither of the boys was seriously hurt, but John was expelled.

His education thus ended, he began to search for adventure, perhaps foreshadowing his daredevil raids during the War Between the States. Never idle for long, he turned to the military for satisfaction of his thirst for excitement, and on June 4, 1846, John joined Company K, a Lexington group of volunteers for the Mexican War. Action at Buena Vista distinguished the entire unit, who were mustered out on June 7 of the following year in New Orleans where they boarded a train for their tumultuous heroes' welcome in Lexington. Before he could find another unit who would reenlist him, the war ended.

On November 21, 1848, Morgan married Rebecca Bruce, a pretty girl whose father owned interests in several firms, including a hemp factory. In 1853, John and his brother, Calvin, entered into a partnership manufacturing ropes and bags from hemp. It was a successful enterprise, but it didn't provide the thrill John had found in the military; consequently, he organized the Lexington Rifles in 1857 and was in command of that unit of the state militia. He was already a captain, having attained that rank from a previous artillery outfit he had formed in 1852, a unit that had disintegrated in 1854 when the state militia was disbanded for three years.

When war broke out at Fort Sumter, Morgan's wife was deathly ill, and this warrior whose comet was to reach its zenith in the coming war made no move to join up. It wasn't because he vacillated. He knew where he stood, and that was squarely with the South, but with Becky's illness at hand and with the state of Kentucky taking a strange stand for nobody, proclaiming itself entirely neutral in the conflict, Morgan was simply in a state of forced limbo.

Two events occurred to shake him form his inactivity. Becky died on July 21, 1861, and the state of Kentucky was taken over by Unionists. The state militia, largely pro-southern, was ordered to turn in its weapons. Morgan went to the armory, hid his guns in hay-filled wagons, and then shipped crates full of bricks – not guns – to Frankfort. The real John Hunt Morgan had emerged, ready to do service for the South.

On September 28, he and his Lexington Rifles left town, headed for Bowling Green, where his more than 250 men would join the Confederate army as a unit under command of Morgan. The twenty-seven days of waiting to be mustered in didn't suit an adventurer like Morgan, so he filled the days with raids behind enemy lines in Kentucky. Riding by moonlight with only ten or twenty handpicked men, he would prowl around the enemy camps, learning of their strength and how best to use it against them. Morgan's raiders attacked the pickets from the woods, isolated small groups from the main body so that they could be attacked, cut communication lines, and generally harassed the Federal army wherever he could.

On October 27, 1861, the twenty-seven days being up, he and his men were sworn in, Morgan being elected captain of a cavalry company. His brother-in-law, Basil Duke, who would later become General Basil Duke, and who would write the history of Morgan's Raiders after the war, became his lieutenant.

John Hunt Morgan, like other cavalry officers, could lead swift attacks upon the flank of an enemy or strike him like a bolt of lightning from the rear while the infantry was moving slowly towards a calculated position. Such was the benefit of the horsemen. General Jeb Stuart, General Jubal Early, and other cavalrymen occasionally made dashes behind enemy lines, striking at communication lines and supply lines, but Morgan differed in that he spent almost the entire war raiding back behind the enemy. It was an exception to his rule when he stayed close to the main army or participated in a joint attack with the main force.

About the time the Yankees thought they had Kentucky muzzled and were moving down into Tennessee, Morgan's Raiders suddenly showed up in central and northern Kentucky, spreading terror to pro-Union communities while liberating prosouthern towns from harsh provost marshals. More than once the Yankee advance had to be stopped until Morgan could be chased out of Kentucky again. He caused much delay in Yankee movements toward Dixie and thwarted numerous battle plans. That was his *modus operandi*.

By April of 1862, only five months after joining the Confederate army, his name had become a household word, North and South. To say that he was adored in the South would be too mild. The very mention of his name was exhilarating. He inspired Southerners with every newspaper account of how he had whipped another bunch of dreaded Yankees. And there were plenty of accounts. The newspapers lauded him at every turn, suggesting that if other officers were as capable as Morgan the war would be carried to the North and won on their soil.

On April 4, Morgan received his commission as colonel. Two days later, his unit was called upon to fight at Shiloh. His cavalry made one major charge in the battle, this with sabers. His mounted men became mixed in with the enemy infantry, and confusion reigned. He never used sabers again, and he never fought in another major battle.

General Bragg's headquarters of the Army of Tennessee had been at Murfreesboro, and it was here that Colonel Morgan met Mattie Ready, daughter of Charles and Martha Ready and one of the most desired belles in Tennessee. During the rest of 1862 theirs was a celebrated romance that would end in marriage on December 14 in an event that eclipsed any social affair known in that part of the country. There were dances, bonfires, receptions, and serenades by two regimental bands. General Leonidas Polk performed the marriage ceremony while Generals Bragg, Hardee, Cheatham, and Breckinridge looked on. President Davis had been there in the afternoon but had to leave before the wedding.

Earlier in the year, July to be exact, Morgan and his cavalry, now 900 strong, made their first extensive raid into Union-held Kentucky, covering over 1,000 miles in 24 days. They disrupted communications, burned railroad trestles, and destroyed government war supplies. They boldly dashed as far north as Cynthiana, a town not far from the Ohio state line, then headed back to Tennessee before any force of Federals could collect the manpower sufficient to subdue them.

His raiding was gaining for him the deep admiration of Southerners who were trapped in a state controlled by Yankees and turncoats. In Lebanon, Kentucky, he perpetuated the Robin Hood image by seizing government warehouses and distributing coffee, meat, flour, and sugar to the citizens of the town. All along the route, citizens of Kentucky met him in the streets with ladies waving handkerchiefs and offering food to his soldiers.

For the first half of his Confederate service, Morgan adhered strictly to the southern code of chivalry, never molesting private property and always paying for the needs of his cavalry in Confederate money; however, an event in Gallatin, Tennessee, coupled with increasing Yankee atrocities, convinced him that retaliation upon the enemy's entire country was not inconsistent with honor and that it was actually honorable to defend the South in that way. The official consensus in Richmond was that he was not acting in an appropriate manner when he attacked targets other than military, but the people were solidly behind him, and he became the only general of the war who could have gotten away with it.

After destroying the Big South Tunnel above Gallatin and wrecking the train, an action which put the Yankee railroad out of service for more than three months, Morgan left town. The Yankees knew that he had been aided by the citizens of the town, so they plundered the town, arrested every male of twelve years and older, and began marching them to Nashville where they were going to hang them all as spies. A twelve-year-old boy raced into Morgan's camp, and within five minutes Morgan's Raiders were in hot pursuit. They came upon the Yankees about halfway to Nashville. The sight of Yankees pushing the Gallatin citizenry at bayonet point was too much. Morgan went after one particular Yankee who prodded an eighty-year-old man along with his bayonet. Running him down the embankment at the side of the railroad, Morgan shot him dead in his tracks, a fate shared by most of the Yankees of that wicked command.

Morgan made several large raids into Kentucky. After December 13, 1862, he made the raids as *General* Morgan with larger forces, though his largest force was no more than 3900 men. His most famous raid was into Indiana and Ohio where he put a righteous fear into Yankee citizens who thought they were safely behind the lines. Streaking across the bottom of both states, he turned northward into east central Ohio but was captured near the Pennsylvania state line at West Point, Ohio. The exultant Yankees threw him and his officers into the Ohio State Penitentiary, but like a caged tiger he resolved to get out, and by November 27, 1863, he and six of his officers had dug their way out, scaled the outside wall, and scattered through the countryside. The penitentiary had held John Hunt Morgan only four months.

The crowds were waiting in Richmond to see this "Francis Marion of the Second Revolution," a man who had escaped a Yankee penitentiary. He was honored in a parade on January 9, 1864 and introduced to the Virginia legislature on January 11, where a formal reception was held for him.

On January 1, he had issued a proclamation calling for the men of his command to reassemble in Decatur, Georgia. Needing about 2,000 recruits, he received over 14,000 responses from men in every branch of the service, but, the fortunes of the Confederacy being on the decline, he was unable to provide 800 of these new horsemen with horses. On his raid into Kentucky in June, the 800 had to walk until a raid at Lexington brought in enough thoroughbreds for all of them, marking the first time Morgan had to move men on foot.

There was another difference in the new raiders. These were not the Dixie Cavaliers he had been used to having in his cavalry. Many of his swashbuckling Kentuckians who made the hills of Kentucky ring with their choruses of Morgan's marching song, *Cheer, Boys, Cheer!*, were not among the new force. Too many of the new recruits were more interested in high adventure than high ideals, making them hard to control. Private property was ransacked, banks were robbed, and goods were stolen, resulting in an inquiry by the Richmond government into Morgan's command.

Morgan asked for a speedy inquiry to clear his name, but ever so impatient, he went on a raid in east Tennessee while awaiting the inquiry. While spending the night in the Williams home in Greeneville, Morgan and some of his staff officers were surprised by a contingent of Union cavalry who raced into town on a little road that had been left unguarded. The main body of Morgan's men were deployed around the entire perimeter of the town, but one little road was left unguarded and discovered by the enemy who made the most of it. Yankees swarmed furiously up and down the streets surrounding the large two-story home with its walled gardens and grape vineyards, where, according to most accounts, Morgan was the only one shot, being the only one who resisted capture.

Mystery still surrounds the death of John Hunt Morgan. Who betrayed him? Was the road left unguarded on purpose? Did the killer know who he was shooting? Was Morgan shot while attempting to escape, or was he murdered after he threw his hands up? How did one man escape this hornet's nest while Morgan, the genius of escapes, fell victim to his foes? Did his pledge to Mattie that he would never again be taken prisoner figure into his death?

The body of John Hunt Morgan was irreverently thrown across the killer's horse, despite protests that it be carried into the Williams house. Amidst coarse yells and cheers, it was paraded through the streets like some hunter's kill, then taken outside of town to the eagerly awaiting Union forces under General Gillem where, to a roar of sadistic cheering, it was once more displayed from the back of a horse.

According to Major Withers, one of Morgan's staff officers taken prisoner, the body was badly abused, and Withers was forced by the Yankees to dismount and view the bloody, mud-covered body, where it lay, mangled and stripped of its clothing, in a ditch. After protest on Withers' part, the body was taken back to the Williams house, where it was washed and dressed.

John Hunt Morgan, the most popular folk hero of the war, was gone. As his loss was mourned throughout the Confederacy. he was given three funerals, the first one being in Abingdon,

Virginia, where Mattie was staying. The date was September 6, two days after Morgan's death. Ten days later, another large funeral was held in Richmond, and the body was laid in a vault there in Hollywood Cemetery, where it would rest until after the war.

General John H. Morgan Monument, Lexington, Ky.

Finally, in April, 1868, Calvin Morgan brought his brother's body back to Lexington for the final funeral, attended by over 2,000 people, many weeping openly for the slain chieftain.

Tributes have been many, but undoubtedly the most impressive memorial to Morgan's memory is the equestrian statue on the courthouse lawn in Lexington, Kentucky, dedicated in 1911 at a public ceremony which drew more than 10,000 faithful admirers.

Tragically, during the Great Purge, city officials in the deracinated city of Lexington removed the equestrian statue of John Hunt Morgan, along with one of John Breckinridge. No longer atop its majestic pedestal where it had remained for 106 years, Morgan's statue was unceremoniously plopped down on a little slab of granite not far off the ground in the local cemetery. Breckinridge's statue fared no better.

SAM DAVIS

When you drive up to the rock gates of the lovingly restored home of Sam Davis, you are greeted by these words, written in stone: SAM DAVIS, THE CONFEDERATE HERO. The Tennessee countryside surrounding the more than 150 acres of the plantation is beautiful, and for those who have not heard the story of Sam Davis, a sort of wondrous anticipation that accompanies any visit to an antebellum home begins to take hold. But this tour will be different, for laughter and gaiety will be left behind as the sad story of a young boy who died for his country begins to unfold in vivid detail. After having read the pitiful letter of farewell to his mother and father, having walked the same floors where his parents waited for days to learn of Sam's fate, and having stood on the same porch where two frantic parents watched the wagon carrying his metal coffin slowly make its way towards them, one will go back through those rock gates with a burdened heart and a hallowed memory which will last as long as sons are sacred to their mothers.

Wars are truly the "times that try men's souls," visiting upon mankind all kinds of cruelty, pestilence, and death. The old expression, the "ravages of war," conjures up things we'd rather forget. But war also has a paradoxical way of demanding the best qualities in an individual, and in war's tragic arena many are called to be heroes. Among these heroic men there usually arises a special person who stands out somewhat apart from the others, one who captures the hearts of the people, one who exhibits bravery and chivalry unmatched – one who gives his life. It is rare to find such qualities in a mature man, much less in a youth, but of such stature was our hero, Sam Davis, who, in the tradition of Revolutionary War hero, Nathan Hale, gave his only life in the cause of freedom.

His home, inside the stone gates, is not the place where he was born on October 6, 1842, but it is his boyhood home. "It is the home from which he rode into the service of his beloved Southland" and the home "to which his body was returned as that of an immortal hero."[47] In 1927, the state of Tennessee bought the plantation which has become a shrine to the young boy who, while facing imminent death, uttered the bravest words of his life, words that have rung down through the years: *If I had a thousand lives, I would give them all rather than betray a friend.*

Sam was one of the most promising boys in Middle Tennessee. He was handsome, friendly, and admired by all of his friends in Rutherford County. In the fall of 1860, when he was eighteen years old, he went away to school. At the Western Military Institute in Nashville, he soon became a favorite with his classmates, many of whom would recall in later years that he was popular and extremely trustworthy. Two of his teachers had a great influence upon him; they would soon be known to the world as Confederate Generals Bushrod Johnson and E. Kirby Smith.

In April, as Sam was nearing the end of his first year of college, the South was struck as by a thunderbolt. Lincoln had provoked a confrontation at Fort Sumter in faraway Charleston Harbor. Shots had been fired, and the first battle of a dreadful war was now history. The enemy would soon be at the door, and Tennessee would have to decide which way to go. There was really little time for deliberation. Tennessee was a southern state and would soon be invaded by hordes of Yankees due to its proximity to several northern states. Kentucky, to the north, would be of only limited help in stopping the murderous onslaught. That poor state was so divided in opinion that its naïve government believed it could remain neutral and so made a declaration to that end, a move which only rendered it defenseless to Lincoln's army of provost marshals who swarmed into the state and usurped the power of civil governments all across Kentucky.

Like Bushrod Johnson and E. Kirby Smith, Sam was aware that his services would be needed and that everybody would be leaving the Institute, but poor Sam had no way of knowing how final his departure would be. One can only imagine the many thoughts that raced through young Sam's mind. He wanted so much to do well in college and make his parents proud of him back in Rutherford County. Maybe he could enlist for six months or a maybe even a year and then return to the Institute. But if the Yankees came – and come they most surely would – there wouldn't be a college anyway. Or any teachers. Sam, like all of the boys in Tennessee, new full well what an invasion of Yankees meant. Yankees had bragged about what they would do. Homes would be burned, schools would be destroyed, and people would be killed. This was war. This was real. And Sam knew it. His father, Charles Davis, was too old to enlist, and Sam, being the eldest son, had to consider the protection of his mother and father as well as his younger brothers and sisters.

The burden lay heavily upon his mind, and he was arriving at the only logical conclusion a southern boy could make in 1861.

A boy of only 19, he bravely returned home to Rutherford County, joining the Rutherford Rifles, which soon became Company I, First Tennessee Infantry, CSA. A saddened mother and heavy-hearted father bade their son farewell as they watched him ride off with the First Tennessee to Virginia, where he would receive his first war experience under the legendary General Stonewall Jackson in the summer and fall of 1861.

Sure enough, while he was away the Yankees got into western Tennessee, and the First Tennessee was rushed back to native soil. These anxious soldiers were directed to Corinth, Mississippi, just south of the Tennessee state line, where they would immediately muster for the looming confrontation over in Tennessee, a clash which would become known as the Battle of Shiloh. It was the bloodiest action of the war up to that time, claiming nearly 11,000 southern casualties in only three days. The northern boys also paid a dear price for their unwelcome visit to Tennessee – nearly 14,000 men killed, wounded, or missing. By this time, Sam had served under three of the ablest generals who ever graced the pages of history: Generals Albert Sidney Johnston, P.G.T. Beauregard, and Stonewall Jackson. Tragically, General Johnston would not survive the battle.

As fall fell on Middle Tennessee in 1862, General Braxton Bragg, who had been given command of the Army of Tennessee after General Johnston's death, organized a special unit of extra-ordinary soldiers to be his "eyes and ears." They were commanded by Captain Shaw, who, to protect his identity, was given the alias of E. Coleman. Confederate officials and his scouts always referred to him as E. Coleman, and the Yankees did not know that he was the same man who meandered frequently within their lines posing as an itinerant herb doctor.

Yankees were all over Tennessee by late 1862, and the state was in danger of being completely lost to the Federals. Sam Davis, possessing splendid soldierly qualities and a reputation

379

for honesty, was fast making his mark in the military. Many accounts of his excellence had made their way home to his ever watchful and waiting parents, so it came then as no great surprise to many that Sam was selected to be a member of the elite close-knit group of men known as Coleman's Scouts. For about a year, these sleuths operated secretly behind enemy lines, collecting vital information for Bragg's army. Once, when Sam was in Yankee-occupied Nashville, he was seated in the dining room of the St. Cloud Hotel at the same table as General Rosecrans, listening with the ears of a Confederate to the plans of an unsuspecting Yankee general; but many times Sam and his compatriots boldly wore their proud Confederate gray trousers and their butternut jackets, making their presence behind enemy lines all the more dangerous.

At home, many a solemn prayer rose from the hearts of two anxious parents.

Discovered details of Yankee movements had contributed to the Confederate victory at Chickamauga in September, 1863, and the Yankees were on an all-out alert to round up these meddling men of Coleman's Scouts. Things were getting tense for the Scouts, and yet they were detailed to find out even more in-formation as to the plan of action of General Grant's army in Middle Tennessee. Their role was extremely vital to General Bragg.

In November, Sam secretly approached his own home to visit the family. Rutherford County was now deep in Yankee-held territory. He came by night and tapped at the dining room window. His mother let him in and gave him an old Federal overcoat which she had dyed with the only dye available at that time: the hulls of the butternut. Now made into a Confederate overcoat, it is the coat Sam would be wearing when captured. Worn over gray trousers, it was part of an outfit widely recognized as sort of a homespun Confederate uniform. The general who would soon condemn Sam to death would, nevertheless, falsely claim that Sam was not in Confederate uniform when captured and that he was, therefore, a spy.

After visiting with his parents and begging a peek at the sleeping children, Sam stole away from his home and family for the last time. Nevermore would he see the love in his father's eyes, nor would he hear his mother's sweet voice as when she tenderly guided him though life's trials. He would never see his brothers and sisters again this side of eternity, and even though he could not have been certain that death would take him, the likelihood of it probably preyed upon his mind as he left his home and disappeared into the night. His father had repaired some boots for him – the boots that would be on his feet as his coffin made its slow, winding way toward home in only a few short weeks.

Sam set out from Smyrna and went northwest to Nashville, a distance of about 18 or 20 miles. He then traveled due south by way of the Franklin pike, and at some point made a rendezvous with Coleman and some of the Scouts. It was here agreed that each man should leave for north Alabama – separately – on Friday night, November 19. Upon reaching north Alabama, they should journey east across that state, perhaps meeting up with each other by chance, finally coming safely within Confederate lines at Chattanooga, Tennessee, where they would give their scouting observations to General Bragg. It was also at this clandestine meeting that Coleman (Captain Shaw) gave Sam Davis the papers for General Bragg, the same papers which were to cost young Davis his life within little more than a week.

Since leaving home that night, Davis had traveled about 100 miles on horseback, all within enemy lines. Upon reaching Giles County down in southern Tennessee, he was captured on November 20 by nervous Yankees at Minor Hill, only seven miles north of the Alabama state line. His Confederate uniform of butternut and gray unmistakably marked him as a Confederate soldier, entitling him to be confined and treated as a prisoner-of-war, not a spy. He was taken at once to Pulaski, eleven miles north of the point of capture. A large part of the Federal army was located in the area, and this picturesque little county seat would soon be forever stained with the horrific death of a defenseless youth in the prime of manhood, a brave boy whose only offense lay in trying to protect his family and his native soil from the invader.

Sam Davis had one week to live. No one will ever know exactly what papers were found upon him, in his haversack, in his saddlebags, or inside the heel of his boots. So many stories have been told by his captors down through the years that nothing but confusion remains; but perhaps that was the plan, for no details were entered in the Yankee provost marshal's books when Sam was imprisoned at Pulaski. The whole sordid affair was handled so shamefully that it is no surprise pertinent facts were intentionally buried. Even the northern soldiers were forbidden to discuss it openly.

Sam had been behind enemy lines for ten days, and it was obvious that much of his information had been obtained by Sam himself; but, together with whatever papers E. Coleman had given him, it was enough to convince the Union general that Sam probably knew the true identity of the elusive E. Coleman. Seizing upon the opportunity afforded by the youthfulness of his captive, the general quickly accused Davis of being a spy so that he could threaten him with hanging if he didn't tell who gave him the papers. The general was laboring under the delusion that E. Coleman must be, in reality, someone on his own staff or very near it, due to the accuracy of the information in the papers, and he was willing to sacrifice a boy's life in order to find that man. In later years, the Yankee general would quote Davis as saying, "I know that I will have to die, but I will not tell where I got the information, and there is no power on earth that can make me tell. You are doing your duty as a soldier, and I am doing mine. If I have to die, I will do so feeling that I am doing my duty to God and my country."[48]

The general held a hasty court-martial in which all of the soldiers in the arresting party testified that Davis was, indeed, dressed as a Confederate soldier – conclusive evidence that he was not a spy. But Union armies in the South were often not held accountable to their superiors in Washington, and being deep in southern territory made it that much easier to hide their evil deeds.

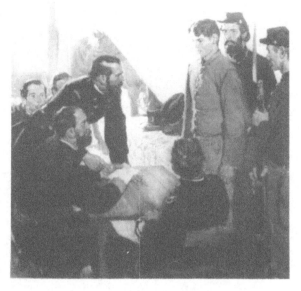

The general needed a death conviction to hold over young Sam's head, and the military commission gave it to him. The commission sentenced Sam Davis to be hung as a spy and set the date for hanging for Friday, November 27, 1863, only one short week after being captured. Thus armed, the general attempted to break Sam down in hopes of finding the true identity of E. Coleman. He assigned Levi Naron, Chief of Scouts for the Union army in Tennessee, to the task. Naron repeatedly offered Sam his freedom in exchange for the information about Coleman, but to no avail. Sam steadfastly informed him that he would never betray the trust placed in him and that if Tennessee could not be restored to the southern Confederacy, he would prefer to die anyway.

This young hero found himself in a tight spot, indeed, for on or about November 20, three of Coleman's Scouts were rounded up and placed in the same jail as Davis. Joshua Brown and W.L. Moore were two of those placed in the jail, but the most ironic twist of all was that the third person arrested was none other than Captain Henry Shaw – alias E. Coleman!

So the man General Dodge was looking for was right under his nose, and he didn't know it. Oh, how easy it would have been for Sam to point out Coleman and save his own neck! So easy! But not for Sam Davis. Sam was raised a true southern boy by Christian parents, and no doubt he knew well the Scripture that he was soon to fulfill: *Greater love hath no man than this, that he lay down his life for his friends.* Can we imagine the whispered conversations between those three Scouts in their jail cells? How breathlessly they must have watched Sam respond to the continual offers of release if only he would name his informants!

Many of the Yankee soldiers, noting Davis's firm resolve, greatly admired the young scout. They often visited him in his cell, begging him to save himself from such a useless death. Sam replied that life was, indeed, sweet and that he did so much want to live, but that he could not betray a friend and would rather die a thousand deaths than do so. Citizens of Giles County visited him, and upon one occasion heard Sam remark, "I do not fear for death, but it makes me mad to think I am to die as a spy." [49]

Chaplain James Young of the 81st Ohio Infantry, was so touched by the plight of this boy – some mother's son – that he spent the final day and night with Sam, going even to the gallows with him. He prayed with him to the end. At Sam's request, on the night before the execution, the chaplain sang with him *On Jordan's Stormy Banks I Stand*. He was there when Sam spoke his last words to Levi Naron, who had made a last-minute offer of freedom if only Sam would betray his friend, E. Coleman. Sam sat down on the lid of his coffin and listened to Naron's last offer. Then, looking him steadily in the eye, Sam replied, "Do you suppose were I your friend that I would betray you? Sir, if you think I am that kind of man, you have missed your mark. You may hang me a thousand times and I would not betray my friends." [50]

What will always remain the mystery of this whole affair is why the commanding general, who was in absolute command, did not, after seeing young Davis's steadfast adherence to his principles, simply call off the bluff and admit a small failure of strategy, thereby saving the life of a boy who had already won the hearts of many a Union man in that outfit. But that wasn't in the make-up of this less-than-masculine officer from Massachusetts who had already managed to shoot himself in the leg early in the war. Holding the power of life and death in his wicked hand, this cowardly creature would not relent.

Approximately two minutes after Sam refused Naron's last offer, it then being twenty minutes after ten in the morning, the noose was tightened, and Sam Davis was launched into eternity. A soldier named John Randal – one of those who had helped capture Sam – said that never in all his life had he witnessed such a pathetic and heroic scene, that he sat on this horse with tears streaming down his face, and that he saw many other Federal soldiers in tears. L.W. Forgrave, another Union soldier, equally distressed by the grisly scene, later recalled the tragic event.

> I was a musician at the headquarters of General G.M. Dodge at Pulaski, Tennessee, and helped to play the dead march at the murder of Sam Davis. With four years of service in the Union army . . . I never witnessed such bravery as was portrayed by him at the time of his killing. This boy Davis was offered a reprieve by a chief of scouts named Chickasaw [Naron] at headquarters if he would tell where his captain was. As I could hear, he told them he would die a thousand deaths first. . . .
>
> I can never obliterate the expression of Davis' face, as he was a boy about my own age. He wore at that time a roundabout or pea jacket and a black slouch hat. I have wondered who his folks were very often, and was glad to know that he was not forgotten. Davis is in Heaven, I trust.[51]

After the execution, fellow prisoners Moore, Brown, and Shaw were sent north to a Yankee prison, but Shaw jumped from the train in Kentucky and resumed his activities as E. Coleman. Sam Davis's death had saved all three of his friends and fellow scouts.

Before he died, Sam gave the overcoat that his mother had dyed for him to his new friend, Chaplain Young. The chaplain kept it until he was seventy-three years old and then sent it to the editor of *Confederate Veteran*, the monthly magazine that served as the main publication and information source for thousands of veterans after the war.

On the day before his execution, Sam wrote a heartrending letter to his parents.

SOUTHERN BY THE GRACE OF GOD

Pulaski, Giles County, Tenn.
Nov. 26, 1863

Dear Mother: O how painful it is to write you! I have got to die tomorrow – to be hanged by the Federals. Mother, do not grieve for me. I must bid you good-bye for evermore. Mother, I do not fear to die. Give my love to all.

Your dear son.

Mother: Tell the children all to be good. I wish I could see all of you once more, but I never will any more.

Mother and Father: Do not forget me. Think of me when I am dead, but do not grieve for me; it will not do any good.

Father: you can send after my remains if you want to do so. They will be at Pulaski, Tennessee. I will leave some things, too, with the hotel keeper for you. Pulaski is in Giles County, Tennessee, south of Columbia.[52]

This letter and the things of which Sam wrote were committed to Chaplain Young for delivery to his mother and father.

Pulaski is about seventy-five miles south of Smyrna, but shortly after the execution, agitation over this heinous crime was so great that word quickly reached Sam's parents about a scout named Davis who had been caught and hanged at Pulaski on November 27. Fearing the very worst, they set about to determine if it was their own Sam. They asked a most trusted and able friend, Mr. John C. Kennedy, to go to Pulaski where he might obtain all of the details possible and, if it were Sam, to bring home the earthly remains of their brave boy. Many years

387

later, Mr. Kennedy recalled that fateful trip.

Mr. and Mrs. Davis were not certain that it was their son who had been executed at Pulaski. They had made diligent efforts through various channels to trace the "grapevine" story that it was their Sam, but were not assured. At last the time was set to start on the search. Mrs. Davis gave me a piece of the plain linsey of that used for his jacket lining, and also described his boots, and told of other things that only a good and loving mother could have thought about. She was interrupted occasionally by suggestions from Mr. Davis.

The start was made with two mules hitched to a very heavy carryall. We had a meal sack containing a boiled ham and about a half bushel of corn pones, on which their son Oscar, a small boy who was to accompany me, and I were to live while gone.

We reached Nashville that evening too late to get a pass, but I procured a metallic case and box and had them put in the conveyance. The next morning I went to General Rousseau, who declined to give me a pass and sent me to General Grant's Adjutant General, who kindly and politely, but positively, refused also, replying to all my pleadings for his mother's sake: "No Sir! No Sir! No Sir!"

I then returned to General Rousseau, whom I had known in my boyhood days, and again asked for a pass. After some boyhood reminiscences not necessary to repeat, he supplied one for myself, the boy, and team to Columbia, which was as far as his lines extended, telling me that was all he could do. I gladly accepted the pass, which was written on a piece of paper elegantly printed and looked like a large bank note.

We entered the lines at Columbia and drove straight through town, not stopping until we reached the picket on the other side, who after looking over our pass, though he could not read it, and seeing the coffin and small boy, permitted us to go on. The same thing occurred when we reached the picket at Pulaski, who permitted us to enter the town. When near the square, I left Oscar to hold to the mules while I went to the Provost Marshal to get a pass or find out what he would do with us. His office was in the Court House. He asked how I got into Pulaski, and I handed him General Rousseau's pass. He looked up and curtly remarked, "This is no account here. What do you want?" I told him I had come for the body of Sam Davis who had been hanged; that his parents wanted it at home.

His manner at once changed and, extending his hand, he said, "Tell them for me that he died the bravest of the brave, an honor to them, and with the respect of every man in this command." He then asked what more he could do to help me. I requested return passes and a permit to take up the body, which he cheerfully gave. I also asked if he thought I would have any trouble or interference while I was at the graveyard, and he replied, "No sir. If you do, I will give you a company . . . yes, a regiment, if necessary."

Taking advantage of his cordial words, I asked him how Sam was captured, as Mr. Davis had requested me to spare no pains to find out how and when he was taken. He said he did not know any of the particulars, but showed me two books in which records were kept in his office, and the only entry, after giving his name and description was, as I remember: "Captured on the Lamb's Ferry Road by

389

Capt. McKenzie's scouts."

Before leaving home I was referred for assistance, if necessary, while in Pulaski, to a Mr. Richardson, who had been (if not then) the County Court Clerk. We found him willing and ready to aid all in his power. The grave digger agreed to take the body up for $20.00. The next morning, together with his assistants, Mr. Richardson, Oscar and I were busy at the grave when four or five Federal soldiers came up. One of them advanced to me, raising his cap politely and in a subdued tone of voice, proffered for himself and comrades to assist, if desired. I thanked him sincerely, for I had not known what their presence might mean, but declined their services. When the box was raised and lid removed, the cap of white was still over his head down to his neck, tied with long strings, which were wrapped around his neck two or three times. His boots were on, but the legs cut off at the ankles. I took from my pocket the piece of his jacket lining and saw that they were alike. When I removed the cap, I found the face was black, but recognizable. We then transferred the body to the metallic case. During all the time the body was being examined and transferred, the Federal soldiers stood in line with caps off, paying tribute in acts if not words. Upon our return from the cemetery, the Provost Marshal said the Chaplain, who was with Sam at the gallows, had some keepsakes for the father and mother. He gave me a little book, in which was a farewell message to his mother, and the buttons from his coat and vest. . . .

We reached Nashville and drove to where the Adams' Express Company's office now is, which was then where our present townsman, Mr. Cornelius, had his undertaking establishment, and turned the body over to him with specific instructions about the shrouding. Mr. Davis had said to me, "If you think it is best that Jane and I should not see him, do as you think best about the matter."

On the evening of the seventh day after leaving home, we drove in the big gate, some distance from the house. Mr. & Mrs. Davis were watching, and when they saw the casket, Mrs. Davis threw her arms above her head and fell. All was sorrow in that home. I had a boy catch my horse to go home to see my old mother and father, and change clothing, etc., but Mr. Davis prevailed upon me to stay and send for what I needed.

The next morning, while standing out in the yard, Mr. Davis came to me, hesitated, then catching his breath almost between each word, said, "John, don't you think it's hard a father can't see the face of his own child?"

I replied that I thought it best he and Mrs. Davis should remember him as they saw him last. He turned and left me. I drove the carryall that afternoon, with the body, across the creek to the old family graveyard where he was buried. [53]

Memorials of every kind, and in great profusion, were generated by the death of the young hero in Tennessee who would be known forevermore as *Sam Davis, Hero of the Confederacy.* The monuments command the most attention, with the most handsome and impressive one being the granite and marble statue south of the courthouse in Pulaski, Tennessee. In 1950, the state of Tennessee dedicated another shrine to the memory of Davis in the form of a stone building which stands upon the exact spot where once stood the hated gallows. Further south, at Minor Hill, there is an inscribed rock where Davis was taken prisoner, and throughout Middle Tennessee bronze markers abound. The

Tennessee Division of the United Daughters of the Confederacy raised money for a stained-glass memorial window, which was installed in the Confederate Museum in Richmond in 1912.

Perhaps the most significant monument, though, is a bronze statue standing on the capitol grounds in Nashville. The state legislature passed an act providing the choicest spot for the statue, having previously allowed only two monuments on the capitol grounds, both of them honoring presidents – Andrew Jackson and James K. Polk. Money for the statue came from every state in the land, and world-renowned sculptor George Julian Zolney was selected to do the likeness. No photographs of Sam were known to exist, so the sculptor had to work from descriptions, using Sam's younger brother as a model. All of the family photographs had been burned when Yankees set fire to a haystack at the Davis home. Mrs. Davis had hidden the photographs in the haystack, fearing the Yankees would burn her home. It was only after 120 years that the photograph used at the beginning of this biographical sketch was discovered. It was found in the old family album of Captain John W. Morton, chief artillerist for Nathan Bedford Forrest. Morton and Davis were the same age and had attended the Nashville Military Academy together. Zolney completed the statue in time for the dedication on April 29, 1909.

The Sam Davis Monument Committee presented the statue, and Governor Patterson made the acceptance speech. Having been present as a school boy at the dedication of the equestrian statue of Andrew Jackson, he proclaimed, "Little did I think then, even in the day dreams of youth, that one day as Governor I would be called upon to accept in the name of the State another figure in bronze erected on this side of the grounds, not of a man on horseback, but of a young man scarcely more than a boy, who belonged to another and later age of our history, who stands without the marks and accoutrements of rank, without any other sign save that of a soldier ready to fight and ready to die. The name and fame of Andrew Jackson filled the mind with wonder and admiration; the memory of Sam Davis, with infinite love and tenderness."[54]

Engraved upon the base of the Sam Davis monument are these words:

"The boys will have to fight the battles without me."

He gave all he had – life;
He gained all he lacked – immortality.

In addition to these lines and other remarks which briefly recall the vital incidents of his short life, the monument contains a few of the inspired lines from the well-known poem of Ella Wheeler Wilcox. The entire poem is so gripping as to require its inclusion in this sketch.

SAM DAVIS

When the Lord calls up earth's heroes
　　To stand before his face,
O, many a name unknown to fame
　　Shall ring from that high place!
And out of a grave in the Southland,
　　At the just God's call and beck,
Shall one man rise with fearless eyes,
　　And a rope about his neck.

For men have swung from gallows
　　Whose souls were white as snow.
Not how they die nor where, but why,
　　Is what God's records show.
And on that mighty ledger
　　Is writ Sam Davis' name —
For honor's sake he would not make
　　A compromise with shame.

The great world lay before him,
 For he was in his youth;
With love of life young hearts are rife,
 But better he loved truth.
He fought for his convictions;
 And when he stood at bay,
He would not flinch or stir one inch,
 From honor's narrow way.

They offered life and freedom
 If he would speak the word;
In silent pride he gazed aside
 As one who h ad not heard.
They argued, pleaded, threatened —
 It was but wasted breath.
"Let come what must, I keep my trust,"
 He said, and laughed at death.

He would not sell his manhood
 To purchase priceless hope;
Where kings drag down a name and crown,
 He dignified a rope.
Ah, grave! where was your triumph?
 Ah, death! where was your sting?
He showed you how a man could bow
 To doom and stay a king.

And God, who loves the loyal
 Because they are like him,
I doubt not yet that soul shall set
 Among his cherubim.
O Southland! bring your laurels:
 And add your wreath, O North!
Let glory claim the hero's name,
 And tell the world his worth.[55]

394

BEAUVOIR.

IX

Southern Sampler

Breathes there a Southerner without a story to tell? One of the oldest pastimes in the world is the art of storytelling. Many an invention – TV, movies, radio, newspapers, magazines, video games – has come along to compete with the personal swapping of tales, but that time-honored genre has survived them all.

When we get together, that's what we do. We begin to tell stories, some short ones, some long ones, but stories all the same. And the funnier, the better – or the more outlandish, the better. We're good listeners, too. But while the other person is telling his tale, in the back of our minds we're racing through our catalogue of good stories, mentally selecting one that ties in with the current line of conversation, silently rehearsing it while the other half of our brain enjoys the tale being told – and surprisingly comprehends what it hears!

What a marvelous thing the brain. For that's where our folklore is stored. Like other cultures of the world, our history is written and stored in archives, but unlike so many of them, ours is told, and told, and retold. Much of our legend and lore will never be written; it simply passes from generation to generation by word of mouth.

Everyone wants to tell his story – or stories. When great-great grandfather came home from the war, he told about it. It was the same war that historians wrote about, but he wanted to tell it his way. Every succeeding generation passes the same story down, each teller rephrasing it in his own style. Thus, the great southern tradition of storytelling is perpetuated, and along with it, our history. I've often wondered why Southerners love to listen to stories about the past. Is it because our history is so interesting, or is it because we tell it so well?

The following selections are but a small representation of the vast amount of material that lends itself to a good southern story. Many good stories have found their way onto paper in the form of letters, diaries, and interviews, and these sources were tapped for some of the tales presented here, but others merely came by word of mouth and are finding their way into print for the first time with the publication of this volume. True to the nature of my southern upbringing, I have been both an avid listener and storyteller, but if my listening took precedence then it gives me pleasure to balance it by relating here some of the tales I've heard.

THE BELL WITCH

There are very few people in Middle Tennessee who don't know about the Bell Witch. It's the favorite ghost story in those parts. My connection with the tale came by way of a visit to the home of some friends in Nashville on a hot night in late

July, 1987. The thermometer had been hitting 100 degrees for several days when I dropped in on Charles and Ginger Turner and found everyone huddled under the air conditioner. A neighbor was there – a young lady by the name of Karen Guy. While introducing us, the Turners mentioned the fact that Karen was the great-great-great-great-great-granddaughter of Andrew Jackson, and it wasn't long before the conversation centered upon stories about the seventh President of the United States. Before the evening was over, Karen gave me an invitation to come out to the old home place at my earliest convenience.

Driving down the old narrow lane with its overhanging trees, back into the woods and occasionally through a pasture, was a relief from the harrowing, everlasting zip-zip-zip of the feverish Nashville traffic. I had been busy, and it was 'way down in the fall now, but I hadn't forgotten about the invitation. Not for a minute. Karen was going to tell me about the Bell Witch, so I had pen and paper in hand when I got out of my Ford pickup in the driveway of a two-story late Victorian house surrounded by large English boxwoods and plenty of shade trees. The house belonged to her aunt, Louise Maxwell, a charming elderly lady who graciously seated us in the parlor which was furnished in Victorian heirlooms. The house itself was a piece of history, for it sits upon the old foundation of Jackson's first home, *Hunter's Hill*, which predates *The Hermitage*. During one of his gambling episodes, Jackson lost *Hunter's Hill* and hundreds of acres that surrounded it. The house burned in 1903, and the house in which we were sitting arose upon its foundation.

Before the storytelling began, Karen's sister Judy arrived, and the story of the Bell Witch began to unfold, a story made all the more intriguing by the fact that Andrew Jackson was involved in an incident with the Witch, plus the revelation made in that parlor that Judy is suspicious as to the Witch's possible visitation upon her own generation of Jackson's descendants due to some strange and unexplained happenings.

The Bell Witch is what most of us would call a ghost

because, unlike a witch, it was not seen – only heard. But the slaves of the Bell family called it a witch, and soon it became known far and wide as the Bell Witch. Betsy Bell saw the Witch in the form of a woman strolling about the orchard, and upon a few occasions her brother and father saw the same apparition, but except for these instances the Witch was merely heard, not seen.

The trouble began about 1817. John Bell saw a strange animal sitting between two corn rows one day. Not being able to identify it, he shot at it only to see it disappear into thin air. Soon, the children began to see strange creatures in the woods, and, before long, the woman appeared in the orchard. Sometime later, there came scratching, knocking sounds at the windows and doors of the house, as if someone was trying to get in; but, upon opening the doors, the Bell family could find no one outside or even near the house. Then came the terrifying realization that the thing was in the house. There were sounds of wings flapping against the ceiling and louder sounds as of dogs fighting inside the house, and eventually the house began to shake as if in a storm. The family was not only frightened out of their wits but afraid that someone in the community would find out about the strange happenings and begin to talk.

The loud noises continued for about a year. Then John Bell came down with a mysterious illness which affected his tongue and jaw, making chewing and swallowing difficult. The continued annoyance affected his nerves, causing the family to seek advice from friends, advice which necessitated divulging the secret in the Bell home. Whether or not this affliction was caused by the spirit in the house was never known, but the family attributed it to the Witch just the same. What is known is that the Witch soon began to talk and threaten the life of John Bell.

At first, friends came one at a time to witness the bizarre events in the house, but as news of the occurrences spread, people came in great numbers. Those who spent the night with the Bells had the sheets yanked from their beds throughout the night while being subjected to loud, derisive laughter. Frank Miles, a close friend of the family, volunteered to try to get hold of the Witch and crush it in his powerful grip. A large, stout man and sure of his ability to defeat the Witch, he frequently spent the night with the Bells awaiting the opportunity to soundly thrash the annoying thing, whatever it was. The bedtick was snatched from under him, his covers were pulled off the bed all night, and finally the Witch struck him about the head with the most forceful blows he had ever sustained. The spirit then screamed out that he would do well to end his pursuit of her because he could not win a struggle with a spirit.

The Bell Witch began to bother several other people in the community, and there are dozens of tales among the people of that area concerning the Witch and its pranks. It would be easier to dismiss the tales as nonsense or mass hysteria or whatever one might wish to call it if the characters in the story were not of the highest reputation and standing in the community. There were ministers of the gospel and doctors who witnessed the strange goings-on in the Bell home, yet none of them could give an explanation as to the cause. In 1849, the *Saturday Evening Post* published a comprehensive sketch of the Bell Witch, and in 1923, *McClure's Magazine* devoted much columnar space to the tale.

The character of the Witch was as mysterious as was her presence. She quoted scripture, preached to various members of the Bell family and sang hymns; yet she disliked them very much and inflicted them with much pain.

She was very selective, reserving most of her evil for John Bell and his daughter, Betsy. She despised the slaves and upon several occasions took great pleasure in whipping them with sticks and rods. Mr. Bell had good slaves who gave no trouble and needed no such discipline. The family had become quite attached to their slaves, yet the Witch had so intimidated them that they were afraid to leave their cabins at night. They were safe in that regard, however, because the Witch's olfactories were so offended by them that she refused to go into their cabins to bother them. One night Mrs. Bell had one of the young girls sleep under her own bed in the house as a method of keeping the Witch out of the room, but the Witch, not to be outfoxed, yelled out that she knew one of the slaves was under the tall, raised bed. The next thing they heard was a loud, continuous spitting sound. Then the girl was rolled out from under the bed like a log, her head covered in spit. Screaming that the Witch was going to spit her to death, she fled from the house back to her cabin.

The only one that the Witch seemed to like was Mrs. Bell, whom she called "Old Luce." She sang sweet songs to her and comforted her with kind words. When Lucy was ill, the Witch prepared the table for the family meals and dropped big bunches of fruit into their laps. The fruit incident happened when visitors were there as well, further adding to the tales that spread across that part of Tennessee.

As the witch talked more and more freely, she told them that she would stay for four years, go away for seven, then return for a little while. Before the four years were up, experts from Europe visited the Bell home, trying to discover the truth about the entire affair. Each time, they went home baffled.

At one point in this sordid saga, Andrew Jackson, who lived about thirty-five miles from the Bells, decided to try his hand at taming the monster. He started out with several horsemen and a covered wagon laden with tents, supplies, and provisions for about a week. On the road near the Bell house, one of his burly companions began to speak slightingly about the Witch. At once, the wheels of the heavy wagon locked and wouldn't budge. The driver, in spite of all of his whipping and exhortation, couldn't make the wagon proceed. The team seemed powerless to move the wheels. Shortly, a sharp voice rang out, "Go on, old General." The wheels moved freely again, and Jackson's party went on.

That night, Andrew Jackson's party slept not a wink. Betsy screamed all night from the slapping and pinching she received from the Witch, and Jackson's covers were ripped from his bed as quickly as he could put them back on. The Witch pulled his hair and slapped the other members of his group until morning; whereupon, the whole expedition was declared a disaster, and Jackson went home.

Young Betsy Bell was in love with one of the finest boys in the country, and it pleased both families when the engagement was told and a distant wedding date was announced. But the Witch had other plans. She told Betsy not to marry Joshua Gardner and began to abuse her frequently by pinching her and slapping her face until it was ready to bleed. At night, she pulled Betsy's hair and twisted it into knots so close to the scalp that it took her mother hours to comb it all out. When Betsy and Joshua persisted with their wedding plans, the Witch would yell at them while they were strolling with friends of having friends over for parties. Between the embarrassment and the persecution, Betsy was beside herself with apprehension, finally agreeing to call off the engagement. Though asked by Betsy and other family members why the marriage shouldn't occur, the Witch would only say that there were some very good reasons which she didn't intend to divulge.

Near the end of the first four-year visit, the Witch began to bother John Bell with terrible physical pain. His face was contorted, and his body was wrenched in agony. At times, he would get better, but the Witch announced that in time she was going to kill him. Near the end, he tried to walk about his yard, but she would knock his shoes off his feet and throw him to the ground. His son, who wrote about the incident years later, tried to tie his shoes back upon his feet as tight as possible, but the Witch would send them flying through the air over and over. Then, in a fit of rage, she beat him terribly about the head and shoulders, sending him to bed and in need of a physician. The doctor prescribed some kind of potion and left, but John began to get violently ill and in a few days was at the point of death. The doctor came back and called for the medicine bottle that he had left with John Bell. In its place, there was a bottle of foul-smelling liquid which defied analysis. The Witch was heard to laugh loudly and to say that she had placed it there. She said old John Bell would soon be dead, and the sooner the better. On December 20, 1820, John Bell was dead.

In 1821, the Bell Witch left, just as it had promised. When it reappeared seven years later, only the two youngest Bell boys were still at home with their mother. The Witch came as it had at the first, with scratching sounds at the window. It stayed only a few weeks this time, bothering no one in the Bell family but announcing its intention to visit others in the neighborhood. The Bell family kept quiet about the second visit and never knew if the neighborhood visits were made or not. A final promise was made by the Bell Witch – a promise to return to Middle Tennessee in 107 years.

The year would have been 1935. Did the Witch return? The Bell homestead was long gone, so did it make a visitation upon another family in the area? If so, did the recipient of the unwanted spirit tell about it or suffer in silence? If it did come back, how long did it stay – or is it still with us?

Judy Guy isn't sure why the Bell Witch bothers some generations and absents itself from others, or if it is even the Witch at all that is causing some current pranks that seem to be more than coincidence. Several years ago, she and sister Karen were out in the barn when a Mason jar, of its own accord, slid from one end of a level shelf to the other with enough speed to send itself crashing into the wall. One of the girls went to the corner where stood a broom, but upon attempting to remove it from its place, found that it would not budge even though it wasn't attached to anything. What happened next? Karen said, "We hightailed it out of there!"

Recently, Judy was in New Mexico late one night on one of those straight highways in the desert. Her car was full of young children who were restless and tired, so she thought of telling them some ghost stories as she drove along. Naturally, she told them about the Bell Witch, ending with the comment that there was probably not a real Bell Witch after all. No sooner had she expressed those doubts than her lights went out and the engine went dead. The car she was following came back and tried to start the engine with jumper cables, but to no avail. Nothing worked, and the suggestion was made to leave the car there until morning. The next day, armed with jumper cables, tools, and an extra battery, Judy and her friends went out to the car again. Just for luck, Judy put the key in the ignition and gave it a turn. The car cranked up immediately. No more trouble.

To compound the occurrences of strange events, the door-knobs in Judy's house began to fall off the doors. That wouldn't seem strange for a 107-year-old house, especially if it had ever happened before – but it hadn't. As soon as the uncle with whom Judy lives left to spend the winter in Texas, seven of the thirteen door knobs fell off in only three days.

Was it circumstance, or has the Bell Witch decided to visit itself upon the eighth generation of Jacksons, beginning with harmless but annoying pranks? Who's to say?

THE DIARY

My grandmother, Eulalie McRae Burkes, lived to be ninety-one years old. Though I was in my twenties and already hopelessly addicted to resurrecting my family's past as far back as humanly possible, I still hadn't learned to ask the most important questions of my grandmother before she passed away – and she was my last living grandparent. Tales of danger and intrigue interested me more than the vital statistics of my grandmother's ancestors, and the one story we kids begged her to tell us time and time again was the one about the Indians shooting at the wagon train when my grandparents were moving from Texas to Indian Territory, which five years later became the state of Oklahoma. I remember her telling me that my granddaddy, Andrew, who was only 27 at the time, remained calm, cautioning the rest of the men not to shoot back. Just leave them alone, he said, and they'd probably move on. And they did.

Now I knew my grandmother well and loved her dearly. I never suspected that she had ever written anything except the many letters and postcards she sent to her seven children and their families. I was aware that she was a genius when it came to crossword puzzles, and I thought she knew more about the Bible than any living human. And then there was this long, nostalgic poem about Texas that we made her say over and over. In fact, that poem will be included in this chapter. But no one, including her seven children, were aware of the little diary she had kept during the move from Texas. Yes, we had heard tales about the trip, but a diary?

I discovered the diary in Texas while visiting my grand-mother's first cousin, Winnie Whited, who at that time was still living on some of the original McRae land near Telephone. This was about two years after my grandmother had passed away, and Winnie was trying to answer questions I should have asked my grandmother. Winnie asked if I had ever seen a copy of the diary. Finding that none of us had heard anything about it, she went into her bedroom and brought out a handwritten version that her mother had copied from the original. Winnie said that my grandmother promised the kinfolks in Texas that she would keep a diary of the trip and send it back to them when she arrived at her destination. Evidently, my grandmother didn't keep a copy for herself.

I was delighted to find my favorite story in the diary,

although it lost part of its Hollywood glamour when the Indians turned out to be . . . well, you'll have to read the diary to find out the rest of the story. I will tell you this: Indian Territory was never the Old West in the tradition of New Mexico and Arizona. My grandmother's wagon train was traveling through the Creek and Choctaw Nations, both of which had been part of the old Confederacy and had raised troops for the Confederate army. But we children were raised on movies of the cowboy-and-Indian days, so we formed mental images of circling wagons attacked by Indians with bows and flaming arrows. My grandmother was telling about an event in the long-ago past, so her recollection of details may not have been razor sharp at that point in her life.

More than 50 people, all kinfolks, left Texas on October 27, 1902, in covered wagons and on horseback, driving their milk cows before them. They were leaving the Elwood and Telephone communities just south of the Red River in northern Fannin County where the McRaes had lived since 1856. Once they crossed the Red River they were in Indian Territory, pushing northward towards the brand new community of Broken Arrow, a distance of approximately 225 miles. It took them two weeks to make the journey.

My grandmother was 22 years old with two small children when she made the trip and wrote the diary.

Several years ago, while my Uncle Clyde was still living, I had the presence of mind to ask him why our side of the family got up and left Fannin County. He answered, "Grandpa McRae told me there was too many kinfolks marryin' kinfolks." This practice was prevalent among the Scotch-Irish clans in the South and was still somewhat acceptable around the turn of the century, but not to Grandpa!

> MONDAY – Oct. 27, 1902. In camps two miles from the river; have just eat supper. Men are dressing squirrels; they killed fifteen this evening. The girls have been gathering pecans. We were about three

hours crossing the river. Three cows fell in the river; they got them out. Wes got one by the ear and pulled her across. Uncle George has an Elm pole for a wagon tongue – he broke his wagon tongue out coming through the bottom. We have a big pot of beans on cooking for dinner tomorrow.

TUESDAY – Oct. 28. In camps one mile south of Blue, twelve or fifteen miles from where we camped last night. The men killed sixteen squirrels this morning; we cooked them for supper tonight. Andrew lost his dog this morning. Edgar has gone back to look for her. If he gets her, Andrew is to pay him five dollars.

WEDNESDAY – Oct. 29. We are now at Caddo Creek, waiting for the rest of the wagons and cows. The sun is about two hours high. One of Uncle George's calves has give out, and he sold it this morning for one dollar. Edgar got back with our dog this morning about ten o'clock. He found her at Telephone. The boys have come with the cows. We will have to go – we want to get to Caddo tonight.

Wednesday night, in camps three miles north of Caddo. We have come about two miles since dark. Have come over some of the roughest road I ever saw. We have been coming downhill and over rocks ever since we left Caddo, and now we are camped down in a hollow. Three or four trains passed us this evening; the mules got scared and tried to run. We were all scared so bad we could hardly sit still.

THURSDAY NIGHT – Oct. 30. In camps eight miles north of Caney. Andrew killed three quails and one rabbit. We put them all in a pot and stewed them and made a big pot of dumplings. They were sure fine! We have had pasture for the cows every night until tonight – just left them out tonight. The grass is about knee high. We crossed a toll bridge at Caney – 25 cents a piece for wagons and buggies, and one cent a piece for the cows. We have been traveling by the railroad. Are camped about one hundred yards from the track now. Five trains have passed since we camped. There comes a train now – I must run or I won't get to see it!

FRIDAY NIGHT – Oct. 31. We are camped tonight two miles from String Town and five miles from Atoka. Have not had much fun today – has been raining ever since before daylight. We have been traveling by mountains all day. The girls went up on one at noon. They said they were almost give out when they got to the top. They got some huckle-berries while they were there; they were the first I ever saw. We crossed another toll bridge today at Boggy. We had cabbage for supper tonight.

SATURDAY NIGHT – Nov. 1. We are camped to-night between Chickie Chockie and Limestone Gap. Have been here all evening. Had to stop and let the cows rest. One of Papa's cows is sick and was almost give out. We women have been washing this evening. The men have been hunting – they killed some birds.

SUNDAY – Nov. 2. In camps three miles from Kiowa. We are camped about half a mile from a place where people have been digging coal. Pearl and Eva Hall went up there and looked in the hole where they have dug out coal and saw a dead horse. Mr. Hall said he read a piece in the paper where a man had been killed, and man, horse, and buggy was all throwed into a pit. We thought that might be the place; we women were scared. One of Papa's cows died today. We crossed another toll bridge today, but did not have to pay for anything but the wagons. It did not seem much like Sunday to us today.

MONDAY NIGHT – Nov. 3. We are camped tonight from McAlester. We are now half way; have been gone one week today. Has been raining all day. The men had to get dinner. We had salmons and hominy for supper; have got a big pot of turnips on cooking for dinner tomorrow.

TUESDAY – Nov. 4. We are camped tonight half mile from Crowder. It is still raining. This is the fifth day it has rained! The men had to get breakfast this morning; it was raining so hard we couldn't get out of the wagons. We have come over the roughest roads today yet. They get a little worse every day – more rocks and bigger ones, more hills and steeper ones. We crossed one branch today and had to double teams to get up the bank. We will get to the South Canadian tomorrow if we have no bad luck. When we get across the river we will be in Creek Nation.

WEDNESDAY – Nov. 5. We are camped tonight in the Creek Nation. We crossed the South Canadian about twelve today. We had to ford it. The river had just begun to rise when we got there. There was a man told us if it rose two inches we could not cross. We had to double teams. We got across all right. We were all scared nearly to death. After we crossed the river we had about two miles of deep sand to pull through. That was one place we didn't have any rocks! I believe the roads are a little worse. Nellie Wyatt has been having the toothache for two or three days; she had it pulled today at Canadian City. It is still raining. This is the sixth day it has been raining, and it looks like it might rain six more. I washed some tonight and had to dry one garment at a time by the fire.

THURSDAY NIGHT – Nov. 6. In camps 8 miles

north of Eufaula. Have been here all evening. Stella and me have been washing. We all taken the things out of the wagons and dried them out. The men have been out hunting – killed some rabbits. We are still having some awful bad roads. We crossed the North Canadian this morning. We had to ford it, too. It was almost as bad as the South. The water was deeper, and there was quicksand on this side. We had to stop in the water and wait for Will to get out, and our wagon began to go down, and old Jude lay down in the water. I was scared so bad I could hardly keep from jumping out in the river. Will found out at dinner today that his coupling pole was broke and had to make a new one.

FRIDAY NIGHT – Nov. 7. We have the nicest camping place we have ever had – plenty of wood and a good spring. We have come about 18 miles today. We camped about two miles from Checota. Today at dinner we had sausage and cucumbers for dinner. I washed the children tonight and combed their heads, and they don't look natural with clean faces and hair platted.

SATURDAY NIGHT – Nov. 8. In camps five miles from Muskogee. Still cloudy and rained some today. We were scared worse this evening than we ever was in our lives. We came through Muskogee about an hour by sun. It is a pretty town about the size of Bonham. We stayed there about an hour or two, and I never saw over two dozen white people. I saw some Indians and more negroes than I ever saw in my life. There was a show in town, and the negroes was so thick we could hardly get through. We had to drive about two hours after dark before we found a place to camp. After we left town there was about two hundred negroes passed us and about half of them drunk. There was a wagon load of negro men passed just before dark, and when they got even with us they began to yell and shoot their pistols. They shot over Aunt Mattie's buggy and over some of the wagons. Edna and Eva were behind in a buggy, and they were nearly scared to death. And so was I. And, after dark, another came from the other way; they shot three or four times. Some of the men said they were white men, but I don't think so. I think it was negroes – it was so dark we could not tell. I don't think there is any white people in this neighborhood. We saw several negro stores and a big fine hotel. The negroes dress fine up here and ride in their fine buggies, and the whites look about like the negroes do in Texas. I forgot to tell you about Will getting lost. He started this morning about daylight to look for his cow. The boys found him about 8 o'clock trying to drive his cow in the opposite direction from camps. When they found him he said he couldn't drive that cow.

SUNDAY NIGHT – Nov. 9. We are camped tonight in the bottom. We crossed the Arkansas River this evening. We got to the river about eleven o'clock, and it was half past two when we got across. We have seen about a dozen white people today. Two white men cam out to our camps tonight and stayed a while. We were glad to see them. I tell you, we are glad to see anybody that looks white. Two or three negroes have passed tonight shooting pistols. One passed with a shotgun and shot just as he got in camps. There was two negro men running the ferry boat on the Arkansas River. They put about 50 negroes across while we were there.

MONDAY NIGHT – Nov. 10. We are camped tonight two miles from Coweta. This is a pretty place to camp, but there is no water here except a pool, and it is thick with mud. We haven't seen but a few negroes today. Have seen lots of white people and saw some Indians at Coweta. I like the country I have seen today very well. We had tomatoes and kraut for supper tonight. I guess you know about how we all eat by this time.

Although it is impossible to identify each of the individuals in this old photograph, this is part of the family who made the trek from north Texas to Broken Arrow, I.T., and it is believed that the photograph was made shortly after they arrived and began picking some of that "fine" cotton of which my grandmother speaks in the last entry of her diary.

TUESDAY NIGHT – Nov. 11. We are at our journey's end, and they say "all is well that ends well." I think I will like this country fine. We are camped on Uncle George's place. Don't know how long we will stay here. Andrew and me will stay until Uncle George builds us a house. Papa and Will haven't got them any place yet, but I don't think they will have any trouble getting a place. We met several men on the road that wanted to rent to us. Uncle George will get to move into his house tomorrow. There is a sight of cotton here to pick, and it is sure fine, too. We have been offered 80 cents. Everybody we have met since we left the river wanted us to stop and pick cotton. Some said they had a hundred acres that had never been touched.

THE RIOT AT SPRING HILL

There's a story they tell in southeastern Alabama about the incident at Spring Hill. If you're driving southeast on the Jefferson Davis Highway (State Highway 6) out of Montgomery, you'll come upon a historical marker just after you cross the Barbour County line near the intersection of County Road 49. It tells about the clash between the Reconstruction scalawags and the citizens of Barbour County, but of course there is much more to the story than the space on a roadside tablet will allow. Upon reading the historical marker, my curiosity led me four miles north to the little settlement of Spring Hill where I learned the rest of the story.

Barbour County lies just across the Chattahoochee River from Georgia, with its county seat in Eufaula. The black population easily outnumbered the white citizenry, presenting the carpetbag government with a golden opportunity for establishing Republican rule in a Democratic county. By 1874, white people had regained the right to vote but were vastly outnumbered by illiterate negroes who were instructed to vote Republican. In addition, the law conveniently allowed a person to vote anywhere in the county, a provision that lent itself to the subversive purposes of the corrupt government in Barbour County. All that was required for the carpetbaggers to win any election was enough transportation to get a large number of negroes to the desired polling place. Some bribery helped, too.

Such was the situation when the general election of 1874 came around. The election was set for November 3, and two particular places were selected for the Republicans to carry – Spring Hill and Eufaula. Word was sent out for the negroes to gather in those two places and vote Republican.

At that time, Spring Hill was a thriving village, and Republicans expected another significant victory. But the citizens of Barbour County had borne indignities, humiliation, and bankruptcy for nearly ten years. An old lady who lives near Spring Hill looked straight into my eyes, as hers narrowed into grim determination, and, with a serious tone of voice that could almost have convinced you she had been one of the players in the actual drama, said, "We were determined to get rid of those Yankees one way or another!"

For several weeks the men of the community had been meeting and making secret plans. There were two vacant store buildings which sat side by side, one of them reserved for the polling place. The other vacant building soon became a storeroom for big boxes filled with pint bottles of whiskey. Each man had donated ten dollars for the purpose. Judge Elias M. Keils, a southern white man who had sold out to the carpetbag government, trading his principles for the judgeship, was superintendent of the election. Although he lived in Eufaula, nineteen miles to the southeast, he sensed the brewing storm up in Spring Hill and requested General Swayne to send down a company of Yankee soldiers from Montgomery.

The soldiers arrived by train more than a week ahead of the

415

election and were met, as usual in such cases, by negroes in old wagons and buggies, ready to carry them to the church and schoolhouse where they were to be quartered. But this time there were others at the depot, waiting in the finest black carriages that could be obtained. These were the white men of the community, who, in the best semblance of hospitality, were accompanied by the ladies of the area. Laden with custards, cakes, and pies, these women of deliberate action greeted the surprised soldiers with smiling faces and well-filled baskets from their kitchens. The plan worked well. Ignoring their negro escorts, the Yankee soldiers opted for the transportation provided by the white people and were thus escorted to their quarters. In an effort to neutralize the soldiers, the courtesies, which even included hunting parties for the enjoyment of the soldiers, were kept up until election day.

On the day of the election, the place was a beehive of activity. People came from everywhere, some riding, some walking. Old Keils, the scalawag judge, was one of the first to arrive. Strutting around the polls, he had brought his sixteen-year-old son, Willie, as protection against violence to himself. Every white man was armed with a pistol or shotgun and a pint bottle from the vacant store on the corner. Spreading out over the town, each man would conspicuously take a drink (or pretend to) from his whiskey bottle, replace the cap, and drop the bottle in plain sight of the negroes. In an instant, the bottle was grabbed and consumed by an overjoyed negro who soon forgot that he was there to vote. They say that even old Dr. Barr, a strict Presbyterian whose deportment confirmed his F.F.V. ancestry, was in the thick of it, raising his arm and exclaiming, "Go it boys. Old Barr is with you."

Before long, most of the "voters" were too drunk to cast their votes, and the scalawag judge began to worry. Already, shots had been fired into the air, causing Judge Keils to frantically summon the soldiers with the old ruse that the white men were killing all of the negroes. Remembering the recent hospitality of the white community and perhaps their marksmanship on the hunting trips, as well, the young soldiers completely rebuffed Keils, sending word that if there weren't enough white men to kill all of the negroes, the soldiers themselves would finish the job. Alarmed, Keils saw his desperate situation and began to beg Dr. Barr to get him out of Spring Hill. Dr. Barr told him that both of them would be killed if they undertook to escape; whereupon, Keils made promises to leave the country and never return – but to no avail.

Brawling and pistol shots punctuated the afternoon hours as the wily old judge became more and more unnerved. Then, night fell. The judge, his scalawag officials, and their guards barricaded themselves inside the old store building and lit the lamps. As they tried to count votes, they could hear threats shouted by angry mobs milling around the streets. There were several men inside that building who would have given anything they owned that night in exchange for a safe ticket out of Spring Hill. Several times the door was broken open in spite of the guards, and tension mounted inside and outside of the polling place.

Suddenly, a tremendous burst of gunfire erupted simultaneously with the sound of crashing doors and windows. The lights were shot out, men started screaming, and the building was full of people who shot wildly through the darkness. The main object of the gunfire was Judge Keils, and the inside of the building was raining lead. When the gunfire died, a lamp was brought in to reveal Keils down on his knees before J.W. Comer, pitifully giving him the Masonic sign of distress. Comer had been shot in the leg by Walter White, who thought he was shooting Keils. A drunk lay under the counter yelling for help, saying he had been shot all to pieces, when in reality not a bullet had touched him. The scalawag Keils was unhurt, but the tragedy of the whole affair was soon apparent when the body of the innocent Willie Keils was discovered in front of his wicked father, riddled with bullets. It was impossible to determine who had shot him, but it was believed by everyone involved that the judge

417

had held his son up in front of him, thinking that no one would fire upon the boy. In the darkness, no one knew the boy was being used as a shield.

The dying boy was taken to the home of Grandma Drewry. The judge was also taken there under heavy guard as there were still some who wanted to kill him. In the early morning hours, the boy's mother, wild with grief, reached Grandma Drewry's. She cried out to her husband, "I begged you not to bring my child here. You did it to shield yourself." Though there was no pity for Judge Keils when the boy died, there was genuine sympathy for Mrs. Keils who was a Christian lady and member of one of the prominent families of Barbour County.

The citizens of the county had finally taken charge of their government. The ballot box had been buried in the woods, and not a scalawag dared to show his face in public. Judge Keils had amassed a fortune embracing the carpetbag government. He had built one of the finest homes in Alabama from money he had taken illegally. But in so doing he had wrecked the life of his wife and lost the life of his son and was eventually run out of the county. It was said that he first went to Dakota Territory, then on to Washington, D.C, where he could be at home among Republicans.

A Congressional inquisition was held, but the bloody riot at Spring Hill marked the end of Republican domination in Barbour County. One woman, joyous over the abrupt end of the carpetbag regime, exclaimed, "Thank God red blood is still flowing in the veins of our Alabama men!"

ALEX HAMILTON

The carpetbaggers profited greatly from dissension in Barbour County – or any county, for that matter. If they could keep the black population hostile toward the whites, the radical Republicans were assured of the total black vote in every election. Fomenting unrest was the best way to perpetuate themselves in their corrupt regimes.

There had been other trouble before the riot at Spring Hill. Undoubtedly, the Republicans were drooling over the prospects of spontaneous disturbances that could augment those of their own making. One such homespun effort was concocted among the negroes, only to be foiled by another negro, a mulatto named Alex Hamilton.

There was a group of eight negroes, four of whom were brothers, who devised a scheme to burn the town of Eufaula. They approached Alex Hamilton, an intelligent negro who proved to be an honest and loyal individual, asking him to help with the proposed plot against the city. Alex had come to Eufaula from Lumpkin, Georgia as a slave to the prominent and respected Crocker family. After being freed, he had remained in their service for quite some time while he also sharpened his skills as a contractor and builder.

In gratitude to the white people of Eufaula, all of whom who had been good to him, Alex confided in local officials who suggested that he pretend to go along with the negroes and learn the details of the anticipated insurrection. For several weeks, the plotters, with Alex among them, gathered on the steps of the John McNab Bank to discuss their plans. A local citizen, Elliott Thomas, hid in the basement where he could hear what each one said, taking notes of the entire scheme. The plans called for breaking into Bray Brothers, a large wholesale and retail hardware store which carried a large stock of firearms and ammunition. After arming a large mob of negroes, the ringleaders would set fire to the store. While the men of the community were fighting the fire, the negroes would be free to rob their homes and set them on fire. With the aid of Alex, Thomas was able to discover their signal for rushing the store.

On the fateful night, when they yelled their signal of "Keno," they were instantly surrounded by more than fifty men who had been waiting in the shadows. Armed with shotguns, rifles, and pistols, the citizens arrested every one of the negroes. They were tried, convicted, and sentenced to the state penitentiary, where they all served terms.

Alex Hamilton, the loyal negro and hero of the town, was given a gold watch and chain by the citizens. In addition, the city of Eufaula gave him a choice lot for the building of a house. Alex built his house and lived there until some time in the 1880s, during which time he built some of the finest homes in Barbour County. He later moved to Atlanta where he built one of the city's largest and finest buildings.

YANKEES IN DIXIE

Yankees do not like to hear these stories. They've never had to experience the brutality that we Southerners experienced – *at the hands of their ancestors!* No one burned their homes, stole their food, killed their animals, violated their women, or quartered horses in their houses of worship. But every one of us down here in Dixie had ancestors who suffered such abuse, and most of us can repeat some of the indignities that occurred in our own family history.

So, upon hearing one of us relate a personal tale of brutish Yankee behavior handed down by our grandparents who heard it from their grandparents, the uneasy modern day Yank, never without a simplistic reply, will usually try to excuse the outrages by letting us know that (1) war is awful, or (2) it was needed to shorten the war, or (3) well, both sides committed such offenses. Never mind that the first excuse is simply evasive and has no bearing on the subject at hand, and never mind that the second excuse is a frivolous attempt to deflect the blame for the war to the women and children who were at home trying to avoid the Yankee torch, and never mind that the third excuse is based upon the demonstrably false premise that our troops invaded and attacked their citizenry.

Nonetheless, here are some brief examples of the kinds of oral accounts that, although never put to pen and paper, will live as long as we pass them down to succeeding generations. As the inscription on a Confederate monument not far from my home says, "Lest we forget."

Walter Tripp told me about the time the Yankees came to his grandmother's home in North Carolina while his grandfather, Jonathan Wylie Tripp, was away with the 44th North Carolina Infantry.

The threat of a visit by the Yankees hung constantly over Southerners' heads. When they appeared at his grandmother's house, Mrs. Tripp and the youngsters were huddled in the yard, terrified at the very sight of these blue-clad devils whose reputation for monstrous deeds had long ago preceded them.

The Yankees must have been rather playful that day. They asked the children if they had ever seen snow. The children, trembling with fright, answered, "No." In the South, many a Southerner had for a mattress what was called a feather bed, a canvas bedtick filled with heaps of chicken or goose feathers. Into the house dashed the Yankees, emerging only minutes later, laughing like hyenas while they dragged all of the feather beds out into the yard. There, before the little mother and her brood, they ripped open the ticking and scattered feathers everywhere. Then, as the last remnants of the family beds were drifting away on the breeze, the Yankees gleefully announced to the horrified children, "There! Now you've seen snow!"

Sometimes even the most charitable among us have to wonder if all mankind truly sprang from the same Adam.

During the war, Yankees were disgustingly well-fed and provisioned from endless supply lines which stretched behind them to their northern sources; however, they were usually allowed to forage at will. They stole animals, eggs, milk, and any type of food they could find from hungry families whose menfolk were away at war. What they couldn't carry they destroyed on the spot so that the women and children would likely starve. It was sort of an outing for the boys in blue giving them something to do between battles.

But I know of one southern lady who once outfoxed the Yankees and kept her children from starving to death. The story was told to me by Georgia Grissom Kennemer, my first cousin twice-removed, and is about her grandmother, Elizabeth Grissom, who happens to be my great-great-grandmother. Georgia, a spry little lady who was in her 87th year when she related this story, said that her grandfather, Joseph Grissom, was away in the war, leaving Grandmother alone with five children to care for. The Yankees were steadily moving deeper into the South and were finally in north Alabama. Word got out one day that they were only a few miles away, and Grandmother knew she must act quickly.

Georgia says, "They had their meat already put up – salt cured, you know. Grandmother and the children took all the meat from the smokehouse and put it between the straw mattress and the feather bed to hide it. The straw mattress was just a bed-tick stuffed with straw that they used as an under mattress, and they laid it on top of that. Then they put the feather bed on top of the meat and smoothed it out. The Yankees came and searched, but they didn't find it. It was all the meat they had for the winter, and Grandmother's quick thinking saved it."

My great-grandfather was one of those children. He was five years old when the war started and nine when it ended. Abraham Jackson Grissom was his name, but he was "Uncle Abe" to Georgia. In 1880, after marrying a Mississippi belle, he left Alabama and moved to the Indian Territory by way of Texas, where he spent a few years. Georgia said he would visit her family while she was living in Hollis, Oklahoma, and, being inquisitive by nature, she would get him to talk about the old days while they sat under a big tree in the back yard.

"You know, he wouldn't stay in the house, so I got my paper and pencil and followed him out to the big tree." According to Georgia, "Uncle Abe told me that he didn't want anything that was made with whole wheat – especially bread. He said that during the war and afterwards they couldn't get good white flour; consequently, his mother would make their bread out of something similar to shorts and bran. She would spoon it out, and the only way they could eat it would be out of cupped hands."

That Mississippi belle was only fourteen when my great-grandfather married her in 1874. In fact, someone wrote across the edge of the page in the marriage book at the courthouse, "Her brother says she is old enough." My great-grandfather himself, was only seventeen years old. Nancy Ann Ferguson was my great-grandmother's name, but they called her Nannie. Her mother had died during the war when Nannie was only five years old, so she was raised by a black mammy on their plantation near Hernando. When she was thirteen, her father, Joseph Ferguson, died, leaving her orphaned during the troublesome days of Reconstruction.

The Fergusons lived in DeSoto County, Mississippi, several miles southeast of Hernando, not too far from the Mississippi River. This is delta country, running south out of Memphis, and, like General Nathan Bedford Forrest, who was a successful planter in DeSoto County, the Fergusons raised lots of cotton. As is too often the case among southern families, ours might have been a wealthy lot had war not come to the inhabitants of the rich delta land, for it was here that cotton was king in every sense of the word. Nowhere in the world did cotton grow better than in the South, and nowhere in the South did it grow better than in the delta. Before the war, Mississippi had more millionaires per capita than any state in the Union.

Joseph also had a cotton gin on the banks of Coldwater Creek and was thus employed in ginning cotton for other planters. He had 500 bales of cotton on hand, ready for shipping, when the Yankees came. Each bale was worth about $500, and it was hard, indeed, to watch the Yankees burn it. And if it wasn't enough to burn a man out, they stole his valuable horses, some of the finest in the county. Joseph had some expensive thoroughbreds which he had hidden down in a thicket, but the Yankees had become so adept at their "profession" that very little escaped their attention. With little more than a trinket, they often bribed a weak slave who pointed them in the right direction. One of

Joseph's servants thus obliged these wicked invaders, and the horses were confiscated. With his fortune gone, my great-great-grandfather became one of thousands who lived the rest of their days in a broken, debt-ridden South, where once they had been blessed by all the comforts their wealth could afford.

In 1975, I found the old homestead in DeSoto County, and to my delight the house that Joseph built in the 1840s was still there, due largely to the practice in the South of roofing buildings with that everlasting tin. The home was not grand, but a rather comfortable-looking, four-room house with a large breezeway, called a dog-trot, running through the center and connecting the front porch with the back. Though the tombstones had been destroyed, the graves of my great-great-grandparents, according to some of the old-timers in the area, remain under a large water oak west of the house.

The land has long since been out of the family, and the old house was being used for a barn. As I stood in the dog-trot, I couldn't help but ponder the consequences of a reversal in the fortunes of the South. What if, instead of a northern invasion of our idyllic Old South, we Southerners had been of a more aggressive breed than what we are and had launched an invasion of the North? Where among the magnates of Wall Street might be the names of Vanderbilt, Morgan, Rockefeller, and Ford? Would these names, synonymous with wealth and riches, even be known to history? Indeed, where might Wall Street itself be? Itta Bena, Mississippi, perhaps?

Alabama suffered heavy destruction during the war, not so much from battle as from the unnecessary and willful wreckage by vindictive northern troops as they passed through the state time after time. Magnificent homes, schools, churches, and business buildings were torched out of pure mischief, and at

Tuscaloosa the beautiful Greek Revival structures of the University of Alabama went up in smoke at the hands of General Croxton.

To human life they assigned little more significance than the property they destroyed. Southerners, with little protection against the roaming bands of Union soldiers, were open to daily insult and violence. Unduly antagonized by these undisciplined mobs of armed men, they were struck down whenever bold enough to protest against the indignities.

In far northeast Alabama, near the Georgia state line, is the small community of Mentone, perched upon the northern stretch of the long ridge known as Lookout Mountain. There we find the story of poor old Eldridge Jones.

The able-bodied men were off in the war, leaving the town virtually unprotected from the Yankee hoards traversing the unfortunate state. There were a few old men who had formed an armed unit called the Home Guard, but of course they were no match for any well-equipped unit of U.S. regulars.

One day, the unwelcome northern soldiers were searching for food in Mentone, a community already hard-pressed to feed itself. One Yankee soldier was caught stealing peaches from a tree in the yard of Eldridge Jones, but that's one brazen bluecoat that wouldn't write home about it. The Home Guard shot and killed him on the spot.

The following day, while Eldridge Jones was innocently repairing his front gate, a U.S. officer rode up and angrily confronted him about the shooting. An argument ensued, with the officer accusing Jones of having threatened to kill the first Yankee that set foot upon the premises – as if Jones had no right to be outraged at the depredations of the U.S. troops in the area. The angry officer picked up a piece of lumber and struck Jones a blow which laid him up in bed.

That night, Union soldiers returned. They broke into the house and dragged Jones from his bed and out into the darkness while his frantic family screamed and pleaded with the Yankees not to hurt him. The next morning he was found dead about three miles from home, his body riddled by sixteen bullets.

Cordelia Lewis Scales put her story in a letter so that there would be no mistake about the details of her experiences with the blue devils in Marshall County, Mississippi. On January 27, 1863, she wrote to her friend, Lou Irby.

"Thirty or forty of the Yankees would rush in at a time, take everything to eat they could lay their hands on, & break, destroy & steal everything they wanted to. . . . I'll tell you what, I thought we would certainly starve. One thousand black republicans, the 26 th Illinois, camped in our groves, for two weeks. . . . The next set that camped on us was the 90th Illinois Irish Legion. . . . "

"The next we had were the Grierson Thieves & the next the 7th Kansas Jay Hawkers. I can't write of these; it makes my blood boil to think of the outrages they committed. They tore the ear rings out of the ladies' ears, pulled their rings & breast pins off, took them by the hair; threw them down & knocked them about. One of them sent me word that they shot ladies as well as men, & if I did not stop talking to them so & displaying my Confederate flag, he'd blow my brains out. I sent him word by the lady that I did not expect anything better from Yankees, but he must remember two could play at that game. . . ."

"Lou, I tell you what, we've been through fiery trials, and if we did not exactly cuss, there is a great many of us *that thought cuss* mighty strong."

Lastly, I wish to relate one of the many accounts I've heard of the desecration of churches throughout the South. The northern army was no respecter of religion. A church house received no more consideration than any other public building. But I think it might be more instructive to let an actual Yankee tell about it, so if my readers will permit this one exception here is what William Wallace, a 31-year-old Wisconsin soldier said about the desecration of an Episcopal church in Virginia. I have not corrected his misspelled words or punctuation in the following narrative.

> After all was settled the wagons was sent to Bolliver for our knap sacks and in the meantime we were quartered in the several churches through the town. It was blowing a perfect gale – cold and piercing. No person would open the church we were sent to. The Major ordered two men to break open the door if the old preacher would not open it. In a few minutes he gave up the key, and we were in the Episcopal Church. At 4 in the evening the wagons got back after night, and then we had to go out in the dark and serch for our knap sacks which was not an easy mater to find, but we got them.
> Made our bed in the pews of the church. It was a curious sight to see so many warlike men in it, the house of the Living God where His Word has often been preached. I felt myself that I was committing a sacralige; but it could not be avoided. The exigences of the time required it, for we could not lay out. The aisles and pews were well carpeted but they were not long that color with the mud and tobacco spit. At this moment it is ridiculous to look at, but the boys says it is owned by rebels and it is no harm. They hardly ever stop playing the organ, while others is playing cards and playing the fiddle and dancing, swearing

all around. This war will ruin many a soul. It is handing it over to Satan each day.

Some of the companies has their tents in the cemetary with the head of the living against the headstone of the dead. The toomstones serves for tables to eat off, and at the same time blaspheming the name of the Redeemer, not thinking how soon they may be in the Land of Forgetfullness.[1]

MALCOLM ALEXANDER McRAE

This is a story the old timers tell around Elwood, Texas. An early settler, and one of the most successful, Malcolm McRae has been featured in *Biographical Sketches of Texas* and *Fannin County Folks and Facts*. He was born in South Carolina to Scottish parents, Hugh Bain McRae and Nancy McDuffey. Following the natural westward migration in America, he eventually settled in Texas. It has been said that he walked into the general store in Elwood in 1843, a gun over his shoulder and $20,000 worth of gold in his knapsack. In 1880, he retired at the age of seventy, giving each of his nine children 100 acres of land. But rather than repeat the story I heard at Elwood, let's let Malcolm tell us in his own words. On April 2, 1896, he wrote to a Bonham, Texas newspaper and told his own story. Eight months later he died at the age of eighty-six and was buried in the local cemetery on land he had given to the community of Elwood for that purpose.

Editor Journal:

It is said multiply and replenish the earth. I was born on the 15th day of May, 1810. I was at one dance at about 17 years of age – my first and last. I have never gambled in my life. I commenced farming in the year 1830 and quit when I was three score and ten. I am now living a retired life, except working my garden.

I was married on the 22nd day of February, 1832. I have raised four sons and five daughters, all living to the age of maturity, and all learning to read and write. No free schools then. I have 44 grandchildren, 75 great grandchildren and one great-great-grand-child. In the time of raising my family I made three long moves, first from Georgia to Southern Missouri. I made one crop and after gathering it I started to Texas on the 18th day of November, 1843. I came on foot and was gone 70 days with my gun and knap-sack. I was in Dallas during the first trip to Texas. There was but one house between Bonham and Dallas.

When I got back to Missouri, I rested two weeks, and found that I weighed 212 pounds. While I stayed in Newton County, Mo., I found 25 bee trees, killed 60 deer and 69 turkeys, made rails and fenced 40 acres of land and made two crops. On Nov. 12, 1844, I started back to Georgia, arriving at my old home on the 8th of January, 1845, having been gone three years and one month.

It is strange to say, the number of years I have been a farmer, and the long moves that I have made, I have never put gears and harness on a pair of horses or mules and hitched them to a wagon and drove

430

them this fashion.

On the 4th of October, 1849, I started to Texas from Georgia in company with 97 persons, but on account of sickness was compelled to stop in Pike County, Arkansas. In 1851 I bought a farm on the main road leading from Little Rock, Ark., to Texas. After remaining until 1856 I resumed my trip to Texas and stopped in Fannin Country, Tex., where I have made my home until the present.

In my travel since coming to Texas, I have visited Ft. Smith, Ark., Ft. Towsend, near Red River in Choctaw Nation, Ft. Graham on the Brazos River, within a few miles of Ft. Arbuckle in Chickasaw Nation, Ft. Riley in the north part of Kansas, Ft. McCullough, Ft. Washita, Ft. McDonald in Kansas. I have crossed the northwest plains in two places: one at the mouth of the A. and R. Ry. tunnel at the timber line on the Rocky Mountains in a snow storm. I was in St. Louis on the 18th day of December and found snow about six inches deep. After returning home I traveled but little. I will be glad to hear from anyone who can beat my record.

M.A. McRae

THE BLOOD-STAINED FLOOR

I guess everyone has a favorite story. Mine is the one they tell at *Carnton*, a stately old mansion in Franklin, Tennessee.

Carnton was one of the most elegant homes in Williamson County when it was completed in 1826 by Randal McGavock, just one year after he finished a term as mayor of Nashville, some twenty miles to the north. The large, two-story home of red brick was surrounded by more than a thousand acres of the estate, and it played host to many notables, among them James K. Polk, Andrew Jackson, and Sam Houston.

In 1987, *Carnton* was being restored by the Carnton Association, an incorporated group of preservationists who acquired the historic old place when the descendants of Randal McGavock deeded it over to them. I have no idea who owns the place now since so much of historic Franklin has been taken over by people who are perverting the history of this southern city and its historic landmarks, but I'm going to proceed with this story as I heard it in 1987. At that time, without any government funds, the Carnton Association flew in, cleaned the place up, and opened the house to the public. The association had had the home for only a few years, and it was nowhere near being fully restored, but they decided to allow folks to tour the house and grounds and see the steady progress being made rather than wait until it was fully restored. Although in 1987 this wonderful old home, situated in a large field that slopes down to a clear-water spring in the woods at the southeast edge of Franklin, was in its infancy as a tourist attraction, 10,000 visitors had already passed through its doors the previous year.

The furnishings, which are being gathered from various sources, are required to be of the 1865 period or earlier. There are several exquisite pieces, including the rosewood piano and the bedroom suites on the second floor. The unusual windows on the first floor, featuring twenty-eight panes each, still contain some of

432

the glass from 1826. And the newly restored two-story brick slave quarters give a good indication of how well Randal McGavock provided for his good servants.

But the most memorable thing about *Carnton* is the appearance of large patches of blood on the wide boards of the hardwood floors. Near the front door is a dark streak of reddish-brown color that looks as if someone had tried years ago to remove it but with little success. The gracious hostess pointed to the blood stain and began to tell the story behind it.

The Battle of Franklin was one of the major engagements of the war. The Yankees had entrenched themselves within the town itself, awaiting a reckless, head-on charge from the impetuous General John Bell Hood and his Army of Tennessee. Not given to strategy and careful execution of separate flanking movements, General Hood obliged his waiting hosts and rammed his army up against formidable fortifications. It was like feeding meat into a sausage grinder. The exposed southern army was mowed down in waves. Five Confederate generals were killed outright, and one was mortally wounded. Never had so many general officers been lost in one battle. Of the soldiers, 1,750 had been killed and 3,800 wounded. Even though Hood was trying desperately to retrieve the waning fortunes of the Confederacy, which in late 1864 were in a precipitous decline, the senseless blood bath was a poor remedy for the situation.

The rear lines of Stewart's Corps were fighting along the lane by the railroad track west of *Carnton* on that cold November day. A steady stream of dying and wounded soldiers stumbled across the lawn and into a grove of trees just south of the house. By the early evening hours, the slaughter now over, there were two hundred pitifully wounded men lying under the barren trees south of the house. Their heart-wrenching cries of pain as they lay bleeding and dying in the cold dark night were distressing to John McGavock and his wife. Before long it began to sleet, and the lot of those bleeding heroes became miserable indeed.

Mrs. McGavock called in the servants and ordered them to

move all the furniture back against the wall. Next, she had them roll up all of the carpets and bring every one of the soldiers inside the house. She turned the back parlor and the upstairs nursery into operating rooms, while they laid horribly mangled men all over the floors in the splendid mansion.

With the help of her servants and several others, Mrs. McGavock turned her home into a makeshift hospital. All through the night they tended to the wounded soldiers. There were no bandages to stop the bleeding, so Mrs. McGavock began tearing up her old linens. The need was always for more, and her extra linens were soon used up. Finally, everything was torn into bandages – her towels, sheets, pillow cases, table cloths, anything that might save a life.

By morning Mrs. McGavock was exhausted. Her skits were stiff with dried blood from working among the injured men. Then, someone stepped up to her and said, "Mrs. McGavock, the bodies of four of our slain generals have been laid out on the back veranda."

The bodies of Generals Adams, Cleburne, Granbury, and Strahl were left at *Carnton* until arrangements for their proper burial could be made. The wounded soldiers remained in the house for several days until a field hospital could be set up in the yard. General Quarles and other wounded officers stayed in the house until February when a Yankee officer came for them. The officer, whose name was Stilwell, marched them out the front door, put them on a wagon, took them to the train depot, and sent them north to prison.

After the Battle of Franklin, Mr. and Mrs. McGavock donated two acres adjoining the family graveyard as a cemetery for the Confederate dead who were resting in temporary graves on the battlefield. In April, 1866, this tranquil cemetery became the final resting place for nearly 1,500 Confederate soldiers from the terrible Battle of Franklin. Through the efforts of Miss M.A.H. Gay, of Macon, Georgia, a handsome wrought iron fence was placed around the hallowed ground, and other Confederate soldiers were buried there later.

Over the years, several attempts were made to remove the blood stains from the floors of *Carnton*, but the blood had soaked into the grain almost immediately and was impossible to remove. Years later, in an effort to cover the stains, the floors were painted, but during the restoration some of the floors were stripped of their paint, revealing the dark red patterns once again. Upstairs, in the southwest bedroom, one can see big drops and smears of dark red blood as clearly defined as the tragic night it was spilled. The directors of *Carnton* have resolved to leave the stains as a stark reminder of our blood-bought heritage, lest we become forgetful of the sacrifices of those who paid so dearly for it. I do hope the blood stains are still visible and the story still told.

THE LOST COLONY OF ROANOKE

Most people love mysteries. They love hearing them and they love telling them. Of all the tales that have come my way, there are three major mysteries that have haunted me most of my life. The first one that caught my fancy was the *Titanic*. I wondered for years and years if they would ever find that ship. Well, much to my surprise, they did. The second one is still unsolved. What ever happened to Amelia Earhart? As afraid of deep water as I am, having resigned myself to never getting on a boat again as long as I live, it bothers me greatly to think of her slipping into the ocean. I can hardly stand the thought of it. The third mystery is one that Southerners have told for more than 400 years, and it, too, goes unsolved. What ever happened to the lost colony of Roanoke is, in fact, America's oldest unsolved mystery.

So here's the story. But before we start, some background is in order.

Sir Walter Raleigh was an English writer, poet, soldier, politician, courtier, explorer, and part of the landed gentry. After Queen Elizabeth ascended the throne in 1558, he rose rapidly in her favor due largely to his efforts in expanding the Protestant religion in Ireland.

Infatuated with Raleigh, she granted him a charter, issued on March 25, 1584, to establish a colony in the New World by 1591 or lose his right to colonization. He was to discover and view the "remote heathen and barbarous lands" across the ocean with the right to hold, occupy, and enjoy whatever portions he was able to settle. It was expected that Raleigh would establish a base from which to send privateers on raids against the treasure fleets of Spain, who at that time was the arch enemy of England. Despite the broad powers granted to Raleigh, he was forbidden to leave the queen's side. Instead of personally leading voyages to the new lands in America, he delegated the missions to his associates and simply orchestrated the operations from London.

Of course Raleigh expected to make a handsome profit from the venture, so he lost no time in organizing an effort to establish a colony in the New World. Within a month, Raleigh sent out an exploratory expedition. It departed England on April 27, 1584, and after exploring the coast around what is now Albemarle Sound and making contact with friendly Indians who controlled Roanoke Island and the mainland between Albemarle Sound and the Pamlico River, the ships returned to England in the autumn of 1584. So impressed was Queen Elizabeth that she knighted Raleigh in a ceremony in 1585, naming the land she had granted to him "Virginia" and proclaiming him "Knight Lord and Governor of Virginia."

Sir Walter Raleigh immediately set about seeking investors to fund a colony in his newly-acquired Virginia. He outfitted seven ships under the command of Sir Richard Grenville to carry colonists and supplies and appointed Ralph Lane, an officer in the court of the queen, as governor of the new colony. The ships were supposed to rendezvous at Puerto Rico and then head north to the outer banks of what later became the state of North Carolina, but a storm off the coast of Portugal separated the ships. The *Tiger*, with Grenville aboard, waited for the other ships to arrive, but only the *Elizabeth* made it to Puerto Rico. Three of the other ships sailed directly to the outer banks and deposited their settlers – all men – on Roanoke Island.

Eventually, Grenville sailed north to Roanoke Island but ran aground as he was approaching the island, ruining many of the supplies he was bringing to the colonists and almost destroying the *Tiger*. After spending the summer repairing his ship, Grenville returned to England, leaving Lane and 107 men at Roanoke. Lane and the colonists survived a rough winter, but when Sir Francis Drake arrived at Roanoke in June and offered the weary colonists a return to England, they readily accepted, arriving back in England on July 28, 1586.

A few days after the settlers departed for England, a supply ship arrived from England but, finding no trace of the settlers, turned around and sailed back to England. Two weeks later another relief fleet, this one under the command of Richard Grenville, arrived. After an extensive search, which included interrogating three Indians, Grenville's fleet returned to England, but not before leaving a detachment of fifteen men to maintain an English presence and to protect Raleigh's claim to Roanoke Island.

Undeterred by the failure of Lane's colony, Raleigh laid plans to send out another group of settlers, this time including women and children, but without an organized military force. Entire families signed up for the second colony while others sailed expecting their families to follow later. Due to the previous hostilities between Governor Lane's group and the Secotan Indians, Roanoke Island was now deemed unsafe. Chesapeake Bay, much farther north, became the recommended destination for the second colony.

On July 22, 1587, the flagship *Lion* and a pinnace, a large boat with both oars and sails, anchored at Croatoan Island just south of Roanoke. Aboard were the newly appointed governor of the prospective colony, John White, his daughter Eleanor, and her husband, Ananias Dare. White planned to take them aboard the pinnace to Roanoke, where he would consult with the fifteen men stationed there by Grenville, before continuing on to Chesapeake Bay. But a dispute arose between White and the captain of the ship, whereupon the captain refused to take the colonists any further, ordering the sailors to put the colonists off on Roanoke Island. And thus we have the beginning of what we know today as *The Lost Colony of Roanoke*.

The following morning, White's party located the site of Lane's old colony on the north end of Roanoke Island. The fort they had built had been dismantled, and their houses stood vacant and overgrown. There was no indication that the fifteen men Grenville left behind the previous year had ever been there except for some human bones that White believed were the remains of one man. No trace of the other fourteen were ever found, nor were any remains ever discovered.

To complicate matters, the settlers found the mainland Indians hostile. Even worse, an accident in landing resulted in the spoilage of much of their food supplies. After taking steps to repair the empty cottages and build new ones, the leaders of the 115 setters, realizing their desperate situation, decided that a direct appeal to Sir Walter Raleigh was needed and that Governor White was the only one to make it.

Before sailing for England, White witnessed the birth and christening of his granddaughter, Virginia Dare, whose name became legendary as the first English child to be born in the New

World. Even today, the North Carolina county which includes the island of Roanoke, is called Dare County.

On August 27, 1587, approximately one month after establishing the colony on Roanoke, John White departed for England to gather a fresh load of supplies that would take the colonists through the winter. Arriving in England two months later, on November 5, White found a major naval war breaking out between England and Spain. Queen Elizabeth called on every available ship to confront the mighty Spanish Armada, leaving White's intended supply mission stranded.

During the winter, the queen granted a waiver, allowing White to outfit two small ships, both unsuited to combat, for re-supplying the colony at Roanoke. Leaving port on April 22, they were soon attacked by French pirates who killed almost two dozen of the crew and looted the supplies bound for Roanoke. A dejected White returned to England, fearful for the lives of his wife, daughter, son-in-law, and new granddaughter, Virginia Dare.

It would be two more years before another supply mission could be made. Even after the defeat of the once-invincible Spanish Armada in August of 1588, England maintained the ban on shipping in order to focus plans on another attack against Spain's warships.

In the summer of 1590, John White was finally given permission to take two ships, the *Hopewell* and the *Moonlight*, to re-supply Roanoke. They anchored August 12 off the northern end of Croatoan Island, one of the long, thin barrier islands that separate the Atlantic Ocean from Pamlico Sound. The Croatoan Indians inhabited Croatoan Island (now called Hatteras) and two other narrow barrier islands further south. Sometimes friendly and sometimes hostile, the Croatoans, along with the Secotan Indians, also inhabited parts of the larger island of Roanoke.

While anchored off Croatoan Island, the crew sighted smoke on August 15 on Roanoke Island. For the next two days, White's crew attempted to sail towards the area where the colony had been established three years earlier. On the 17th, they again sighted smoke on the north end of the island and rowed towards it, but arriving after dark they decided not to risk going ashore. They spent the night loudly singing English songs in hopes the colonists would hear and realize who they were.

The next morning White and his men made landfall and began their search. They saw fresh tracks in the sand but came into contact with no people. Upon reaching the site of the colony, they found it abandoned without a trace of any of the colonists. White found that the colonists had enclosed the area with a palisade for protection, but within the palisade the search party found that the houses had been dismantled and anything that could be carried away had been removed. Several large metal trunks, including three of White's, had been dug up and the contents removed. None of the colony's boats could be found along the shore. On one of the posts of the palisade, White found that someone had carved the word "CROATOAN." Nearby, carved into a tree were three letters: "CRO." This was the only clue as to what might have become of the colonists, and it would be debated and discussed and investigated into the present age without any resolution of the mystery.

Sure enough, the colonists had agreed in 1587 to leave a secret token indicating their new location should they decide to move, or leave a cross pattée as a sign of duress. Finding no sign of a cross pattée, the questions then centered upon the word "CROATOAN" carved into the post. Did that mean that the colonists had relocated to the barrier island of Croatoan? Or did it mean that out of desperation for food during the winter they had taken up residence with the Croatoan tribe? Or, could it mean that the Croatoans had taken them prisoner and moved them to another location? Or perhaps slew them? One thing of which we can be rather sure: They had left White a sign that they wanted to be found, dead or alive.

The search party returned to the *Hopewell* that evening with plans to resume the search the next day, but the ship's anchor cable broke, and the mission could not continue without considerable risk of shipwreck. The *Moonlight* set sail for England, but the *Hopewell* headed for the Caribbean where it could be repaired during the winter for a return trip and resumption of the search in the spring. But, as fate would have it, the *Hopewell* was blown terribly off course, forcing the crew to try to stop for supplies in the Azores. When winds prevented it from landing in the Azores, the ship was forced to head back to England where it arrived on October 24.

There was one final expedition to locate the colonists, this one made in 1603 by an English mariner named Bartholomew Gilbert. He decided to drop anchor farther north in Chesapeake Bay and conduct a wider search, but bad weather forced him to land in an unspecified location. Going ashore, he and his landing team were murdered by Algonquian Indians, forcing the remaining crew to return to England empty-handed.

Theories abound. One theory suggests that the colonists, realizing their desperate situation, boarded their pinnace and headed back for England only to be lost at sea. That could account for both the absence of people and their boat. It is plausible that the colony included sailors qualified to make the voyage in the pinnace that was left behind in 1587, and of course ships of its size were capable of making the trip, although they typically did so alongside larger vessels.

But then there are local legends that refer to an abandoned settlement called Beechland, located along the Alligator River on the mainland, west of Roanoke Island. There have been reports of finding small coffins, some with Christian markings, in that area which is now located within the Alligator National Wildlife Refuge in Dare and Hyde counties.

Another theory, more recent that the rest, is that the colonists may have split into two groups, one going northwest onto the mainland, where they lived among an Indian tribe, and one going southeast onto Croatoan Island. Archaeologists have found evidence at both places that seem to sustain that theory. At

Cape Creek, about 50 miles south of Roanoke discovery was made of a slate with the number "M" barely visible on it. Beside it was a lead pencil, clear evidence that it was a European artifact. Additionally, Spaniards sailed up and down the outer banks trying to find the English settlement, suspecting that it was to be used as a base for raiding their ships. Although never finding the colony, they reported seeing native Indians waving from the shore and making music on European-style musical instruments.

To the northwest, about 50 miles from Roanoke Island, some fragments of English pottery and some weapons have been uncovered. The location of this site, now called Site X, was selected for excavation in 2011, when a patch on a map drawn by John White in 1585 was discovered to have a tiny four-pointed star, resembling a fort, beneath the patch. The challenge here is to rule out the possibility that the artifacts are from the failed Lane colony of 1585 or from a trading post established in the 1650s by Nathaniel Batts.

Of course, an obvious guess is that the colonists were annihilated by unfriendly Indians. The problem with that theory is that no remains have ever been found. If the settlers were slaughtered at their compound on Roanoke, it's not likely that the attackers would drag the bodies of 115 people to another location but would rather leave them where they fell, and yet no bones have ever been discovered.

Pestilence is always a consideration. If an epidemic swept the colony, then where are the graves of those who died? Cremation was not a practice among Christians, so there would surely be graves with some type of headstones, whether rock or wood, to mark the resting places of the victims. But none were found. And it is reasonable to assume that even if the headstones were made of wood portions of them would still be visible after only three years.

The most intriguing theory, in my estimation, is the one I first heard in my youth many years ago: eyewitness reports of blue-eyed Indians. From the early 1600s clear up into the mid-

1750s, colonists from Europe reported meeting gray-eyed Indians who claimed descent from white settlers. In 1696, French Huguenots left records of having met blond-haired, blue-eyed Indians soon after their arrival along the Tar River, about 60 miles southwest of Roanoke. In 1709, John Lawson, in his book *A New Voyage to Carolina*, records Croatoans living on Croatoan Island who claimed that they used to live on Roanoke Island and claimed to have white ancestors.

The main focus of that theory is that the colonists moved onto Croatoan Island and began living among the Croatoans, eventually adopting the Indian lifestyle and assimilating into the tribe. The settlers who founded Jamestown, Virginia in 1607 were well aware of the vanished colonists of Roanoke, and several reports reached them over the years of Indians with gray or blue eyes as well as tales of Europeans living among Indians. William Strachey, secretary of Jamestown, claimed in 1612 that he saw four men, two boys, and one girl – all Europeans – living with the Eno tribe as slaves, but there is no evidence that they were descendants of the Roanoke colonists.

With the development of modern technology, solving the mystery may now be more possible than ever before with DNA testing. Currently, there is a DNA project underway to test the Croatoans – or Croatans – most of whom now live in the three North Carolina counties of Cumberland, Sampson, and Harnett. So far, however, none of the testing has been able to identify any descendant of the Lost Colony of Roanoke. Even if European blood is found among the Croatans, there are no bones available from the colonists with which to narrow the European DNA down to members of the Lost Colony.

Adding to the intrigue is the discovery of what have come to be called the Dare Stones. In 1937, a tourist found an inscribed stone and brought it for authentication to Dr. Haywood Pearce at Emory University. Although Dr. Pearce could not determine the authenticity of the stone, the message did not contradict what was known at the time. The message was purportedly inscribed by John White's daughter, Eleanor Dare, stating that her husband and daughter were dead and asked whoever found the stone to tell her father. Consistent with the phrasing of the time, it read:

Ananias Dare &
Virginia Went Hence
Unto Heaven 1591
Anye Englishman Shew
John White Govr Via

The other side of the stone reported that only seven of the colonists were left in 1591 and that the Indians had murdered all the rest. It was signed EWD.

Could the information left on this stone support the claim of Powhatan, who told Captain John Smith at Jamestown in 1607 that he had killed all the colonists at Roanoke in retaliation for their living among another tribe that had refused to align itself with him? Smith, who had been interested in finding the lost colonists, was shown a musket barrel and a brass mortar and pestle which Powhatan said he took when he slaughtered the colonists. William Strachey in *The Historie of Travaile Into Virginia Britannia*, seemed to back up this story when he reported that Powhatan claimed he had murdered the colonists because of a prophecy that he would be conquered and overthrown by people living on Roanoke Island. And yet, even though no bodies or archeological evidence has ever been found to support that claim, the story has persisted for more than 400 years.

In 1940, forty-seven more stones were found. Attributed to Eleanor White Dare, they purportedly told the story of what happened to the Roanoke colonists, but upon inspection they were found to be a hoax, having been inscribed with a drill. Historians believe, however, that the first stone is absolutely authentic. Not only is in couched in the language of the day, the colonists would have had the tools that were used to make the inscription.

What is troubling about all these theories is that an entire colony of 115 people – of all ages – could simply vanish within three years. Gone, without a trace. After 400 years of speculation without the discovery of any physical evidence upon which to come to a satisfactory conclusion of the matter, I fear that this is one mystery that will never be solved. But then I thought they would never find the *Titanic*.

PAPA AND THE KKK

No one can doubt the effectiveness of the original Ku Klux Klan. Without it we might never have shaken off the curse of the carpetbag-scalawag regimes which had us bound hand and foot after the war. But there arose another Klan sometime before World War I, and Southerners have viewed it with both admiration and skepticism ever since. And it wasn't only Southerners who made up the ranks of the 20th century Klan. It spread into the north, where it found strongholds in Indiana, Illinois, and Pennsylvania, and then reached as far west as the state of Washington. It even put on large parades in Washington, D.C., such as the one on August 8, 1925, where reports of between 40,000 and 50,000 robed Klansmen marched for three hours down Pennsylvania Avenue, the street lined with cheering spectators.

The 20th century Klan was created for entirely different purposes than the original Ku Klux Klan. The carpetbaggers were gone by 1877, so the old KKK disbanded. But the malevolent media, whose grasp of history is as weak as their claim to objective reporting, work feverishly in their delirium to conflate the

445

two, operating with malicious intent or perhaps out of certifiable ignorance. Nevertheless, my readers are vastly more intelligent than those who read the news every evening on TV, so let us proceed with the narrative.

This photograph of the KKK parade on August 8, 1925, was made at the far end of Pennsylvania Avenue, where the ranks of approximately 40,000 to 50,000 Klansmen can be seen stretching all the way back to the U.S. capitol, which can be dimly seen in the background. According to *American Heritage* magazine, half the marchers were from Pennsylvania and New Jersey. The streets were lined by enthusiastic spectators who kept up a steady stream of applause.

The period surrounding World War I brought to American shores what came to be called the "Red Scare." Europe was in political turmoil and socialism was on the rise. The communists had taken over Russia in 1917 during the Bolshevik Revolution, and America was experiencing an influx of Eastern European immigrants with communist sympathies. Further fueling the fears of American citizens was a political demagogue named Eugene V. Debs. Elected as a Democrat to the Indiana State Assembly in 1884, Debs had carved out for himself a reputation as a radical socialist who, in 1905, would help found the Industrial Workers of the World, an organization of militant unionists, socialists, anarchists, and labor radicals who employed crippling strikes against the railroads and other businesses who failed to comply with their demands. Five times he would run as the candidate of the Socialist Party of America for the Presidency. Under his withering influence, the labor movement in America was turning violent and the country was looking more like socialism than anything since the days of Reconstruction.

As a result, the average American became suspicious and uneasy about all liberal movements and demands for social change. The times were just right for a militant, patriotic response, and the Ku Klux Klan stepped forward to fill the bill. Most Southerners – in fact, most Americans – agreed with the Klan's stand against communism. In addition, the Klan did a tremendous amount of benevolent work among the poor. By the early 1920s, it was even fashionable to avow membership in the Klan, and as its numbers grew nationwide to almost four million, many a politician was elected by the powerful clout of the Ku Klux Klan. At least eight governors and a dozen U.S. Senators were elected with the backing of the Klan.

In the 1970s, our preacher told about the Klan arriving at the church in Alabama where his daddy was preaching. In the middle of the sermon, the back doors of the little church house opened wide, and there stood several Klansmen in their white robes. No one said a word as the hooded men walked slowly down the aisle. When they approached the contribution baskets, they opened up a container full of money and dumped it into the baskets. Without a word, they turned and walked slowly back out of the church; whereupon, the preacher resumed his sermon as if nothing had happened.

My grandfather lived on an eighty-acre farm in Hughes

County in the east central portion of Oklahoma. Across the road was the schoolhouse where he sent his four children to school and drove one of the school buses. He was also on the school board and was known far and wide as a man of integrity – one who couldn't be moved when he knew he was right. We called him "Papa."

Six miles to the north, in the heart of the Creek Nation, is the county seat of Hughes County, a town called Wetumka, named for an old Creek town in Alabama. As in most of the South, the Ku Klux Klan was quite active in the area. During the first World War, it vigorously enforced the rationing that was necessary to the war effort. Aunt Norma told me about the man who went into Wetumka in a wagon and started back out to Pleasant Ridge with several more bags of sugar than he was allotted. She was about twelve years old at the time, and it made a lasting impression upon her when the Ku Klux Klan stopped the man and gave him a thrashing. They poured his sugar out all over the road, and he never tried to cheat on the rationing again.

Then there were the IWW's. Aunt Norma said it stood for "I Won't Work." In reality, it was Debs' Industrial Workers of the World, but the people of Hughes County had the right idea. Aunt Norma used to tell how the IWW threatened to poison Wetumka's water supply during the first World War. She told how the Ku Klux Klan came to the rescue, placing guards around the lake twenty-four hours a day.

But there were flies in the ointment, so to speak. As most of the newly arrived immigrants from Eastern Europe were Catholics and Jews, they tended to settle in the North where there were already large populations of both religions. The suspicion of communist influence among them led to hooded intimidation and even violence against both Jews and Catholics, and the Klan, partly for that reason, began to lose its credibility towards the end of the 1920s. Even though the Klan was so widely accepted that members could march with their face flaps turned up, as they did in the parades in Washington, the hoods could provide a measure of dangerous anonymity to thugs and criminals who eventually destroyed the effectiveness of the Klan. If someone had a personal score to settle, he could hide his misdeeds under a hood, and the Klan would get the blame. The Klan was powerless to control criminals who were thus utilizing its famous costume, and as its reputation began to suffer its prominent citizens withdrew from the circle.

This is the KKK parade of September 13, 1926, in Washington, D.C. The U.S. Capitol can be seen at the far end of Pennsylvania Avenue.

One night, the Ku Klux Klan came for Papa. There were three of them dressed in white robes and hoods, standing in the front yard near the porch. My grandmother heard them hollering for Papa to come outside and talk to them. My dad was about ten years old then, and he knew by the sound of my grandmother's voice that something was wrong. Papa stepped out on the front porch, and the men raised their voices in anger, telling him that he was going to go with them. My dad watched through the open door as Mama grew white with fear. As quick as a flash, Papa jumped back inside and grabbed a great big pistol. Then he leaped back out onto the porch, leveled the gun at their heads, and told them to disrobe or they'd be dead men. According to Daddy, "That's when Mama fainted."

The men threw their hands above their heads but were a little hesitant about removing their cowardly hoods. Papa jumped off the porch and waded into them, jabbing the pistol into their ribs a few times as he walked among them. He told them to get those hoods off pronto or he would kill all three of them. As my dad watched from the safety of the house, he saw Papa making them show their guilty faces. Papa found just what he expected. There stood three of the sorriest humans in that little country community. One of them had previously threatened him because he didn't stop the school bus in the right place for his daughter; one was trying to get back at him for refusing to hire a woman of loose morals to teach at the school; the other was a constant complainer about all of his school board decisions.

None of them were members of the Ku Klux Klan, but had Papa not disrobed them the Klan would have caught the blame. Papa had no more trouble out of them, and Mama was revived, but the Klan began to disintegrate from incidents such as this.

A TRIBUTE TO TEXAS

In the last half of the nineteenth century, someone had a story to tell about Texas, a story which found expression in the form of a poem and life in the heart of my grandmother. The author remains unknown to me, but he or she had to be someone who loved Texas as much as my grandmother did.

My grandmother, Eulalie McRae Burkes, left Texas with this poem of her youth indelibly etched in her mind. She was twenty-two when she bade farewell to her native state. For the next seventy years she kept us all entertained with the recitation of this poem about Texas. We grandchildren often coaxed her into saying it while we sat on the floor in rapt attention at her feet, hanging on to every word as it proceeded so effortlessly from her Texas soul. At times, as she grew older, a line or two would be skipped, but she knew it and would say, "Right here is where I get mixed up," and then she'd back up and take another run at it.

We were never able to find a copy of the poem, and as she advanced into her upper 80s, we were afraid it would slip from her mind and be gone forever. Finally, Aunt Hazel began to sit down with pencil and paper every time my grandmother said the poem. Eventually, what we believe to be the entire poem was on paper, just as my grandmother remembered it down through the years. Like the author, the title remains a mystery as well.

> Missouri is a grand old state
> In history we are told;
> She is one among the many,
> Her sons among the bold.
> She was foremost in the struggle
> We have often heard it said,
> And many of her patriots
> Are numbered with the dead.

SOUTHERN BY THE GRACE OF GOD

But now that time is passed away
And she's at peace again
While St. Louis and Kansas City
Spread abroad her righteous fame.
Oh yes, she's rich and powerful,
Her people grand and free,
But with all of her pomp and glory
She is not the home for me.

Illinois, too, does well to boast
And be exceeding glad,
For a brighter prospect to her size
No other state has had.
Calmly and serenely,
Chicago, her crowning star,
Stands upon Lake Michigan
And spreads her fame afar.
But what is grandeur and splendor
Where the heart cannot be free?
With all of her magnificence,
She is not the home for me!

But Texas is a model state;
Her sons are statesmen, too,
No people half so free as hers,
No hearts are half so true.
She has no St. Louis of which to boast,
Or no Chicago grand,
But, among the pretty cities are hers;
She's the most promising in the land.
She's the home of fruits and flowers,
Likewise of meadows green;
And all that's pleasing to the eye
In Texas can be seen.
Her soil is rich and fertile —

Her prairies broad and fair,
Bedecked with natural ornaments
With which none can compare.

Yes, Texas is a grand old state,
And grander yet she'll be.
For all the days that I may live
Texas is the home for me.
Texas bright and fair!
Grant me this wish, I trust:
That when my body turns to clay
It shall mingle with her dust.

THE MYSTERY OF JOHN HUNT COLE

In the early 1970s, I stumbled onto one of the most bizarre tales I have ever heard. It stuck with me partially because of its bold claim, but additionally and perhaps mostly because of the incredible aggregation of evidence with which the teller proceeded to validate his claim.

The story took flight on November 8, 1899 upon the death of one John Hunt Cole near Vian, Indian Territory. Only a few people in the world have ever heard this tale, and I relate it here just as it came to me, followed by uncanny details produced upon further inquiry.

453

First, the story.

While teaching school, I had the good fortune to be associated with a congenial football coach named Darvis Cole. When attempting to organize a local chapter of the Sons of Confederate Veterans, of which membership requires proof of a Confederate military ancestor, I made mention of it to Coach Cole. At once interested, he said, "I have a good Confederate ancestor; in fact, he's a general, and he's my great-grandfather."

Realizing immediately the amount of prestige that would accrue to my new local chapter by virtue of enrolling a direct descendant of a Confederate general, not to mention the pleasure I would personally take in fraternizing with such "royal blood," I quickly responded, "Who is it?"

"Have you ever heard of General John Hunt Morgan?" His question-answer dropped my mouth wide open. Had I ever heard of John Hunt Morgan – the dashing, daring John Hunt Morgan? Dixie cavalier. Kentucky's favorite son. Oh, yes, I most certainly had heard of John Hunt Morgan and his famous Raiders, whose heroic exploits were known far and wide. Now, nothing would do but to enroll Darvis Cole in my SCV camp immediately – if not sooner!

"There is a problem, though," he interrupted. "I can't prove it." The great-grandson of John Hunt Morgan, and he couldn't prove his lineage only three generations back? I guess the question must have asked itself by the look on my face, for he continued, "History books tell us that General Morgan was killed near the end of the war, leaving only one child who died before she bore any children, so there are supposedly no descendants. But he didn't die in 1864 as supposed. He escaped, changed his name to Cole, and came to Oklahoma."

There are a lot of people, myself included, who would like to claim descent from a famous Confederate hero, and to be quite honest I became a little skeptical at that point in his story, fearing that someone had invented the tale and had passed it off to Coach Cole as truth. Evidently, skeptics had frowned before, so

454

he was next suggesting, "You might want to talk to my brother's wife. She has all of the details."

I lost little time in contacting brother Darrel and his wife, June. She was well versed in her husband's genealogy, and the story began to unfold.

It seems that the surprise attack upon the house where Morgan and his staff officers were sleeping on September 4, 1864 and the resulting confusion, which is well-documented, afforded General Morgan a chance to escape – which is not documented. According to the story June was telling, he changed coats with an aide in an effort to confuse his foes in the event they tried to capture or kill him.

During the melee, shots rang out from every direction, and Morgan caught one in the side. Managing to effect his escape, he slipped away and received help from a negro family in the area. After recuperating, he rode north to locate Maggie Critzer, a woman he had met on a business trip into Illinois, presumably before the war when he was exporting woolen goods and hemp products.

Changing his all-too-familiar name to John Hunt Cole, he married Maggie, and the couple lived with her parents who were running a grist mill at the time. The name John Hunt Morgan was notorious in the North, and it was commonly known that many Yankees had sworn to kill him on sight. Even after the change in surname, five men showed up one day saying that they had discovered his true identity. A fight ensued and several men were killed.

Having been discovered in Illinois, John Hunt Cole realized the necessity of an immediate move. With his wife and the Critzers, he made a drastic dash to the wide open plains of Kansas, settling on the Cottonwood River between the towns of Florence and Marion, where Mr. Critzer again operated a grist mill. Early in 1879, Cole and his wife moved to a rural area near South West City, Missouri, a small community that sits virtually astraddle the border with Indian Territory. The move was made in response to Maggie's failing health, but she passed away soon after arriving in Missouri.

Cole now had five children who needed a mother. On May 8, 1879, he remarried, this time to Carolyn Reardion. She would bear him four sons, although none of them would live past childhood.

Having more education than most of the men in the remote area of southwestern Missouri and Indian Territory, Cole began practicing medicine and soon became known in those parts as Dr. Cole. He was also distinguished by his marksmanship with a pistol and his love for horses, being always in possession of at least one good horse.

One of Cole's younger boys, Charles Alexander, married while living near South West City. The court records show, on March 3, 1892, that John Hunt Cole gave his written permission for the marriage, his permission being required because Charles was not of age.

Shortly thereafter, the family moved to the area around Vian, Indian Territory, deep in the heart of the old Cherokee Nation. Even though that had been pro-Confederate territory, Cole kept his secret and continued to practice medicine as Dr. Cole. Sometimes a man would come from a long way off, always arriving after dark. Neighbors could see lamps burning in the Cole house all night long, and before daylight the visitor would depart. In relating this part of the story, June Cole told me that one of John Hunt Morgan's brothers knew about the escape, and most of the family have always believed the visitor was that brother.

In the autumn of 1899, the wife of Cole's oldest son became ill. Though Cole himself was also sick, he saddled a horse and rode over to care for the ailing woman. It was a fateful ride, for she died and Cole contracted pneumonia from the trip.

Suspecting that he would not survive the pneumonia, John Hunt Cole decided to divulge the long-held secret of his identity and suggested that the family be summoned. Probably fearing that he would become irrational or unconscious before the family arrived, he had only his oldest son, John Morgan Cole, and John's wife, Carolyn, at his bedside when he took pen and paper and signed *John Hunt Morgan*. Some friends may have been present, but the other family members did not arrive in time. Handing the signature to the person closest to his bed, he said, "This is who I really am." On November 8, 1899, the real John Hunt Morgan died.

Why he chose to write his true identity rather than verbalizing it will never be known. He may have intended to leave a sample signature for comparison with earlier signatures of John Hunt Morgan, or perhaps he merely wished to heighten the drama. Whatever the reason, he actually left the family a perfect tool for substantiating his claim. His wife kept the paper for a while, but it disappeared before comparisons could be made.

Long before he died he had confided in his wife and his oldest son, thus the deathbed revelation was no surprise to those two trustworthy confidants. And there was a Mr. McKee, who lived near Stilwell, Indian Territory, who claimed to have known the secret, although no one ever knew just how he came by his knowledge of it.

So ends the story.

Well, at least part of the story ends there, for in reality, the story will never end until it is proven beyond the shadow of a doubt, or until the descendants of John Hunt Cole can find some antecedents for him. The recurring dead end with the genealogy of John Hunt Cole only serves to strengthen the Cole family's theory that Cole actually was John Hunt Morgan.

So what kind of evidence do they have other than the apparent lack of parentage for John Hunt Cole? For starters, they have the testimony of Cole's oldest son, John Morgan Cole, who once asked his father why he kept holding the secret after the fear of imprisonment or assassination had passed, to which Cole answered that it would bring much dishonor to the proud Hunt and Morgan names in Kentucky as he was legally married to

Mattie Ready of Murfreesboro, Tennessee. Matters were further complicated when Mattie, thinking Morgan was dead, married Judge James Williamson of Lebanon, Tennessee.

Then, too, there is the testimony of Cole's daughter-in-law, who was the wife of Cole's fourth child, Charles Alexander, and the grandmother of my source, Darrel Cole. One thing that struck me as more than coincidence is that Darrel learned to plait ropes from his grandmother who was taught to plait by John Hunt Cole himself. Darrel's grandmother stated that while Dr. Cole was teaching her to plait ropes he told her that he had been in the hemp business years earlier and had sold ropes plaited from hemp. And was it mere coincidence that Morgan and six of his officers scaled the penitentiary wall in their escape by making a strong rope, according to Morgan biographer James Ramage, out of the bedticking?

When I requested more evidence, they mentioned the interesting similarity between Morgan, Hunt, and Cole family names. The most obvious repetition was found in the name of Cole's first son, John Morgan Cole. His second child, a daughter, was named Margaret Charlotte Cole. John Hunt Morgan had an aunt named Margaret and a brother named Charlton. Cole's fourth child was named Charles Alexander. Could this child have been named after John Hunt Morgan's uncle, Alexander, and his brother Charlton, whom his father called "Charly"?

The question of Morgan's choice of Cole as his pseudonym came up. Grandson, Wiley Cole, said that his grandfather had selected the name because one of his aides was named Cole. Indeed, the Adjutant General's report shows a John Cole assigned to Morgan's Kentucky Cavalry. In addition, Pollard's *Southern History of the War* refers to a Captain Coles, on page 212 of Volume II, as an officer in Morgan's command. (See page 155 of this book.)

The plausibility of Morgan's escape from the Williams home in Greenville also required some rationale before I could consider myself a convert. I must admit that here the Cole family had certainly done its homework. It was recalled that Morgan had made a solemn vow to his wife, Mattie, that he would never be taken prisoner again, a pledge alluded to several times by biographer Ramage, who points out Morgan's affirmation of that oath in the last letter he would ever write to Mattie. The letter was written the day before his death – or the death that historians acknowledge.

The contention that Morgan made good his escape by changing coats with an aide, and thereby changing roles, is supported at least in logic by several illustrations. Morgan's biographers, of whom there are several, have alluded to his proclivity towards masquerading as someone else, at times for military advantage while at others seemingly for the mere satisfaction he derived from deceiving someone, especially when it called for posing in the guise of a Yankee – a ruse he frequently employed.

Although Morgan's fame was evident, he was living in an age devoid of television and mass media, a factor that worked to his advantage in that his physical likeness was not widely known. He managed to avoid capture more than once due to the inability of his enemies to identify him by facial features or physical appearance. Again, Ramage portrays a classic example of Morgan's subterfuge on page 155 in his biography, *Rebel Raider*. A Federal cavalry detachment dashed into McMinnville, Tennessee, surprising Morgan and a small force of forty men. Morgan and most of his men escaped due to the deceptive action of Major Dick McCann, who surrendered to the Yankee force, proclaiming himself as the unfortunate General Morgan, a story swallowed hook, line, and sinker by the unsuspecting Federals. A singular characteristic of Morgan's men is their undying allegiance to their intrepid commander, and they were ready at any given moment to divert danger their way in order to save his valuable neck.

June Cole provided me with a description of John Hunt Cole, the information having come to her from Darrel's grandmother. Cole was described as six feet tall, weighing 180 pounds, and having grayish-blue eyes. The grandmother's account is corroborated by Ramage on page one of *Rebel Raiders*, where the description of Morgan matches that of Cole except for Morgan's weight, listed at 185 pounds rather than the 180 reported by the grandmother.

Similarities between even the facial features of Cole and Morgan continue to fuel the belief that the men are one and the same. Upon request, a photograph of Cole in his sixties was provided, and when compared to one of the last available pictures of Morgan, both bore remarkable similarities.

The mystery of the man named McKee tends to thicken the plot when it is remembered that Morgan's commander in the Mexican War was Col. William R. McKee from Lexington, Kentucky.

And what about the Critzer family from Illinois? Cole's second child, Margaret Charlotte, was born in 1867 in East St. Louis, Illinois. And what about the Cole family story that John Hunt Cole's in-laws, the Critzers, moved to Kansas along with John and his wife, Maggie? Is it only coincidence that when Darrel and June Cole visited the Kansas home site they found local residents referring to an area called Critzer's Ford? It may even be pure happenstance that two unmarked graves were identified by area inhabitants as those of Mr. and Mrs. Critzer who did not make the move to South West City, Missouri in 1879, but it seems rather hard to dismiss those connections altogether.

It is also worth mentioning that the strange story of John Hunt Cole caused enough controversy early in the 20th century as to draw a response from Richard Morgan, brother of John Hunt Morgan, and to command mention by the popular Morgan biographer, Cecil Fletcher Holland. Disclaiming the story, he writes, "Even more fanciful was a story current some years after Morgan's death that he was not killed at all but escaped and went to Kansas where it was said he lived under the name of Dr. J.W. Cole until his death in 1899. At a Confederate reunion in

Oklahoma in 1915, a Mrs. L.F. LaRue was reported to have made a speech in which she claimed to be the daughter of General Morgan by a wife he married in Kansas." [2] Holland says that Richard Morgan accused the woman of laboring under a hallucination. The Cole family verified the speech as having been made by Cole's third child, Lizzie.

Was the coffin opened at the funeral on September 6? If so, was it not clearly Morgan's body? If not, was even his burial service a well-planned subterfuge to quell the relentless deadly pursuit of John Hunt Morgan? Was the casket opened ten days later at the funeral service in Richmond? In 1868, when Morgan's body was removed from the vault in Richmond to be transported back to Kentucky, Morgan's brother, Calvin, attended to all of the arrangements, accompanying the body everywhere it went, including the final stops between Covington and Lexington – but the casket was closed, and a guard sat up with the body at night. The guard was composed of several members of Morgan's former staff, including Major Withers, who had helped wash and dress the body shortly after the killing in Greenville, Tennessee.

Could a cover-up for Morgan's escape have been this elaborate? Was Calvin the brother who visited John Hunt Cole in later years? And is it not significant that Major Withers, in sworn testimony that is recognized by all to be the most authentic account of the killing of General John Hunt Morgan, stated that Morgan, rather than make a dash back inside the Williams house for safety – where he surely would have been taken prisoner – shook hands with Withers and parted company with him there in the garden, saying, "You will never see me again"? [3]

Admittedly, much of the evidence seems to be circumstantial, yet there remains the haunting feeling that the abundance of coincidental material lends a certain credibility to the whole strange story. It would have been easier to dismiss the case from my mind as something of a coincidence had I not looked

461

upon the actual tombstone of John Hunt Cole at Vian, Oklahoma. There was just something cold and convincing about that gray granite birth date of *June 1, 1825* – the exact date of the birth of John Hunt Morgan.

THE HANGIN' AT ADA

At this late date in history, there isn't a person left who is old enough to remember the days when hangings settled the question of what to do with a murderer, but there are still some who grew up in the shadow of the most sensational hanging, and one of the last, in the Southwest. This outright lynching, which occurred in 1909, is the one the old-timers still talk about.

Ada, Oklahoma is a community quite representative of what you might call the rural South. Even though it has a small state college and a permanent population of about 16,000, it is the only town of any size in Pontotoc County. Surrounded by small towns, Ada is situated eighty miles from the nearest metropolitan area and is located in an area of Oklahoma comprising roughly the southeastern one-third of the state known quite proudly as "Little Dixie." After the war, this section of Indian Territory was settled nearly exclusively by people from the old Confederate states, many of whom were Confederate veterans or the sons and daughters of Confederate soldiers. In 1954, the local newspaper, the *Ada Evening News*, ran a survey of the 205 people who had lived in Ada since 1903, asking them to list the states from which they had emigrated. Various towns within Indian Territory were listed by the native-born residents, with others giving their home states as Tennessee, Texas, Arkansas, Alabama, Mississippi, and Missouri. One lone soul admitted that he came to Ada from Kansas.

Today Ada's street names reflect those Old South roots: Forrest, Johnston, Stonewall, Texas, Mississippi, Arlington. A typically rural southern town, you'll see magnolias, oaks, dogwoods, and crape myrtles; and in mid-May the whole town is delightfully perfumed with the heavenly smell of honeysuckle. And of course every mother's boy in town can be found on a baseball diamond at least every summer night – all of them, that is, except those who are fishing in someone's farm pond out in the country. Ada is a nice town.

But it hasn't always been that way. You see, Indian Territory not only presented a good opportunity for ruined Southerners to start over; it soon became a haven for criminals who could get away with literal murder due to the laxity of territorial law. The whole territory had become a refuge for people running from the law. An elderly neighbor of mine once told me that when he was growing up around here you never asked a man where he was from – he might have come here to get out of trouble.

By the turn of the century, Ada, now only seven years old, had gained the reputation of being one of the roughest places in the Southwest. If you disliked someone intensely and had a little money to invest in his discomfort, you could hire a killer with near impunity.

When statehood arrived in 1907, things didn't get appreciably better. In 1908 alone there were thirty-six murders in the Ada vicinity. Over in Pauls Valley, a criminal lawyer named Moman Pruiett was notorious for getting desperadoes off the hook. Of the 343 persons he defended against murder charges, he won 303 acquittals. Only one of his clients was ever sentenced to death, and even this one was saved by presidential clemency.

Ada was being ridiculed in state newspapers as a lawless, dangerous place to be, a reputation not wholly deserved by this young town of 5,000. There were fine Christian families, law-abiding citizens, and businessmen who were tying to establish some semblance of law and order in the community. But even their own lawmen were ineffective when the state courts were so lax that men were permitted to murder for a price. Long-suffering Ada was getting fed up.

Ada's particular problem was rooted in an ongoing war between two factions. A.A. Bobbitt owned a large spread of cattle in Pontotoc County. He was always at odds with the owners of another large ranch – Joe Allen and Jesse West. Both sides had the largest bunch of gunfighters they could hire, and Ada was holding its breath, waiting to be the scene of an all-out war between them. The anticipated gunfight never did explode on the streets, and, quite unexpectedly, A.A. Bobbitt began to court the law-abiding element in the town. He had a few things in his favor as he began to improve his image. He had been a U.S. marshal at one time; he was a Mason; and he had a family which included a handsome twenty-year-old son who was the fancy of all the young ladies.

When Ada's society responded, hoping its acceptance of Bobbitt would defuse the situation, Joe Allen and Jesse West threw in the towel and moved their ranching and gunslinging operations to Canadian, Texas. In addition, one of Ada's most notorious gunmen went over to the side of the now somewhat respectable Bobbitt, and the community breathed a sigh of relief. Bobbitt was a little more wary than the city fathers, however, and he fully expected more trouble from the recently departed Allen and West. Bobbitt was especially hated by West, who had always believed that Bobbitt had had something to do with the killing of West's teenage son; consequently, Bobbitt lost no time in drawing up a will in which he left a thousand dollar reward for the capture of the guilty party in the event that he was killed.

As if in fulfillment of a prophecy, the will would soon be

executed. It was an afternoon in February, 1909. Bobbitt was headed back out to his ranch southwest of Ada. When he was within a half mile of the house, a shotgun blast ripped open his left side. With deadly accuracy, his shotgun resting in the fork of a tree, the killer quickly fired the second barrel, then jumped on a horse and dashed away. Bobbitt's hired hand, Bob Ferguson, was driving a second wagon just behind Bobbitt and got a good look at the fleeing killer and the horse he was riding.

When word of this violent, cowardly ambush reached Ada, the community was livid. Having no faith in its peace officers or the courts, a large crowd met and resolved to take action. A reward fund was set up, and citizens left the meeting in search of the killer.

Soon, the killer's horse turned up at John Williamson's farm near Francis, a small town northeast of Ada. Jailed at Ada, Williamson gave a statement saying that he had loaned the mare to his uncle who had admitted to killing Bobbitt. Ada probably wasn't prepared for what it learned. Williamson's uncle was one of the deadliest and most feared outlaws in the country, a man by the name of Jim Miller. He had killed over thirty men in Texas and New Mexico Territory and had arranged the killing of Pat Garrett, the famous peace officer who shot Billy the Kid – and now he was in Ada!

But Ada had a new weapon in its arsenal. It was a man by the name of Robert Wimbish, who just happened to be the county attorney, Ada's first since statehood. And he was just new enough to dare to do right. Wimbish sought Jim Miller with a vengeance, and before long a surprised Miller was caught near Fort Worth by Ada's police chief, George Culver. Miller had influential friends in Texas who could get him out of trouble about as easily as he could get into it, and he probably expected to ease out of this killing in Oklahoma. He just didn't know that Ada was mad, and this was the last straw with them. They would have justice, and they weren't afraid of Jim Miller even if the rest of the Southwest was!

During the meantime, details of Bobbitt's murder were coming to light. Oscar Peeler had made some arrangements ahead of Jim Miller's arrival in Ada – like renting him a house. When Peeler was thrown into jail, he talked, and Ada's vigilantes learned who they were really after: Joe Allen and Jesse West. Those two hoodlums had hired Miller to kill Bobbitt, and a professional bondsman named B.B. Burwell had acted as go-between. Soon both Allen and West were in Ada's jailhouse, and when Burwell showed up to make bail for them he was thrown in, too. All five were in the jail together – Allen, West, Miller, Burwell, and Peeler. Ada wasn't joking around.

To make matters worse, or as we might say, to add insult to injury, Jim Miller behaved like an exiled prince. He threw his money around even while in his cell, and Ada took note of it all. He wouldn't eat the regular fare at the jail, but instead ordered porterhouse steaks from the Elite Cafe for himself and the other prisoners. He shaved every day, and he wore stiff-bosomed shirts which he sent out to the laundry, along with a $5 tip to the jailer each time. He had fresh linen sent up for the beds, and the jail smelled of incense. He even had rugs brought in for the floors of his cell. He seemed to be laughing at Ada – and Ada grew quiet. Mysteriously quiet.

Letters and telegrams poured in, praising him and vouching for his sterling character. These came from judges and prominent people, including Texas Rangers. Jim Miller was awaiting another quick "ho-hum" trial in a state known to go easy on contract murder, and with all of his Texas character references he would be out in no time and back to his nefarious deeds. Or, so he thought.

On a Sunday night in April – a misty night, characteristic of Oklahoma in the spring – things were especially quiet. By midnight the town was deep in slumber. By some coincidence (or was it?) county officials had made themselves scarce. The sheriff found urgent business over in Arkansas, and several deputies were "out of town." It had been two months since the murder of

A.A. Bobbitt, and the men responsible were safely locked in the city jail. An unsuspecting jailer and a deputy blew out the lights about midnight and went to sleep on cots in the hall of the jailhouse.

About 2:30 in the morning, the jailer and deputy awoke to a command of "Git up and dress" and found themselves surrounded by about fifteen masked men who tied the two up with baling wire. Finding the keys to the cell block, the men entered the cells holding Allen, West, Burwell, and Miller, telling them to get dressed. Peeler was left alone because he had turned state's evidence against the killers at the preliminary hearing three weeks earlier. Jim Miller, arrogant even in the face of death, took all the time he wanted in dressing, putting on a stiff-bosomed shirt and tie complete with diamond stickpin. While he combed his hair slowly and deliberately, the crowd was growing, numbering about forty by this time. It was also growing impatient. Finally, Miller stepped out of his cell and made some wisecrack, although he did go along peacefully. Burwell and Allen, realizing the jig was up, gave no trouble. Jesse West was a different story. He came out fighting, trying to slug his way through the mob. He was pistol-whipped until he fell unconscious, then dragged along behind the other three to the Frisco livery stable next door to the jail.

It wasn't far, and it didn't take long. Inside the barn, the suspects' hands were tied behind their backs with baling wire. Then their feet were tied. The mob tired to make them talk about the murder, but none of them would cooperate. Jim Miller was the only one who would say anything. "Let the record show I killed fifty-one men!" is all he said, bragging about his murderous past to the very end.

Ropes were put around their necks and tightened. Then, the other end of each rope was thrown across a rafter. One by one the doomed suspects were hauled up into the air and left hanging. One account has it that the hangmen formed their small ropes into simple loops instead of hangman's knots, meaning the

467

This is the scene captured on April 19, 1909 by Ada photographer, N.B. Stall, who waited at the barn until morning brought enough light for him to take this famous picture. Hanging, from left to right, are Jim Miller, Joe Allen, B.B. Burwell, and Jesse West. Men and boys can be seen peeking through the wooden gates and spaces between the board walls. Just above and to the right of Burwell can be seen some of the curious who climbed up into the loft for a better view. Afraid that famous defense attorney Moman Pruiett of Pauls Valley might be brought to Ada in an effort to get the criminals freed on a technicality, outraged citizens had taken swift action.

four murderers slowly strangled to death. Jim Miller was the first to go up. After his body stopped wiggling, someone picked up his hat and put it on his head. Allen was second, and Burwell was third. West was last.

Their job done, the mob, numbering nearly fifty, disappeared into the misty night. The gray light of dawn brought curious men and boys to the barn for a peep through the slatted doors and cracks between wall boards. Some of the braver and more agile climbed up into the loft for a bird's-eye view, while the town photographer waited for enough light to snap an early morning picture of the bizarre scene. It's been said that he made a small fortune from his picture and the penny postcards that followed.

News of the hanging spread like wildfire across the nation's telegraph wires, each story growing a little larger than the one before. As it made the rounds, some newspapers in other parts of the country castigated Ada for its "frontier justice." They didn't understand the lawlessness that had preceded the hanging, nor were they aware of Ada's patience worn thin. But it didn't matter to Ada what those newspaper editors halfway across America thought. On that April night in 1909, Ada had begun to gain control over the killers and outlaws that were stalking its citizens. That one determined community may well have rung down the final curtain on killers in many a frightened town throughout the Southwest, for it seemed that the courts tightened up almost overnight in Oklahoma; and many were the telegrams of congratulations from individual citizens and whole communities throughout Texas, New Mexico, and Arizona, who had suffered at the hands of Jim Miller and his gang for years. Soon, Ada disposed of three more of its notorious hoodlums, one being sent to prison, one being sentenced to hang, and the other being shot in a pool hall by Ada's police chief.

Forty-two years later, Oklahoma City's newspaper giant, the *Daily Oklahoman*, left no doubt as to how it felt about the hanging at Ada. In 1951, it wrote, "So many were the fruits of this hanging that it can be written down as one mob action in America entirely justified in the eyes of God and man. . . . Echoes of the hanging still resound throughout Oklahoma, and those who took part in it have no reason today to be ashamed or conscience-stricken. . . . Those four men hanging in the gray light of dawn symbolized the end of America's old west in the sense of men murdering and being murdered without full justice thereafter." [4]

But the direct effects upon Ada's citizens were more than symbolic. When one of the local old-timers is asked for his reaction to the celebrated lynching, he usually answers quite simply, "Well, it sure straightened up Ada."

Recent interviews with several Ada citizens, including A.A.

Bobbitt's granddaughter, have revealed some interesting reflections upon that event of one hundred and eleven years ago. To this day, no one knows the name of any of the participants in the hanging. It is not sure that anyone outside the circle ever knew who participated, and as they wore hoods or masks, the participants themselves might not have been fully known to each other, although Bobbitt's granddaughter believes that her dad knew who some of them were.

The most widely-held belief among the citizens of Ada is that the Masons did the hanging. In support of this opinion, they point to the story that the men, whoever they were, met prior to the hanging at the Masonic Hall, an upper floor meeting room with an outside stairway. As the story goes, the men came down the steps of the two-story building two by two, each group having a special duty to perform. One group went to the city's electric plant and forced the engineer to turn off Ada's lights between 2 and 3 a.m. Others cleared the streets of anyone who might happen to be out at that dark hour. Although no definite proof has ever been found tying the Masons to the hanging, one thing is certain: It was a well-organized group, and one that surely could keep a secret.

THE PALMYRA MASSACRE

During the War Between the States, emotions ran high both North and South, but they rode at fever pitch in the border states of Missouri, Kentucky, and the western counties of Virginia, which would be railroaded into seceding from Virginia in 1863 to form a new state within the U.S. government, an operation full of hypocrisy considering Lincoln's vociferous rhetoric that secession upon the part of the southern states was the very reason he continued to perpetuate a bloody conflict.

Perhaps one of the major reasons for the bitter tension that pervaded those border states was their awkward juxtaposition between North and South. Unlike the lower South which was united in its opposition to the Federal invasion, there was great division of opinion, at least early in the war, between citizens of the border states. Differing viewpoints and opposite loyalties were especially pronounced in northern Kentucky and Missouri.

Nowhere was this discord more graphically and grotesquely illustrated than in the small northeastern Missouri town of Palmyra in 1862. The story first came to my ears in 1980, but it would be seven more years before I began a serious pursuit of the historical facts. I am indebted to Bob Ravenscraft, County Clerk of Marion County, and Corbyn Jacobs, local historian, for supplying me with further details of the horrific tale known as The Palmyra Massacre.

On September 12, 1862, Col. Joe Porter and his Confederate cavalry made a raid on Palmyra, endeavoring to liberate the town and free some Confederate soldiers who were being held in the jail. They captured several Union soldiers, all of whom were immediately paroled outside of town in Summer's pasture. They had also captured a man by the name of Allsman, a sixty-year-old citizen of Palmyra who had been the cause of much disturbance in the area. In the fall of 1861, Allsman had enlisted in the 3rd Missouri Cavalry of Union forces but was soon discharged due to his age, his inability to undergo active military service and, more importantly, the belief among the Federal officers that he could better be used as an informant.

An ardent, outspoken, and stubborn old man of Union sentiment, he had lived in Palmyra for over thirty years, having relocated from Kentucky when he was younger. He knew the area well. It was said that "he knew every hog path and every man's politics" in Marion County. [5] Many a time, he had led forces to the home of a person of southern sentiment, and many a time a home had been ransacked upon his pointing of the finger. He often led Federals to the homes of people for foraging purposes and to search for firearms.

Quite frequently, Allsman was called upon to testify as to the loyalty or disloyalty of certain individuals, and if he said a man was a Rebel the authorities believed him without question. The accused men were thrown into jail upon the slightest provocation while their families were robbed at home by Union soldiers. Understandably, there was a deep resentment of this old spy among the citizens of the area. Many swore revenge on him, and before the cavalry left with Allsman as prisoner, certain of the ladies of Palmyra said to Colonel Porter, "Don't let old Allsman come back."[6]

So stood the situation upon the third day of Allsman's detainment. It was the 15th of September. Colonel Porter's command was camped at Whaley's Mill on the banks of the South Fabius River, about 20 miles northwest of Palmyra, when Union General McNeil suddenly attacked and dispersed most of Colonel Porter's troops. Porter and a squad of cavalrymen were able to gain the rear of McNeil's forces and escape into Lewis County, where they encamped for the night on Troublesome Creek, about 25 miles northwest of Palmyra. Allsman accompanied Porter's small cavalry force voluntarily. He could have escaped. No one was restraining him. But he clung to the Confederates out of fear that he might be shot by stragglers or by someone who might recognize him and take the opportunity to mete out some vigilante justice.

As a result of the overwhelming defeat at Whaley's Mill, Porter was forced to change plans and begin a permanent retreat southward towards Arkansas. He informed Allsman that his original plan of carrying the old tattle tale off into another state had been thwarted by the unexpected defeat and that Allsman was now at liberty to go wherever he pleased. This was not altogether good news for Allsman, and he replied that he was afraid to go back, telling the colonel, "There are enemies of mine here who will kill me if they have the slightest chance." [7]

Colonel Porter was unwilling to drag him along, suggesting instead that he choose six of Porter's men as an escort to the home of some Union sympathizer. Allsman chose three or four men whom he had known, making no objection to the remainder. They started off in the evening toward Marion County but were soon overtaken by others who had followed them from camp. The guard was changed, and Allsman became worried. Before long, the party stopped in the woods, and Allsman was told that he was going to pay for his evil deeds. He was shot by three men, then his body was covered with brush and leaves in the dense underbrush of the thicket. To this day, his body has never been found, nor were his executioners ever identified.

Even the fact that he had been killed was not known until long thereafter. It was assumed by everyone back in Palmyra that he was still in the custody of Colonel Porter, although the whereabouts of Porter and his cavalry was unknown at the time. After more than two weeks had passed with no word of Allsman, the talk began, and the union newspaper in Palmyra, the *Courier*, fanned the flames into a raging fire by assuming a murder had occurred. The newspaper called for avenging the murder, and the Union citizens of the town took up the cry.

Had Colonel Porter wanted, he could have killed old Allsman at any time, and there were men under his command who, having families that had suffered from the old man's meddling, had urged the colonel to shoot him. Porter reproved

473

his men for their vilification of the old man and ordered the guard to prevent anyone from harming him, saying, "The Federals are the ones who shoot prisoners; let General McNeil have a monopoly on that sort of work if he desires it."[8]

In reality, the Unionists in Palmyra were correct in believing that Allsman had met with foul play, but no one could say for sure. On October 8, there was published in the *Palmyra Courier* a notice from General McNeil, now in command of Missouri's new pro-Union state militia, to Colonel Porter that he must produce Mr. Allsman, unharmed, within ten days, or rest assured that ten Confederate prisoners in Marion County jails would be shot in retaliation. A supplementary notice was sent to Porter's wife, although it is highly unlikely that she knew her husband's whereabouts or even had a way to forward McNeil's demand to him as he fled southward with the remainder of his command.

Even though the pro-Union citizens of the town had at first followed the hysterical lead of the newspaper, they could not believe the order to shoot ten men would actually be carried out. They saw it only as a threat intended to obtain the return of old Allsman. Earlier, a delegation of citizens of Confederate proclivities had started out to visit Colonel Porter's camp to effect Allsman's release, but, not finding the camp, they returned empty-handed. When it became clear that General McNeil's order was in earnest, an uneasiness gripped Palmyra.

In the jail at Palmyra, there were twelve mighty worried men who remembered the murder of Colonel McCullough and fifteen of their comrades in August at the direction of Union authorities in Kirksville, only seventy miles to the northwest. Lined up and shot. No trial, no jury, no court, no appeal. Just lined up and shot.

Some in town thought that Yankee General Merrill might intervene from his headquarters at Macon and save the men in the Palmyra jail from the same fate. After all, Merrill was McNeil's superior and could have stopped the whole sordid affair with the stroke of a pen. But the waiting prisoners thought otherwise. They remembered how he had executed ten "oath-breakers" on September 25 in Macon for simply not swearing allegiance to a government in which they had no faith.

In addition to these hard facts, the Palmyra prisoners were well aware of the reputation of the unsavory characters who held their lives in the balance. That fact alone was enough to strike mortal fear into the hearts of all twelve of the men locked in the jail, none of whom yet knew for sure if he was to be among the ill-fated ten who would have to die if Allsman were not produced pretty quickly.

General McNeil's published notice and directive to Colonel Porter had been issued by William R. Strachan, provost marshal of northeast Missouri. When approached by people who pled for revocation of the order, the red-faced Strachan, who was more often than not intoxicated, blustered that the ten men would be shot according to the notice. With him there was no appeal. His authority came from McNeil who, with a wave of his hand could have averted the calamity. But McNeil, puffed up with pride over his new appointment as head of the state militia, chose to rebuff even citizens of northern sympathies who begged him to stop this macabre ordeal. His curt answer to their pleas of mercy: "My will shall be done."[9] The prisoners certainly had reason to fear.

On the ninth day after the publication of the death order, when it became apparent that ten days would elapse without the appearance of Andrew Allsman, the hideous certainty of it dawned upon Palmyra. Entreaties continued by local citizens, but they fell on deaf ears. They were under military rule and all they could do was beg. Neither General McNeil nor Provost Marshal Strachan had the slightest compunction about slaying ten innocent men. It had been done before and the Yankee government had given them the right, so they were willing actors in the tragedy that was about to unfold.

Local citizens were helpless, and no one could produce Allsman. Colonel Porter had been making his way southward since before the threat was issued, and it is doubtful that he had ever seen or heard of General McNeil's ultimatum. It was a gloomy, desperate situation.

It was Friday evening, October 17. General McNeil ordered Strachan to go to the jail and select ten men, notifying them to prepare for death the following day. He knew most of the men, and Strachan knew them all, for they were all from neighboring counties and had families in the area. McNeil was probably satisfying a jealousy when he instructed Strachan to select the "worst rebels," his definition being those who could read and write, were educated above the others, and were of higher military rank. He further directed that those who could not read or write were to be left alone, taking instead those "of the highest social position and influence."[10] A case of malicious envy if ever there was one.

Strachan walked into the jail where twelve trembling souls awaited their fate. Only five would be selected from among them, while five others were being called to their graves from out of the jail at Hannibal. Those poor souls were started on a late night journey to Palmyra, where, through no fault of their own, they would be shot the next day. There was an exceptionally mean undercurrent in the occupation of northern Missouri, and most of the men and boys in the jails were being held there for nothing more than holding different political views from those of their new Yankee overlords. Others were bona fide Confederate soldiers who had been taken in battle – all native residents of the area.

With eyes as cold as steel, his mouth turned up at the corners in a wicked smile of satisfaction, Strachan called all of the prisoners to attention, reading off the names of all ten men who were selected to die. "You and each of you will be shot tomorrow at 10 o'clock in the forenoon as a punishment for your crimes and in retaliation for the murder of Andrew Allsman." [11]

It was an awful moment. The five condemned men and their fellow prisoners stood for a few moments as if suspended between Heaven and earth. Silence. Deathly silence. Then when the horror of the thing burst upon them like a cannon blast from the depths of Hell, men broke down and wept as if their very hearts would explode inside their manly chests. Some prayed, their faces buried deep in their hands, remembering their scenes of childhood, their families, their boyhood chums, and their sweethearts. In less than twenty-four hours, those minds, now wild with despair, would never think another thought. So much had be crowded into such little time now.

Soon, the five prisoners from Hannibal arrived, and by and by came a Baptist preacher. Next morning came a minister of the Christian Church, doing what he could to console and prepare them for eternity. Together, these men of the cloth tried to persuade the unfortunate souls to forgive their executioners and be ready to meet the Lord in the hereafter, at length being assured that the poor doomed prisoners had, indeed, forgiven their assassins. All, that is, except old Willis Baker.

Willis Baker, a sixty-year-old man who was not even remotely suspected of being religious, stormed and swore that he had done nothing to deserve being shot like an animal and that he would see "old McNeil and Strachan miles in Hell" before he would forgive them.[12] Baker was a resident of nearby Lewis County and had never been in the Confederate service, but he had two sons who fought the Federals like tigers. Mr. Baker was charged with harboring them and their companions, and when a Union man turned up murdered in the area, old Willis was charged with complicity in that crime. He was known to be loud and profane in his denunciation of the Yankees, and the death sentence did little to quieten him down. He would denounce them to the very end.

The names of the other nine men selected that night were: Capt. Thomas A Sidenor, from Monroe County; Thomas Humston, from Lewis County; Morgan Bixler, from Lewis County; John Y. McPheeters, from Lewis County; Herbert Hudson, from Ralls County; John M. Wade, from Ralls County; Francis W. Lear, from Ralls County; Eleazer Lake, from Scotland County; and William T. Humphrey, from Lewis County.

All nine of them were soldiers in the regular service of the Confederacy. All were church members and small farmers, men of limited means but upright citizens in their communities. Thomas Humston presented a particularly pathetic scene. He was only nineteen years old. Although the youngest of the lot and just approaching the prime of manhood, this single boy, whose life might have lay full ahead of him, tried to be the bravest of them all. He simply said, "A man has to die sometime, and I suppose one time is as good as another."[13] Contrary to McNeil's stipulations, Humston could neither read nor write, yet Strachan got away with choosing him for the slaughter. The poor boy was in jail only because he had been picked up by a scouting party on routine duty.

Captain Sidenor had been in the service under General Sterling Price, but after seeing his troops decimated at Whaley's Mill he decided he had seen enough of war and disbanded the rest of his command. To elude the Yankees, he disguised himself as a woman and headed for Illinois and, hopefully, civilian life. At Shelbyville, he was discovered and sent to the Palmyra jail. Like the others, he sat down and wrote messages of farewell, one to his fiancée back in Monroe County.

The very first name Strachan put on the death list was that of William T. Humphrey. He had been captured, then paroled, promising to stay in the vicinity. When Colonel Porter's raid occurred, culminating in the disappearance of old Allsman, Strachan had Humphrey thrown into jail, unjustly accusing him of joining Porter and engaging in bushwhacking.

Up in her little cabin home in Lewis County, Mary Humphrey got the tragic news of her husband's impending execution. She was only twenty years old and unlearned in many ways, but she determined to beg for her husband's life and sought out her brother-in-law to drive her to Palmyra. With her two little stepchildren and her two-weeks-old baby, she rushed to the office of the provost marshal, only to hear Strachan tell her to go to McNeil. With only hours remaining, she raced to General McNeil, finding the grim Nova Scotian determined to kill her husband. At length, however, she succeeded in convincing him that her husband, although invited by Porter's men to rejoin them, refused, fearing that his parole would be revoked. Once assured of the veracity of her statement, McNeil sent word to Strachan to choose another man to replace Humphrey.

It was 8 o'clock Saturday morning when the decision was made to grant Humphrey's reprieve. The execution was delayed and rescheduled for 1 o'clock. Back at the jail, old Willis Baker was somewhat more calm than before, only occasionally calling down an imprecation upon the Yankees. He was seated in one corner of the jail, telling a young boy named Hiram Smith what to tell his family after he was gone. Tears streamed down young Hiram's face as he listened to the old man speaking in low, sad tones. How he dreaded relating all this to the tortured faces of Willis Baker's wife and sons.

From the hallway came the jailer, who stepped near the cell and called out in a loud voice, "Hiram T. Smith!" Brushing the tears from his eyes, young Hiram walked to the cell door and looked through the bars. At that moment Provost Marshal Strachan appeared, asking, "Is your name Hiram Smith?"

"Yes, sir," was the polite reply.

"Well, then, you will prepare yourself to be shot with the other men today at 1 o'clock." [14]

Silence fell like a rock. Then, as Smith's fellow prisoners tried to comfort him, William Humphrey, reprieved but saddened at Strachan's diabolical choice of another youth who could neither read nor write, offered to write a letter to his family. His parents were dead, so young Hiram Smith dictated a letter to his sister, written in detail by the man whose place he would take before the firing squad.

Shortly after 12 o'clock, three wagons pulled up in front of the jail. There were three rough, pine coffins in each of the wagons, with the exception of one wagon which held four. The condemned men bade farewell to their companions and shook hands with their kind jailer, Captain Reed, who cried like a child as each man told him goodbye. Like Marie Antoinette in her tumbrel, each man was made to sit upon his coffin and ride to his fate in the back of an open wagon.

Down the streets of old Palmyra went this mournful cavalcade. Few persons witnessed it at all. A sickening horror gripped the citizens of this stricken community, and they closed their shutters against such a barbarous act – an act committed by full authority of the United States government which was, incredibly, demanding their fidelity and devotion. Now and then, a woman's voice could be heard, wailing as one laments the dead. Draped windows and vacant streets told of the mourning in Palmyra as that death train slowly wound its way to the fairgrounds.

East to Main Street, then south as far as the livery stable. East again, the creaking old wagon wheels adding their own music to the dirge that all nature seemed to be singing for these brave, sad hearts. Shortly, the slow moving cortège entered the Hannibal Road as the beauty of the countryside appeared. Rural Marion County. How could she be the scene of such gore?

The fences were thrown down when the wagons reached the fairgrounds, and the last leg of that fateful journey was completed when the conveyances were halted within the circular ring of the amphitheater. Only about a hundred people watched in ghastly horror, but it was enough to remind one of the days of Rome when Christians were slaughtered as mere entertainment.

The prisoners huddled together as their coffins were removed from the wagons and placed in a row about six feet apart, just to the east of the bandstand in the center of the ring. Next, the helpless men were made to sit upon the ends of their respective coffins. They were offered blindfolds, but only two accepted. A minister came forward and the doomed men knelt upon the grass between their coffins and their executioners while one last prayer was offered up to their Heavenly Father, who must have stood at the Gate, ready to welcome them Home.

A gruesome execution by firing squad. Although this was probably not part of the execution at Palmyra, this photograph was made at some place during the war and is of the same time period. To further humiliate the condemned man, he was always made to sit upon his coffin while riding to his execution, then made to stand up, or in some cases made to sit on his coffin, such as at Palmyra, while a squad of Union soldiers -- in this case, thirteen of them -- shot the poor soul to death.

At the conclusion of the prayer, they all resumed their seats upon their coffins. The minister shook hands all around, and the disgusting miscreant, Strachan, followed suit. When Strachan reached Willis Baker, who was as defiant as ever, Baker looked him straight in the eye and, refusing his hand, said, "Every dog shake his own paw!" [15]

It was a horrible scene, straight out of the depths of Hell. Seventy-five men were drawn up in dread array with rifles at their sides, as they stood only thirty feet back from those ten defenseless men who were being forced to pay for a deed in which they had no part. There were thirty soldiers in the front line, forty-five behind them as reserves. It was as if Goliath had come to do battle with little David.

There in the fairgrounds arena, a place reminiscent of community merriment, the deadly spectacle was about to begin. Ten pitiful human beings looked straight at their killers who were waiting for the order to shoot. Captain Sidenor, a handsome man, engaged to be married, was attired in his best suit of broadcloth with a shining white vest. He placed his hand over his heart and called out to his executioners, "Aim here, please." [16] The other men, simply dressed in plain clothing, swallowed hard – or tried to, their mouths and throats dry with exhaustive fear. Wild thoughts undoubtedly raced through their minds. Would they be killed with one shot? Would they only be wounded and have to go through another volley at their vital organs? Would they be conscious and suffer great pain? Would bullets crash into their brains?

"Ready!" The rattle of musket-locks almost stopped the heartbeat of every soul there. "Aim!" Thirty gun barrels were raised and aimed at the gently sobbing men who tried to think of mother and home and at the same time tried to appear as brave as possible. The next word must have echoed around the whole Christian world. "Fire!"

What an irregular crashing and discharge of bullets! Thirty men, and so many of their shots went wild. Some believed there was poor understanding among the soldiers as to when to fire. It was evident that many of them were extremely nervous, having never killed in cold blood before. War is one thing, but this was another. Some probably fired astray purposely in hopes of standing faultless on the Judgment Day.

Whatever the reasons, only three men were killed outright. Captain Sidenor's request had been met only too well. He fell forward with his hands clasped upon his bosom, his left leg drawn up and his muscular chest torn all to pieces. He did not move again. Two of the others fell backward upon their coffins, dead. All of the remaining prisoners fell forward upon the ground. Morgan Bixler had not been hit at all but in the despair of the moment fell forward with the rest. It must have been a gruesome thing, indeed, for him to watch as the reserves moved in to finish the job.

An example of a similar execution, hideous and revolting. Poor Alex Johnson, an Alabama boy, was executed by Yankees near Corinth, Mississippi on July 23, 1863.

With revolvers, they moved up to the wounded "rebels," as they called them, and fired at close range into their writhing bodies. "They walked among the fallen men, firing bullet after bullet into their quivering bodies, while the blood streamed out and saturated the earth."[17] The sight of their struggling and the sound of their moaning was sickening. They were "put out of their misery" like wounded horses. Old Willis Baker died the hardest, gazing upon his assassins as they shot him seven times. The Palmyra *Courier*, which had sounded the drumbeat for this occasion, smugly reported, "The other seven were not killed outright; so the reserves were called in who dispatched them with their revolvers." [18]

At last, when all of the lifeless bodies were pronounced dead, their mangled corpses were gathered up from the blood-soaked arena, dumped unceremoniously into their coffins, and returned to town where friends and relatives claimed their precious remains.

Sometime after the war, when the troops were gone, the managers of the fair association refused to hold any more fairs on the old grounds. The place had become an Aceldama, and the citizens would no longer attend functions there. By 1883, all that was to be seen in its place was a wheat field. A new fairgrounds was built in the northern part of town.

The news of the Palmyra Massacre sent shock waves around the world. The leading journals of the North reported it with comment in New York, Philadelphia, Boston, and elsewhere. The newspapers of London, the *Times*, the *Star*, and the *Herald*, published accounts and wrote editorials about the affair. It was a topic of discussion at two of Lincoln's cabinet meetings, and the South was ablaze with indignation and revulsion over the grisly killings. President Davis made a written demand upon the United States authorities to deliver General McNeil into his hands, with the warning that ten Union officers would be executed if McNeil were not surrendered forthwith. The demand was refused, but the Confederate government could not bring itself to duplicate the dastardly deed and, consequently, did not follow through with the promised executions.

General McNeil was generally censured for his authorship and perpetration of the crime. He was denounced from the pulpit, in the papers, and from the hustings. "His unholy act followed him as an avenging Nemesis through life, and his crime was a stench in the nostrils of men wherever it was known."[19] On the other side, the occupying forces rallied to his support. General Merrill, his superior, stationed at Macon, fully approved and congratulated him. The Union newspapers of northeast Missouri applauded him, hard-bitten Union sympathizers signed petitions to retain him as commander of their local troops, and Lincoln rewarded him with a fat promotion, reassigning him from command of the state militia to Brigadier General of U.S. Volunteers. In 1880, President Hayes nominated him for U.S. Marshal, but bitter opposition quickly developed over his part in the Palmyra Massacre, and his confirmation by the U.S. Senate, whose membership once again included the southern states, was subsequently defeated.

"My will shall be done" was the reply of the pompous McNeil to the people of the town who begged him to rescind his order of execution. For his savage deed, McNeil would forever be known to history as The Butcher of Palmyra.

As to the utterly profligate Strachan, his subsequent actions proved his unmitigated depravity. On Sunday, less than twenty-four hours after the execution, the young Mrs. Humphrey called upon him in an effort to secure the release of her husband. Although his name had been removed from the execution list, there were the wildest rumors circulating throughout northeast Missouri that McNeil was going to shoot ten men every Saturday until old Allsman showed up unharmed. Nearly beside herself after the horror at the fairgrounds, Mrs. Humphrey was grasping at every straw to save her husband from such a fate.

Strachan seized upon the weakness of the terrified young woman, who was there all alone with her small children. He reminded her that he could either have Mr. Humphrey released or shot as he well pleased. There was nothing she wouldn't do to save the father of her little children, and Strachan knew it. The perverted price this demon demanded became known almost immediately. Some passing soldiers observed the little step-daughter crying outside Strachan's building. They investigated at once and learned enough know that Strachan had forced the young mother to submit to him. Word spread among the soldiery, where there was scathing denunciation of him.

Even after such display of his base character, politics under military rule in Missouri were so absurd that he was elected to the House of Representatives in that state and often considered for the speakership of that strange body. A New Yorker by birth, he had lived in Missouri most of his forty-four years. In addition to his other sins, he had been in the business of extracting money from prisoners in return for their release and other favors. Finally, in 1863, a Union officer brought charges against him during his term in the House of Representatives. Other officers, having the utmost disdain for him, began to aid in the collection of evidence against him, shunning him socially and professionally at every chance. At the trial, he was charged with multiple offenses, including embezzling, demanding large sums of money from prisoners, drunkenness, gross immorality, and placing levies upon the citizenry for release of certain prisoners.

Strachan was found guilty on two counts: embezzlement and prostituting his position as an officer for base and immoral purposes. He was sentenced to imprisonment for one year and fined $680; but General Rosecrans, commander of the military district at that time, said that he was the victim of persecution and ordered him released.

It was January, 1864, fifteen months after the Palmyra Massacre, and Strachan set out for the occupied city of New Orleans. Fortunately, for the good of humanity, the depraved reprobate wouldn't live long. He rambled around between New Orleans and Old Mexico for a while, before dying of consumption in a hotel in New Orleans on February 10, 1866, friendless and alone.

In 1901, the noble citizens of Palmyra formed The Palmyra Confederate Monument Association and began raising funds to memorialize the ten heroes who were murdered there forty years earlier by McNeil and Strachan. In 1907, they unveiled a stately monument of granite, topped by a marble statue of a Confederate soldier. On the south side of the sacred shrine is the date of the awful event, *October 18, 1862.* The north side contains two crossed swords and two olive branches. On the west face are the words: *Erected by the Confederate Monument Association and its Friends, Feb. 25, 1907.* But the most important feature is the list of names graven upon the front of the granite pedestal:

Capt. THOMAS A SIDENOR
WILLIS T. BAKER
THOMAS HUMSTON
MORGAN BIXLER
JOHN Y. McPHEETERS
HIRAM T. SMITH
HERBERT HUDSON
JOHN M. WADE
FRANCIS W. LEAR
ELEAZER LAKE

Confederate Monument, Palmyra, Mo.

In a lonely little cemetery in Lewis County rest the remains of young Hiram T. Smith. For years the grave remained
unmarked, but sometime around the turn of the 20th century a
modest marble shaft was placed at its head by the son of the
man in whose place Hiram died. The shaft bears the following inscription:

HIRAM SMITH

This Monument is Dedicated
to the Memory of
HIRAM SMITH
Who was shot at Palmyra
October 18, 1862
As a Substitute for
WILLIAM T. HUMPHREY
My Father

X

Researching Your Confederate Ancestors

Before reading this chapter, please read the caution label very carefully. The author is not responsible for any Yankee ancestor uncovered while using the tools described in this chapter.

WARNING: GENEALOGICAL RESEARCH MAY BECOME ADDICTIVE!
THERE IS NO KNOWN CURE FOR THIS DISEASE.

The following symptoms may occur: burning, itching eyes; tired feet; lack of sleep; confusion; temporary loss of memory; hallucinations; writer's cramp; rapid heartbeat; uncontrollable urge to visit courthouses; inordinate desire to walk through cemeteries; longing to speak with the dead; tendency to live in the past; habitual inclination towards excessive questioning; unnatural desire to take long trips; internet addiction; computer fatigue; aching fingers; back pain; frustration; exhaustion; manic-depression; and telephonitis.

If symptoms persist, contact a professional genealogist.

How well we know it! Once bitten by the genealogy bug, you're hooked for good, and those of us who once equated libraries with absolute drudgery will sit for hours, yea days, reading microfilmed census reports, marriage records, and ships' passenger lists. Sometimes the results are immediately gratifying. Sometimes it takes weeks to find a tidbit or two. But the satisfaction of seeing the pieces of the puzzle fall into place, no matter how long it takes, is enough to keep you following the next clue. And now with the internet, you can run down rabbit trails as long as you can hold your eyes open.

Southerners love a good story, especially if it's about someone we know, or better yet, if it's about some of our kinfolks. And kinfolks might be someone living now or someone who lived a hundred and fifty years ago. It makes no difference to a Southerner – they're all kinfolks, and we want to know all we can about them. To a Southerner, it's those family stories that we latch onto. That's what we like to pass down to the younger generations. The birth and death dates, names of children, and places of residence are what we write down, but the questions we most want answered are things like: What was he like? What color were his eyes, and his hair? Was he good-natured? What did others think about him? What was his religion? Was he brave? And, of course if he was a Confederate soldier, are there any tales from the war? What was my great-great-grandmother like? Was she pretty? Did she leave a diary? Did she have to fend off the Yankees during the war? The answers to those questions are the ultimate goal in our pursuit of genealogy, for therein lie the stories, and the stories are what make our ancestors come to life. So, "lookin' up your family tree," as we call it down South, is a fabulous journey into the past, and it pays wonderful dividends to those who are brave enough to take the trip.

Most of us have a sort of haunting curiosity about our past. Even if it never causes us to start looking up our family tree, nearly all of us wonder where we came from and what kind of blood flows in our veins. If we happen to be lucky, some great-aunt or third cousin might have done all of the hard work for us, and all we have to do is ask for xerox copies. But if we aren't so fortunate, as most of us aren't, we have to depend upon ourselves to make the long, diligent search which may or may not end with satisfactory results.

So, how does a novice begin – from scratch? Having been there, I can give you a few guidelines. The very first place to start is right at home. Ask your mother and father what they know about their family trees – names, dates, stories. Write down the facts. Record the stories on a tape recorder, or I guess in this modern age I should say, do a video. I don't know if you can even buy tape recorders any more. If you have the patience, write the stories down, and make a note of the date and who told the story. My dad remembered nearly all of the stories told by his parents and the two grandparents who were living when he was a child. He could tell an entire story, but he didn't ask questions as to who was who and how they were kin. So there were lots of stories, but not so many genealogical details. My mother knew only one set of grandparents, the ones on her mother's side of the family. Her own daddy died when she was three years old, and his daddy died when he was only five, so very few names or stories were available to me from that side of the family. Even on her mother's side of the family, where Mother knew her grandparents and aunts and uncles, she said she grew tired of hearing those old folks talk; consequently, she hardly remembered a story!

The next step is to backtrack until you have talked to your oldest living relative. Obviously, that relative is going to remember further back than anyone else – unless he, too, was bored with hearing the old folks talk! I waited until all of my grandparents were gone before learning the right questions to ask. It was then that I had to turn to collateral kin (aunts, uncles, cousins) for further information. Even though your main interest centers on your lineal ancestors (parents, grandparents, great-grandparents, etc.) don't overlook queries to your aunts and uncles, for they have the same parents as your mother or father.

If any family member, no matter how distant the relation, is in possession of an old family Bible, find it and look for the records that so often were kept there (births, baptisms, marriages, and deaths). One of my lucky breaks came when I looked through the old family Bible belonging to my grandmother's first cousin who remained in north Texas when my grandmother left there in 1902. It contained information which took me back five generations to the year 1810.

After gathering as many names, dates, and places as you can, it is time to visit a genealogical library where you will find sundry lists of people of the past, among which you will probably find some of your ancestors. The census roles usually produce the richest initial yield. By utilizing them, you can begin to narrow the location to state, then county, and eventually, to precinct. In this day and age, the internet can also produce much the same information if you know where to look.

Based upon the foregoing information, a trip to the appropriate county courthouse can produce good results. Some counties provide photo copies at a minimal charge in answer to requests by mail. Courthouses are rich in public records (marriages, deaths, court actions, wills, probates, etc.). Some courthouses contain cemetery records for the county, although the public library in the county seat is a better bet for those compilations. Bound copies of county and community histories are usually to be found in libraries and can sometimes offer a biographical sketch of the ancestor in question. And finally, tombstones themselves can sometimes reveal a wealth of information that can lead you to another generation further back.

The internet is a poor substitute for a courthouse search. Someone has to take the time to transcribe the documents and put them in a digital file on the internet, and to date I have found no genealogical site that has made that kind of Herculean effort. Yes, some marriage records and a few court records have been transcribed and digitized for internet use, but you will find much more information from a personal visit to the actual courthouse.

The preceding outline is admittedly a brief treatment of a complex procedure, but it will get you started, and it is understood that the family sleuth will certainly devise many ways of his own once he begins the journey backwards into his own personal past. At least it provides a basic method by which we can approach the main topic of this chapter: *how to find a Confederate ancestor*.

One of the primary objectives of a Southerner's investigation of his pedigree (yes, humans have pedigrees, too) is to confirm that he has an ancestor who served in the Confederate military – or as we say, "fought in the war." Not only does the discovery and authentication of such an ancestor thrill the descendant and, of course, add to his or her life a measure of prestige, it qualifies the descendant for membership in one of the two national societies of Confederate descendants, the United Daughters of the Confederacy and the Sons of Confederate Veterans.

The procedure is much the same as searching for any ancestor. Find out what you can from your primary sources until you have the name of a man who would have been of age for military duty between 1861 and 1865. Most of the men in the Confederate military were young men in their twenties or early thirties, meaning that they were born in the 1830s or 1840s, so it's a good bet that any male ancestor born during those years in any southern state was a Confederate soldier. But it must be remembered that the shortage of manpower in the South led to the enlistment of able-bodied males in every conceivable age group, as long as they could shoulder a gun. I've found soldiers as young as eleven and twelve and soldiers who were in their fifties. I've seen many a Confederate tombstone with a birth date of 1847 or 1848, making that soldier a mere fourteen or fifteen in the first or second year of the war. Of course, many of the young boys joined during the last year or two of the war, making them sixteen or seventeen when they joined the service. I've seen a few

Confederate tombstones with a birth date of 1850, which means that if that soldier joined in 1864 or early 1865 he would have been only fourteen or fifteen at the time of his enlistment. So, my rule of them is: Check out any male whose birth date is between 1820 and 1850.

The next step is to determine from your information at hand the state in which he was living at the time of the war. Most men initially joined units within their own states, though there were exceptions. Using the addresses provided in the following pages, write to the appropriate agency in the state of his probable enlistment, requesting his military unit designation. There may be a reasonable charge for the search, but many times there is not. I found a great-great-grandfather named Hugh James McRae in the 1860 census of Fannin County, Texas, so I wrote to the Texas State Library in Austin, who, in turn, wrote back with his unit designation: Co. C, 31st Regiment, Texas Cavalry, CSA.

If, in the case of the border states of Kentucky, Missouri, and Maryland, you do not find your ancestor in a Confederate unit there – and you know that he lived in one of those states in 1860 – then write to the surrounding southern states. Although each of those states, especially Missouri and Kentucky, furnished many soldiers to the Confederacy, some of the men crossed into the seceded states to enlist. For example, many of the volunteers from Maryland joined Virginia and North Carolina units upon Lincoln's rapid invasion of Maryland and subsequent suppression of civil government in that state.

If you prefer using the internet rather than writing each state, much of the same information is available online now. At the end of this research outline, I will list the websites that I use.

Another approach you might take involves searching the Confederate pensions granted to needy Confederate veterans after the war. The individual southern states provided the pensions in the wake of refusals upon the part of the national government to aid our aging, destitute veterans, so you will need to determine where the veteran was living after the war because he had to reside in the state in which his pension was granted. If he was living on a meager income and had little in the way of assets, he would have qualified for a pension in any southern state. Those pension applications contain a wealth of information about the soldier. Detailed affidavits were required of the applicant, and those documents reveal various types of information about the individual, including, of course, the unit or units in which he had served. Write the appropriate state agency and request a search of its pension records. Some states, including Texas and Oklahoma, have indexes online, and some of the states even have the actual applications online.

When you have acquired your ancestor's military unit designation, you have the information which qualifies you for membership in the SCV or the UDC; however, you will probably have been bitten so severely by the genealogy bug by this time that you will crave more information for your personal satisfaction. It is then that you begin an in-depth search which could lead in several directions.

A primary source of military information is the National Archives. From this source, I obtained the muster rolls of my great-great-grandfather, and from those rolls I learned several interesting things: color of eyes, complexion, height, weight, enlistment date, rank, date of rank, when present for duty and on leave, military pay, and illnesses.

Another source is the *unit history*. This is a history someone has compiled about a Confederate military unit, such as, shall we say, the 11th Alabama Infantry. The history of the unit will usually contain a list of battles in which the unit participated, a list of the officers and enlisted men in the unit, and other pertinent information, including perhaps some personal stories. Your ancestor just might be mentioned by name in one of these histories, but if not you will at least be able to determine the battles in which he participated by tracing the movements of his unit. Some of the unit histories are short but rich in genealogical information. Most of these can be found in local libraries or in larger bookstores that feature books about the war.

A reminder: Don't forget about those collateral ante-cedents. If you cannot authenticate a Confederate record for a lineal ancestor, and your purpose is to qualify for membership in the UDC or the SCV, then pursue the records of your uncles who would be in the appropriate generation for Confederate military service. It they are blood kin, as opposed to kin by marriage, their military records will qualify you for membership in either of those two organizations.

The following list contains the addresses of some of the main repositories of material concerning Confederate soldiers. There are many smaller collections to be found throughout the South in city libraries, county and city historical societies, ge-nealogical libraries, county courthouses, and museums; how-ever, it is virtually impossible to list all of them in this volume. The larger research centers in this guide will be more likely to contain the information you seek and can more readily direct you to some of the smaller repositories in their areas.

Keep in mind that all of these places have hundreds of additional items, such as manuscripts, books, diaries, occasional cemetery lists, old newspaper clippings, and other sources that might be pertinent to your search.

For several reasons, difficulties may be encountered in your search for Confederate records. Many courthouses and city halls were put to the torch by Yankee soldiers during the war, and many valuable records went up in smoke. Subsequent fires, though purely accidental, destroyed more records. In addition, official records from commanders in the field are incomplete due partially to the neglect in writing reports and to the nature of the desperate movements of the armies toward the end. Following the war, the vengeful Radical Republican Congress placed such blame upon Confederate military leaders as to cause many Confederate officers to destroy or hide their military records. Some were only recently discovered under the floor of a Georgia bank.

SOUTHERN BY THE GRACE OF GOD

And I am going to be perfectly blunt. As more and more blacks take over county and state agencies in the South, it is not unreasonable to expect Confederate records to disappear. Already, they have broken into the national headquarters of the United Daughters of the Confederacy in Richmond, setting fire to the valuable Confederate records and historical artifacts housed in that building.

Department of Archives & History
P.O. Box 300100
Montgomery, Alabama 36130

https://archives.alabama.gov/referenc/newform2.html

Auburn University Libraries
231 Mell Street
Auburn, Alabama 36849

https://etd.auburn.edu/xmlui/handle/10415/2014

Birmingham Public Library
2100 Park Place
Birmingham, Alabama 35203

http://www.bplonline.org

499

Public Library of Anniston and Calhoun County
108 East 10th Street
Anniston, Alabama 36201

https://publiclibrary.cc/info

Huntsville Public Library
915 Monroe Street
Huntsville, Alabama 35801

https://hmcpl.org

University of Alabama Library
Box 870266
Tuscaloosa, Alabama 35487

https://www.lib.ua.edu/#/home

Arkansas State Archives
900 West Capitol Avenue
Little Rock, Arkansas 72201

http://archives.arkansas.gov/ArkansasStateArchives/home

SOUTHERN BY THE GRACE OF GOD

University of Arizona
1510 East University Blvd
Tucson, Arizona 85721

https://new.library.arizona.edu

Florida State Archives
500 South Bronough St.
Tallahassee, Florida 32399

https://dos.myflorida.com/library-archives

University of South Florida
P.O. Box 117005
Gainesville, Florida 32611

https://cms.uflib.ufl.edu/spec/pkyonge

Georgia Archives
5800 Jonesboro Road
Morrow, Georgia 30260

https://www.georgiaarchives.org

Kentucky Department for Libraries & Archives
300 Coffee Tree Road
Frankfort, Kentucky 40601

https://kdla.ky.gov/records/e-archives

Kentucky Historical Society
100 West Broadway Street
Frankfort, Kentucky 40601

https://history.ky.gov

Murray State University
200 Pogue Library
Murray, Kentucky 42071

https://libguides.murraystate.edu/c.php?g=54398&p=351677

Western Kentucky University
1906 College Heights Blvd.
Bowling Green, KY 42101

https://www.wku.edu/library/information/departments/dlsc

Louisiana State Archives
8585 Archives Avenue
Baton Rouge, Louisiana 70809

https://www.sos.la.gov/HistoricalResources

New Orleans Public Library
219 Loyola Avenue
New Orleans, Louisiana 70112

http://nolalibrary.org/branch/1/main-library

Maryland State Archives
350 Rowe Boulevard
Annapolis, Maryland 21401

https://msa.maryland.gov

Mississippi Department of Archives & History
200 North Street
Jackson, Mississippi 39201

https://www.mdah.ms.gov/genealogy

University of Southern Mississippi Library
118 College Drive
Hattiesburg, Mississippi 39406

http://www.lib.usm.edu/spcol/collections//#genealogy

North Carolina Department of Archives & History
109 East Jones Street
Raleigh, North Carolina 27601

https://archives.ncdcr.gov/about/visit/visit-state-archives-north-carolina

Oklahoma Historical Society
800 Nazih Zuhdi Drive
Oklahoma City, Oklahoma 73105

https://www.okhistory.org/research/udc

https://www.digitalprairie.ok.gov/digital/collection/pensions

South Carolina Department of Archives & History
8301 Parklane Road
Columbia, South Carolina 29223

https://scdah.sc.gov/research-and-genealogy/resources

Tennessee State Library & Archives
403 Seventh Avenue North
Nashville, Tennessee 37243

https://sos.tn.gov/products/tsla/tennessee-confederate-soldiers-home-applications-and-ledgers

https://tslaindexes.tn.gov/database-military-records/members-confederate-relief-and-historical-association-memphis

https://sharetngov.tnsosfiles.com/tsla/history/military/pension2.htm

Texas Heritage Museum
Hill College
112 Lamar Drive
Hillsboro, Texas 76645

https://www.hillcollege.edu/museum

Texas State Library
1201 Brazos Street
Austin, Texas 78701

https://www.tsl.texas.gov/apps/arc/pensions

Houston Public Library
500 McKinney Street
Houston, Texas 77002

https://houstonlibrary.org/research

Library of Virginia
800 East Broad Street
Richmond, Virginia 23219

https://www.lva.virginia.gov/public/guides/Civil-War/Veterans-
Memorials.htm

United Daughters of the Confederacy
328 North Boulevard
Richmond, Virginia 23220

https://hqudc.org

Sons of Confederate Veterans
P.O. Box 59
Columbia, Tennessee 38402

https://scv.org

In addition to the previous list, the following websites have also been useful in locating information about Confederate soldiers. All of the previous listings, as well as the following web pages, are up to date as of 2020, but keep in mind that many of them will continue, for various reasons, to change both physical and website addresses.

https://www.nps.gov/civilwar/soldiers-and-sailors-database.htm

https://www.findagrave.com

https://www.fold3.com

https://broadfootpublishing.com

https://www.familysearch.org

https://www.ancestry.com

Renè Beauregard

Courtesy of *White Pillars*, by J. Frazer Smith, © 1941

XI

Southern Poetry

It may come as a shock to modern school children that the South ever produced an author or poet of any note. In my school days of the 1950s and early 1960s, we were exposed to writings, much of which are little more than average verse, by the so-called literary giants of New England. We were forced to read works by Massachusetts novelists, essayists, and poets such as Henry Wadsworth Longfellow, Henry David Thoreau, Emily Dickinson, and Ralph Waldo Emerson.

Longfellow was an abolitionist, Thoreau was an abolitionist and transcendentalist who likened the execution of bloody John Brown to the crucifixion of Christ. Emily Dickinson, also described as a transcendentalist, was a recluse in Amherst, Massachusetts, who spent most of her life sitting in a room dribbling out little pieces of odd verse that were published posthumously. Ralph Waldo Emerson, another transcendentalist and rabid abolitionist, referred to Christianity as a myth, deploring it as a religion that "dwells with a noxious exaggeration about the *person* of Jesus." While awaiting the execution of the serial murderer John Brown, Emerson emoted, "The Saint whose fate yet hangs in suspense, but whose martyrdom, if it shall be perfected, will make the gallows as glorious as the Cross."[1] And yet we were required to study the works of these folks, along with those of Walt Whitman, a New Yorker whose fame rests upon his poetry collection, *Leaves of Grass,* called by most critics pornographic and obscene, as if they were the best America has to offer.

But not a single entry in our high school literature books about South Carolina's Paul Hamilton Hayne, William Gilmore Simms, or Henry Timrod, whose *Ode to the Confederate Dead at Magnolia Cemetery* is recognized as the most perfect ode in the English language. And what about Judd Mortimer Lewis, the poet laureate of Texas? Or what about Georgia's Sidney Lanier? Or Maryland's James Ryder Randall? Or Albert Pike of Arkansas or Abram Joseph Ryan, the "Poet-Priest of the Confederacy" who wrote many of the postwar poems about the South? And then there's Douglas Southall Freeman, of Virginia who won Pulitzer Prizes for his biographies of Robert E. Lee and George Washington? His *Lees' Lieutenants: A Study in Command* established Freeman as the preeminent military historian in the country.

Never heard of any of them. By the time we impressionable students finished the course, it was pretty much assumed that America's literary illuminati were exclusive to New England, and we went on our merry way. It was only as an adult and much later in life that I discovered the deception.

The South has produced first-rate novelists, essayists, biographers, historians, and poets, and fortunately it is now within the scope of this current project to present some of the long-buried talent of the poets. A good poem has to rhyme. If it doesn't, then it's not poetry. It's prose. It takes much more intellect and mental agility to say what needs to be said and make it rhyme than to jot down some random thoughts flitting through the brain. The poetry which follows is excellent rhyme. Most of it deals with the war, for that is the source of much of our most

510

moving poetry.

For the convenience of the reader, who may later wish to refer to poems used in this book, I have repeated in this chapter four poems that are found in earlier pages.

I can think of no better poem with which to start than Timrod's *Ode to the Confederate Dead at Magnolia Cemetery.* Written to be sung upon the occasion of decorating the graves in Charleston's Magnolia Cemetery in the spring of 1867, its last stanza has probably been engraved on more Confederate monuments than any one piece of poetry.

Ode to the Confederate Dead at Magnolia Cemetery

Sleep sweetly in your humble graves,
    Sleep, martyrs of a fallen cause;
Though yet no marble column craves
    The pilgrim here to pause.

In seeds of laurel in the earth
    The blossom of your fame is blown,
And somewhere, waiting for its birth,
    The shaft is in the stone!

Meanwhile, behalf the tardy years
    Which keep in trust your storied tombs,
Behold! Your sisters bring their tears,
    And these memorial blooms.

Small tributes! but your shades will smile
    More proudly on theses wreaths to-day,
Than when some cannon-moulded pile
    Shall overlook this bay.

Stop, angels, hither from the skies!
    There is no holier spot of ground
Than where defeated valor lies,
    By mourning beauty crowned.

— Henry Timrod
(1828-1867)

A Georgia Volunteer

Far up the lonely mountain-side
  My wandering footsteps led;
The moss lay thick beneath my feet,
  The pine sighed overhead.
The trace of a dismantled fort
  Lay in the forest nave,
And in the shadow near my path
  I saw a soldier's grave.

The bramble wrestled with the weed
  Upon the lowly mound; —
The simple headboard rudely writ,
  Had rotted to the ground;
I raised it with a reverent hand,
  From dust its words to clear,
But time had blotted all but these —
  "A Georgia Volunteer!"

I saw the toad and scaly snake
  From tangled covert start,
And hide themselves among the weeds
  Above the dead man's heart;
But undisturbed, in sleep profound,
  Unbleeding there he lay;
His coffin but the mountain soil
  His shroud Confederate gray.

I heard the Shenandoah roll
  Along the vale below,
I saw the Alleghenies rise
  Towards the realms of snow.

513

The "Valley Campaign" rose to mind —
    Its leader's name – and then
I knew the sleeper had been one
    Of Stonewall Jackson's men.

Yet whence he came, what lip shall say —
    Whose tongue will ever tell
What desolated hearths and hearts
    Have been because he fell?
What sad-eyed maiden braids her hair,
    Her hair which he held dear?
One lock of which perchance lies with
    The Georgia Volunteer!

What mother, with long watching eyes,
    And white lips cold and dumb,
Waits with appalling patience for
    Her darling boy to come?
Her boy! Whose mountain grave swells up
    But one of many a scar,
Cut on the face of our fair land,
    By gory-handed war.

What fights he fought, what wounds he wore,
    Are all unknown to fame;
Remember, on his lonely grave
    There is not e'en a name!
That he fought well and bravely too,
    And held his country dear,
We know, else he had never been
    A Georgia Volunteer.

He sleeps – what need to question now
    If he were wrong or right?

SOUTHERN BY THE GRACE OF GOD

He knows, ere this, whose cause was just
   In God the Father's sight.
He wields no warlike weapons now,
   Returns no foeman's thrust —
Who but a coward would revile
   An honest soldier's dust?

Roll, Shenandoah, proudly roll,
   Adown thy rocky glen,
Above thee lies the grave of one
   Of Stonewall Jackson's men.
Beneath the cedar and the pine,
   In solitude austere,
Unknown, unnamed, forgotten, lies
   A Georgia Volunteer.

— Mary Ashley Townsend
(1832-1901)

Forget It

If you see a tall fellow ahead of a crowd
   A leader of men, marching fearless and proud,
And you know of a tale whose mere telling aloud
   Would cause his proud head in anguish be bowed,
     It's a pretty good plan to forget it.

If you know of a skeleton hidden away
   In a closet and guarded, and kept from the day
In the dark, and whose showing, whose sudden display
   Would cause grief and sorrow and pain and dismay
     It's a pretty good plan to forget it.

515

SOUTHERN BY THE GRACE OF GOD

If you know of a tale that will darken the joy
  Of a man or a woman, a girl or a boy,
That will wipe out a smile or the least bit annoy
  A fellow, or cause any gladness to cloy,
    It's a pretty good plan to forget it.

— Judd Mortimer Lewis
(1867-1945)

Little Giffen

Out of the focal and foremost fire,
Out of the hospital walls as dire,
Smitten of grape-shot and gangrene,
(Eighteenth battle, and *he* sixteen!)
Spectre! Such as you seldom see,
Little Giffen, of Tennessee.

"Take him – and welcome!" the surgeons said;
"Little the doctor can help the dead!"
So we took him and brought him where
The balm was sweet in the summer air;
And we laid him down on a wholesome bed —
Utter Lazarus, heel to head!

And we watched the war with abated breath —
Skeleton boy against skeleton death.
Months of torture, how many such!
Weary weeks of the stick and crutch;
And still a glint of the steel-blue eye
Told of a spirit that wouldn't die.

SOUTHERN BY THE GRACE OF GOD

And didn't. Nay more! In death's despite
The crippled skeleton learned to write.
"Dear Mother," at first, of course; and then
"Dear Captain," inquiring about the men.
Captain's answer: "Of eighty-and-five,
Giffen and I are left alive.

Word of gloom from the war, one day;
"Johnston pressed at the front, they say."
Little Giffen was up and away;
A tear – his first—as he bade good-by,
Dimmed the glint of his steel-blue eye.
"I'll write, if spared!" There was news of the fight;
But none of Giffen. He did not write.

I sometimes fancy that, were I king
Of the princely knights of the Golden Ring,
With the song of the minstrel in mine ear,
And the tender legend that trembles here,
I'd give the best on his bended knee,
The whitest soul of my chivalry,
For Little Giffen of Tennessee.

— Francis Orray Ticknor
(1822-1874)

(This poem is true in every detail. The young soldier boy, in such pitiful condition in one of the makeshift hospitals in Columbus, Georgia that his case was declared hopeless, caught the attention of the wife of Dr. Ticknor. She took him home and watched him slowly regain his health, while teaching him to write so that he could write to his mother. Little is known about the boy even today, the only known piece of information being that his father was a blacksmith in the mountains of East Tennessee. Upon hearing from his captain, he left the Ticknors and promised to write if spared. He was never heard from again.) [2]

Somebody's Darling

Into a ward of the whitewashed walls
    Where the dead and the dying lay —
Wounded by bayonets, shells, and balls —
    Somebody's darling was borne one day.
Somebody's darling! so young and so brave,
    Wearing still on his pale sweet face —
Soon to be hid by the dust of the grave —
    The lingering light of his boyhood's grace.

Matted and damp are the curls of gold
    Kissing the snow of that fair young brow,
Pale are the lips of delicate mould —
    Somebody's darling is dying now.
Back from the beautiful blue-veined brow
    Brush the wandering waves of gold;
Cross his hands on his bosom now —
    Somebody's darling is still and cold.

Kiss him once for Somebody's sake;
    Murmur a prayer soft and low;
One bright curl from the cluster take —
    They were Somebody's pride, you know.
Somebody's hand hath rested there;
    Was it a mother's soft and white?
And have the lips of a sister fair
    Been baptized in those waves of light?

God knows best. He has Somebody's love;
    Somebody's heart enshrined him there;
Somebody wafted his name above,
    Night and morn, on the wings of prayer.

SOUTHERN BY THE GRACE OF GOD

Somebody wept when he marched away,
    Looking so handsome, brave, and grand;
Somebody's kiss on his forehead lay;
    Somebody clung to his parting hand; —

Somebody's watching and waiting for him,
    Yearning to hold him again to her heart;
There he lies – with the blue eyes dim,
    And the smiling, child-like lips apart.
Tenderly bury the fair young dead,
    Pausing to drop on his grave a tear;
Carve on the wooden slab at this head,
    "Somebody's darling slumbers here!"

— Marie Ravenel de la Coste
(ca. 1843-1936)

C.S.A.

Do we weep for the heroes who died for us,
Who living were true and tried for us,
And dying sleep side by side for us;
        The Martyr-band
        That hallowed our land
With the blood they shed in a tide for us?

Ah! fearless on many a day for us,
They stood in front of the fray for us,
And held the foeman at bay for us;
        And tears should fall
        Fore'er o'er all
Who fell while wearing the Gray for us.

519

How many a glorious name for us,
How many a story of fame for us
They left: Would it not be a blame for us
    If their memories part
    From our land and heart,
And a wrong to them, and shame for us?

No, no, no, they were brave for us,
And bright were the lives they gave for us;
The land they struggled to save for us
    Will not forget
    Its warriors yet
Who sleep in so many a grave for us.

On many and many a plain for us
Their blood poured down all in vain for us,
Red, rich, and pure, like a rain for us;
    They bleed — we weep,
    We live — they sleep,
"All lost," the only refrain for us.

But their memories e'er shall remain for us,
And their names, bright names, without stain for us,
The glory they won shall not wane for us,
    In legend and lay
    Our heroes in Gray
Shall forever live over again for us.

               — Abram Joseph Ryan
                (1838-1886)

A Land Without Ruins

Yes, give me the land
    Where the ruins are spread,
And the living tread light
    On the heart of the dead;
Yes, give me the land
    That is blest by the dust,
And bright with the deeds,
    Of the down-trodden just.

Yes, give me the land
    Where the battle's red blast
Has flashed on the future
    The form of the past;
Yes, give me the land
    That hath legend and lays
That tell of the memories
    Of long-vanished days.

Yes, give me the land
    That hath story and song
To tell of the strife
    Of the right and the wrong;
Yes, give me the land
    With a grave in each spot
And names in the graves
    That shall not be forgot.

Yes, give me the land
    Of the wreck and the tomb;
There's grandeur in graves —
    There's glory in gloom.

For out of the gloom
    Future brightness is born;
As, after the night
    Looms the sunrise of morn.

And the graves of the dead
    With the grass overgrown,
May yet form the footstool
    Of Liberty's throne;
And each simple wreck
    In the way-path of might
Shall yet be a rock
    In the temple of Right.

— Abram Joseph Ryan
(1838-1886)

The Old Wash Place

She was such a little mother —
So absurdly young – that while
Tears are trembling on my lashes
At her memory, I smile
At the very youngness of her.
Just a little girl she seems,
Smiling at me from the distance,
Singing to me in my dreams
Lullabies we all remember;
But I mostly see her face
Smiling through the clouds of steam
That almost hid the old wash place.

SOUTHERN BY THE GRACE OF GOD

Sometimes in my dreams a dogwood
Blossom glimmers in her hair.
I hear a redbird whistle
And the dream is free from care.
Then a man comes in the picture —
In the dream — and goes away,
Waving to the little mother
From the ranks of men in gray.
And from then the dogwood blossom
Never glimmers any more
And the redbird sings no longer
'Round the wash place as of yore.

Three of us and just that little
Bit of mother to the brood,
Singing while her heart was breaking
In the woodland's solitude.
With the homely tubs and kettles,
The soap gourd and the stick —
The old battling stick! — the memory
Catches at my throat so quick
That I scarce can choke the sob back
At the picture of her face,
Smiling bravely from the distance
Through the smoke of the old wash place.

Yes, I carried water for her
While the baby went to sleep,
With the songs that sister sang her
Where the wash lay in a heap;
And I sought dry sticks and piled them
'Neath the kettle. All the joy
In the dreams that come back to me
Is that I was born a boy

And could help the little mother —
And was glad to help her, too!
In the tasks about the wash place
Where there was so much to do.

Can wee babies understand it —
When a heart's about to break?
We were babies, but we seemed to know,
Somehow, for Mother's sake,
We must help to bear a burden
Which we could not comprehend,
And our puny arms about her
Seemed to strengthen and to lend
Her a strength no little bit o' mother
Could have got elsewhere,
As she toiled about the wash place
With her heart bowed down with care.

Sometimes tasks seemed over-dreary
And the days seemed over-long,
But she'd catch our eyes fixed on her
And would tremble into song.
But the world of heartbreak throbbing
Through the counterfeited joy
 Somehow would play on the heart-string
Of the little girl and boy
And baby sister;
And we'd snuggle face to face,
Heart to heart, her arms about us,
Kneeling at the old wash place.

Then one morning came a message —
Came in with the morning gleam —
How it came is lost or hidden

In the shadows of the dream.
But with it, hope went out from her
And she seemed to hark no more
For a voice across the distance,
For a footstep at the door.
And she knelt there at the wash place,
Kneeling with sister girl and me,
And I know now that that moment
Was her soul's Gethsemane.

Then the washings came more often, —
There were other heaps of clothes;
Day by day the clouds of steam
From the old kettle rose.
Day by day her love grew stronger,
And in the worry and the smart
Of her heartaches, she would rush to
And would clasp us to her heart.
And she'd strive to coax her lips
Into a snatch of song,
But the wash place called and called her,
And its tasks were hard and long.

Not long since I heard a woman
Say — in sneering tones and low —
"Humph! His mother did our washing,
For my mother told me so."
Whiter than the dogwood blossom,
Sweeter than the air could be,
Shone the truth of that vile whisper,
For she did it all for me
And for sister girl and baby!

Oh, the whisper — it was base!
But a soul was born in heaven
From that lowly old wash place.

Why it seems that Mother was not
Quite grown-up when she died, —
Such a little bit of mother.
Oh, the years are long and wide
Since she went away and left us
With the old smile on her face,
Leaving us with just the memory
Of that lowly old wash place.
I know that Father beckoned to her
By the look that o'ercrept her sweet face;
But we still miss her —
Shall as long as life shall last.

— Judd Mortimer Lewis
(1867-1945)

A Song for the South

O peerless land of tears and smiles,
  Of fragrant glooms and golden hours,
Where summer's hand with endless wiles
  Entwines the feet of Time with flowers,
Howe'er the tide of fortune flow,
  Thou hast my heart where'er I go!

No blot of shame thy record mars
  In senate-hall or lurid fight;
Thy spotless fame shines like the stars
  That guard thee through the balmy night.

526

SOUTHERN BY THE GRACE OF GOD

In weary wanderings to and fro,
Thou hast my heart where'er I go!

Thy maids are fair, thy warriors brave,
And those at peace beneath the pine.
Hymned through the air by wind and wave, —
Their glory needs no song of mine.
O native land! through weal and woe,
Though hast my heart where'er I go!

— Samuel Mintern Peck
(1854-1938)

The Wizard of the Saddle

It was out of the South that the lion heart came,
From the ranks of the Gray like the flashing of flame,
A juggler with fortune, a master with fame —
The rugged heart born to command.

And he rode by the star of an unconquered will,
And he struck with the might of an undaunted skill,
Unschooled, but as firm as the granite-flanked hill —
As true and as tried as steel.

Though the Gray were outnumbered, he counted no odd,
But fought like a demon and struck like a god,
Disclaiming defeat on the blood-curdled sod,
As he pledged to the South that he loved.

SOUTHERN BY THE GRACE OF GOD

'Twas saddle and spur, or on foot in the field,
Unguided by tactics that knew how to yield;
Stripped of all, save his honor, but rich in that shield,
Full armored by nature's own hand.

As the rush of the storm, he swept on the foe;
It was " Come! " to his legions, he never said " Go! "
With sinews unbending, how could the world know
That he rallied a starving host?

For the wondering ranks of the foe were like clay
To these men of flint in the molten day;
And the hell-hounds of war howled afar for their prey,
When the arm of a Forrest led.

For devil or angel, life stirred when he spoke,
And the current of courage, if slumbering, woke
At the yell of the leader, for never was broke
The record, men wondering read.

With a hundred he charged like a thousand men,
And the hoof-beats of one seemed the tattoo of ten;
What bar were burned bridges or flooded fords when
The wizard of battles was there!

But his pity could bend to a fallen foe,
The mailed hand soothe a brother's woe;
There was time to be human, for tears to flow —
For the heart of the man to thrill.

Then " On! " as though never a halt befell,
With a swinging blade and the Rebel yell,
Through the song of the bullets and plowshares of hell —
The hero, half iron, half soul!

SOUTHERN BY THE GRACE OF GOD

Swing, rustless blade in the strong right hand —
Ride, soul of a god, through the dauntless band —
Through the low green mounds or the breadth of the land —
Wherever your legions dwell!

Swing, Rebel blade, through the halls of fame,
Where courage and justice have left your name;
By the torches of glory your deeds shall flame
With the reckoning of Time!

— Virginia Frazer Boyle
(1863-1938)

The Conquered Banner

Furl that Banner, for 'tis weary:
Round its staff 'tis drooping dreary;
    Furl it, fold it, it is best;
For there's not a man to wave it,
And there's not a sword to save it,
And there's not one left to lave it
In the blood which heroes gave it;
And its foes now scorn and brave it;
    Furl it, hide it — let it rest!

Take that Banner down! 'tis tattered;
Broken is its staff and shattered;
And the valiant hosts are scattered;
    Over whom it floated high.
Oh! 'tis hard for us to fold it;
Hard to think there's none to hold it;
Hard that those who once unrolled it
    Now must furl it with a sigh.

SOUTHERN BY THE GRACE OF GOD

Furl that Banner! furl it sadly!
Once then thousands hailed it gladly,
And ten thousands wildly, madly,
   Swore it should forever wave;
Swore that foeman's sword should never
Hearts like theirs entwined dissever,
Till that flag should float forever
   O'er their freedom or their grave!

Furl it! for the hands that grasped it,
And the hearts that fondly clasped it,
   Cold and dead are lying low;
And that Banner — it is trailing!
While around it sounds the wailing
   Of its people in their woe.

For, though conquered, they adore it!
Love the cold, dead hands that bore it!
Weep for those who fell before it!
Pardon those who trailed and tore it!
   But, oh! wildly they deplored it!
   Now who furl and fold it so.

Furl that Banner! True, 'tis gory,
Yet, 'tis wreathed around with glory,
And 'twill live in song and story,
   Though its folds are in the dust;
For its fame on brightest pages,
Penned by poets and by sages,
Shall go sounding down the ages —
   Furl its folds though now we must.

Furl that Banner, softly slowly!
Treat it gently — it is holy —
   For it droops above the dead.

SOUTHERN BY THE GRACE OF GOD

Touch it not — unfold it never,
Let it droop there, furled forever,
  For its people's hopes are dead!

— Abram Joseph Ryan
(1838-1886)

Texas

Missouri is a grand old state
In history we are told;
She is one among the many,
Her sons among the bold.
She was foremost in the struggle
We have often heard it said,
And many of her patriots
Are numbered with the dead.
But now that time is passed away
And she's at peace again
While St. Louis and Kansas City
Spread abroad her righteous fame.
Oh yes, she's rich and powerful,
Her people grand and free,
But with all of her pomp and glory
She is not the home for me.

Illinois, too, does well to boast
And be exceeding glad,
For a brighter prospect to her size
No other state has had.
Calmly and serenely,
Chicago, her crowning star,
Stands upon Lake Michigan
And spreads her fame afar.

But what is grandeur and splendor
Where the heart cannot be free?
With all of her magnificence,
She is not the home for me!

But Texas is a model state;
Her sons are statesmen, too,
No people half so free as hers,
No hearts are half so true.
She has no St. Louis of which to boast,
Or no Chicago grand,
But, among the pretty cities are hers:
She's the most promising in the land.
She's the home of fruits and flowers,
Likewise of meadows green;
And all that's pleasing to the eye
In Texas can be seen.
Her soil is rich and fertile —
Her prairies broad and fair,
Bedecked with natural ornaments
With which none can compare.

Yes, Texas is a grand old state,
And grander yet she'll be.
For all the days that I may live
Texas is the home for me.
Texas bright and fair!
Grant me this wish, I trust:
That when my body turns to clay
It shall mingle with her dust.

— author unknown

Lines on a Confederate Note

Representing nothing on God's earth now,
    And naught in the waters below it,
As the pledge of a nation that's dead and gone,
    Keep it, dear friend, and show it.

Show it to those who will lend an ear
    To the tale that this trifle can tell
Of Liberty born of the patriot's dream,
    Of a storm-cradled nation that fell.

Too poor to possess the precious ores,
    And too much of a stranger to borrow,
We issued today our promise to pay,
    And hoped to redeem on the morrow.

The days rolled by and weeks became years,
    But our coffers were empty still;
Coin was so rare that the treasury'd quake
    If a dollar should drop in the till.

But the faith that was in us was strong, indeed,
    And our poverty well we discerned,
And this little check represented the pay
    That our suffering veterans earned.

We knew it had hardly a value in gold,
    Yet as gold each soldier received it;
It gazed in our eyes with a promise to pay,
    And each Southern patriot believed it.

But our boys thought little of price or of pay,
    Or of bills that were overdue;

We knew if it brought us our bread today,
    'Twas the best our poor country could do.

Keep it, it tells all our history o'er,
    From the birth of our dream to its last;
Modest, and born of the Angel Hope,
    Like our hope of success, it passed.

                 — S.A. Jones

The Confederate Cross of Honor

As even a tiny shell recalls
    The presence of the sea,
So gazing on the cross of bronze
    The Past recurs to me.

I see the Stars and Bars unfurled,
    And like a meteor rise
To flash upon a startled world,
    A wonder in the skies.

I see the gathering of the hosts,
    As like a flood they come —
I hear the shrieking of the fife —
    The growling of the drum.

I see the tattered Flag afloat
    Above the flaming line —
Its ragged folds, to dying eyes,
    A token and a sign.

SOUTHERN BY THE GRACE OF GOD

I see the charging hosts advance —
   I see the slow retreat —
I hear the shouts of victory —
   The curses of defeat.

I see the grass of many fields
   With crimson life-blood wet —
I see the dauntless eyes ablaze
   Above the bayonet.

I hear the crashing of the shells
   In Chickamauga's pines —
I hear the fierce, defiant yells,
   Ring down the waiting lines.

I hear the voices of the dead —
   Of comrades tried and true —
I see the pallid lips of those
   Who died for me and you.

With back to earth, wherever raged
   The battle's deadliest brunt,
I see the men I loved — thank God,
   With all their wounds in front.

The many varied scenes of war
   Upon my vision rise —
I hear the widow's piteous wail,
   I hear the orphan's cries.

I see the Stars and Bars unfurled,
   Unstained, in Glory's hand,
And Peace once more her wings unfold
   Above a stricken land.

SOUTHERN BY THE GRACE OF GOD

All this and more, this little Cross
  Recalls to heart and brain —
Beneath its mystic influence
  The dead Past lives again.

And friends who take a parting look
  When I am laid to rest,
Will see beside the cross of Christ,
  This cross upon my breast.

— Henry Lynden Flash
(1835-1914)

The Southern Cross of Honor

This is an oversize sketch of the Southern Cross, the subject of Henry Lynden Flash's poem. The southern soldier came home to desolation, wreck, ruin, and the grave. There were no federal pensions or medals for soldiers who wore the gray, but southern states, laboring under severe financial burdens, still managed to provide small pensions for destitute veterans. In 1900, the UDC began presenting a medal of valor to Confederate veterans who had served honorably during the war. The bestowals were to end in 1913, but in 1912, after 78,761 medals had been awarded, the UDC voted to extend the bestowals indefinitely. The Cross of Honor is made of bronze and is a little less than two inches square, just right for wearing on the lapel. The soldier's name was inscribed on the bar across the top, and each and every cross was numbered and recorded in the UDC headquarters in Richmond.

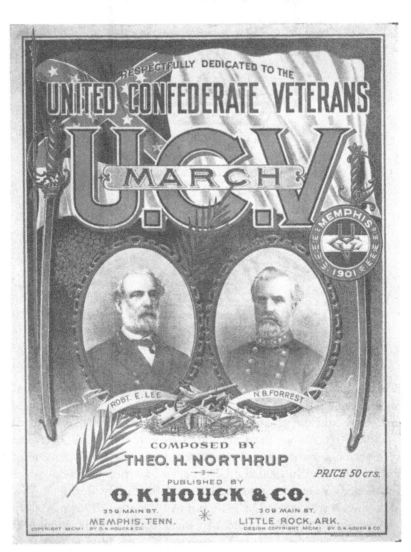

XII

Recommended Reading

Since the War Between the States, a regrettable effort has been made to grind out histories of the period which reduce that complex era into a morality play between good and evil, the North representing the good and you-know-who cast as the eternal villain. The skewing of the facts was evident immediately following the war. Alarmed at the prospect of history books which would teach southern children a lie, several capable Southerners set about writing their own accounts of the war. Jefferson Davis, one of the ablest of the southern writers, finished his scholarly work, *The Rise and Fall of the Confederate Government*, in 1881. Edward Pollard was quick to publish his *Southern History of the War* in 1866 and *The Lost Cause* in 1867. Many of the Confederate officers, including several generals, wrote their memoirs, in which invaluable information pertaining to the battlefield was faithfully recorded for posterity. Some enlisted men wrote of their experiences as soldiers in the ranks, one of the best-known works being Private Sam Watkin's *"Co. Aytch."*

With the passing of time, it is disconcerting to note that the situation has not improved but, moreover, has worsened. The

539

willful distortions grow more flagrant every year. There seems to be no honor among historians of today, most of whom shamelessly fill textbooks with political propaganda against anything and everything Southern. No wonder we now see anarchists destroying statues and historical monuments reminiscent of gangs in third-world countries. After all, many of these insurrectionists are youth who have been through Duke, UNC, and scores of other formerly reputable institutions where they learn their history – and I use that term loosely in this case – from bogus books and history courses taught by professors who instruct them in such worthwhile subjects as "how to topple a monument."

Of course, we know that victors write the histories, and we know that, whether accurate or not, those histories are always perpetuated with the approval and support of the government of the victors. And it is certain, we have learned, that the victorious will reject, deny, and hide the truth when it comes to the Southern War for Independence. One of their favorite methods of obfuscation is to explain to those of us who believe in facts that history must be constantly reinterpreted in light of the moral values – and again I use the term loosely – of the day, so that nothing actually stands upon the actual truth of the matter. In 2020, as I prepare this new edition, the entire epoch of the war has been reinterpreted as an attempt by the South to maintain involuntary servitude. Nothing else. No consideration of the burdensome tariff. No consideration of the Republican promise to prevent a southern terminus for the proposed transcontinental railroad. No acknowledgement of federal appropriations for bridges, harbors, and roads, most of which were located in the North but were funded by taxes raised in the South. No recognition of the political domination of the sparsely settled South by the heavily populated states of the industrial North. No, none of that. None of the actual reasons the South wanted to be free from association with the North. The media, the politicians – both Republican and Democrat – the universities, and sadly, most of the churches, have reduced the South's attempt to break free from Northern domination to a cartoonish formula: white people oppressing black folks. That is precisely why the insurrectionists are destroying our statues, our monuments, and virtually everything, whether connected to the war or not, that has to do with the white race. And yet these pseudo-intellectuals and religious practitioners still promote the false narrative.

History should stand upon its own record. It was Voltaire who said that history is a set of tricks we play upon the dead. He meant that as a joke, or perhaps as a criticism against such abuse, but, as in the case of George Orwell who tried to warn us of the totalitarian state in his novel, *1984*, the precautionary advice of both men has been turned into an actual blueprint for the regrettable state of affairs we see today.

It is especially unfair to indoctrinate our southern school children with modern, northern-produced textbooks that portray with increasing venom the South as an evil force which has always been a little out of step with democracy, and which, if not for the jaws of the Union Army in the 1860s, would have completely destroyed the much-ballyhooed American dream. Hogwash? Balderdash? Twaddle? Of course, but that's what southern children are raised to believe.

Add to that the spurious spewings of blacks who now try to legitimize fables and fairy tales by getting them into print. I give but one example. A recent review of a new book by some unknown black writer, the name of which I do not remember, carried an outlandish quote that some New Orleans restaurant – no name given, of course – offered a free ham to every policeman in the city who "killed a black man in the line of duty." The review goes on to state that even "a black police officer came in to claim his ham." And how does the black writer document this absurd tale? He simply begins with "According to a rumor . . " And yet when the eyes of the unsuspecting reader fall upon those remarks, it begins to churn around in the mind until it gains an illegitimate color of truth, or at the very least remains lodged there, and it becomes yet another part of the useful false narrative – all because the rumor made it onto the pages of a book.

The subversive media leads the march. The talking heads of television have absolutely nothing to gain from this false narrative except the satisfaction they obviously derive by promoting the destruction of western culture, the bedrock of which has always been the traditional South.

Unless Southerners are quite willing to take on the media, the education system, and the weathervane politicians, about all we can do is read and educate ourselves. Then, armed with knowledge, we can pass on to succeeding generations the real history of our people. Like little David of old, perhaps we can slay the Goliaths of the media and the educational institutions with a well-slung rock of truth.

Southern history encompasses much more than the subject of The War Between the States, and southern literature is a vast and varied field; however, most of the following recommendations are pertinent to the war era for all of the reasons discussed in this book. In some instances, I have found it helpful to include remarks about the selection. I have read most of the books listed here but have included a few other selections upon the suggestion of southern scholars and historians interested in disseminating truth about the South.

There are thousands of other good books by southern authors, books which space alone will not permit me to include. This meager offering is simply intended to assist the beginner in acquiring a substantial amount of knowledge about his inimitable Confederate heritage with the admirable goal of instilling in him an unending loyalty to the ideals of the Lost Cause.

While many of the older books in this list have been reprinted by university presses and private individuals, some still remain out of print. A google search can help you locate many of them, and Amazon lists lots of original books for sale by individuals. Another source for locating rare and out-of-print books is Bookfinder. [https://www.bookfinder.com] Then there is Hathitrust [https://www.hathitrust.org] a digital library where you can actually read scanned copies of an original book. There are other digital library websites, as well.

A Confederate Girl's Diary, Sarah A. Morgan, Houghton Mifflin Co., New York, 1913. (This is a large book and valuable for its information, but as far as diaries of the war, this is not one of the best ones.)

A Defense of Virginia and the South, Robert L. Dabney, Sprinkle Publications, Harrisonburg, Va., 1991. (Dabney's incisive treatise on slavery, with an exhaustive study of the religious argument is unsurpassed. Originally published in 1867.)

A Diary From Dixie, Mary Boykin Chesnut, edited by Ben Ames Williams, Harvard University Press, Cambridge, Mass., 1980. (This is the expanded edition of Mrs. Chesnut's diary, nearly twice as long as the original publication. Her wit, charm, intelligence, sarcasm, and southern loyalty combine to make this not only the most popular diary of the war but one of the most fascinating.)

A Fool's Errand, Albion W. Tourgee, New York, 1879. (Written anonymously by a carpetbag judge from Ohio, this work perfectly depicts the high-handed, self-righteous attempt by northerners to "reform" the South after the war. In fact, when Tourgee first published the book, he introduced it as *A Fool's Errand,* by One of the Fools.)

SOUTHERN BY THE GRACE OF GOD

A History of Morgan's Cavalry, Basil W. Duke, Indiana University Press, Bloomington, Indiana, 1960. (General Duke was a brother-in-law to General Morgan and took over his command after the death of General Morgan.)

A Rebel Private, Front and Rear, W.A. Fletcher, Austin, Texas, 1954. (A realistic account of soldier life in Hood's Texas Brigade.)

A Southern Woman's Story, Phoebe Pember Yates, edited by Bell I. Wiley, Mockingbird Books, St. Simons Island, Ga., (This is a 1959 version of the 1879 original. Through the eyes of a thirty-seven-year-old Jewish lady, this account provides an interesting look at Richmond's *Chimborazo,* the world's largest hospital, where she was matron during the war.)

A Woman's Civil War, Cornelia Peake McDonald, University of Wisconsin Press, 1992. (Southerners need to be wary of northern reprints of southern writings. Invariably, Yankee publishers dig up some axe-grinding liberal, in this case a woman, to write a new introduction to an old work. This introduction, true to form, goes on for endless boring pages, telling us what the diarist said but didn't mean or meant but didn't say. She calls Mrs. McDonald a racist, rails against men, and concludes that it was the women who were the only ones who had anything worthwhile to say. But even a bad introduction can't ruin the wonderful, lucid account left by Cornelia McDonald. This is a gripping story, so just sail past the introduction and read Mrs. McDonald's diary.)

American Terrorists: Lincoln's Armies in the South, Michael Andrew Grissom, Little Dixie Pub., 2015, Wynnewood, Okla. (If you have the idea that the war was nothing more than a North-South ballgame, then this is a must-read. If you think that Lincoln sent some nice boys in pretty blue uniforms down South to shoot across a field at some of our boys, then retire to their tents at night and listen to the band play "Yankee Doodle," then you're in for quite a surprise.)

An Untutored Genius: The Military Career of General Nathan Bedford Forrest, Lonnie E. Maness, Guild Bindery Press, Oxford, Miss., 1990.

Antebellum Slavery: An Orthodox Christian View, Gary Lee Roper, Xlibris, 2009.

Authentic History of the Ku Klux Klan, 1865-1877, Susan Lawrence Davis, W.G. Mori Pub., Birmingham, Ala., 1998. (This is an excellent reprint of the original edition which Davis published herself in 1924. She gives us a lot of valuable information concerning the original KKK, information to which she was especially situated to know at the time of its operation. Her dedication reads: *"To my mother, Sarah Ann (McClellan) Davis, and the other Southern women who designed and manufactured with their own fingers the regalia for the Ku Klux Klansmen and the trappings for their horses, and to the Ku Klux Klan 1865-1877, both the living and the dead, this history is gratefully dedicated."* This book can also be read online at www.hathitrust.org.)

Autobiographical Sketch and Narrative of the War Between the States, Jubal A. Early, Philadelphia, 1912. (This work is largely a compilation of General Early's articles in the Southern Historical Society Papers.)

Autobiography, Eppa Hunton, Richmond, 1933. (Colonel Hunton's history of Garnett's brigade includes a discussion of Long-street's responsibility for the failure at Gettysburg.)

Caddo: 1,000, Viola Carruth, Shreveport Magazine Publishing, Shreveport, La., 1970. (The history of Shreveport and Caddo

Parish, this book contains two excellent chapters on the War and Reconstruction in north Louisiana.)

"*Co. Aytch*", Sam Watkins, Morningside Press, Dayton, Ohio (This is the 1982 reprint of the 1882 edition. Watkins, an enlisted man, wrote his own history of the war as he saw it from the ranks of Company H, 1st Tennessee Infantry.)

Confederate Echoes, Albert T. Goodloe, Zenger Publishing Co., Washington, D.C. (This is a 1983 reprint of the 1893 original by a Confederate lieutenant who became a Methodist minister after the war. Concerned by the northern distortion of facts that had found their way onto the pages of history texts, Goodloe wrote his account in an effort to give Southerners the straight story.)

Confederate Flags Matter: The Christian Influence on the Flags, H. Rondel Rumburg, Society for Biblical and Southern Studies, Appomattox County, Virginia, 2015.

Confederate Military History, twelve volumes, edited by General Clement A. Evans, Confederate Publishing Co., Atlanta, 1899. (Now available from Broadfoot Press, Wilmington, N.C.)

Confederate Scrapbook, Lizzie Cary Daniel, Dixie Press, Nashville, 1996. (Compiled during and after the war, these poems, songs, newspaper clippings, and bits of trivia were first published in 1893.)

Confederate Veteran. (This was a magazine primarily intended for Confederate veterans. It began as a monthly magazine in 1893 under the editorship of S.A. Cunningham and soon became the official publication for the United Confederate Veterans, the United Daughters of the Confederacy, and the Sons of Confederate Veterans. It continued in print until 1932.

In 1986, Broadfoot Publishing Company of Wilmington, North Carolina, published a complete 40-volume reprint of the magazine, including a 3-volume index to the publication. It contains war reminiscences, battle accounts, and virtually anything of interest to the aging veterans. There are 20,000 pages, 4,000 photos, and more than 5,000 obituaries. The reprint carries a price tag of $1500, but you can view the magazine online at www.hathitrust.org.)

Confederate War Poems, edited by Walter Burgwyn Jones, Bill Coats Ltd., Nashville, 1984. (An excellent collection of poetry from the war era. Includes the *Ode to the Confederate Dead at Magnolia Cemetery,* considered the most perfect ode ever written. Alfred Lord Tennyson declared that its author, Henry Timrod, deserved to be called the "laureate of the South.")

Confederate Women of Arkansas in the Civil War, 1861-1865, compiled by the United Confederate Veterans of Arkansas, H.G. Pugh Printing, Little Rock, 1907. (A series of first-hand accounts written by women who lived through the war. Some of the ladies' stories are laced with gruesome details of Yankee atrocities.)

Detailed Minutiaé of Soldier Life in the Army of Northern Virginia, Carlton A. McCarthy, Richmond, Va., 1882.)

Diary of a Southern Refugee During the War, Judith W. McGuire, University of Nebraska Press, Lincoln, 1995. (Some of the best writing to come out of the war period are the women's diaries, and this one is as entertaining as any. A good read.)

Dixie After the War, Myrta Lockett Avary, Houghton-Mifflin Co., Boston, 1937. (Originally published in 1906. This work has long been recognized as one of the most gripping accounts of the horrors of Reconstruction, although Mrs. Avary, herself, admits that even she hadn't seen the worst of it. Her book is flawed, however, by an unrealistic portrayal of Lincoln as the kind, fatherly overseer of the human race, who had very little to do with the war. If it sounds out of context for a southern woman, it can be recalled that Reconstruction was so terribly cruel that Southerners were forced to dwell upon the "what if" to the extent that over a period of years a belief was conjured up that had old Honest Abe lived he would have been magnanimous after the war. His assassination aroused a measure of sympathy, and some Southerners bought into the carefully scripted portrayal of him as a kind old country philosopher who couldn't possibly have prosecuted such a bloody invasion of the South.

It should also be noted that Mrs. Avary moved north for a while where she worked as a journalist. Living in the land of Lincoln, she was undoubtedly caught up in the postwar effort to canonize the man. Wishing to get along with her associates and out of a sincere desire to foster good relations between North and South, perhaps she accepted the glorification of the war president under a barrage of social pressure. Who knows? But something caused her to become protective of Lincoln's image, and in editing Mary Chesnut's diary for publication in 1905 Mrs. Avary removed many of Mrs. Chesnut's derogatory references to Lincoln, all of which were restored in the 1980 edition of the Chesnut diary.

Still, this look at Reconstruction by Mrs. Avary fills a void in that field and is heartily recommended to modern readers. It is impossible to read this gripping account without drawing a parallel between the persecution of the white South during that period and similar events unfolding today, a parallel Mrs. Avary could not have foreseen in 1906.

Dixie After the War has been widely quoted by historians and has been called the literary forerunner of *Gone With the Wind*.)

Embattled Confederates: An Illustrated History of Southerners at War, Bell Irvin Wiley and Hirst D. Milhollen, Bonanza Books, New York, 1964. (An interesting collection of southern photographs pertaining to the war.)

Facts the Historians Leave Out, John S. Tilley, Bill Coats Ltd., Nashville, 1993. (A small book of refutations of myths found in history textbooks.)

Farewell to the Accent, Michael Andrew Grissom, Little Dixie Publishing Co., 2005, Wynnewood, Okla. (A small paperback which takes a look at why the southern brogue has faded so quickly and what might be done to yet save it.)

Father Ryan's Poems, Abram Joseph Ryan, John L. Rapier & Co., Mobile, 1879. (The wonderful collection of the poems of Ryan, who was called "The Poet-Priest of the Confederacy.")

Five Tragic Hours, James Lee McDonough and Thomas L. Connelly, University of Tennessee Press, Knoxville, 1982. (The story of the disastrous Battle of Franklin.)

Florida Breezes; or Florida, New and Old, Ellen Call Long, Ashmead Brothers, Jacksonville, Fla., 1883. (A semi-fictional account of antebellum life primarily set in middle Florida, widely regarded as one of the best primary source accounts of the planter class lifestyle in Florida.)

Four Years in the Stonewall Brigade, John Overton Casler, Morningside Press, Dayton, Ohio, 1983.

Four Years with General Lee, Walter H. Taylor, New York, 1877.

Full Many a Name, Mabel Goode Frantz, McCowat-Mercer Press, Jackson, Tenn., 1961. (The story of Sam Davis.)

Generals in Gray, Eliza J. Warner, Louisiana State University Press, Baton Rouge, 1959. (An easy to use reference, providing a thumbnail sketch of each of the 425 Confederate generals. Warner is no southern admirer, and the book should be used only as a starting place. He also did a work called *Generals in Blue.*)

Gray Fox, Burke Davis, Fairfax Press, New York, 1981. (This is a reprint of the 1956 edition. *Gray Fox* is a must for the student of Lee and the fighting in Virginia. It is concise, easy to read, and riveting. Once the reader begins, it is hard to put this book down. Highly recommended.)

Gray Ghosts and Rebel Raiders, Virgil Carrington Jones, Mockingbird Books, Atlanta, 1956. (For those who have wondered about the activities of Col. John S. Mosby, the "Gray Ghost," this book outlines vividly his daring career behind enemy lines. In addition, other raiders and partisan rangers are treated herein. Northern troops are shown to be the devils they were in the Virginia theater of war. Jones paints a vivid picture of Yankee Gen. Phil Sheridan as he laid waste the Shenandoah Valley. It is unfortunate that the author was not more judicious in the use of cursing throughout the narrative, so be aware.)

Heroines of Dixie, Katherine M. Jones, Bobbs-Merrill Co., New York, 1955. (More first-hand accounts of the war written by southern women who recorded them as they happened.)

History of Marion County, Missouri, R. I. Holcombe, E.F. Perkins Pub., St. Louis, 1884. (An old, hard-to-find local history that is nevertheless valuable for its story of the wicked Palmyra Massacre, the cold-blooded slaying of ten southern soldiers by official Yankee orders.)

History of the Coles-Cooke Brigade, Henry W. Thomas, Atlanta, 1903.

History of the Twentieth Tennessee Regiment, William J. McMurray, Elder's Bookstore, Nashville. (This is the 1976 reprint of the 1904 edition.)

Hood's Texas Brigade, J.B. Polley, New York, 1908. (A history of General John Bell Hood's Brigade, with the most detailed and informative material on the Gettysburg action at Devil's Den and Little Round Top.)

I Rode With Stonewall, Henry Kyd Douglas, Chapel Hill, 1940. (A personal first-hand account by one of Jackson's staff officers.)

I'll Take My Stand, Harper & Row Pub., New York. (The 1962 edition of the famous 1930 essays by twelve southern writers whose association centered around Vanderbilt University at Nashville. Five of them were poets, two were novelists, one was a professor of English, two were historians, one was a journalist, and one was a psychologist. The scholarly essays have one thing in common: They articulately advocate the old southern way of life and warn of the urban, industrial melting pot psychosis that was already at work in 1930. Excellent reading.)

In and Out of the Lines: An Accurate Account of the Incidents During the Occupation of Georgia by Federal Troops in 1864-1865, Frances Thomas Howard, Neale Publishing Co., New York, 1905. (A grueling account of the atrocities suffered at the hands of the invaders.)

In Memory of Self and Comrades: Thomas Wallace Colley's Recollections of Civil War Service in the 1st Virginia Cavalry, Michael Shaffer, University of Tennessee Press, 2018.

Inside the Confederate Government, Robert Garlick Hill Kean, Louisiana State University Press, Baton Rouge, 993. (Head of the Bureau of War, Kean gives us an insider's look at the war through his carefully kept diary in war-torn Richmond. Some observations on why the Confederacy did not use negroes as soldiers.)

Jefferson Davis, Herman S. Frey, Frey Enterprises, Nashville, 1978. (A good, short book on the life of our great president. This is the version usually found in souvenir shops at historic attractions throughout the South. It contains the seldom seen photograph of the enormous funeral procession in New Orleans that astounded northerners, who thought Southerners had been "reconstructed" to the point of rejecting their loyalty to and the memory of President Davis.)

Jefferson Davis: American Patriot, Hudson Strode, Harcourt, Brace, and Co., New York, 1955.

Jefferson Davis, Constitutionalist: His Letters, Papers, and Speeches, edited by Dunbar Rowland, Mississippi Dept. of Archives & History, 1923.)

Jefferson Davis: Private Letters, 1823-1889, edited by Hudson Strode, Harcourt, Brace, & World Pub., 1966. (The letters selected by Strode present an opportunity to look into the mind of Davis. One cannot help but be impressed with the intelligence, compassion, and sincerity of the Confederate president after reading the words he penned to his wife, his children, and friends. Despite two cruel years of imprisonment, there are no words of bitterness to be found in his correspondence.)

Jefferson Davis: Tragic Hero, Hudson Strode, Harcourt, Brace, & World Pub., New York, 1964.

SOUTHERN BY THE GRACE OF GOD

John Bell Hood and the War for Southern Independence, Richard M. McMurry, University Press of Kentucky, Lexington, 1982.

John Pelham of Alabama: The Gallant Chief of J. E. B. Stuart's Horse Artillery, H. Rondel Rumburg, Society for Biblical and Southern Studies, Appomattox County, Virginia, 2005.

Kentucky Cavaliers in Dixie, George Dallas Mosgrove, McCowat-Mercer Press, Jackson, Tenn., 1957. (Reminiscences of a Confederate cavalryman.)

Kirby Smith's Confederacy – The Trans-Mississippi South, 1863-1865, Robert L. Kerby, Columbia University Press, New York, 1972.

Last Ninety Days of the War in North Carolina, Cornelia Phillips Spencer, Watchman Publishing Co., New York, 1866. (Mrs. Spencer lost no time in getting into print her brutally honest account of the Yankee depredations in her state. She was especially incensed by the vainglorious boasting of Union Major Nichols in his *Story of the Great March,* and it was partly to this early, spurious account that she addressed herself In *Last Ninety Days of the War in North Carolina.* Nichol's falsehood's and demeaning attitude could not go unanswered, and this lady was more than up to the challenge.)

Lee's Last Campaign, Clifford Dowdey, Little, Brown & Co., Boston, Mass., 1960.

Life and Campaigns of Major-General J.E.B. Stuart, H.B. McClellan, Richmond, 1885.

Life and Labor in the Old South, Ulrich B. Phillips, Little, Brown & Co., Boston, 1963. (Phillips is *the* authority on slavery, much to the chagrin of the current proponents of the false narrative who try to dismiss him as "part of the old school historians."

A much-neglected book in today's craving for the sensational and the prurient, this book is the culmination of three decades of research and reflection on the social and economic systems of the antebellum South The history of the cotton industry and its work force are examined in scholarly fashion by Phillips, who concluded that even though plantation slavery produced great wealth it was a dead end proposition that left the South bypassed by the industrial revolution underway in the North. By turning away from the political debates about slavery that divided North and South, Phillips made the economics and social structure of slavery the main theme in 20th century scholarship. Together with his highly eloquent writing style, his new approach made him the most influential historian of the antebellum South. This is a reprint of the 1929 original.)

Life of General Nathan Bedford Forrest, John Allan Wyeth, Morning-side Press, Daytona, Ohio. (This is the 1975 reprint of the well-known biography of 1899.)

Lincoln Takes Command, John S. Tilley, Bill Coats Ltd., Nashville, 1991. (A reprint of the 1941 version, written by the capable Montgomery lawyer who gave us *Facts the Historians Leave Out* and *The Coming of the Glory.* In this exhaustive analysis of the Fort Sumter affair, Tilley exposes the chicanery of Lincoln in maneuvering the South into firing the first shot.)

Lost Mansions of Mississippi, Mary Carol Miller, University Press of Mississippi, 1996.

Memoirs of the Civil War, William W. Chamberlaine, Washington, 1912. (Chamberlaine was a soldier in Gen. A.P. Hill's corps, Army of Northern Virginia.)

Memoirs of the Confederate War for Independence, Heros von Borcke, New York, 1928. (The Prussian baron volunteered for service

SOUTHERN BY THE GRACE OF GOD
in the Confederate military and rode with Jeb Stuart.)

Military Memoirs of a Confederate, E.P. Alexander, Morningside Press, Dayton, Ohio. (A 1974 reprint of the 1907 edition.)

Morgan and His Raiders, Cecil Fletcher Holland, The MacMillan Co., New York, 1942.

Mosby's Memoirs, Col. John S. Mosby, J.S. Sanders & Co., Nashville, 1995. (Another great reprint from the Sanders Company, this is the autobiography of Mosby, first published shortly after his death in 1917.)

Nashville, the Occupied City, Walter T. Durham, Tennessee Historical Society, Nashville, 1985.

Natchez, Harnett T. Kane, William Morrow & Co., New York, 1947.

Old Baldhead: General R.S. Ewell, Percy Gatling Hamlin, Strasburg, Va., 1940.

Old Jube: A Biography of General Jubal A. Early, Millard Kessler Bushong, Boyce, Va., 1955.

Pat Cleburne, Confederate General, Howell and Elizabeth Purdue, Hill Junior College Press, Hillsboro, Texas, 1973. (The definitive work on Pat Cleburne, the Irish-born Confederate general who earned the sobriquet, "The Stonewall Jackson of the West.")

Personal Reminiscences of General Robert E. Lee, J. William Jones, New York, 1875. (Written by the same man who wrote the first biography of Jefferson Davis. Jones was a close friend of Lee, serving as chaplain at Washington College while Lee was its president. The work is valuable for its first-hand view of the legendary southern knight and the attitudes of his contemporaries towards him.)

Race and Reason, Carleton Putnam, Howard Allen Enterprises, Cape Canaveral, Fla., 1980. (Although this book does not deal with the events of the war directly, it deals with them indirectly, for some of the same issues were to be fought again, ironically, during the centennial of The War Between the States. The issue of states' rights was to play out its final scenes in the integration crisis of the 1950s and 1960s, and it was to that doctrine which the beleaguered southern states turned for their protection from northern antagonists precisely as they had done in the 1850s and 1860s, the unfortunate results being somewhat the same. Was it coincidence that integration orders came amidst enthusiastic celebration by Southerners of their hundred-year-old experiment in independence? The mixing of Confederate flags and racial turmoil in the 1960s, whether instigated or incidental, has served today's anti-South propagandists well. Southerners, who hear only one side of the school crisis, need to read Putnam's account of why the South was unable to defend itself and how he, a New England-born, Columbia-educated Yankee, came to do battle for the South and to define so clearly the South's position in its centennial calamity.

And in the Great Purge of 2020, where everything dear to Southerners and Americans in general is being swept aside in what has become an insurrection, race is the ram with which the doors of America are being battered. Putnam's book is a must-read for anyone who thinks Southerners – or anyone else for that matter – can continue being javelin catchers for those throwing them.)

R.E. Lee, Douglas Southall Freeman, Charles Scribner's sons, New York, 1934. (Recognized as the major work on Lee, it was published in four volumes and is considered the ultimate biography of Lee. Freeman won a Pulitzer Prize for this work.)

Rebel Rose, Ishbel Ross, Mockingbird Books, St. Simons Island, Ga., 1954. (One of several inspiring books about an almost forgotten heroine of the war, Rose O'Neal Greenhow. It holds one's attention through suspense and intrigue, for it is about a southern woman who chose to stay in Washington after secession of the southern states, acting as a spy for the new Confederacy. It was a dangerous mission as she moved in the highest of Washington's social and political circles. The dignified Mrs. Greenhow was imprisoned, threatened, followed, and eventually banished to the Confederacy. Her untimely end came off the coast of North Carolina while in the service of her beloved Confederacy. She drowned trying to make her way ashore with enough gold sewed into her clothing to weight her body down in the rough seas. A true heroine of the South. Highly recommended reading.)

Recollections and Letters of General Robert E. Lee, Robert E. Lee, Jr., New York, 1905.

Recollections of Alexander H. Stephens, edited by Myrta Lockett Avary, Doubleday, Page, & Co., New York, 1910. (In 1911, *The Outlook,* a weekly newspaper in New York, one of whose contributing editors was Theodore Roosevelt, reviewed Mrs. Avary's new book about Stephens, former vice-president of the Confederacy. Here is the review in its entirety:

The Recollections of Alexander H. Stephens, consists of a brief biographical introduction by the editor, Myrta Lockett Avary and Mr. Stephens' "diary when kept a prisoner at Fort Warren, Boston Harbor, 1865, giving incidents and reflections of his prison life and some letters and reminiscences." It is a valuable addition to American history. It is not altogether pleasant reading to a Northern man, but we wish that it could be not only read but carefully digested by that happily decreasing number of men who keep alive their hostility to the South as a section lately in rebellion, and regard as traitors Southerners who took part, either as soldiers or statesmen, in the Confederacy. Probably, however, it would do them no good. Could they, for example, understand the following sentence? "I told them that if, in solemn convention, the State [Georgia] should determine to assume her delegated powers, and assert her sovereign and independent rights, I should be bound to go with her; to her I owed ultimate allegiance; her cause would be my cause, her destiny mine. I thought the step a wrong one – it might be fatal; and exerted my utmost power to prevent it; but when it was taken, though against my judgment and counsel, I, as a good citizen, could but share the common fate, whatever it might be." We do not envy the man who can read that sentence and not realize that the act of Mr. Stephens (and this is equally true of thousands whom he represented) was that of a man absolutely loyal to his own convictions and to the government to which he believed his allegiance was primarily due. As in the American Revolution the Tory was loyal to the mother country, and the revolutionist to the Colonial government, so in the secession movement General Lee and Mr. Stephens were loyal to the State Government, and General Grant and General Sherman were loyal to the Federal Government. The question at issue between them was, to which Government was the loyalty primarily due? Even he who cannot understand this simple principle can hardly fail, in reading this diary, to realize that he is listening to a soul at once devout and conscientious, who may be criticized, if you will, for an error of judgment, but cannot be condemned for a moral obliquity.

This book has been reprinted by the LSU Press, but the full text can be read online. A google search will help locate the digital library where it can be found.)

Recollections of a Confederate Staff Officer, Moxley G. Sorrell, New York, 1917.

Seventy Years in Dixie, F.D. Srygley, Gospel Advocate Publishing Co., Nashville, 1891. (This 400-page book is a delightful read. At the age of 75, T.W. Caskey, a minister of the Christian Church, collaborated with F.D. Srygley, associate editor of the *Gospel Advocate,* to write his recollections of the Old South, from 1820 through 1890. If you can't find the book, you can read it online at www.hathitrust.org.)

Reminiscences of the Civil War, John B. Gordon, Morningside Press, Dayton, Ohio. (This is a 1985 reprint of General Gordon's 1903 work. An interesting book. Gordon was with General Lee's army at the end.)

Robert Devoy: A Tale of the Palmyra Massacre, Frank H. Sosey, Sosey Brothers, Palmyra, Mo., 1903. (This is a partly fictionalized account of the Palmyra Massacre with characters and dialogue, but based entirely upon the real incident.)

Robert E. Lee, John Esten Cooke, New York, 1871. (Although the book may be hard to find, it is worth the search. Cooke was an antebellum writer by profession and the cousin of Jeb Stuart's wife.)

Sack and Destruction of the City of Columbia, S.C., William Gilmore Simms, The Daily Phoenix Press, Columbia, 1865. (The most comprehensive account of the destruction of Columbia, this narrative was prepared by Simms, an author and poet, whom Edgar Allen Poe called, "the best novelist America has ever produced." Simms's own plantation home, *Woodlands,* which held 10,700 books – one of the largest libraries in the United States – was burned when the Yankees came through Barnwell County.)

Sam Davis, Hero of the Confederacy, Edythe Johns Rucker Whitley, Blue & Gray Press, Nashville, 1971. (Although the first part of this book gets bogged down in genealogy, the story of Sam Davis is there – all of it. Drawing upon rich sources, Mrs. Whitley spins the pitiful tale and includes many touching tributes in the last chapter. This book needs to be read.)

Southern History of the War, Edward A. Pollard, Fairfax Press, New York, 1977. (Originally published as a two-volume work in 1866, it is now available in a handsome one-volume edition of 1,255 pages. If you want a feel for the times, this is the book to read. Pollard was the editor of the *Richmond Examiner,* and he wrote the book as the war was happening. At war's end, he was ready to publish, and we soon had a southern version to offset the barrage of cover-ups that flowed from the northern press. We are indebted to Pollard for sharing the great wealth of information he had at his command as editor of a newspaper in the Confederate capital. He is sharp with his criticism of Yankee barbarity but too sharp in his constant disagreement with President Davis over almost everything the President said or did. A stricken South could have been better served after the war by kind words for a president who was imprisoned in Fortress Monroe during the time that Pollard was producing his history. Allowing, however, for his personality conflict with President Davis, *Southern History of the War* is an absolute must for the modern reader. In fact, it may be the place to start.)

Southern Side; or Andersonville Prison, R. Randolph Stevenson, Turnbull Brothers, Baltimore, 1876. (A good answer to those who would perpetuate the myth of southern cruelty at the Confederate prison in Georgia.)

Stonewall Jackson and the American Civil War, George F.R. Henderson, New York, 1936. (A standard work, it is valued for its discussion of the inability of Lee to return to his successful and daring tactics after Jackson's death. A thorough study of the warfare waged during Stonewall's brief time in the conflict.)

Story of the Confederate States, Joseph D. Terry, Arno Press. (A 1979 reprint of the 1895 edition which was published in Richmond by B.F. Johnson.)

The Army of Tennessee, Stanley F. Horn, University of Oklahoma Press, Norman, 1952. (High on the recommendation list, Horn's *Army of Tennessee* is the definitive work on the major Confederate army outside the Richmond theater. Horn is the recognized authority on the Army of Tennessee. This is a must for the study of the Confederate army, its victories, and its defeats.)

The Artillery of Nathan Bedford Forrest's Cavalry: "The Wizard of the Saddle," John Watson Morton, Publishing House of the Methodist Episcopal Church South, Nashville and Dallas, 1909. (John W. Morton was Chief of Artillery in Forrest's Cavalry. I found the full text of this book at www.archive.org, but the website is somewhat difficult to search.)

The Battle of New Market, William C. Davis, Doubleday & Co., Garden City, N.Y. 1975.

The Battles and Campaigns of Confederate General Nathan Bedford Forrest 1861-1865, John R. Scales, Savas Beatie Pub. Co., 2017.

The Civil War Day by Day, An Almanac, 1861-1865, E.B. and Barbara Long, Doubleday & Co., Garden City, N.Y., 1971. (This book is as essential to the avid reader of the history of the war as is a dictionary to a writer. The major events of the war years are chronicled day by day. In addition, there are several special studies at the end of the book, making the entire work an excellent reference that will be used over and over. The only drawback is that the authors are not southern, and the bias, though subtle, shows. Confederate successes are downplayed while Yankee routs are merely "orderly retreats." Southerners, who are used to reading around the bias, will find this volume a handy tool.)

The Clansman, Thomas Dixon, Jr. University of Kentucky Press, Lexington, 1970. (Reprinted from the 1905 original, this book is a revelation to most modern Americans who are never exposed to the truth about times in the South after the war. In his own description of the book, Dixon says it is a "historical romance" of the era. The characters are fictional, but the story is based on the happenings of his childhood. His characters are mirror images of people he knew. The book was so controversial that it was reportedly "banned in Boston" and, conversely, widely acclaimed in the South. It became so popular that it inspired the epic silent film of 1915, *The Birth of a Nation.* The fly in the ointment is Dixon's strange affinity for Lincoln. He labors through a good part of the first half of the book to convince his southern readers of the "goodness" of the man who brought them the horrors of war, failing to make the obvious connection between Lincoln and the ensuing afflictions of an occupying army and the impudent freedmen Dixon so despised. For all its puzzling, drifting beginning, though, it is an essential book for understanding the plight of the white South after the war. Dixon is a master at developing a story.)

The Coming of the Civil War, Avery Craven, University of Chicago Press, Chicago, 1974. (An excellent study of the events leading up to the war. Craven, himself a northerner, has put together a marvelous book for Southerners who need to understand slavery in its historical context. And he makes a convincing argument that race is important and that the agitation for abolition was a major factor contributing to the outbreak of war.)

The Coming of the Glory, John S. Tilley, Bill Coats Ltd., Nashville, 1995. (Tilley covers three major topics: slavery, secession, and Reconstruction. Oddly enough, he begins with a ringing denunciation of slavery but eventually notes that the institution's most odious aspect was the negative, unhealthy, and burdensome effects it had upon the white Southerner who was surrounded by these alien laborers.)

The Confederate Reader, Richard B. Harwell, David McKay Co., New York, 1976. (This potpourri of wartime material is good, light reading for either the beginning student of the war or for those who have studied regularly and are looking for genuine entertainment. Included among its short, assorted entries are poems, articles from wartime newspapers, excerpts from diaries, orders to the troops, private letters, humorous anecdotes, and eyewitness accounts of various events. This collection was originally compiled in 1957.)

The Confederate States of America, E. Merton Coulter, Louisiana State University Press, Baton Rouge, 1950.

The Death of a Nation, Clifford Dowdey, Alfred A. Knopf Pub., New York, 1958. (Hooray for Clifford Dowdey! He writes for us! You don't have to wonder who's side he's on. After reading this book, you'll agonize over the defeat at Gettysburg and realize how close we came to victory. Well worth the reading, even if it does have an unpleasant end.)

The Flags of the Confederacy: An Illustrated History, Devereaux D. Cannon, Jr., St. Luke's Press, Memphis, and Broadfoot Publishing, Wilmington, N.C., 1988. (This is the latest, most inclusive, and informative work on the subject.)

The History of the United Daughters of the Confederacy, by a committee of their membership, Garrett and Massie Pub., Richmond, 1938. (A very readable and informative book about the UDC – its origin, goals, rules, and impressive accomplishments through 1938.)

The Land They Fought For, Clifford Dowdey, 1955. (When this was reprinted in 1992 by Barnes & Noble Books, for some reason it underwent a title change: *A History of the Confederacy.* The change did not affect Dowdey's marvelous narrative, though, and this hefty book has earned high praise.)

The Last of the Confederate Privateers, David and Joan Hay, Crescent Books, Great Britain, 1977. (An interesting tale of Captain John Clibbon Brain of the Confederate States Navy.)

The Last Rebel Yell, Michael Andrew Grissom, The Rebel Press, Nashville, Tennessee, 1991. (This is the second volume in the Southern Trilogy which began with *Southern By the Grace of God.* A rare find nowadays, having been printed only two times.)

The Leopard's Spots, Thomas Dixon, Jr., Irvington Publishers, New York. (A 1979 reprint of the 1902 edition by the same author who wrote *The Clansman.*)

The Long Surrender, Burke Davis, Random House, New York, 1985.

The Lost Cause, Edward A. Pollard, E.B. Treat & Co., New York, 1867. (This good account of the war appeared one year after Pollard's *Southern History of the War,* but it is not as lengthy.)

The Memorial Volume of Jefferson Davis, J. William Jones, W.M. Cornett & Co., Dallas, 1890. (This 672-page book, a wonderful testament to President Davis, is now a rarity. I have been able to find only two copies. Information written on the flyleaf of each book indicates that one was purchased in Beef Creek, Indian Territory in 1890, while the other was bought at an auction in Hillsboro, Texas on September 22, 1891, for 65 cents. It is not known how many of these were published, but Jones was the first to get out a biography after the death of Jefferson Davis, which occurred on December 6, 1889. The biography, with the blessing of Mrs. Davis, was released in 1890, and due to the remarkable popularity of the deceased President of the Confederacy, it must have sold in record numbers. A most valuable work, done by a man who knew Davis well, it contains extraordinary details concerning the funeral and burial of the president. Letters of condolence, dispatches from notables, and invaluable records of who attended and where they rode or marched in the funeral procession are preserved for posterity in this volume.)

The Orphan Brigade: The Kentucky Confederates Who Couldn't Go Home, William C. Davis, Doubleday & Co., Garden City, N.Y., 1980.

The Real Lincoln, Thomas J. DiLorenzo, Three Rivers Press, New York, 2002. (A good exposé of Abraham Lincoln by a professor of economics at Loyola College in Maryland.)

The Rise and Fall of the Confederate Government, Jefferson Davis, D. Appleton & Co., New York, 1881. (This monumental and celebrated work that Davis wrote at *Beauvoir,* his seaside home in Mississippi, is a thorough explanation of how and why the Confederacy came into being and an authoritative analysis of the trials it experienced during its four short years. Be careful to look for the two-volume work. There is an abridged version of only one volume on library shelves now. No one should have tampered with President Davis's work. Every word was chosen with great care by this intellectual, and no one is adequate to an abridgment of his work.)

The Secret Six, Otto Scott, Uncommon Books, Murphys, Calif., 1993. (Not an easy read, full of details, but a valuable one because it reveals the dark inner workings of the abolitionists and the vicious nature of their main leaders.)

The Seven Days, Clifford Dowdey, Little, Brown, & Co., Boston, 1964.

The Southern Tradition at Bay, Richard M. Weaver, Arlington House, New Rochelle, N.Y., 1968. (Written in the 1940s, this is Weaver's great work, considered by many to be the ultimate statement of the Southern position. Oft-quoted, it is a must for the serious student of the South.)

The Story of a Cannoneer Under Stonewall Jackson, Edward A. Moore, J.P. Bell Co., Lynchburg, Va., 1910.

The Story of a Confederate Boy in the Civil War, David E. Johnston, Portland, Ore., 1914.

The Story of the Confederacy, Robert Selph Henry, Peter Smith Publishing Co., Gloucester, Mass. (A 1970 reprint of the 1930 original edition.)

The Story of the Great March, George W. Nichols, Corner House, Williamstown, Mass., 1972. (This is not a southern book. It is pure Yankee through and through. Written by Brevet Major Nichols, aide-de-camp to the infamous General Sherman, it was published in 1865 as soon as the narcissistic Nichols could get to a printer. Its value to us as Southerners is in the revelation of the northern attitude towards the southern race. Nichols had utter disdain for Southerners, considering them an inferior order of humanity. He uses words like "extermination" and "annihilation" as he revels in the fun of burning and destroying southern property. The "judgment of the

Christian world," writes Nichols, had justified Sherman in his barbarity. "This rebel horde should be swept from the earth." Those who doubt that our ancestors contended with arbitrary death at the hands of the invaders need to read this book. Nichols and others like him saw themselves as the instruments of God in bringing the "terrible swift sword" of Julia Ward Howe to the South. If that meant genocide, then so be it. Nichols was a product of the anti-South psychosis that had permeated the North for years. Such frenzied, fanatic passion tends to push people over the brink, directly into the waiting arms of a Sherman or a Hitler. Read Nichol's book and you'll draw some parallels.)

The Tragic Era, Claude G. Bowers, Houghton Mifflin Co., Cambridge, Mass., 1957. (Originally published in 1929, this is the scholarly, amply-documented, standard work on Reconstruction, touching especially upon the political corruption which made this era so tragic.)

The Traitor, Thomas Dixon, Jr., Grosset & Dunlap, New York, 1907. (The closing volume in Dixon's trilogy on Reconstruction, a series which began with *The Leopard's Spots.* His second volume, *The Clansman,* was by far the most significant of the three, causing a tremendous uproar throughout the North.)

The War the Women Lived, edited by Walter Sullivan, J.S. Sanders & Co., Nashville, 1995. (The horrors of war and the exigencies of life during the war years, faithfully recorded in various diaries, come alive in this fine sampling. The reader will be shocked at the barbarous treatment of southern women at the hands of U.S. soldiers.)

The Women of the South in War Times, Matthew Page Andrews, 1920.

This Band of Heroes, James McCaffrey, Eakin Press, Austin, Texas, 1985.

Those 160 Days, John M. Gibson, Bramhall House, New York, 1961.

Three Months in the Southern States, Lt. Col. Arthur J. Fremantle, University of Nebraska Press, Lincoln, 1991. (First published in the London newspapers in 1863, this is the vivid, readable account of a British officer's travels in the Confederacy, who he met, and what he saw. Highly recommended.)

Through Some Eventful Years, Susan Bradford Eppes, J.W. Burke Co., Macon, Ga., 1926. (A very good read. Mrs. Eppes provides a rare look at the war and Reconstruction in north Florida.)

Uncle Remus: His Songs & His Sayings, Joel Chandler Harris, D. Appleton & Co., 1881. (A reprint of the original edition can be found at www.confederateshop.com.)

War Crimes Against Southern Civilians, Walter Brian Cisco, Pelican Pub. Co., Gretna, La., 2013.

War Years With Jeb Stuart, William Willis Blackford, LSU Press, 1993. (This is the reprint of the original 1945 edition.)

When the Devil Came Down to Dixie: Ben Butler in New Orleans, LSU Press, Baton Rouge, 1997.

When the South Was Southern, Michael Andrew Grissom, Pelican Pub., Gretna, La., 1994. (A photographic look at the South of yesteryear, with photographs going all the way back to the War Between the States. This book is the culmination of Grissom's Southern Trilogy that began with *Southern By the*

Grace of God. A rare find today as only two bona fide printings were made, both of which are printed on glossy enamel stock such as you see in college yearbooks. One substandard edition, printed on inexpensive offset paper was issued by Pelican. That version can readily be identified by its dark blue cover, while the two standard versions have handsome red covers stamped in gold foil.)

When the World Ended: The Diary of Emma LeConte, edited by Earl Schenck Miers, University of Nebraska Press, 1987. (A small paperback detailing the burning of Columbia as seen through the eyes of a young lady – as it was happening. Once again, though, this northern publisher appoints a crusading feminist to grind out a useless introduction to this poignant diary. An effort is made to convince the reader that poor little Emma really didn't mean to be so angry with the nice Yankees who were burning the town down over her head. Little bits of conversation from Emma's later life are misused to claim that Emma had virtually rejected her former southernness and in so doing had become a much better woman, at least in the opinion of this introductionist. Still, the diary speaks for itself and is high on the recommended list.)

Will Rogers, Kenneth G. Richards, Children's Press, Chicago, 1968.

Yankee Autumn in Acadiana, David C. Edmonds, Center for Louisiana Studies, Lafayette, 2005. (A recital of the enormities suffered by the inhabitants of south Louisiana when the U.S. army pushed up through Acadiana from Morgan City. Murders, home burnings, theft, plunder, and all that characterizes an undisciplined army were on full display in this expedition.)

CONFEDERATE POSTAGE STAMPS

These ornately decorated stamps, bearing the likenesses of George Washington, Jefferson Davis, Andrew Jackson, and Thomas Jefferson, are shown here approximately 275% larger than the actual stamps. Postmaster-General John H. Reagan established the Confederate postal system under the most trying circumstances of war and a blockaded coast, but, to the amazement of the South and other watchful eyes, he soon had it operating so efficiently that not only did it break even, it showed a modest profit as well.

Acknowledgement

I once read that no one writes a book all by himself, and while I can't vouch for everyone I can say that it is certainly true in my case. In addition to my mother and daddy, Elba and Alma Grissom, who suffered through this whole thing with me, and my brother, Patrick, who supplied me with several necessary things, including a home xerox machine and a loan that enabled me, an unknown writer, to pay for my first printing, I wish to thank the following institutions and individuals for their important contributions, no matter how great or small, to this work now completed:

The governors of all of the southern states in 1987, with a special thanks to Governor Hunt of Alabama and former Governor Edwards of Louisiana.

The librarians and staff of the many libraries I visited during the preparation of this volume, including especially the Nashville Metropolitan Libraries; the Public Library of Wynnewood, Oklahoma; the Metropolitan Libraries of Oklahoma City, the Bizzell Memorial Library at the University of Oklahoma; the County Bookmobile of Garvin County, Oklahoma; the Carnegie Library of Eufaula, Alabama; the Public Library of Norman, Oklahoma; the Pontotoc County Historical & Genealogical Society Library and the Public Library of Ada, Oklahoma; Linscheid Library of East Central State University of Oklahoma;

Linebaugh Library of Murfreesboro, Tennessee; and the State Library and Archives of Tennessee.

The Board of Directors of the Sam Davis Association; the Oklahoma Division, United Daughters of the Confederacy; and the General Joseph E. Johnston Camp, Sons of Confederate Veterans, Nashville, Tennessee.

Norman Burns (Manager, Sam Davis Home), Mary Vaughan Gallagher (President, Oklahoma Division, UDC), Bernice Seiberling (Director of *Carnton*), Delores Kestner (Curator, Carter House), James Hoobler (Executive Director, Tennessee Historical Society), Ralph Green (Commander-in-Chief, SCV), Roberta Robertson (President, Tennessee Division, UDC), Dr. James Edwards (Chief of Protocol, Military Order of the Stars and Bars), Mrs. Donald Perkey (President-General, UDC), Mildred Logan (Assistant Editor, OU Press), Dr. William D. McCain (President Emeritus, University of Southern Mississippi), and Charles Smith (Lt. Commander-in-Chief, MOSB).

Also, Jamie Walton, Sharon Burkes, Cheryl Smith, Joyce Jordan, Curtiss Baker, Troy Tipton, Ruth Hamernik, Betty Bobbit Poe, Jessie Glover, Leonora Beverly, Verna Dell Tolson, Velma Zinn, Mr. & Mrs. Dean Isaac, Mamie Farnham, Richard Shacklett, Dr. & Mrs. William F. King, Mr. & Mrs. Paul Mott, Marilyn Geiger, Mr. and Mrs. Roger Risenhoover, Delphia McNeill, Ouida Elliott Jones, Maynita Warren, James Cochran, Sharon Schantz, Beverly Cady, Devereaux Cannon, Mr. & Mrs. Lanier Merritt, Mr. & Mrs. Darrel Cole, Ginger Turner, Joann Schnorrenberg, David Holland, Ron Johns, Kemper Kimberlin, Carolyn Pruett, Jody Baltz, Darvis Cole, Karen Guy, Judy Guy, Louise Maxwell, Mrs. John Farringer, Jr., Corbyn Jacobs, Rob Ravenscraft, Rob Hager, Mr. & Mrs. Ed Joe Mitchell, Elizabeth Baker, Leta Ferguson, Georgia Kennemer, Sharon Calhoun, Howard Kelley, Leta Rae McClain, Carolyn Fox, Hazel Dunn, Steve Rogers, Jackie Purdy, Marthalie Johns, Albert Baxendale, Betty Earl, Cam Cox, Annie Meek, Jesse Wayne, Mr. & Mrs.

Cletues Dixon, Mr. & Mrs. Conley Shirley, Al Thomas, Gene Andrews, Dr. James L. Jackson, and Nathan Roper.

A special word of gratitude goes to my friend, Leona Holland, formerly my high school English teacher, who constantly encouraged and urged me to write this book.

In addition, I am eternally indebted to Lucy Booker Roper, of Southaven, Mississippi, who assisted me in preparing the 2020 reprint of this enduring classic.

Rattle and Snap

Courtesy of *White Pillars*, by J. Frazer Smith, © 1941

Notes

INTRODUCTION

1. Clayton, Victoria V., *White and Black Under the Old Regime*, p. 51
2. Burnham, Stanley, *America's Bimodal Crisis: Black Intelligence in White Society*, pp. 51-52
3. Brimelow, Peter, *Alien Nation*, p. 108
4. *Century Magazine, Vol. XXXIX, No. 6*, pp. 826-828
5. *Ibid.*, p. 834
6. *Ibid.*, pp. 828-831
7. Coulter, E. Merton, *A History of the South: Vol. III, The South During Reconstruction 1865-1877*, p. 50
8. Shay, *Judge Lynch*, pp. 82, 83
9. Murphey, Dwight D., *Lynching – History and Analysis: A Legal Studies Monograph*, p. 21
10. Clark, Thomas D., *The South Since Reconstruction*, p. 313
11. Coulter, E. Merton, *A History of the South: Vol. III, The South During Reconstruction 1865-1877*, p. 49
12. Cutler, James Elbert, *Lynch-Law: An Investigation into the History of Lynching in the United States*, p. 205
13. *Ibid.*
14. Ayres, Edward L. ,*Vengeance and Justice*, pp. 232, 252
15. Murphey, Dwight D., *Lynching – History and Analysis: A Legal Studies Monograph*, p. 21

PREFACE

1. *Gone With the Wind*, MGM, from the introduction to the movie.
2. Pollard, Edward A., *The Lost Cause*, p. 752.

CHAPTER I

1. *My Mammy*, Joe Young, Sam Lewis, and Walter Donaldson, © 1920, Irving Berlin Music, New York.
2. *Detroit City*, Danny Dill & Mel Tillis, © 1963, Cedarwood Publishing Co., Nashville.
3. *Don't It Make You Want To Go Home*, Joe South, © 1969, Lowery Group Publishers, Atlanta.
4. *Precious Memories*, J.B.F. Wright, © 1936, Hartford Music Co., Hartford, Arkansas.
5. Purdue, Howell and Elizabeth, *Pat Cleburne, Confederate General*, p. 108.
6. *You Ain't Just Whistling Dixie*, David Bellamy, © 1979, Famous Music Corporation and Bellamy Brothers Music, New York.
7. Davis, Burke, *The Civil War: Strange and Fascinating Facts*, p. 13.
8. Ryan, Abram J., *Father Ryan's Poems*, pp. 53-54.

CHAPTER II

1. *My Home's in Alabama*, Teddy Gentry and Randy Owen, © 1980, Maypop Music, Nashville.
2. *Southern Style*, Knoxville, Tenn., July/August, 1987.
3. *Southern Partisan*, Volume III, No. 3, 1986, p. 7.
4. Mitchell, Steve, and Rawls, Sam, *How to Speak Southern*, p. 43.

CHAPTER IV

1. Chesnut, Mary Boykin, *A Diary From Dixie*, p. 19.
2. *Ibid.*, p. 235.
3. *Ibid.*, p. 268.
4. Pollard, Edward A., *Southern History of the War*, p. 40.
5. These two lines are from the last stanza of Henry Timrod's *Ode to the Confederate Dead At Magnolia Cemetery,*

CHAPTER V

1. Chesnut, Mary Boykin, *A Diary From Dixie*, pp. 113-114.
2. Altman, James David, *Mr. Lincoln's War on the South*, p. 9.
3. *Ibid.*, p. 5.
4. Ross, Ishbel, *Rebel Rose*, p. 90.
5. *The War of the Rebellion: Official Records of the Union and Confederate Armies*, Volume I, Part 1, p. 294. The letter from Maj. Robert Anderson, USA, to Col. Lorenzo Thomas, Adjutant-General, US Army, is dated April 8, 1861.
6. Nichols, George W., *The Story of the Great March*, pp. 68, 81, 119, 139, 268, 277.
7. Tilley, John S., *Facts the Historians Leave Out*, p. 39.
8. *Ibid.*, p. 50.
9. *Ibid.*
10. Pollard, Edward A. *Southern History of the War*, p. 59.
11. Tilley, John S., *Facts the Historians Leave Out*, p. 51.
12. Dowdey, Clifford, *The Death of a Nation*, pp. 41-42.
13. *Ibid.*, p. 42.
14. Alexander, E. P., *Military Memoirs of a Confederate*, p. 223.
15. Davis, Burke, *Gray Fox*, p. 131.
16. Dowdey, Clifford, *The Death of a Nation*, p. 45.
17. *Histories of the Several Regiments & Battalions from North Carolina in the Great War, 1861-1865*, Volume 5, p. 264.
18. Chesnut, Mary Boykin, *A Diary From Dixie*, p. 495.
19. Jones, Virgil Carrington, *Gray Ghosts and Rebel Raiders*, p., 104.
20. Pollard, Edward A., *Southern History of the War*, p. 20.

21. Davis, Burke, *The Civil War: Strange and Fascinating Facts*, p. 34.

22. Pollard, Edward A., *Southern History of the War*, pp. 298-210.

23. *The War of the Rebellion: Official Records of the Union and Confederate Armies*, Volume XXVII, Part 3, p. 943.

24. Dowdey, Clifford, *The Death of a Nation*, p. 8.

25. Pollard, Edward A., *Southern History of the War*, pp. 628-629.

26. *The Lanyard*, Volume XIII, No. 5, p. 5.

27. Chuenut, Mary Boykin, *A Diary From Dixie*, p. 534.

28. *Ibid.*, pp. 92-93.

29. Burkhardt, George S., *Confederate Rage, Yankee Wrath: No Quarter in the Civil War*, p. 25.

30. Dowdey, Clifford, *The Death of a Nation*, p. 46.

31. Chesnut, Mary Boykin, *A Diary From Dixie*, p. 122.

32. Davis, Burke, *Gray Fox*, p. 110.

33. The *Leaf-Chronicle*, Clarksville, Tennessee, July 14, 1996, page 5.

34. Pollard, Edward A., *Southern History of the War*, p. 105.

35. *Ibid.*, pp. 105-106.

36. *Appleton's Cyclopaedia of American Biography*, p. 391.

37. Pollard, Edward A., *Southern History of the War*, p. 119.

38. *The Lanyard*, Volume XIII, No. 5, p. 5.

39. *Ibid.*

40. Chamberlain, Joshua, *The Passing of the Armies*, pp. 258-265.

41. Cooke, John Esten, *Life of Gen. Robert E. Lee*, p. 461.

CHAPTER VI

1. *The Official and Statistical Register of the State of Mississippi*, Vol. I, Mississippi Department of Archives & History, 1904, page 619. (This is a quotation from Judge Jere Black.)

2. *Ibid.*, pp. 618-619.

3. *Ibid.*

4. *Ibid.*

5. Pollard, Edward A. , *Southern History of the War*, p. 656.

6. Stucker, Augustin, *Lincoln & Davis: A Dual Biography of America's Civil War Presidents*, p. 265.

7. Pollard, Edward A., *Southern History of the War*, Vol. II, pa. 142.

8. *Ibid.*, p. 365.

9. *Ibid.*, p. 365.

10. *Ibid.*, pp. 365-366.

11. Current, Friedel, and Williams, *A History of the United States Since 1865*, p. 10.

12. Caruth, Viola, *Caddo: 1,000*, p. 73.

13. *Ibid.*

14. *The Lanyard*, Volume XIV, No. 5, p. 2.

15. Current, Friedel, and Williams, *A History of the United States Since 1865*, p. 8.

16. Caruth, Viola, *Caddo: 1,000*, p. 73.

17. Adams, James Truslow, The March of Democracy, Vol. III, p. 204.

18. Caruth, Viola, *Caddo: 1,000*, p. 70.

19. *Ibid.*, p. 80.

20. *Ibid.*, p. 83.

21. *Southern Partisan*, Volume IV, No. 4, 1984, p. 56.

22. *Red Shirt Shrine*, p. 4.

23. *Southern Partisan*, Volume IV, No. 4, 1984, p. 55.

24. Current, Friedel, and Williams, *A History of the United States Since 1865*, p. 29.

25. Watkins, Sam, *"Co. Aytch."*, p. 49.

CHAPTER VII

1. Jackson, Robert, *Fade In, Crossroads: A History of the Southern Cinema*, page 160.

2. *Ibid.*, page 161.

3. This quotation is a bit confusing. Part of it seems to come from an interview with Stephens Mitchell in the Atlanta Constitution on Oct. 22, 1978, page 244, yet, some of it appears to come from Pyron's biography of Margaret Mitchell. It is unclear who is quoting who.

4. *Confederate Veteran*, Volume XXXI, page 161.

5. Eppes, Susan Bradford, *Through Some Eventful Years*, pp. 343, 354-355.

CHAPTER VIII

1. Jones, J. William, *The Memorial Volume of Jefferson Davis*, pp. 27-28.

2. *Ibid.*, p. 52.

3. *Ibid.*, p. 54.

4. *Ibid.*, p 55.

5. *Ibid.*, p. 61.

6. *Ibid.*, p. 28.

7. *Ibid.*, p. 110.

8. *Ibid.*, p. 212.

9. *Ibid.*, p. 301.

10. *Ibid.*, p. 340.

11. Strode, Hudson, *Jefferson Daivs: Private Letters, 1823-1889*, p. 123. This is part of the letter from Jefferson Davis to Varina Davis, written from Montgomery, Alabama, on Feb. 20, 1861.

12. Jones, J. William, *The Memorial Volume of Jefferson Davis*, p. 317.

13. Watkins, Sam, *"Co. Aytch."*, 228.

14. Jones, J. William, *The Memorial Volume of Jefferson Davis*, p. 352.

15. *Ibid.*, p. 340.

16. *Ibid.*, p. 653.

17. *Ibid.*, p. 493.

18. *Ibid.*, p. 212.

19. Purdue, Howell and Elizabeth, *Pat Cleburne, Confederate General*, p. 39.

20. *Ibid.*, p. 60.

21. *Ibid.*, pp. 74-75.

22. *The War of the Rebellion: Official Records of the Union and Confederate Armies*, Volume X, Part 1, p. 584.

23. McKinnon, John L., *History of Walton County*, pp. 299-300.

24. Purdue, Howell and Elizabeth, *Pat Cleburne, Confederate General*, p. 392.

25. *Ibid.*, p. 75.

26. *Ibid.*, p. 419.

27. *Ibid.*, p. 420.

28. *The Land We Love*, Vol. II, p. 460.

29. Davis, Burke, *Gray Fox*, p. 9.
30. *Ibid.*, p. 5.
31. Jones, J. William, *The Memorial Volume of Jefferson Davis*, p. 310.
32. Davis, Burke, *Gray Fox*, p. 164.
33. *Ibid.*, p. 280.
34. *Ibid.*, p.250.
35. Jones, J. William, *The Memorial Volume of Jefferson Davis*, p. 309.
36. Chesnut, Mary Boykin, *A Diary From Dixie*, pp. 330-331.
37. *Appleton's Cyclopaedia of American Biography*, p. 391.
38. Chesnut, Mary Boykin, *A Diary From Dixie*, p. 261.
39. Morningside Bookshop Catalogue, No. 16, p. 42.
40. Chesnut, Mary Boykin, *A Diary From Dixie*, p. 341.
41. Davis, Burke, *Gray Fox*, p. 353.
42. Wyeth, John Allan, *Life of General Nathan Bedford Forrest*, p. 128.
43. *Ibid.*, p. 135.
44. *Ibid.*, p. 393.
45. *Ibid.*, p. 425.
46. *Ibid.*, p. 628.
47. Whitley, Edythe Johns Rucker, *Sam Davis, Hero of the Confederacy*, p. 217.
48. *Confederate Veteran*, Volume III, p. 182.
49. Whitley, Edythe Johns Rucker, *Sam Davis, Hero of the Confederacy*, p. 136.
50. *Ibid.*, p. 158.
51. *Ibid.*, p. 139.
52. Letter from Sam Davis to Charles and Jane Davis, Nov. 19, 1863. This heartbreaking letter can be seen at the small museum located behind the Sam Davis Home near Smyrna, Tennessee.
53. *Confederate Veteran*, Volume IV, pp. 35-36.
54. *Ibid.*, Volume XVII, p. 280.
55. *Ibid.*, Volume XVI, cover of the December, 1908 issue.

CHAPTER IX

1. *William Wallace's Civil War Letters: The Virginia Campaign,* edited by John O. Holzheuter.
2. Holland, Cecil Fletcher, *Morgan and His Raiders,* p. 347.
3. Thomas, Edison H., *John Hunt Morgan and His Raiders,* p. 109.
4. The *Daily Oklahoman,* March 4, 1951. The article was written by Welborn Hope.
5. Holcombe, R.I., *History of Marion County, Missouri,* p.491.
6. *Ibid.,* page 491.
7. *Ibid.,* page 492.
8. *Ibid.,* page 491.
9. *The Palmyra Massacre,* p. 8.
10. Holcombe, R.I., *History of Marion County, Missouri,* p. 497.
11. *Ibid.,* page 499.
12. *Ibid.,* page 500.
13. *Ibid.,* page 500.
14. *Ibid.,* page 506.
15. *Ibid.,* page 508.
16. *Ibid.,* page 508.
17. Sosey, Frank H., *Robert Devoy: A Tale of the Palmyra Massacre,* p. 130.
18. Pollard, Edward A., *Southern History of the War,* Vol. I, pp. 525-526.
19. *Ibid.,* p. 140.

CHAPTER XI

1. Scott, Otto, *The Secret Six,* pp. 116, 120, 140.
2. This is the paragraph that usually accompanies this melancholy poem. Dr. Ticknor passed away in 1874, but in 1909, when his widow was in her 80th year, Lucian Lamar Knight, reported more details about the young man in a Georgia history publication. From a sketch written by Col. Charles J. Swift, a resident of the City of Columbus and a promi-

nent member of the Georgia bar, we learn that the young lad's name was Isaac Newton Giffen and that his daddy was a blacksmith in East Tennessee. Newton and Dr. Ticknor's eldest son, Douglas, who was about six years younger than the soldier, became chums and companions. Douglas recalled that as Newton's health improved he was very industrious, gave a great deal of attention to the wrapping of the apple trees to keep the rabbits from eating the bark, and that both of them went forth on occasions to pick blackberry leaves to make green tea. Douglas described Newton as having very light hair, a fair complexion, and was unusually tall for his age, and very thin.

The soldier, true to the story in the poem, bade the Ticknors a tearful farewell and left to rejoin his comrades at war. In describing his leaving, Col. Swift wrote, "On the morning when Newton Giffen left *Torch Hill* on his way to his company, passage was taken on an old gray army horse, Newton riding in front and Douglas riding behind. Getting near to Bull Creek bridge, about half way between *Torch Hill* and Columbus, they found the waters of the creek at flood height and covering all the lower lands on the side of their approach to the bridge. The old horse, getting a little off the road where the water covered it, fell into a big washout and in struggling to extricate themselves, both of the boys were unhorsed, and came near being swept down the stream and drowned. Douglas Ticknor and the horse got ashore on the side next to home. Little Giffen was carried by the current to a point where he gained a footing close to the bridge. About the time the excitement and danger was over, a negro drove up with a four-mule team on his way to Columbus. He kept in the track of the submerged road and met with no mishap such as that to the boys and the old gray horse. With no other possession than his dripping and muddy clothes, Little Giffen climbed into the four-horse wagon and standing up waved a last farewell to his friend, Douglas, on the other side of the raging waters." Col. Swift concluded his narrative with the following remarks:

"It is practically certain that Little Giffen fell in battle soon after leaving *Torch Hill*. The character of the lad, his promise to write if spared, the kindness which was lavished upon him by devoted friends, the sense of gratitude which he must have felt for favors received, and the long silence which followed his departure, preclude the supposition that he could possibly have survived the clash into which he was again plunged. Doubtless he was numbered among the unknown dead in one of the battles which occurred soon thereafter; but Doctor Ticknor has happily rescued the lad's name from oblivion and blazed it immortally upon the heights of song."

In 2020, I did some research of my own. Going to the Tennessee census of 1850, I found him in Dickson County, Tennessee. He is listed there as Isaac N. Giffin, his age given as five. His daddy was Isaac Giffin, and, indeed, the daddy's occupation was "blacksmith." In the census of 1860, the family is living in Montgomery County, just north of Dickson County. In that census, Isaac was 13 years old, which means he was born in 1847, making him sixteen years old in 1863, exactly as Dr. Ticknor states in the poem. If this truly is Little Giffen, of which I am fairly certain, then the part about "East Tennessee" has been wrong all along. Dickson and Montgomery counties are in Middle Tennessee.

Bibliography

PUBLISHED BOOKS

Adams, James Truslow, *The March of Democracy*, Charles Scribner's Sons, New York, 1933.

Alexander, E.P. *Military Memoirs of a Confederate*, New York, 1907.

Augspurger, McLemore, and Shafer, *United States History for High Schools*, Laidlaw Brothers, River Forest, Illinois., 1961.

Avary, Myrta Lockett, *Dixie After the War*, Houghton-Mifflin Co., Boston, 1937.

Ayers, Edward L., *Vengeance and Justice*, New York, Oxford University Press, 1984.

Botkin, B.A., *A Civil War Treasury of Tales, Legends, and Folklore*, Promontory Press, New York, 1960.

Burkhardt, George S., *Confederate Rage, Yankee Wrath: No Quarter in the Civil War*, Southern Illinois University Press, Carbondale, 2007.

Carruth, Viola, *Caddo: 1,000*, Shreveport Magazine Publishing, Shreveport, La., 1970.

Chamberlain, Joshua, *The Passing of the Armies*, New York, 1915.

Chesnut, Mary Boykin, *A Diary From Dixie*, edited by Ben Ames Williams, Harvard University Press, Cambridge, Mass., 1980.

Clark, Thomas D., *The South Since Reconstruction*, The Bobbs-Merrill Company, Indianapolis, Indiana, 1973.

Clayton, Victoria V., *White and Black Under the Old Regime*, The Young Churchman Co., New York, 1899.

Cooke, John Esten, *Life of Gen. Robert E. Lee*, D. Appleton & Co., New York, 1871.

Current, Friedel, and Williams, *A History of the United States Since 1865*, Alfred A. Knopf, New York, 1967.

Cutler, James Elbert, *Lynch-Law: An Investigation into the History of Lynching in the United States*, Patterson Smith, Montclair, N.J., 1969.

Davis, Burke, *The Civil War: Strange and Fascinating Facts*, The Fairfax Press, New York, 1960.

Davis, Burke, *Gray Fox*, The Fairfax Press, New York, 1956.

Davis, Jefferson, *The Rise and Fall of the Confederate Government*, D. Appleton & Co., New York, 1881.

Dowdey, Clifford, *The Death of a Nation*, Alfred A. Knopf, New York, 1958.

Duke, Basil W., *A History of Morgan's Cavalry*, Indiana University Press, Bloomington, Ind., 1960.

Eppes, Susan Bradford, *Through Some Eventful Years*, The J.W. Burke Co., Macon Georgia, 1926.

Freeman, Douglas Southall, *R.E. Lee*, Charles Scribner's Sons, New York, 1934.

Gibson, Arrell M., *Oklahoma, A History of Five Centuries*, Harlow Publishing Co., Norman, Okla., 1965.

Hay, David and Joan, *The Last of the Confederate Privateers*, Crescent Books, Great Britain, 1977.

Holcombe, R.I. *History of Marion County, Missouri*, E.F. Perkins, St. Louis, 1884.

Hope, Welborn, *Four Men Hanging*, Century Press, Oklahoma City, 1974.

Horn, Stanley, *The Army of Tennessee*, University of Oklahoma Press, Norman, Okla., 1952.

Jackson, Robert, *Fade in, Crossroads: A History of the Southern Cinema*, Oxford University Press, 2017.

Jones, J. William, *The Memorial Volume of Jefferson Davis*, W.M. Cornett & Co., Dallas, 1890.

Jones, Virgil Carrington, *Gray Ghosts and Rebel Raiders*, Mockingbird Books, Atlanta, 1956.

Jordan, Robert Paul, *The Civil War*, National Geographic Society, 1969.

Kantor, MacKinlay, *If the South Had Won the Civil War*, Bantam Books, New York, 1960.

Kirwan, Albert D., *The Confederacy*, Meridian Books, New York, 1959.

Knight, Lucian Lamar, *Georgia's Landmarks, Memorials and Legends*, The Byrd Printing Company, Atlanta, 1914.

Logsdon, David R., *Eyewitnesses at the Battle of Franklin*, Kettle Mills Press, Nashville, 1991.

Long, E.B. and Barbara, *The Civil War Day by Day, An Almanac, 1861-1865*, Doubleday & Co., Garden City, New York, 1971.

Lytle, Andrew Nelson, *Bedford Forrest and His Critter Company*, G.P. Putnam's Sons, New York, 1931.

McKinnon, John L., *History of Walton County*, Atlanta, 1911.

Miers, Earl Schenck, *The Golden Book History of the Civil War*, Golden Press, New York, 1963.

Mitchell, Steve, and Rawls, Sam, *How to Speak Southern*, Bantam Books, New York, 1976.

Nichols, George W., *The Story of the Great March*, Corner House Publishers, Williamstown, Mass., 1972.

Pember, Phoebe Yates, *A Southern Woman's Story*, edited by Bell I. Wiley, Mockingbird Books, St. Simons Island, Ga., 1959.

Phillips, Ulrich B., *Life and Labor in the Old South*, Little, Brown & Co., Boston, 1963.

Pollard, Edward A., *Southern History of the War*, Fairfax Press, New York, 1977.

Pollard, Edward A., *The Lost Cause*, E.B. Treat & Company, New York, 1867.

Poppenheim, Merchant, McKinney, White, Wright, Hyde, Campbell, Woodbury, and Lawton, *The History of the United Daughters of the Confederacy*, Garrett and Massie, Inc., Richmond, 1938.

Pratt, Fletcher, *Civil War in Pictures*, Garden City Books, Garden City, New York, 1955.

Purdue, Howell and Elizabeth, *Pat Cleburne, Confederate General*, Hill Junior College Press, Hillsboro, Texas, 1973.

Ramage, James A., *Rebel Raider*, University Press of Kentucky, Lexington, 1986.

Richards, Kenneth G., *Will Rogers*, Children's Press, Chicago, 1968.

Ross, Ishbel, *Rebel Rose*, Mockingbird Books, St. Simons Island, Ga., 1954.

Ryan, Abram J., *Father Ryan's Poems*, John L. Rapier, Mobile, Ala., 1879.

Scott, Otto, *The Secret Six*, Uncommon Books, Murphys, Calif., 1993.

Shay, Frank, *Judge Lynch: His First Hundred Years*, Patterson Smith, Montclair, New Jersey, 1938.

Sosey, Frank H., *Robert Devoy: A Tale of the Palmyra Massacre*, Sosey Brothers, Palmyra, Mo, 1903.

Stockard, Henry Jerome, *A Study in Southern Poetry*, Neale Publishing Company, New York and Washington, 1911.

Strode, Hudson, *Jefferson Davis: Private Letters, 1823-1889*, Harcourt, Brace, & World, 1966.

Stucker, Augustin, *Lincoln & Davis: A Dual Biography of America's Civil War Presidents*, Author House Publishing, 2011.

Thomas, Edison H., *John Hunt Morgan and His Raiders*, University Press of Kentucky, Lexington, 1975.

Tilley, John Shipley., *Facts the Historians Leave Out*, The Paragon Press, Montgomery, Ala., 1951.

Tilley, John Shipley, *Lincoln Takes Command*, University of North Carolina Press, Chapel Hill, 1941.

Warner, Ezra J., *Generals in Gray*, Louisiana State University Press, Baton Rouge, 1959.

Watkins, Samuel Rush, *"Co. Aytch,"* Cumberland Presbyterian Publishing House, Nashville, 1882.

Whitley, Edythe Johns Rucker, *Sam Davis, Hero of the Confederacy*, Blue & Gray Press, Nashville, 1971.

Williams, T. Harry, *P.G.T. Beauregard: Napoleon in Gray*, Louisiana State University Press, Baton Rouge, 1954.

Wright, George C., *Racial Violence in Kentucky, 1865-1940*, LSU Press, Baton Rouge, 1990.

Wyeth, John Allan, *Life of General Nathan Bedford Forrest*, Harper Brothers, New York, 1899.

BOOKLETS, PAMPHLETS, ESSAYS, NEWSLETTERS

Altman, James David, *Mr. Lincoln's War on the South*, Charleston, S.C., 1987.

SOUTHERN BY THE GRACE OF GOD

Confederate Veteran, Hattiesburg, Miss., Volumes XXIX and XXX.

Gone With the Wind, MGM, 1939.

McCain, William D., Confederate Memorial Day address at Little Rock, Ark., April 1976.

Murphey, Dwight D., *Lynching – History and Analysis: A Legal Studies Monograph,* Council for Social and Economic Studies, Washington, D.C., 1995.

Napier, Cameron Freeman, *The First White House of the Confederacy,* The First White House Association, Montgomery, Ala., 1986.

Red Shirt Shrine, UDC, Edgefield, S.C., 1945.

The Lanyard, Memphis, Tenn., Volumes XIII, XIV, XV, and XVI.

The Palmyra Massacre, The Palmyra Confederate Monument Association, Palmyra, Mo., 1903.

The Rebel Yell, Oklahoma City, Okla. Volumes V, XI, and XII.

What is the Sons of Confederate Veterans? Hattiesburg, Miss., March 25, 1979.

DIARIES AND LETTERS

Diary of Eulalie McRae Burkes, Oct. 27 – Nov. 11, 1902, in possession of Winne Whited.

William Wallace's Civil War Letters: The Virginia Campaign, edited by John G. Holzheueter, Wisconsin Magazine of History, Vol. 57, No. 1, Autumn, 1973.

MAGAZINES, NEWSPAPERS, PERIODICALS

Blue and Gray, Columbus, Ohio, Vol. IV, No. 2, 1986.

Confederate Veteran, Nashville, Tenn., Volumes III, IV, XVI, and XVII.

Morningside Bookshop Catalogue, No. 16, Dayton, Ohio, Jan. 2, 1985.

Southern Partisan, Columbia, S.C., Volumes IV,V,VI, and VII.

Southern Style, Knoxville, Tenn., July-Aug. issue, 1987.

The Bonham Journal, Bonham, Texas, April, 2, 1896.

SOUTHERN BY THE GRACE OF GOD

The Clarksville Leaf-Chronicle, Clarksville, Tenn., July 14, 1996.
The Daily Oklahoma, Oklahoma City, Okla., March 4, 1951.
The Land We Love, Volume II, 1867.
The Memphis Daily Appeal, Memphis, Tenn., April 28, 1870.
The Nashville Banner, Nashville, Tenn., May 13, 1905.
The Outlook, New York, 1911.
The Philadelphia Press, Philadelphia, Penn., June 7, 1917.
The Sparrow Hawk, Centreville, Ala., Vol. III, No. 3, 1978.
The Sunday Oklahoman, Oklahoma City, Okla., Jan. 11, 1987.

GENERAL REFERENCE WORKS

Appleton's Cyclopaedia of American Biography, James Gran Wilson and John Fiske, Appleton & Co., New York, 1888.
Confederate War Poems, edited by Walter Burgwyn Jones, Bill Coates, Ltd., Nashville, 1984.
Dictionary of American Biography, edited by Allen Johnson, Charles Scribner's Sons, New York, 1957.
Histories of the Several Regiments & Battalions from North Carolina in the Great War, 1861-1865, edited by Walter Clark, Raleigh, N.C., 1901.
The War of the Rebellion: Official Records of the Union and Confederate Armies, Washington, 1884.
The Official and Statistical Register of the State of Mississippi, Mississippi Department of Archives & History, Jackson, Mississippi.

INDEX

591

592

213, 576, 589
Goolsby, B.F., 237
Gordon, John B., 146, 559
Govan, Daniel, 335
Granbury, Hiram B., 335, 434
Grant, Ulysses S., xxxix, 137, 148-149, 168, 170, 180, 182, 210-211, 220-222, 320, 333, 347-348, 380, 388, 558
Greencastle, Penn., 151, 160
Greely, Horace, 129
Greenhow, Rose O'Neal, 133-134, 174, 309, 352, 557
Greensboro, N.C., 326
Greenville, Tenn., 461
Grenville, Sir. Richard, 437-438
Grierson Thieves, 427
Griffith, D.W., 224-225
Grissom, Abraham Jackson, 423
Grissom, Avis, 74
Grissom, Elizabeth, 422
Grissom, Fred, 78, 448
Grissom, Ida, 82
Grissom, Joseph, 423
Guerin, F.W., 268
Guerin Studio, 268
Guiney's Station, Va., 355
Guy, Judy, 399, 404
Guy, Karen, 399, 404

Haden, Preston, 242, 281
Hall, Mrs. L.S., 147
Hale, Nathan, 124, 377
Hall, Arthur, 409
Hall, Eva, 409
Halpine, Charles G., 164
Hamilton, Alex, 419-420
Hannibal, Mo., 476-477, 480
Hannity, Sean, xliii
Hardee, William J., 332, 370
Hardeman, Etta, 255
Harnett County, N.C., 443
Harper's Ferry, Va., 163, 340, 344, 352
Harris, Isham, 336, 358
Harris, Phil, 20
Harrisburg, Penn., 344
Hawkins, James, 237

Hayes, Rutherford, 222-223, 484
Hayne, Paul Hamilton, 510
Hays, William Shakespeare, 113
Heath, John, xxvi
Helena, Ark., 329-331, 335-336
Henry Holland Studio, 247
Henry, Patrick, 124, 222, 230, 305
Hermitage, 292, 398
Hermitage, Tenn., 39
Hernando, Miss., 44, 358, 423
Hill, _____, 334
Hill, A.P., 344, 554
Hill, Daniel, 151, 337, 344
Hindman, T.C., 329
Hoke, Mr. _____, 141
Holland, Cecil Fletcher, 460-461
Holland, Virginia, 44
Hollingsworth, James, 218, 221
Hollis, Okla., 423
Homer (ancient Greek poet), xxxii
Hood, John Bell, 171-172, 334-335, 433, 544, 551, 553
Hooker, Joseph, 345-346, 354
Hooks, Matthew O., iv
Hopewell (ship), 439-441
Hopkins, Octave, 250
Hot Springs, Ark., 258
Houghton, Sir Henry, 104
Houston, Sam, 431
Houston, Texas, 60, 506
Howard, William, xxvii
Howell, Madeline, 167-168
Howell, Thomas, 167
Howell, Varina, 167, 291, 314, 316, 322, 326, 580
Hudson, Herbert, 476, 487
Hughes County, Okla., 447
Hughes, S. H., 249
Humphrey, Mary, 477, 486
Humphrey, William T., 478-479, 489
Humston, Thomas, 477-478, 487
Hunt, Henrietta, 367
Hunt, John Wesley, 367
Hunter's Hill, 398
Hurricane Camille, 265, 291
Hyde County, N.C., 441

McLendon, Marty, 65, 265
McLendon, Will D., 65
McLendon, William Elisha, 65
McMinnville, Tenn., 459
McNab, John, 419
McNabb, Edgar, 408
McNeil, John, 472, 474-479, 484-487
McPheeters, John Y., 477, 487
McRae, Alexander Franklin, 407
McRae, Hugh Bain, 429
McRae, Hugh James, 496
McRae, Malcolm Alexander 429
McRae, Pearl, 409

Macon, Ga., 82, 255, 314, 326, 434, 568, 586
Macon, Mo., 474-475, 485
Macon Telegraph and Messenger, 314
Madison, Fla., xxiii
Madison, James, 89, 124, 305
Manassas Gap Railroad, 176
Manassas, Va., 174, 317, 352
Margaret _____, 252, 458
Marietta, Ga., xxvii
Marilyn _____, 116
Marion County, Mo., 471-472, 474, 480
Marion, Francis, 372
Marion, Kansas, 455
Marshall County, Miss., 427
Marshall, Texas, 219
Martin Brothers Studio, 243
Maryland, 8, 32, 140, 159, 344, 496, 503, 510, 565
Mason, George, 124
Masons, 330, 417, 469-470
Mason-Dixon Line, 1, 2, 5, 113
Massachusetts, xlii, 193, 199, 215, 385, 509
Massey, _____, 251
Maxwell, Louise, 398
Meade, George, 346
Meigs, Montgomery C., 341
Memhis Daily Appeal, 326
Memphis, Tenn., xxxi, xlii, 80, 205, 320, 326, 331, 336, 358, 361, 363-365, 424, 505, 563, 589-590

Mennonite, 26
Mentone, Ala., 426
Merion, _____, 152-154
Merrill, Lewis, 474, 485
Methodist, 21-22, 27, 42, 76, 195, 275, 331, 546
Metropolitan Brigade, 217-218, 220
Mexican War, 91, 240, 313-314, 340, 367, 460
Mexico, 101, 179, 314, 352, 362, 487
Mexico City, 179
Michigan, 211, 452, 531
Miles, Frank, 401
Milledgeville, Ga., xxvii
Miller, Jim, 465-469
Minden Democrat, 219
Minnesota, 45, 211
Minor Hill, Tenn., 381, 391
Miss America, 41
Miss Clifford, 42-43
Miss Debbie, 44
Miss Gertrude, 44
Miss Irene, 42
Miss Jane, 44
Miss Louisiana, 45
Miss Mississippi, 41
Miss Oklahoma, 41
Miss Pearl, 43
Miss Sallie, 43
Mississippi, xix, xxi, xl, 14, 27, 44-45, 61, 94, 106, 109, 121, 140, 167, 171, 186-187, 211, 245, 265, 289, 291, 294, 309, 312, 314-316, 326, 335, 357-358, 361-362, 379, 423-425, 427, 463, 483, 503-504, 552, 554, 565, 572-573, 578, 590
Mississippi River, 85-86, 183, 312-313, 314, 329, 424
Missouri, xliii, 120, 140, 159, 197, 227, 235, 251, 268, 283, 296, 430, 451, 455-456, 460, 463, 471, 474-476, 485-486, 496, 531, 550, 582, 586
Mitchell, Bob, 243-244
Mitchell, Ed, 243
Mitchell, Margaret, iii, xlvii, xlviii, 260, 579
Mitchell, Stephens, 260

601

603

Taylor, Zachary, 305, 313-314
T.E. Hudson Studio, 276
Teich, Frank, 267
Telephone, Texas, 406-407
Tennessee, 3, 5, 11, 16, 30, 32, 39, 46-47, 97, 113, 120, 140, 156, 170-172, 183, 199, 205-206, 225, 229-230, 238, 240, 242, 253, 257, 284, 289, 292, 306, 333-334, 357-358, 363-364, 367, 369-371, 373, 376-381, 383, 386-387, 391-392, 397, 402, 404, 432, 457, 458-459, 461, 463, 505-506, 516-517, 546, 549, 551, 555, 564, 572, 578, 581, 583-584
Tennessee River, 170, 332, 362
Texas, xxx, sli, 4, 7, 11, 17, 25, 31, 44, 60, 61, 63, 84, 101, 121, 140, 199, 211, 219, 227, 236-237, 244-245, 248, 252, 255, 267, 277, 287, 289, 292, 317-318, 327, 339-340, 405-407, 412-413, 423, 429-431, 451-453, 463-466, 469, 494, 496-497, 505-506, 510, 532, 544, 551, 555-565, 568, 587, 589
Texas (poem), 451, 531
Texas Rangers, 466
Thackerville, Okla., xxx
The Blackwood Brothers, 12
The Birth of a Nation (movie), 224-225
The Clansman (book), 224
The Confederate Cross of Honor (poem) 534
The Conquered Banner (poem), 102, 529
The Dixie Echoes, 12
The Gray Ghost (TV show), xliv
The Happy Goodmans, 12
The Jazz Singer (movie), 1
The Old Wash Place (poem), 522
The Rebel (TV show), xliv
The Wilderness, 170, 347
The Wizard of the Saddle (poem), 527
Thomas, Al, 62, 65, 82, 573
Thomas, Elliott, 419-420
Thompson, Eva, 412
Thomson, Ken, 284
Thoreau, Henry David, 509
Three Oaks, 270
Ticknor, Douglas, 583
Ticknor, Francis Orray, 517, 582-583, 584
Tiger (ship), 437
Tilden, Samuel, 222

Timrod, Henry, 308, 510-512, 457, 577
Tippah County, Miss., 357
Titanic (ship), 435, 445
Tombstone, Ariz., xxvi
Toombs, Robert, 228
Torch Hill, 583
Tourgee, Albion W., 229, 543
Townsend, Mary Ashley, 515
Transylvania College, 312, 367
Tripp, Jonathan Wylie, 421
Tripp, Walter, 421
Tulsa, Okla., xxii, 264
Turchin, John B., 150
Turner, Charles, 398
Turner Falls, 257
Turner, Ginger, 398
Turner, Mazeppa, 257
Turner, Nat, 162
Turner, Ted, 46
Tuscaloosa, Ala., 425
Tyler, John C., 97, 305

Union, S.C., xix
Union County, S.C., xix
United Confederate Veterans, 245, 261, 289, 298, 546-547
United Daughters of the Confederacy, ii, xxxvi, 163, 267, 287, 301, 392, 495, 497, 498-499, 506, 537, 547, 564, 572, 587, 589
United States Military Academy at West Point, 312-313, 315, 339-340, 351
University of Alabama, 425
University of North Carolina, 540
University of Oklahoma, 31, 561, 571, 586

Vallandigham, Clement L., 193
Vanderbilt, Cornelius, 424
Van Dorn, Earl, 97, 170
Vashti _____, 27
Venable, Richard, 250
Vera Cruz, Mexico, 340, 352
Vian, I.T., 453, 456, 461
Vicksburg National Military Park, xxxix
Vicksburg, Miss., 14, 171, 241, 314, 316, 321, 326

605

Oklahoma Division of the United Daughters of the Confederacy
State Officers, 1964-1965

Halftime at an Ole Miss football game in the 1960s. The band spells
out *DIXIE* while a giant Confederate flag is floated down the field.

ABOUT THE AUTHOR

MICHAEL ANDREW GRISSOM, recipient of the Oklahoma Heritage Distinguished Service Award, and the United Daughters of the Confederacy's prestigious Jefferson Davis Medal, is the author of twelve books. In 1996, he wrote the inscription for Tennessee's Confederate monument in Vicksburg National Military Park, and in 2004 he wrote the inscription for the Confederate monument in Wynnewood, Oklahoma. He has earned two degrees from the University of Oklahoma and has lived in both Tennessee and Oklahoma.

OTHER BOOKS BY THE AUTHOR

American Terrorists: Lincoln's Armies in the South
    https://amzn.to/2NXkoET

Billie Jo (a novel)
    https://amzn.to/3a9VA5w

You Might Be Southern If . . .

Farewell to the Accent: A Humorous Look at a Serious Problem

The Last Rebel Yell (out of print)

Good Ol' Southern Home-Cookin'

When the South Was Southern (out of print)

Standard Songs of the Church

Can the South Survive? (out of print)

*Things I Learned the Hard Way: Practial Advice for the
    Modern Young Man*

The Southern Book of Quotes
    (co-authored with Christopher Erik McBroom)
    https://amzn.to/38470pu

Made in the USA
Las Vegas, NV
30 September 2021